JUL - - 2021

DISCARD *volume* **1**

ASADORA!

NAOKI URASAWA

Chapter 1 ● The Girl Who Ran Past

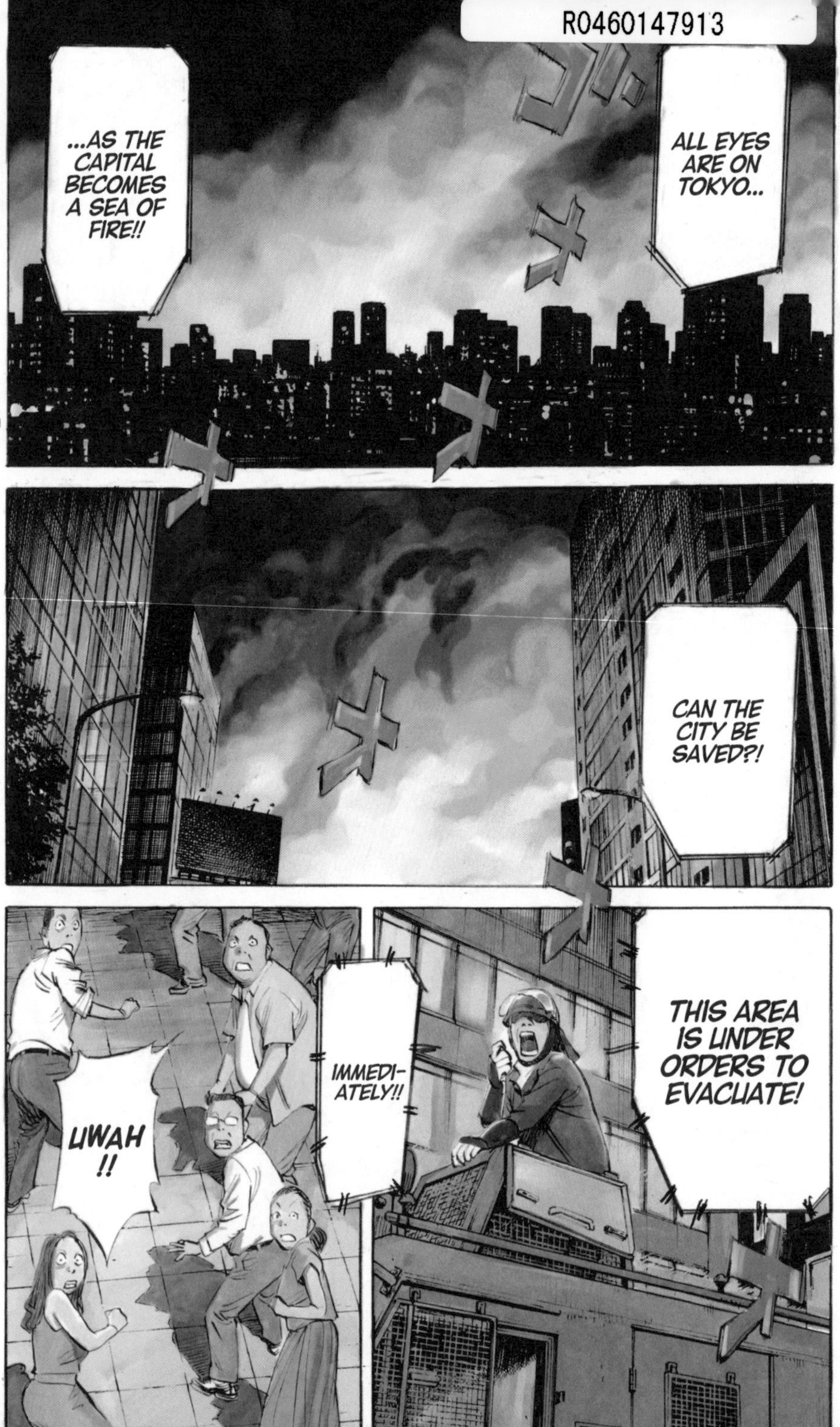
ALL EYES ARE ON TOKYO...
...AS THE CAPITAL BECOMES A SEA OF FIRE!!
CAN THE CITY BE SAVED?!
THIS AREA IS UNDER ORDERS TO EVACUATE!
IMMEDI-ATELY!!
UWAH!!

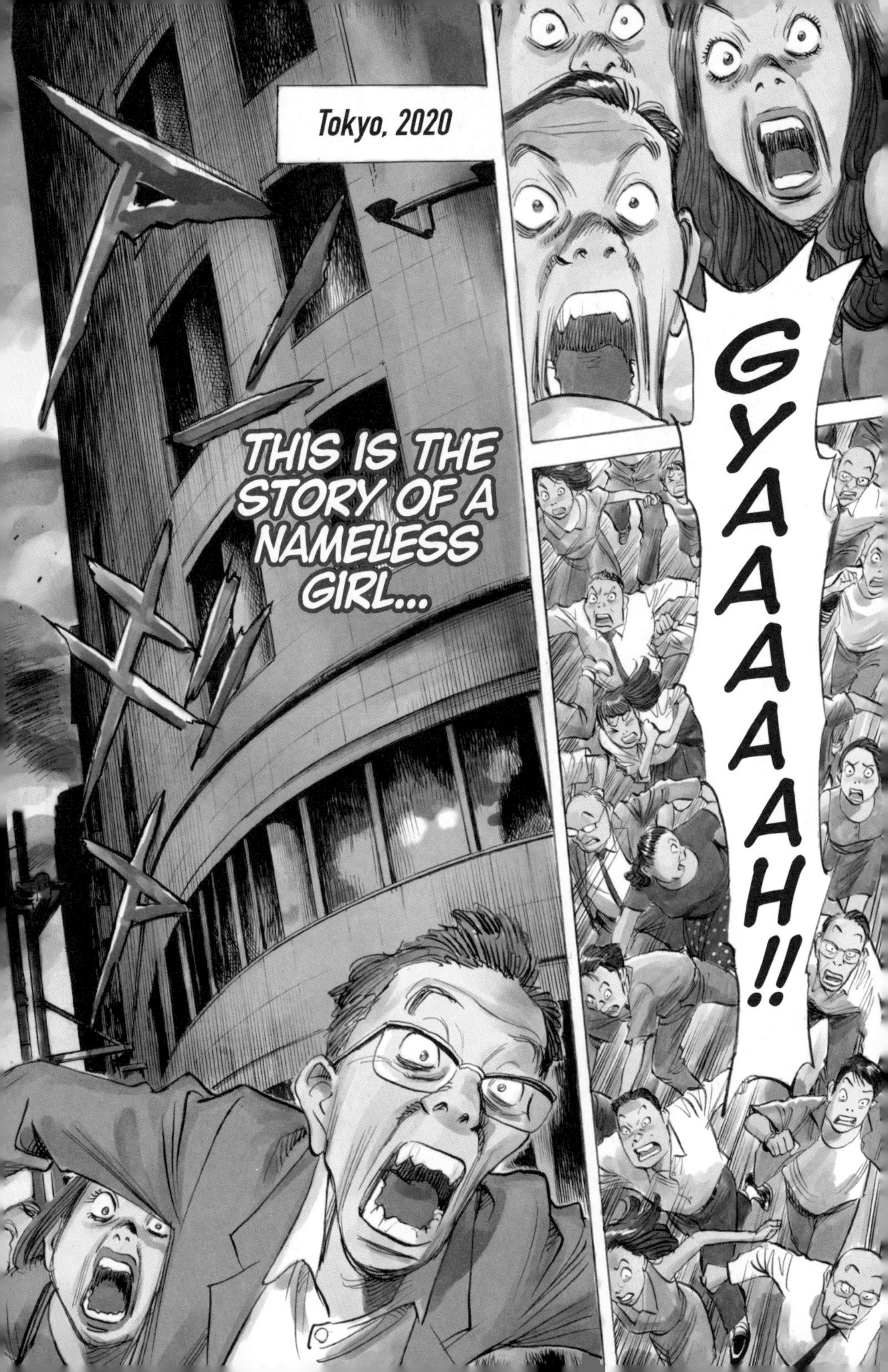
GYAAAAAH!!
Tokyo, 2020
THIS IS THE STORY OF A NAMELESS GIRL...

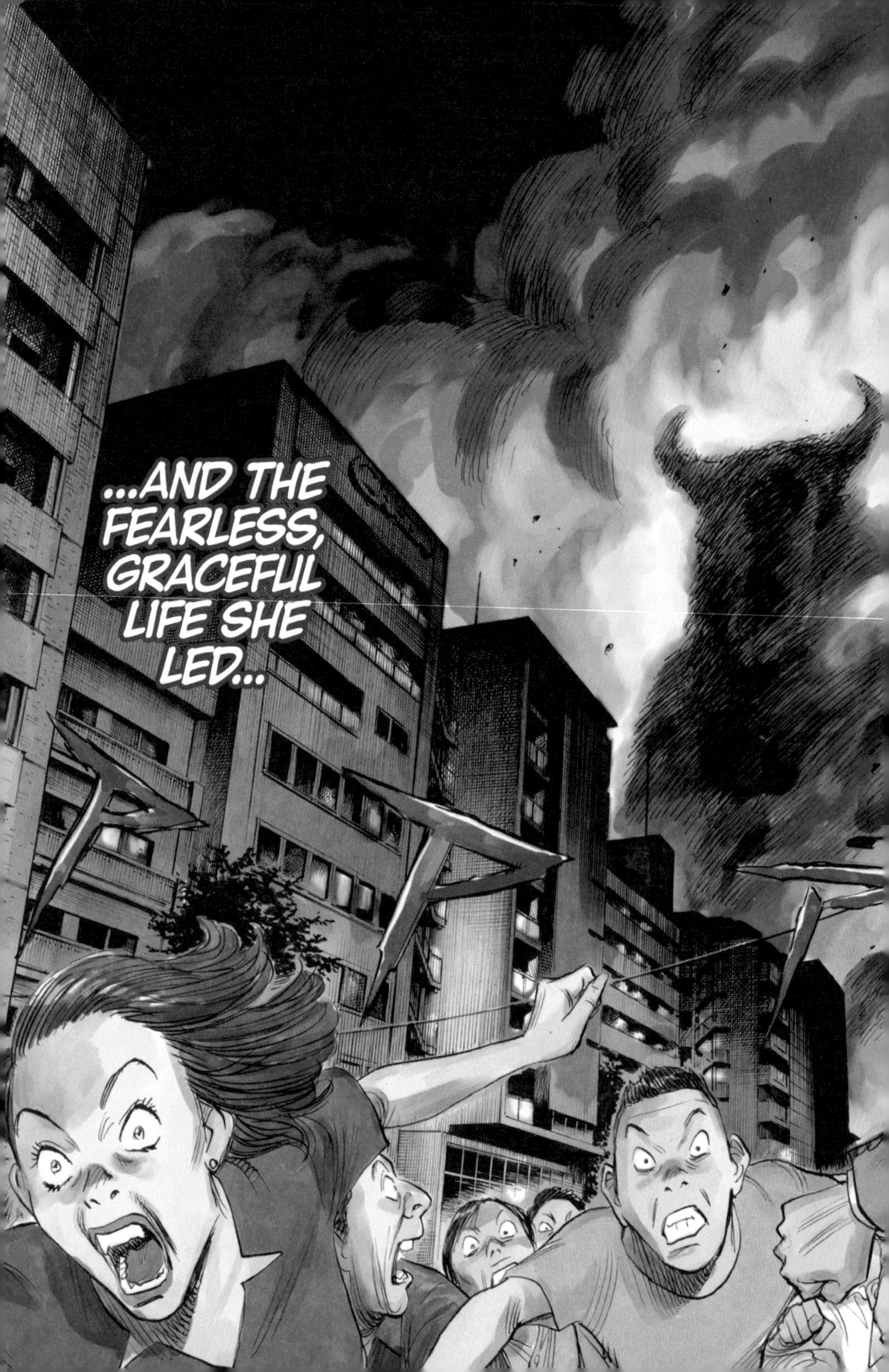
...AND THE FEARLESS, GRACEFUL LIFE SHE LED...

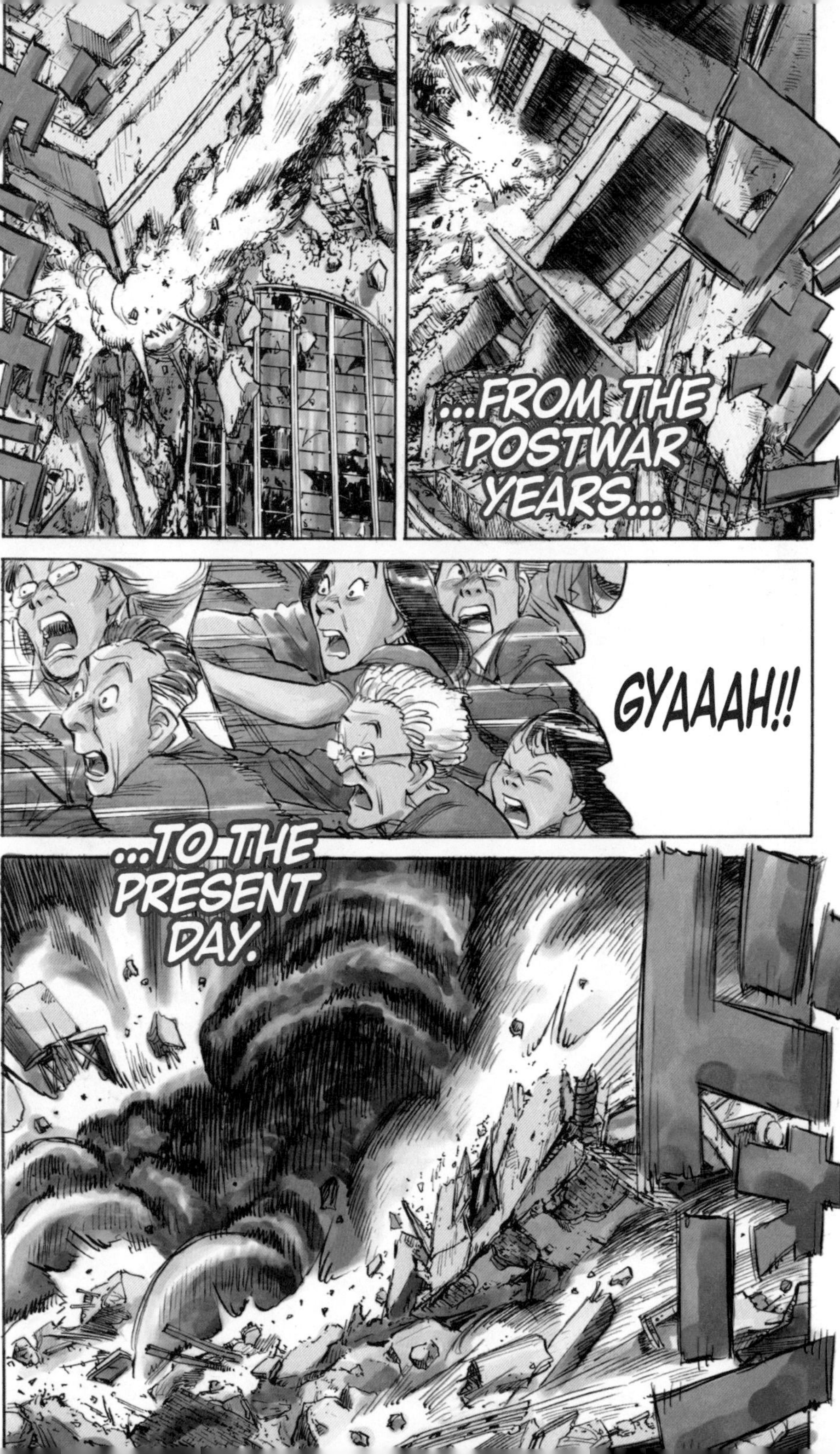
...FROM THE POSTWAR YEARS...
GYAAAH!!
...TO THE PRESENT DAY.

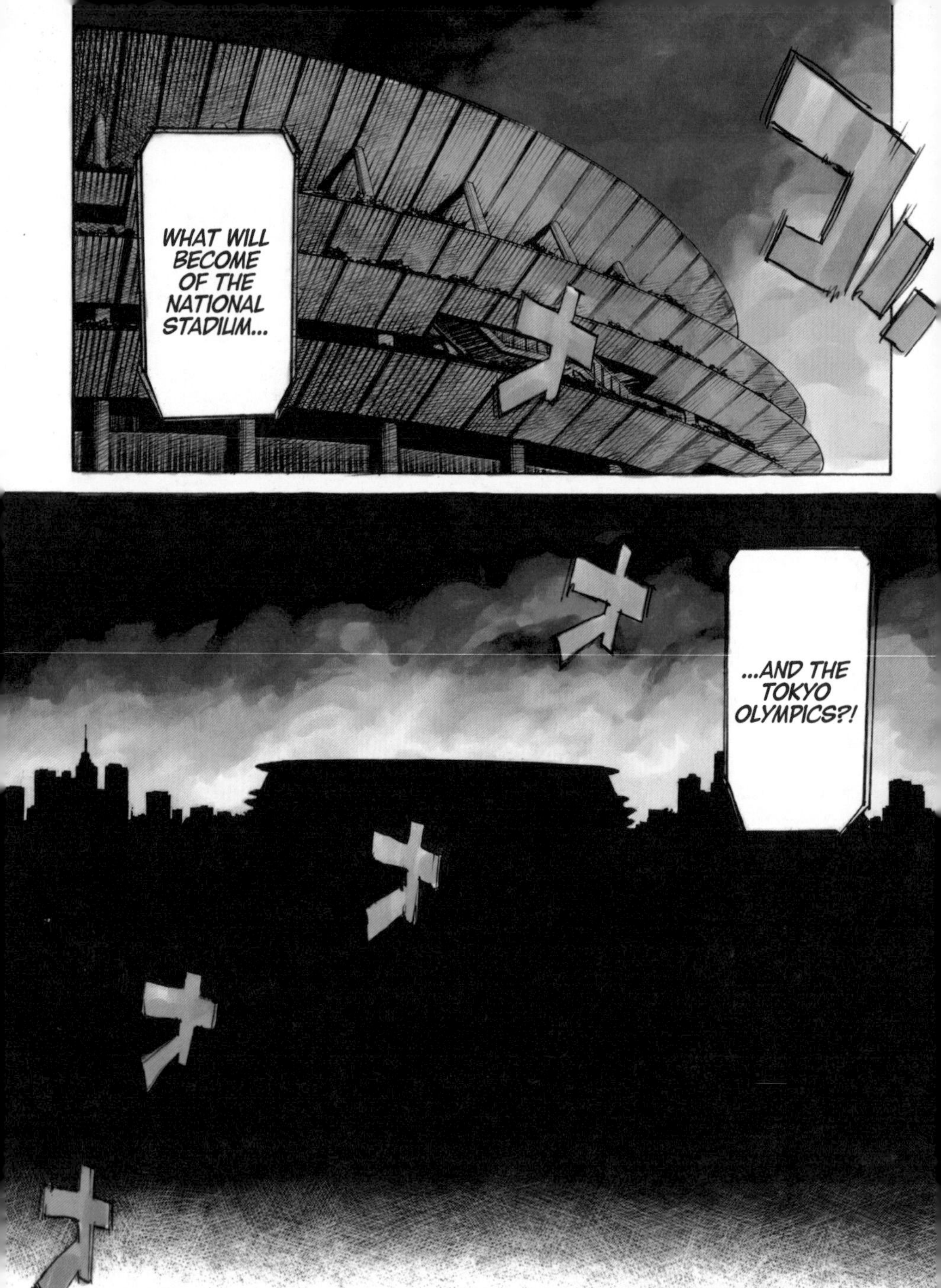
WHAT WILL BECOME OF THE NATIONAL STADIUM...
...AND THE TOKYO OLYMPICS?!

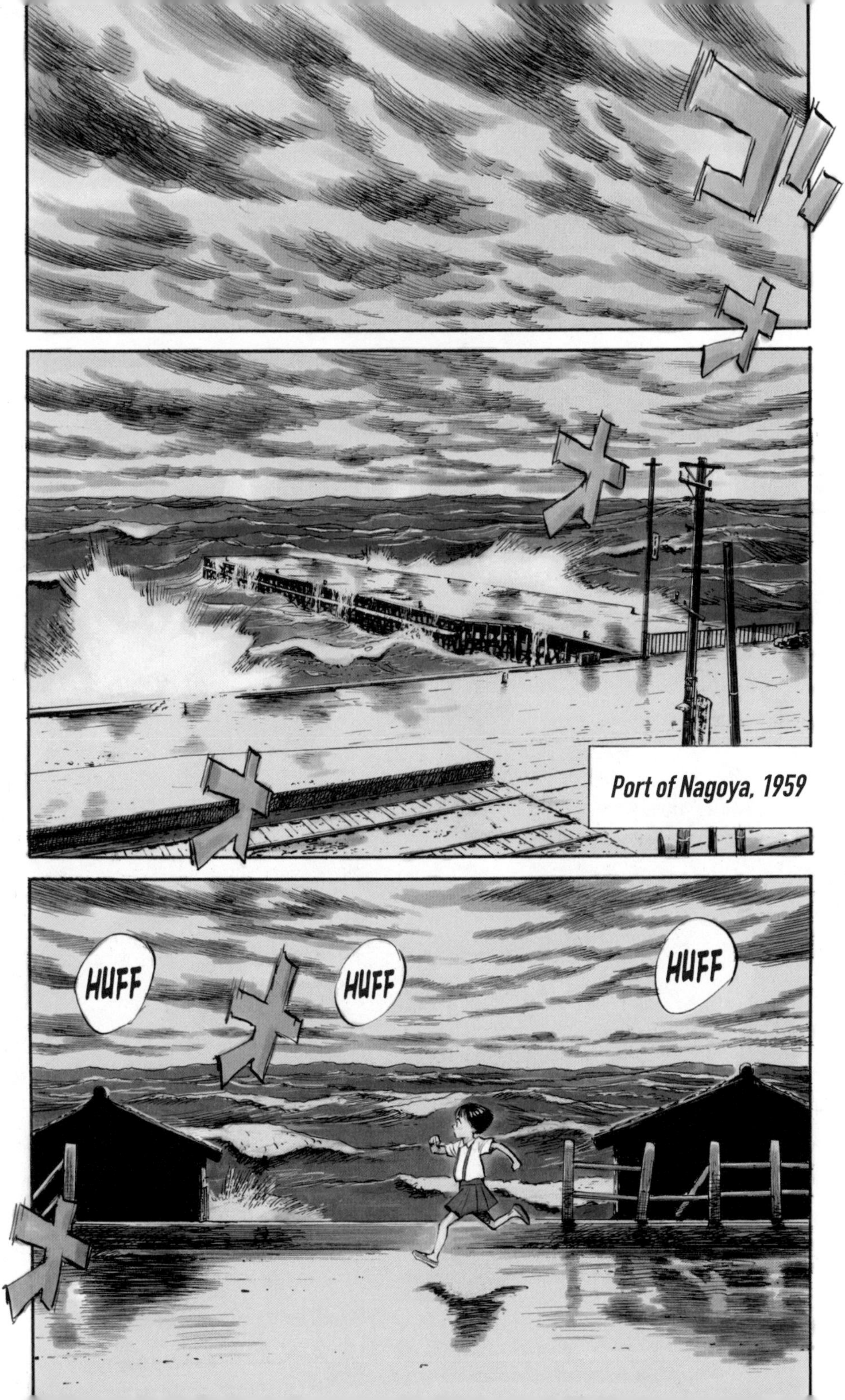
ゴオオオオオ
Port of Nagoya, 1959
HUFF
HUFF
HUFF

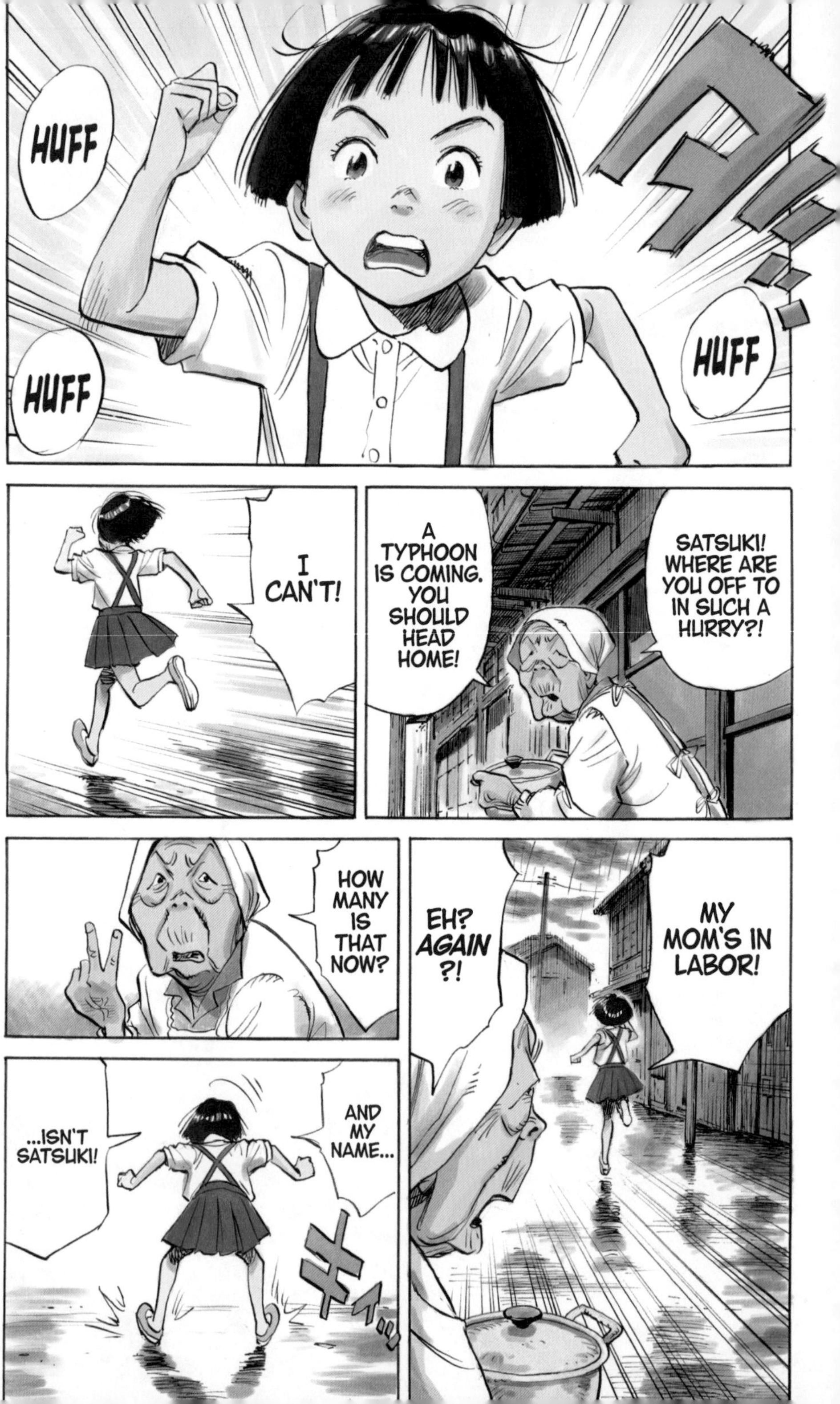
HUFF
HUFF
HUFF
SATSUKI! WHERE ARE YOU OFF TO IN SUCH A HURRY?!
A TYPHOON IS COMING. YOU SHOULD HEAD HOME!
I CAN'T!
MY MOM'S IN LABOR!
EH? AGAIN ?!
HOW MANY IS THAT NOW?
AND MY NAME...
...ISN'T SATSUKI!

Chapter 1 ◉ The Girl Who Ran Past

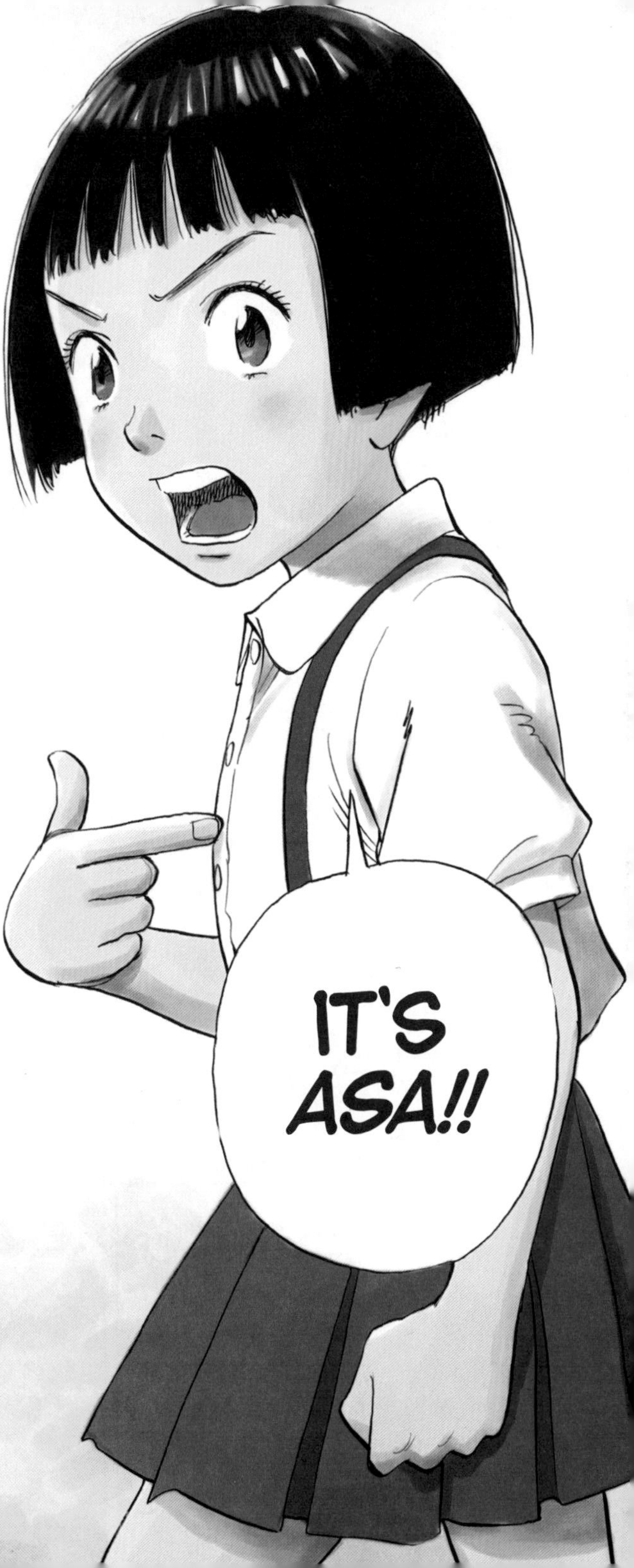
IT'S ASA!!

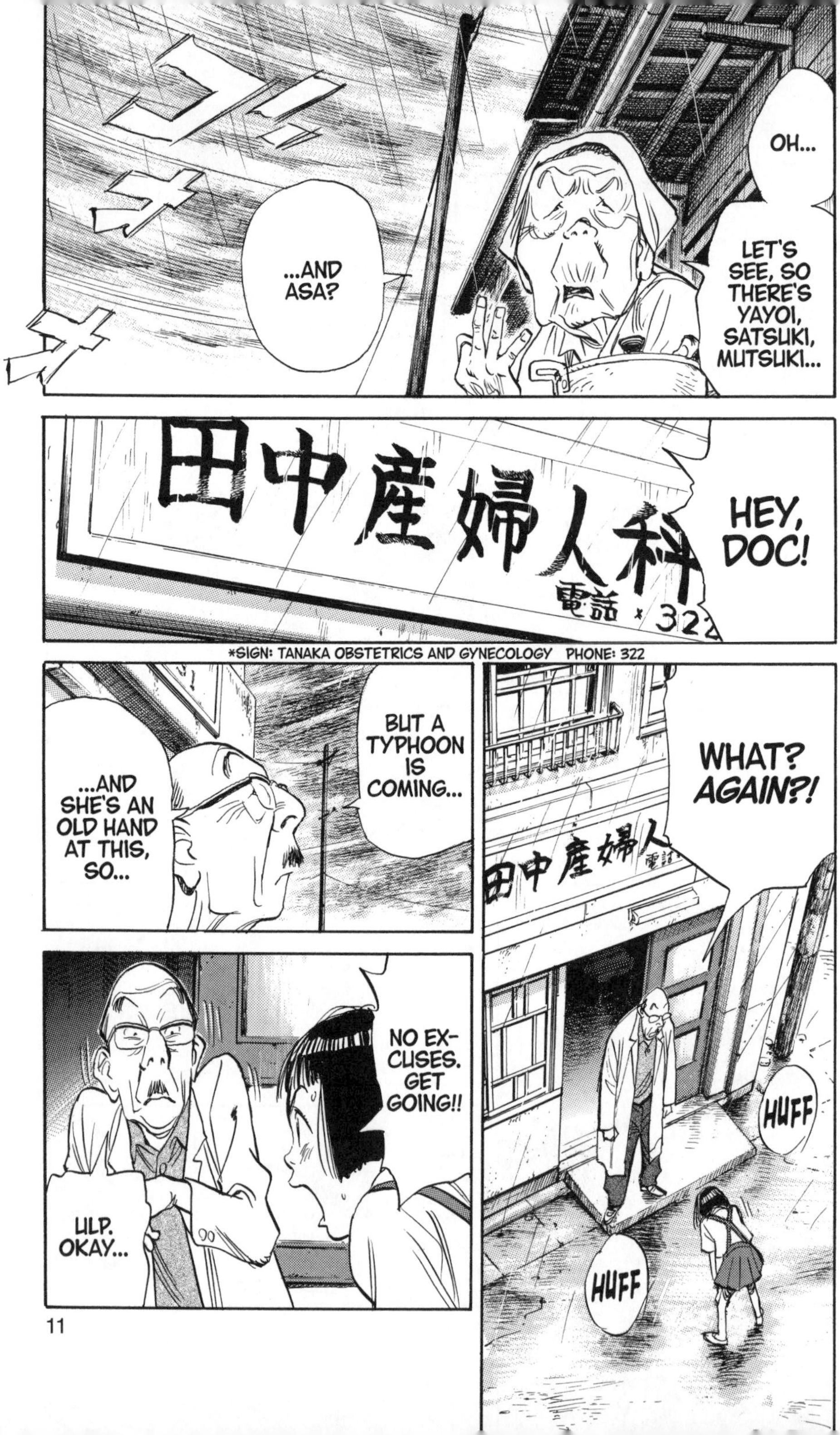
OH...
LET'S SEE, SO THERE'S YAYOI, SATSUKI, MUTSUKI...
...AND ASA?
田中産婦人科
電話 322
HEY, DOC!
*SIGN: TANAKA OBSTETRICS AND GYNECOLOGY PHONE: 322
WHAT? AGAIN?!
田中産婦人
HUFF
HUFF
BUT A TYPHOON IS COMING...
...AND SHE'S AN OLD HAND AT THIS, SO...
NO EXCUSES. GET GOING!!
ULP. OKAY...

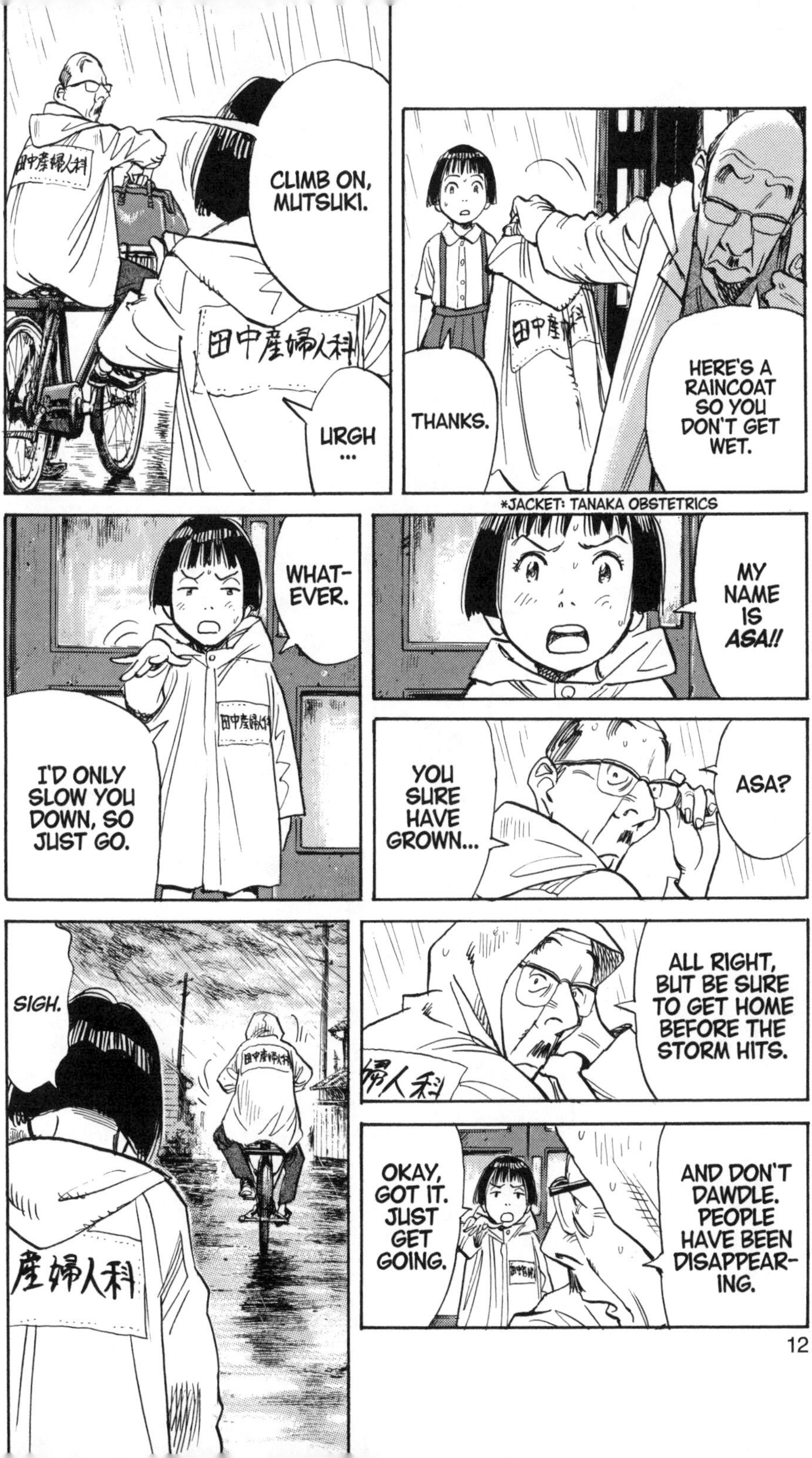
田中産婦人科
HERE'S A RAINCOAT SO YOU DON'T GET WET.
THANKS.
*JACKET: TANAKA OBSTETRICS
CLIMB ON, MUTSUKI.
田中産婦人科
URGH ...
MY NAME IS ASA!!
ASA?
YOU SURE HAVE GROWN...
WHAT-EVER.
I'D ONLY SLOW YOU DOWN, SO JUST GO.
ALL RIGHT, BUT BE SURE TO GET HOME BEFORE THE STORM HITS.
AND DON'T DAWDLE. PEOPLE HAVE BEEN DISAPPEAR-ING.
OKAY, GOT IT. JUST GET GOING.
SIGH.
産婦人科

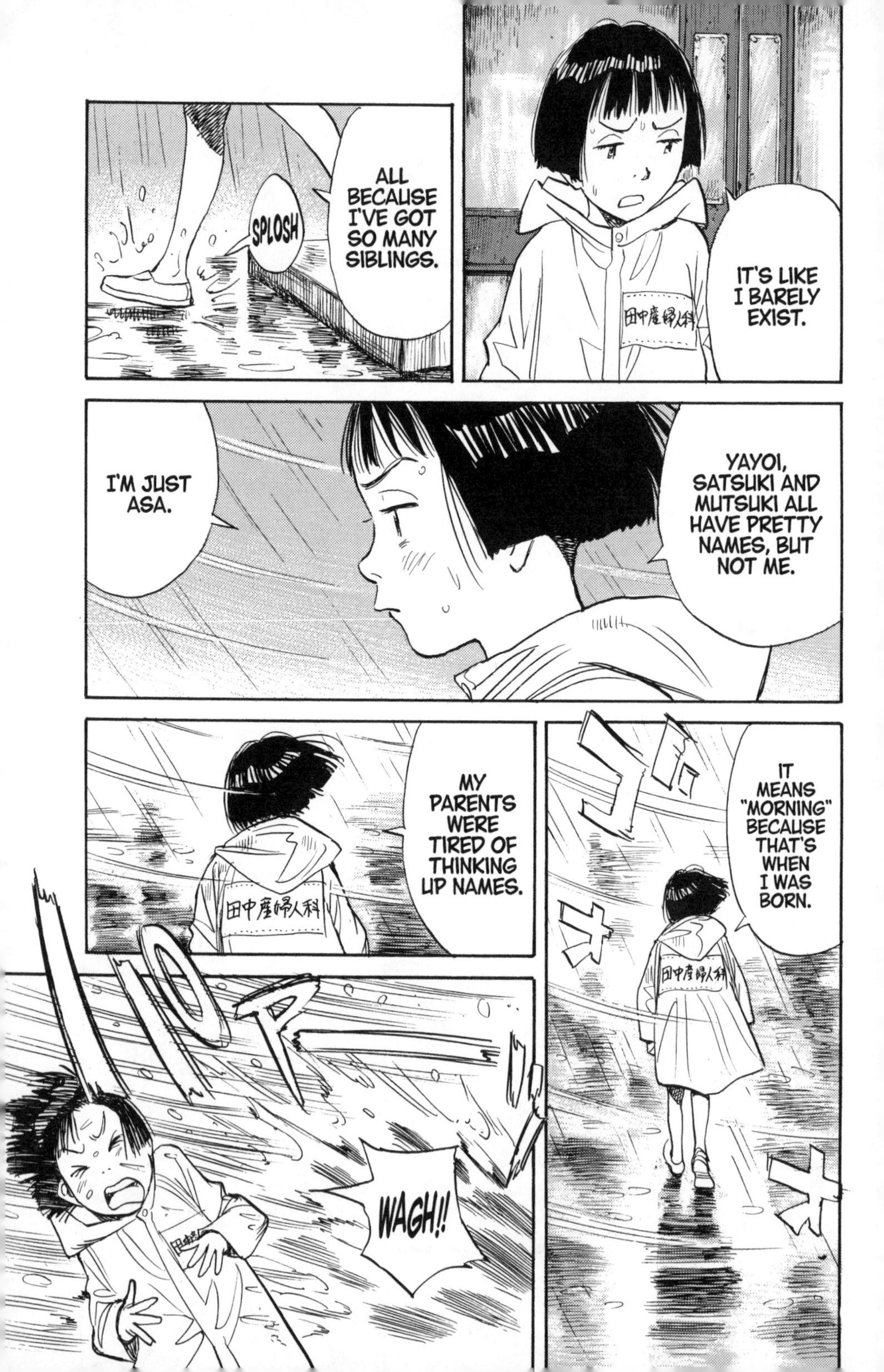
IT'S LIKE I BARELY EXIST.
田中産婦人科
ALL BECAUSE I'VE GOT SO MANY SIBLINGS.
SPLOSH
YAYOI, SATSUKI AND MUTSUKI ALL HAVE PRETTY NAMES, BUT NOT ME.
I'M JUST ASA.
IT MEANS "MORNING" BECAUSE THAT'S WHEN I WAS BORN.
MY PARENTS WERE TIRED OF THINKING UP NAMES.
WAGH!!

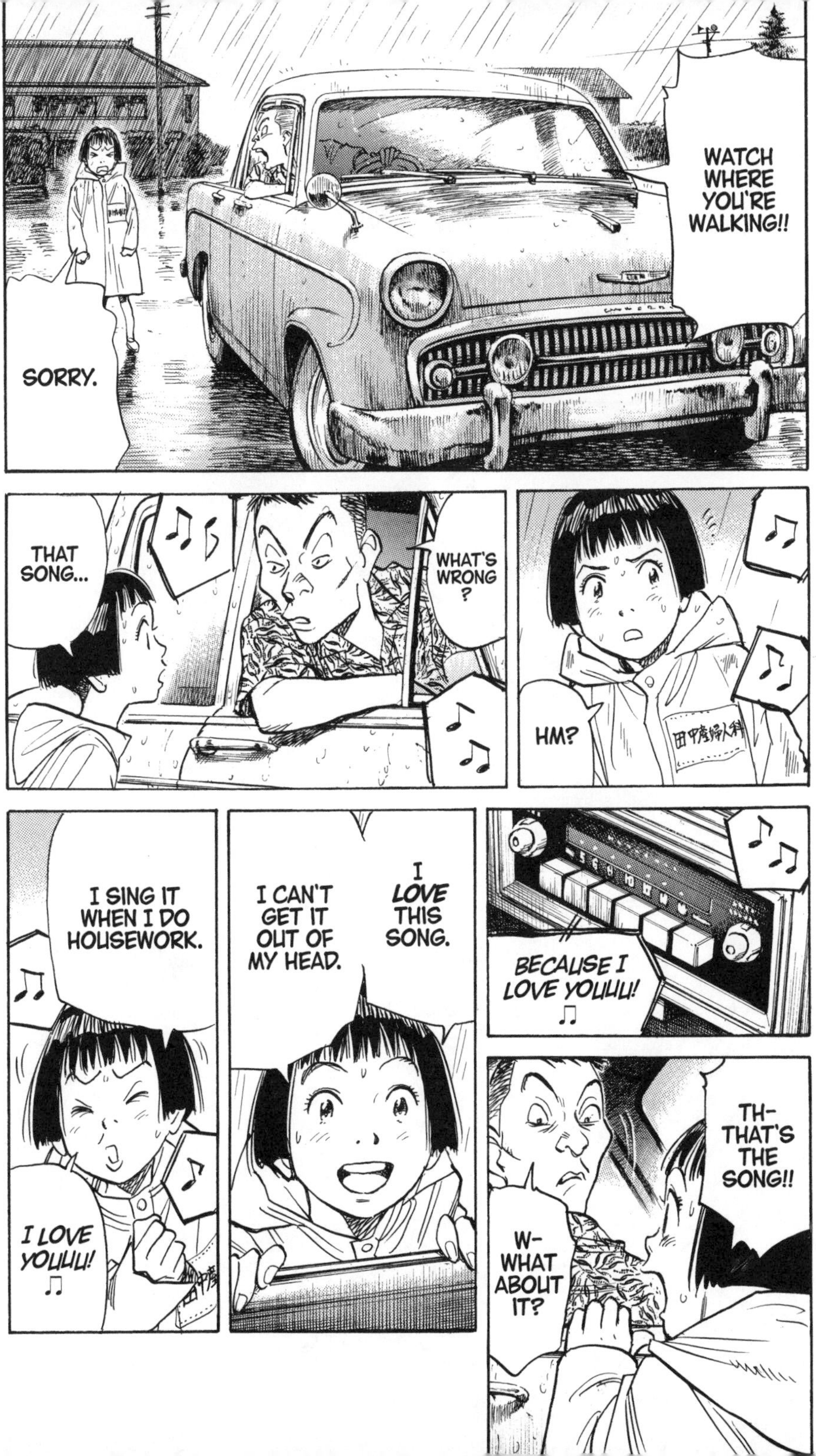
WATCH WHERE YOU'RE WALKING!!
SORRY.
HM?
田中産婦人科
WHAT'S WRONG?
THAT SONG...
BECAUSE I LOVE YOUUU! ♫
TH- THAT'S THE SONG!!
W- WHAT ABOUT IT?
I *LOVE* THIS SONG.
I CAN'T GET IT OUT OF MY HEAD.
I SING IT WHEN I DO HOUSEWORK.
I LOVE YOUUU! ♫

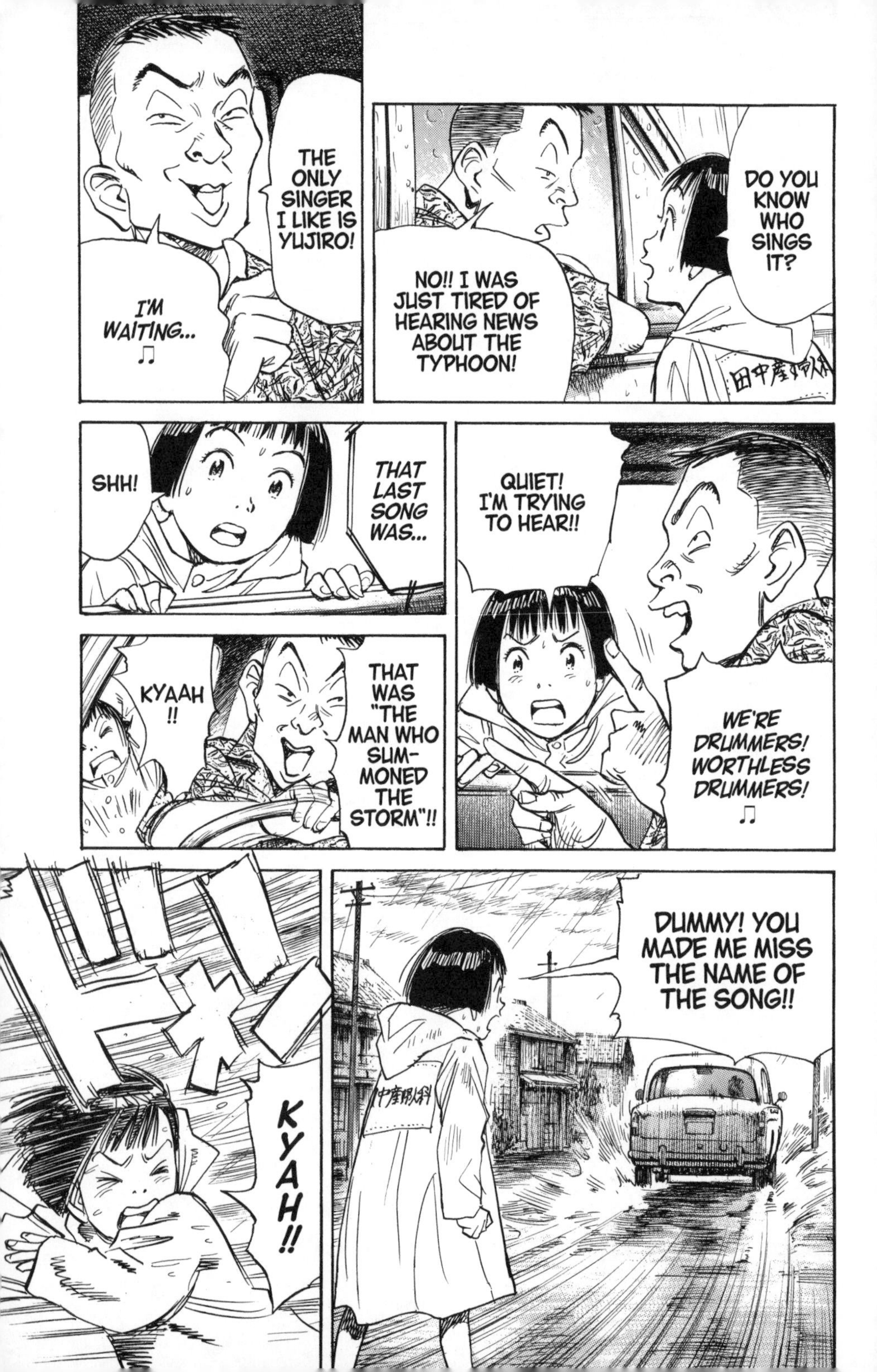
DO YOU KNOW WHO SINGS IT?
NO!! I WAS JUST TIRED OF HEARING NEWS ABOUT THE TYPHOON!
THE ONLY SINGER I LIKE IS YUJIRO!
I'M WAITING... ♫
QUIET! I'M TRYING TO HEAR!!
WE'RE DRUMMERS! WORTHLESS DRUMMERS! ♫
THAT LAST SONG WAS...
SHH!
THAT WAS "THE MAN WHO SUMMONED THE STORM"!!
KYAAH!!
DUMMY! YOU MADE ME MISS THE NAME OF THE SONG!!
KYAH!!

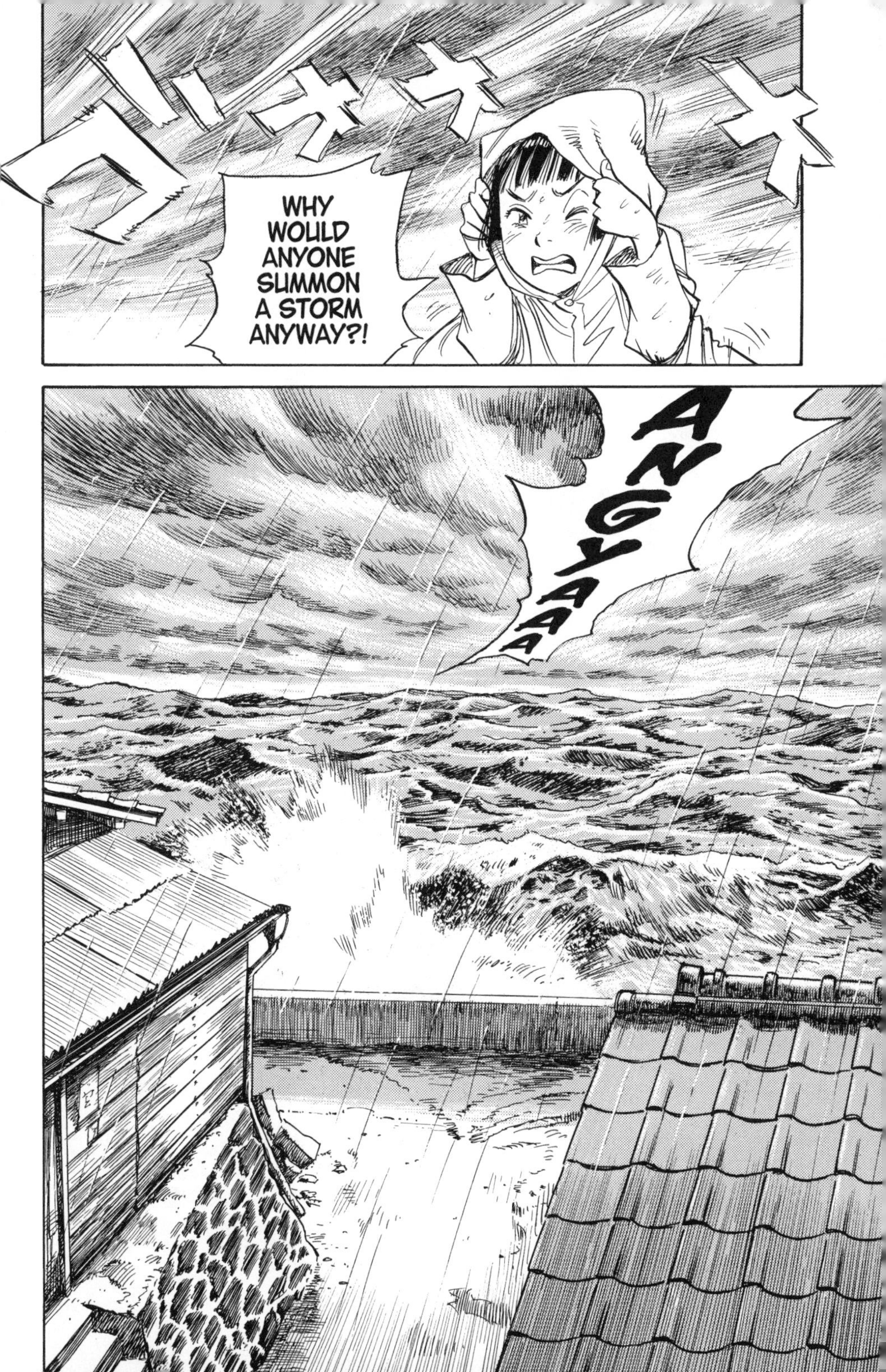
WHY WOULD ANYONE SUMMON A STORM ANYWAY?!
ANGYAAAA

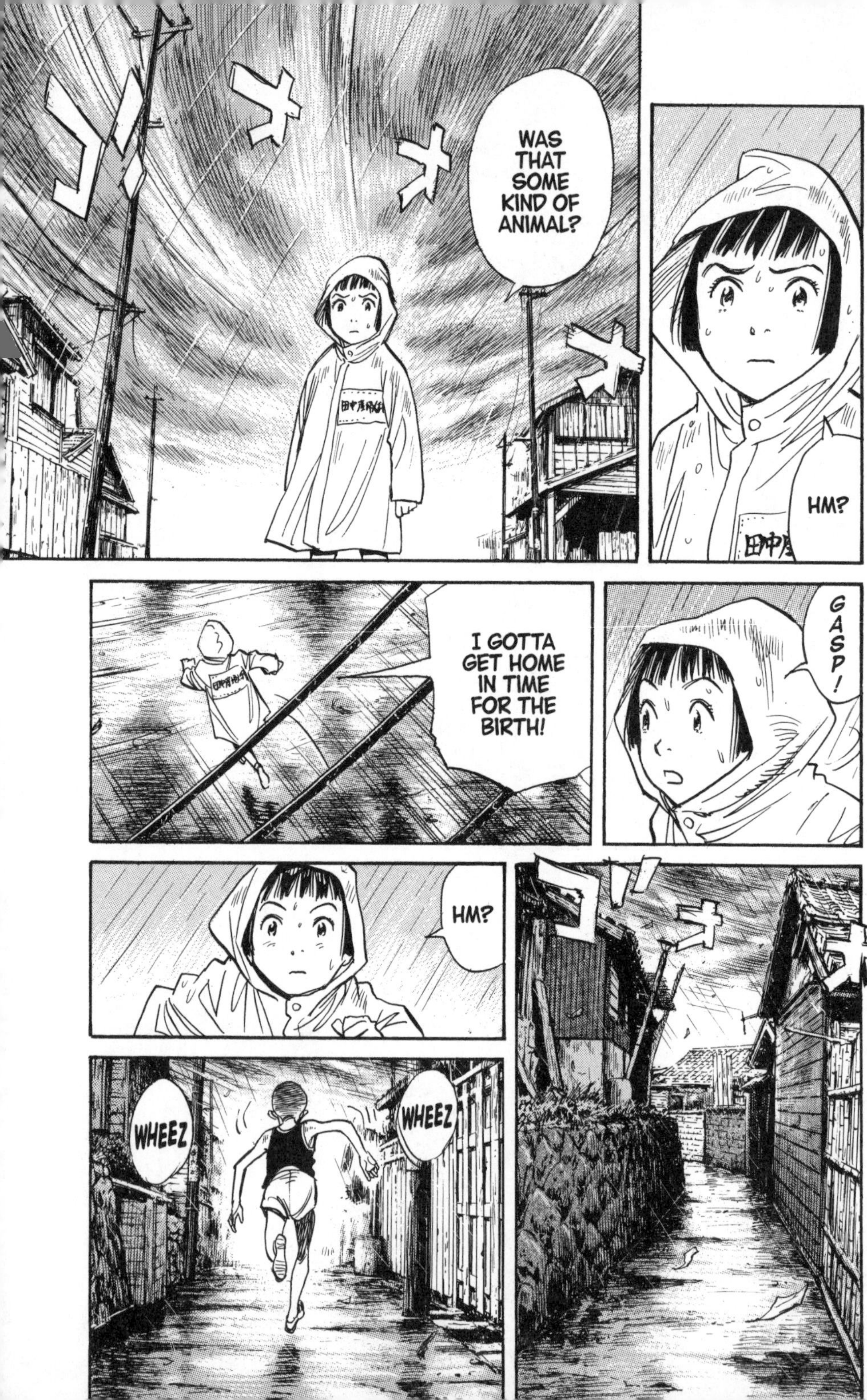
HM?
WAS THAT SOME KIND OF ANIMAL?
GASP!
I GOTTA GET HOME IN TIME FOR THE BIRTH!
HM?
WHEEZ
WHEEZ

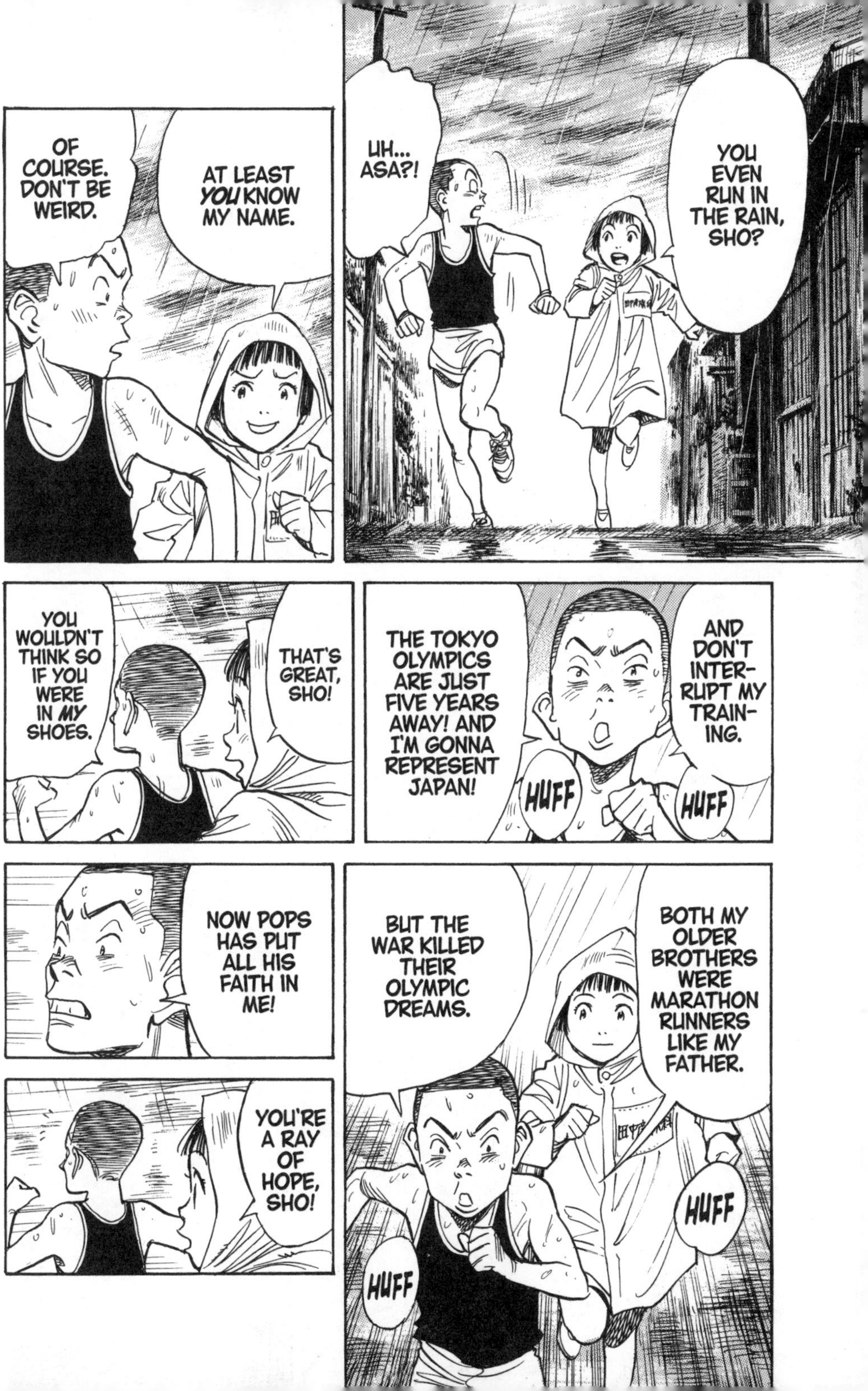
YOU EVEN RUN IN THE RAIN, SHO?
UH... ASA?!
AT LEAST YOU KNOW MY NAME.
OF COURSE. DON'T BE WEIRD.
AND DON'T INTERRUPT MY TRAINING.
HUFF
THE TOKYO OLYMPICS ARE JUST FIVE YEARS AWAY! AND I'M GONNA REPRESENT JAPAN!
HUFF
THAT'S GREAT, SHO!
YOU WOULDN'T THINK SO IF YOU WERE IN MY SHOES.
BOTH MY OLDER BROTHERS WERE MARATHON RUNNERS LIKE MY FATHER.
BUT THE WAR KILLED THEIR OLYMPIC DREAMS.
HUFF
HUFF
NOW POPS HAS PUT ALL HIS FAITH IN ME!
YOU'RE A RAY OF HOPE, SHO!

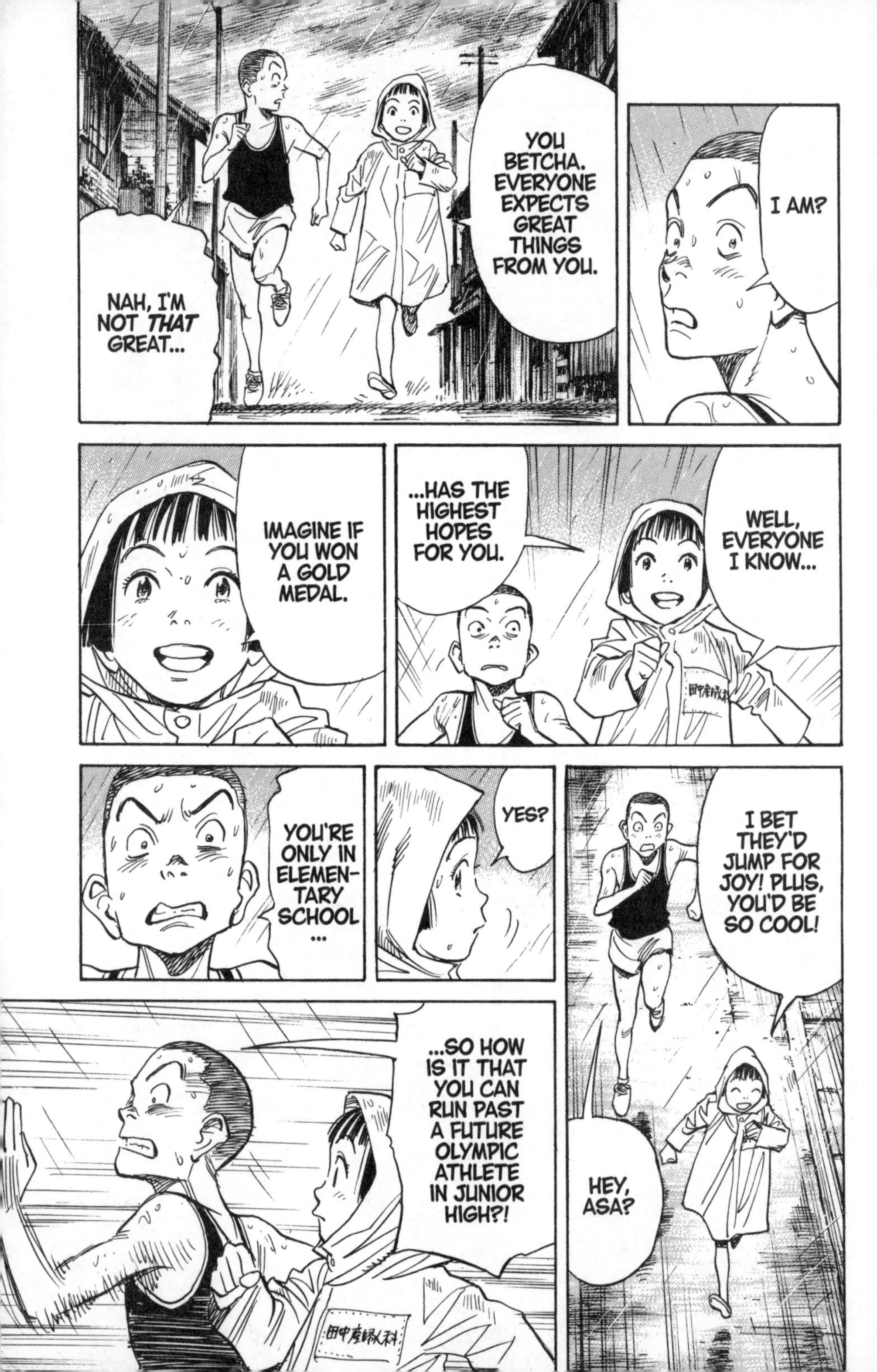
I AM?
YOU BETCHA. EVERYONE EXPECTS GREAT THINGS FROM YOU.
NAH, I'M NOT *THAT* GREAT...
WELL, EVERYONE I KNOW...
...HAS THE HIGHEST HOPES FOR YOU.
IMAGINE IF YOU WON A GOLD MEDAL.
I BET THEY'D JUMP FOR JOY! PLUS, YOU'D BE SO COOL!
HEY, ASA?
YES?
YOU'RE ONLY IN ELEMENTARY SCHOOL ...
...SO HOW IS IT THAT YOU CAN RUN PAST A FUTURE OLYMPIC ATHLETE IN JUNIOR HIGH?!

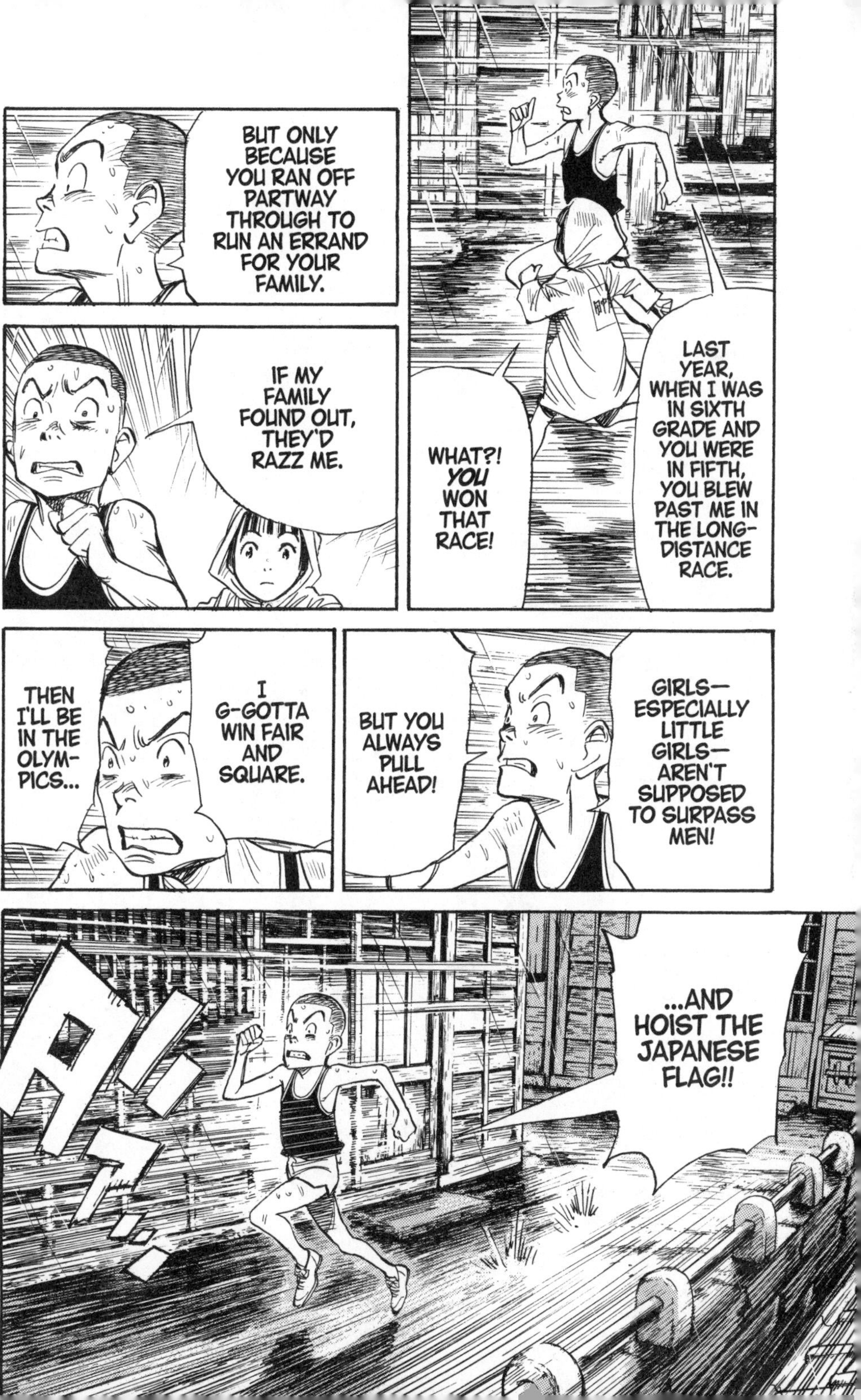
LAST YEAR, WHEN I WAS IN SIXTH GRADE AND YOU WERE IN FIFTH, YOU BLEW PAST ME IN THE LONG-DISTANCE RACE.
WHAT?! *YOU* WON THAT RACE!
BUT ONLY BECAUSE YOU RAN OFF PARTWAY THROUGH TO RUN AN ERRAND FOR YOUR FAMILY.
IF MY FAMILY FOUND OUT, THEY'D RAZZ ME.
GIRLS—ESPECIALLY LITTLE GIRLS—AREN'T SUPPOSED TO SURPASS MEN!
BUT YOU ALWAYS PULL AHEAD!
I G-GOTTA WIN FAIR AND SQUARE.
THEN I'LL BE IN THE OLYMPICS...
...AND HOIST THE JAPANESE FLAG!!

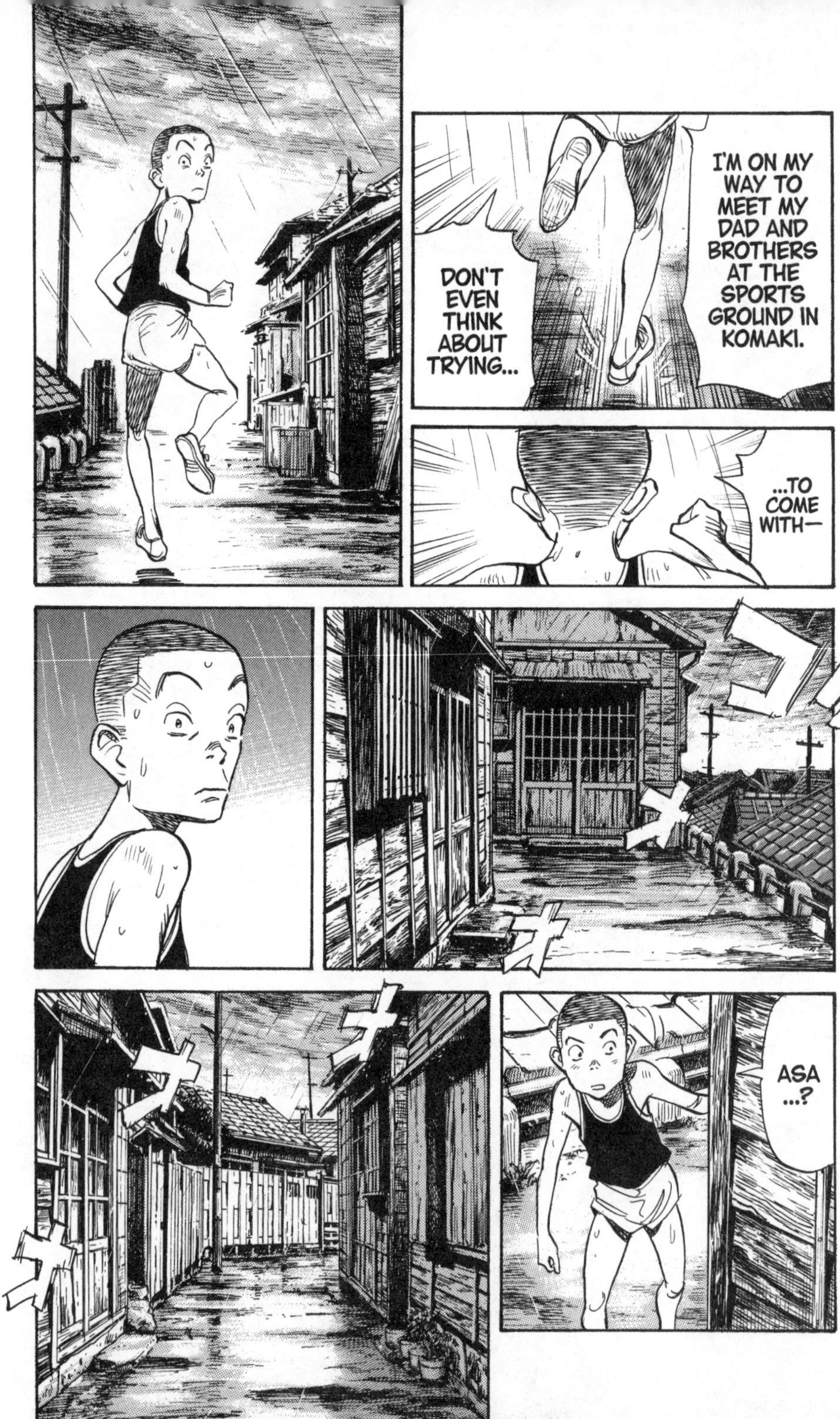
I'M ON MY WAY TO MEET MY DAD AND BROTHERS AT THE SPORTS GROUND IN KOMAKI.
DON'T EVEN THINK ABOUT TRYING...
...TO COME WITH—
ASA ...?

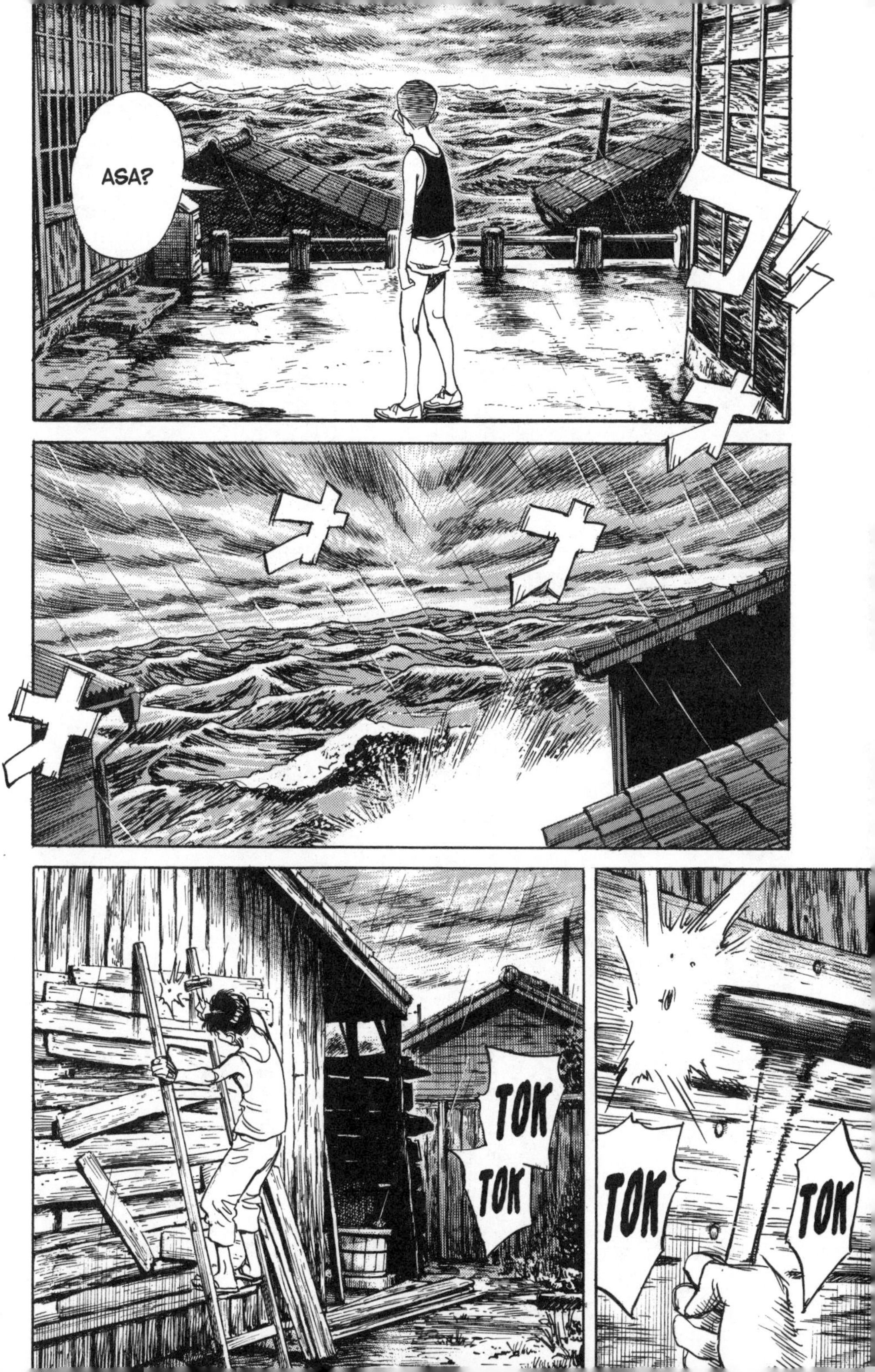
ASA?
TOK
TOK
TOK
TOK

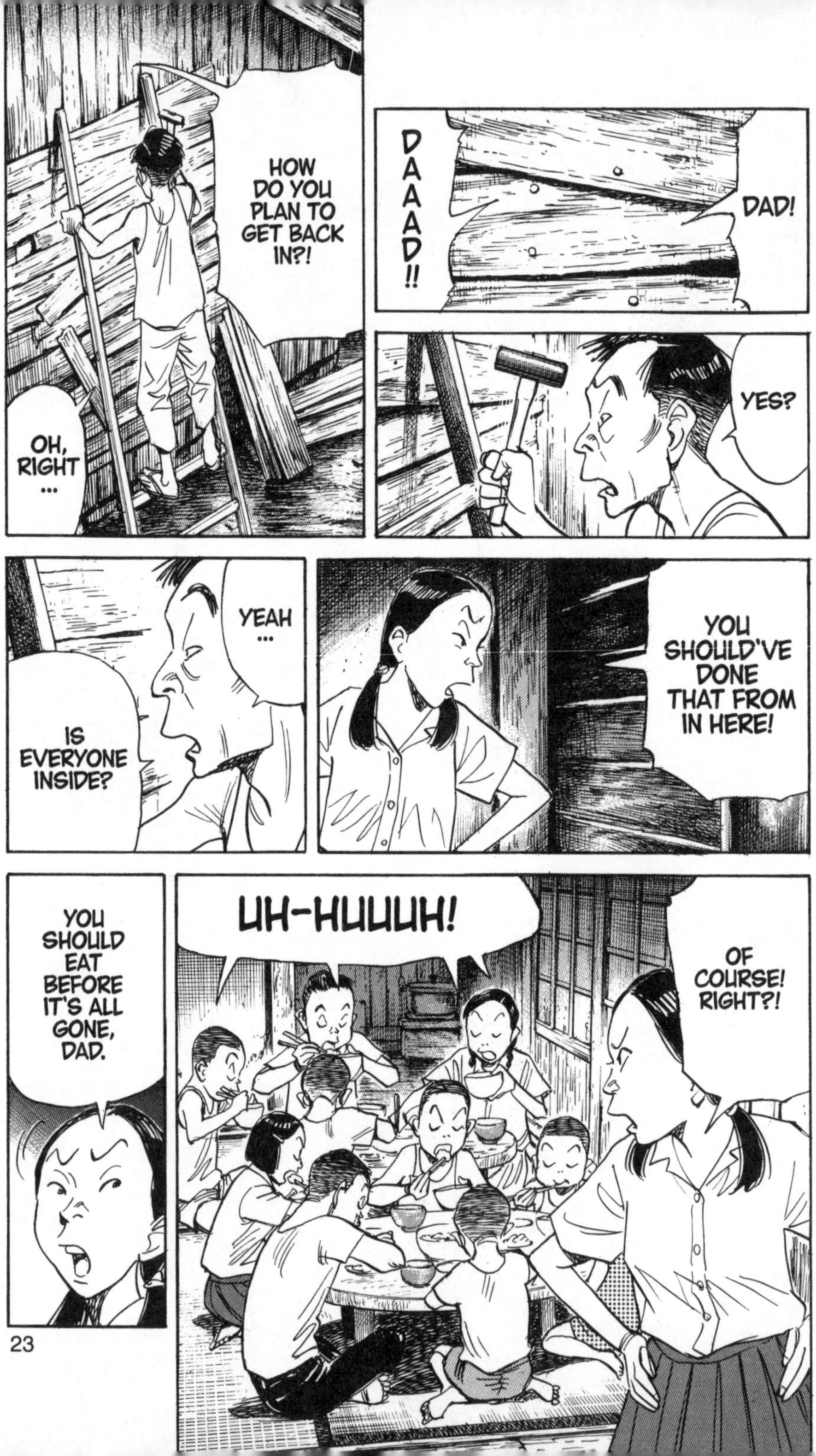

DAD!
DAAAD!!
YES?
HOW DO YOU PLAN TO GET BACK IN?!
OH, RIGHT ...
YOU SHOULD'VE DONE THAT FROM IN HERE!
YEAH ...
IS EVERYONE INSIDE?
OF COURSE! RIGHT?!
UH-HUUUH!
YOU SHOULD EAT BEFORE IT'S ALL GONE, DAD.

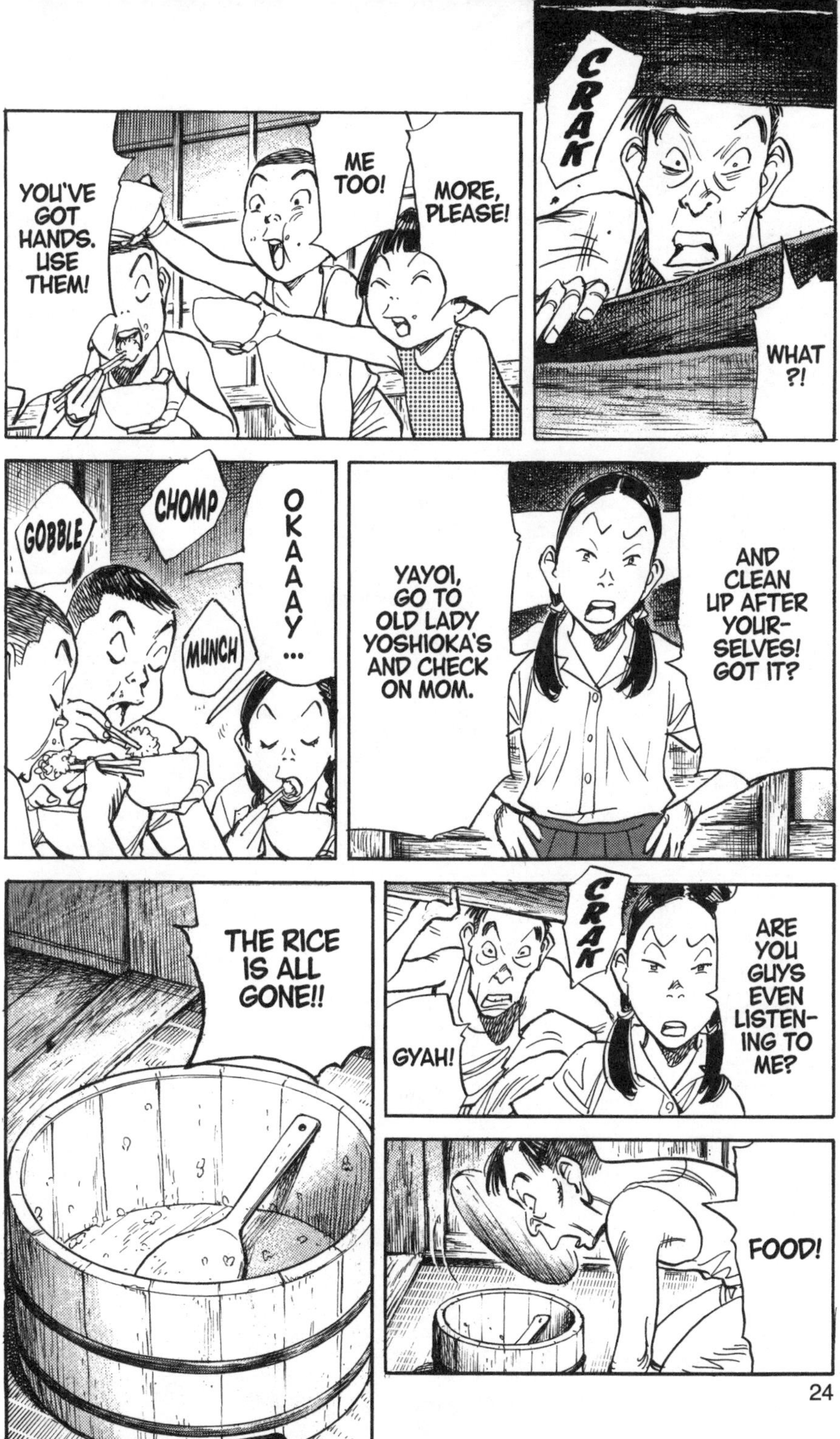
CRAK
WHAT ?!
MORE, PLEASE!
ME TOO!
YOU'VE GOT HANDS. USE THEM!
AND CLEAN UP AFTER YOUR-SELVES! GOT IT?
YAYOI, GO TO OLD LADY YOSHIOKA'S AND CHECK ON MOM.
OKAAAY...
CHOMP
GOBBLE
MUNCH
CRAK
ARE YOU GUYS EVEN LISTEN-ING TO ME?
GYAH!
FOOD!
THE RICE IS ALL GONE!!

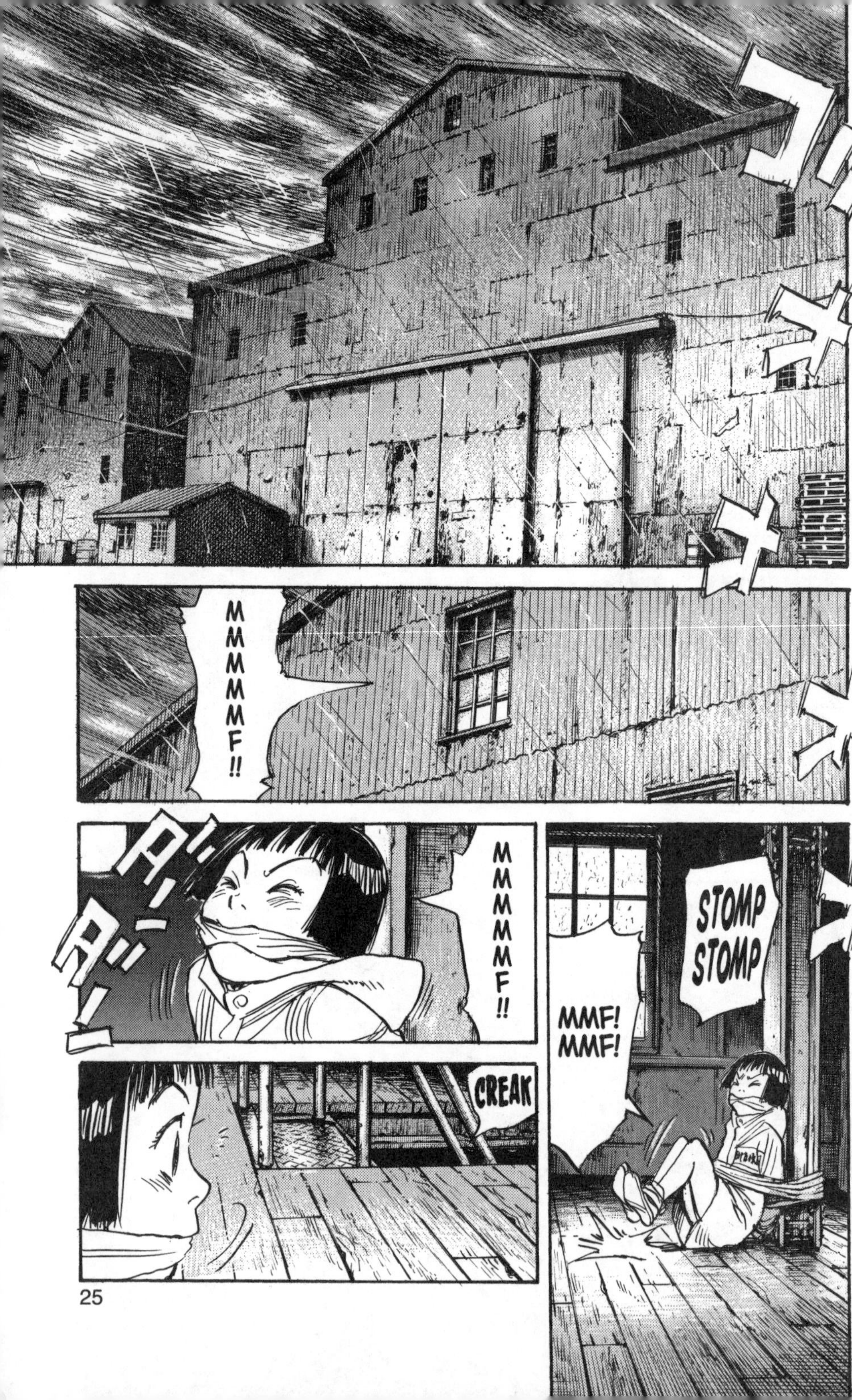
MMMMMMF!!
STOMP STOMP
MMF! MMF!
MMMMMMF!!
CREAK

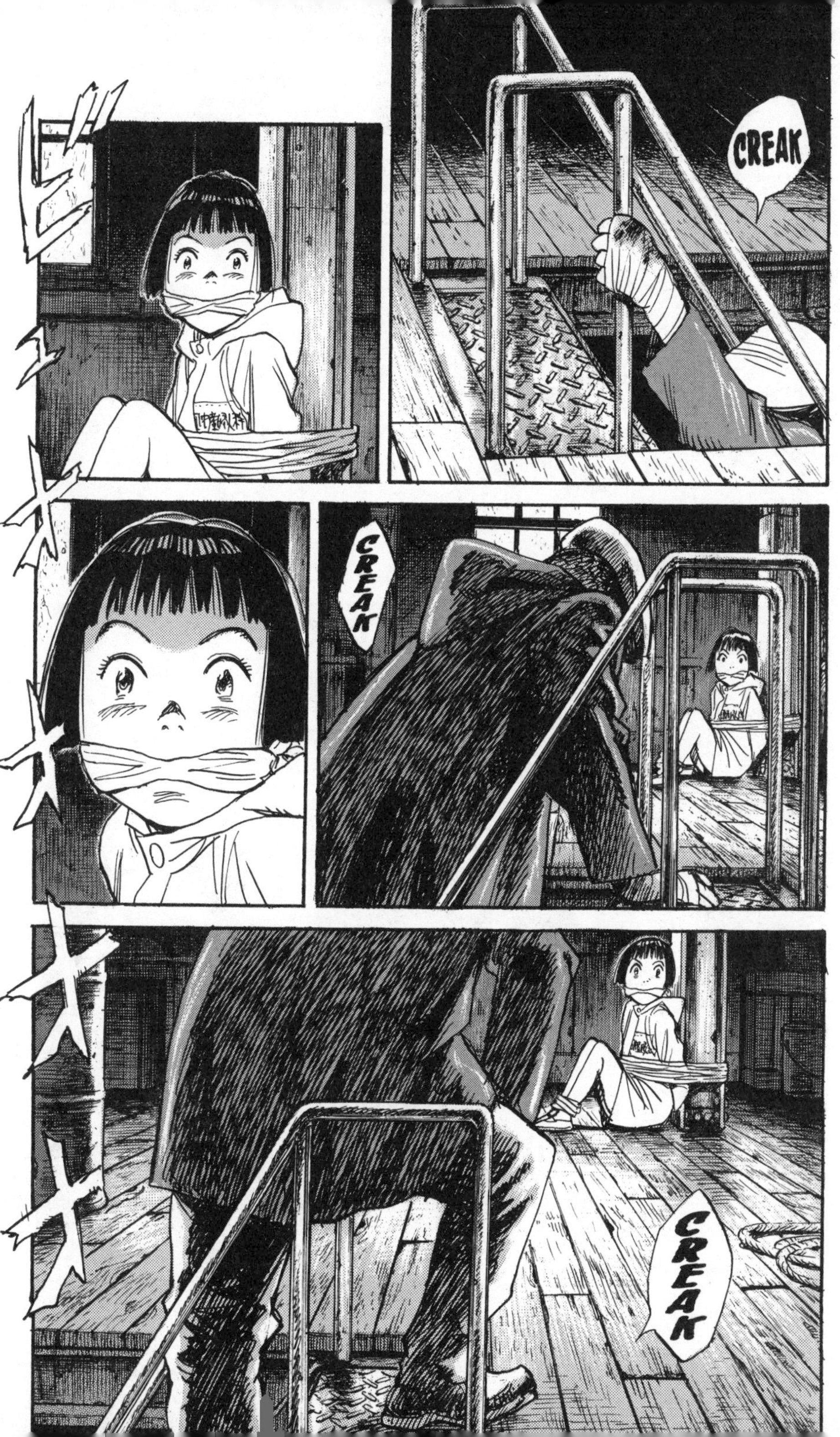
CREAK
CREAK
CREAK

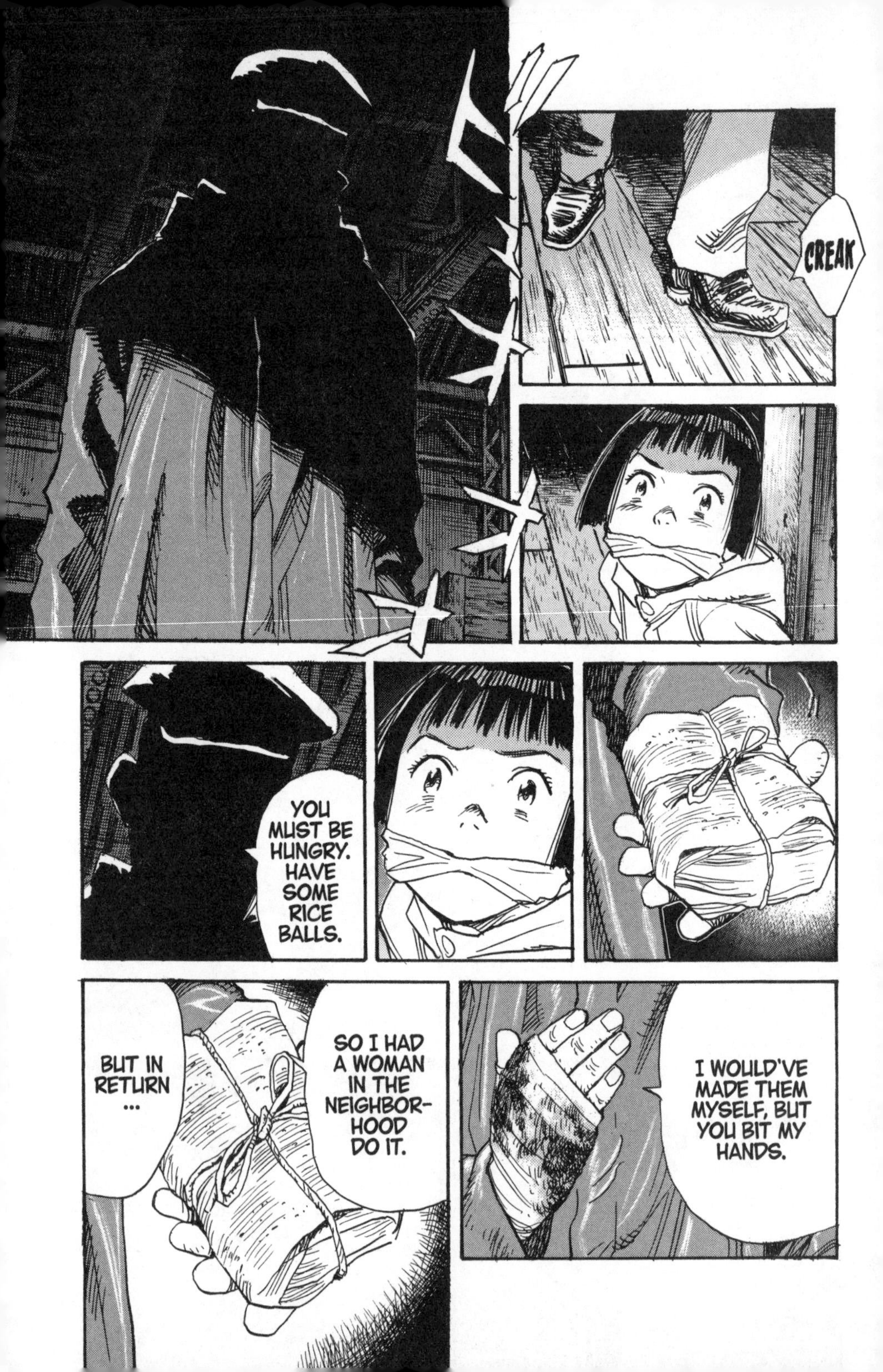
CREAK
YOU MUST BE HUNGRY. HAVE SOME RICE BALLS.
I WOULD'VE MADE THEM MYSELF, BUT YOU BIT MY HANDS.
SO I HAD A WOMAN IN THE NEIGHBOR-HOOD DO IT.
BUT IN RETURN ...

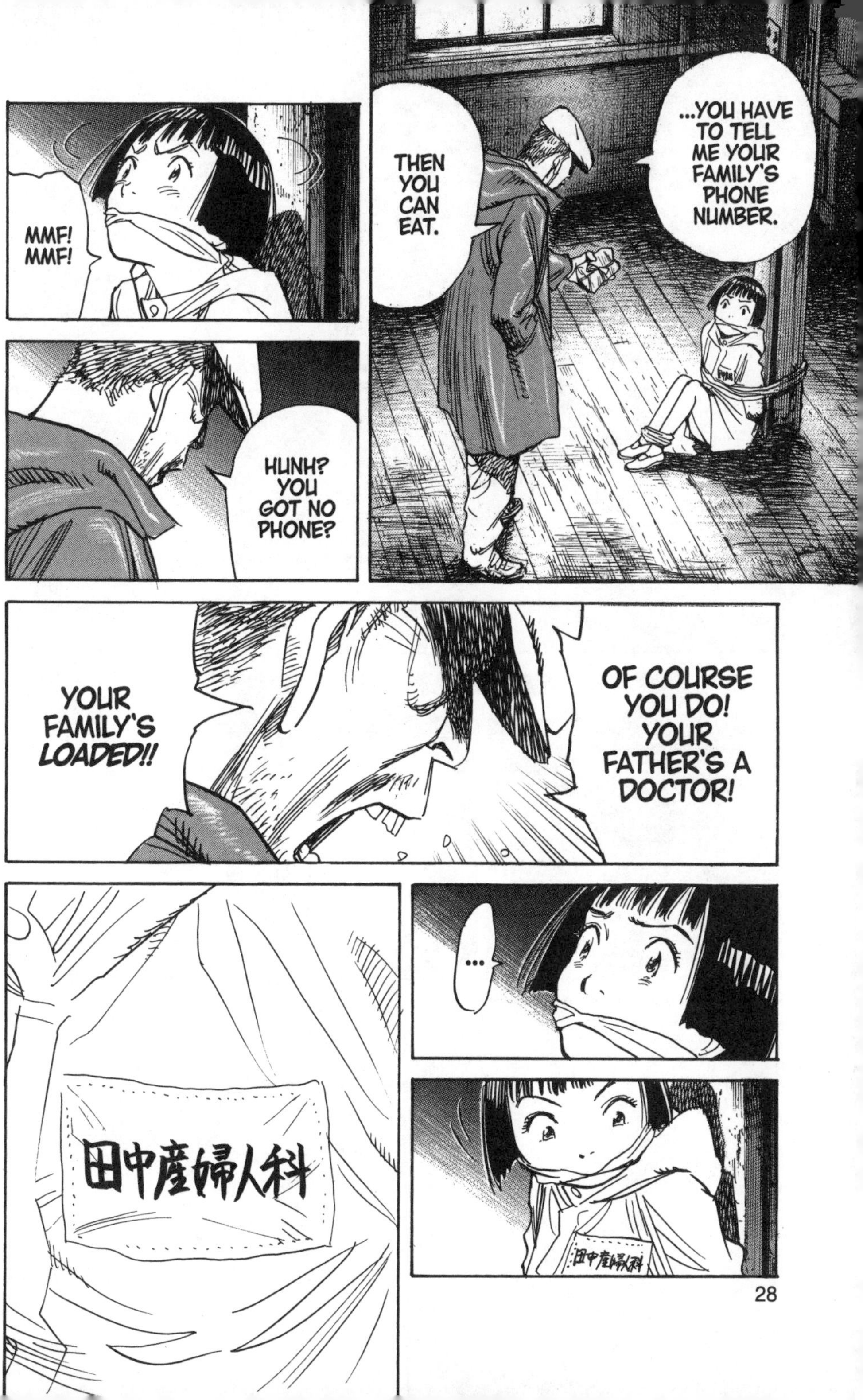
...YOU HAVE TO TELL ME YOUR FAMILY'S PHONE NUMBER.
THEN YOU CAN EAT.
MMF! MMF!
HUNH? YOU GOT NO PHONE?
OF COURSE YOU DO! YOUR FATHER'S A DOCTOR!
YOUR FAMILY'S *LOADED!!*
...
田中産婦人科
田中産婦人科

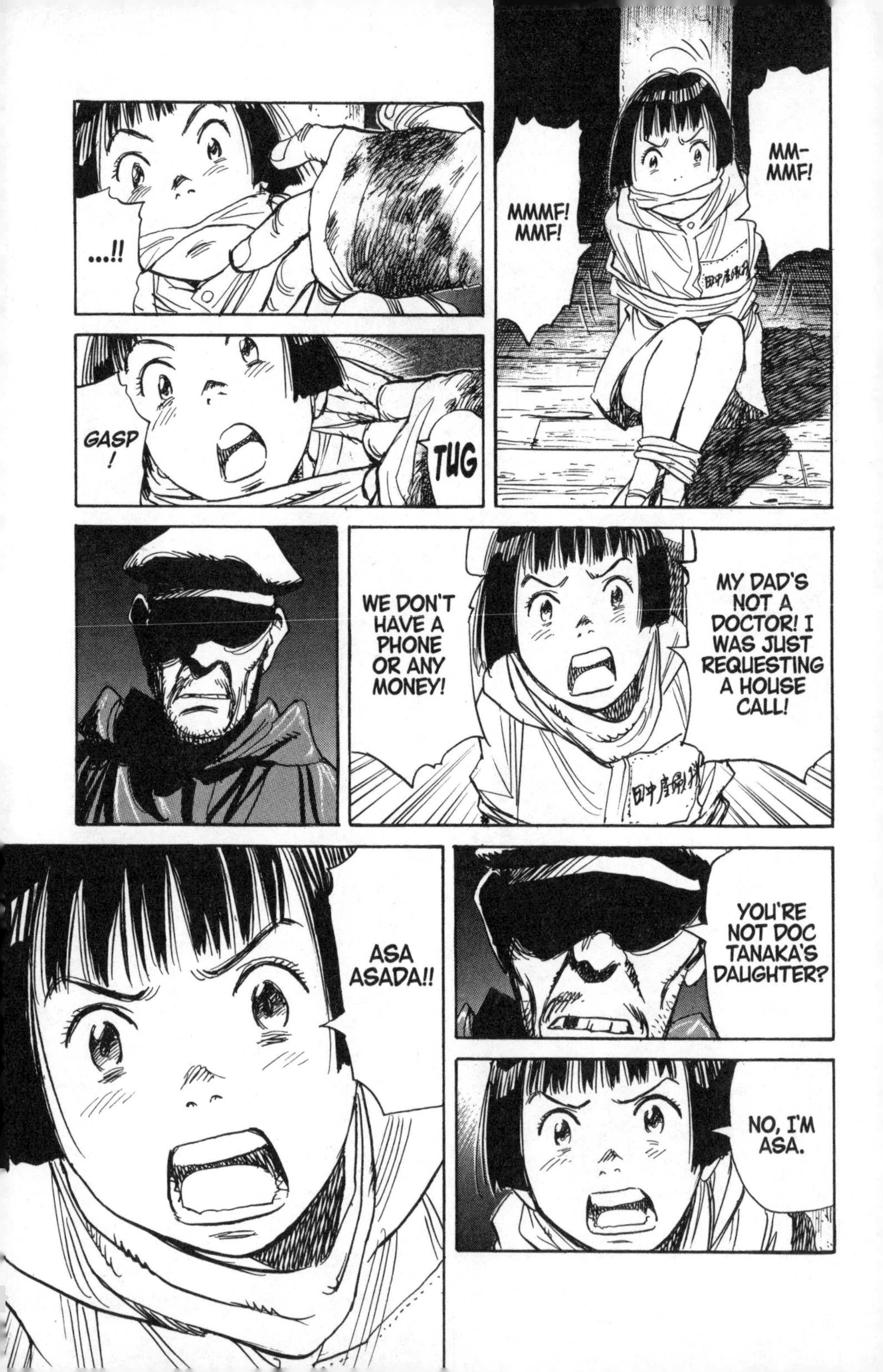
MM-MMF!
MMMF! MMF!
...!!
TUG
GASP!
MY DAD'S NOT A DOCTOR! I WAS JUST REQUESTING A HOUSE CALL!
WE DON'T HAVE A PHONE OR ANY MONEY!
YOU'RE NOT DOC TANAKA'S DAUGHTER?
NO, I'M ASA.
ASA ASADA!!

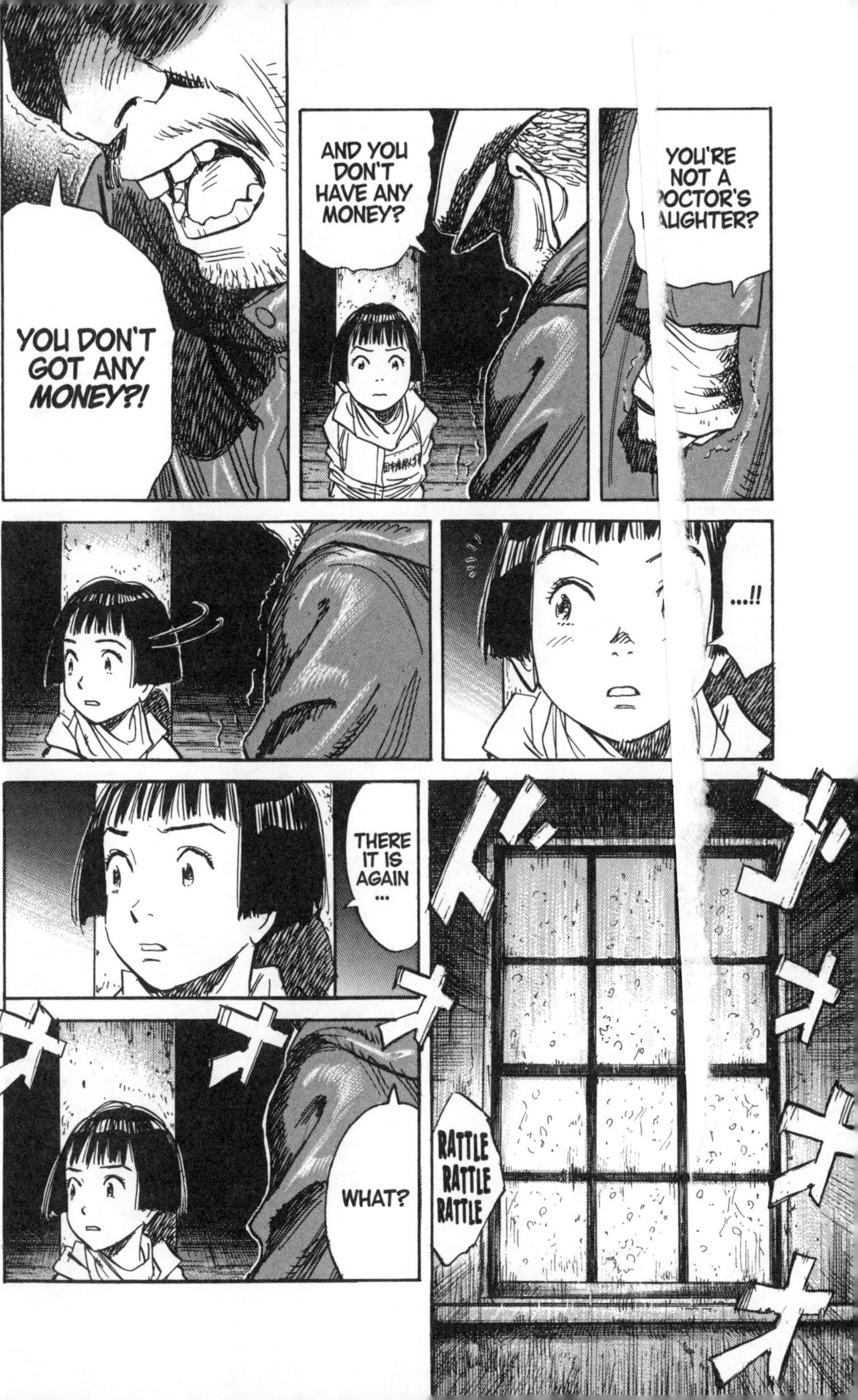
YOU'RE NOT A DOCTOR'S DAUGHTER?
AND YOU DON'T HAVE ANY MONEY?
YOU DON'T GOT ANY *MONEY?!*
...!!
RATTLE RATTLE RATTLE
THERE IT IS AGAIN ...
WHAT?

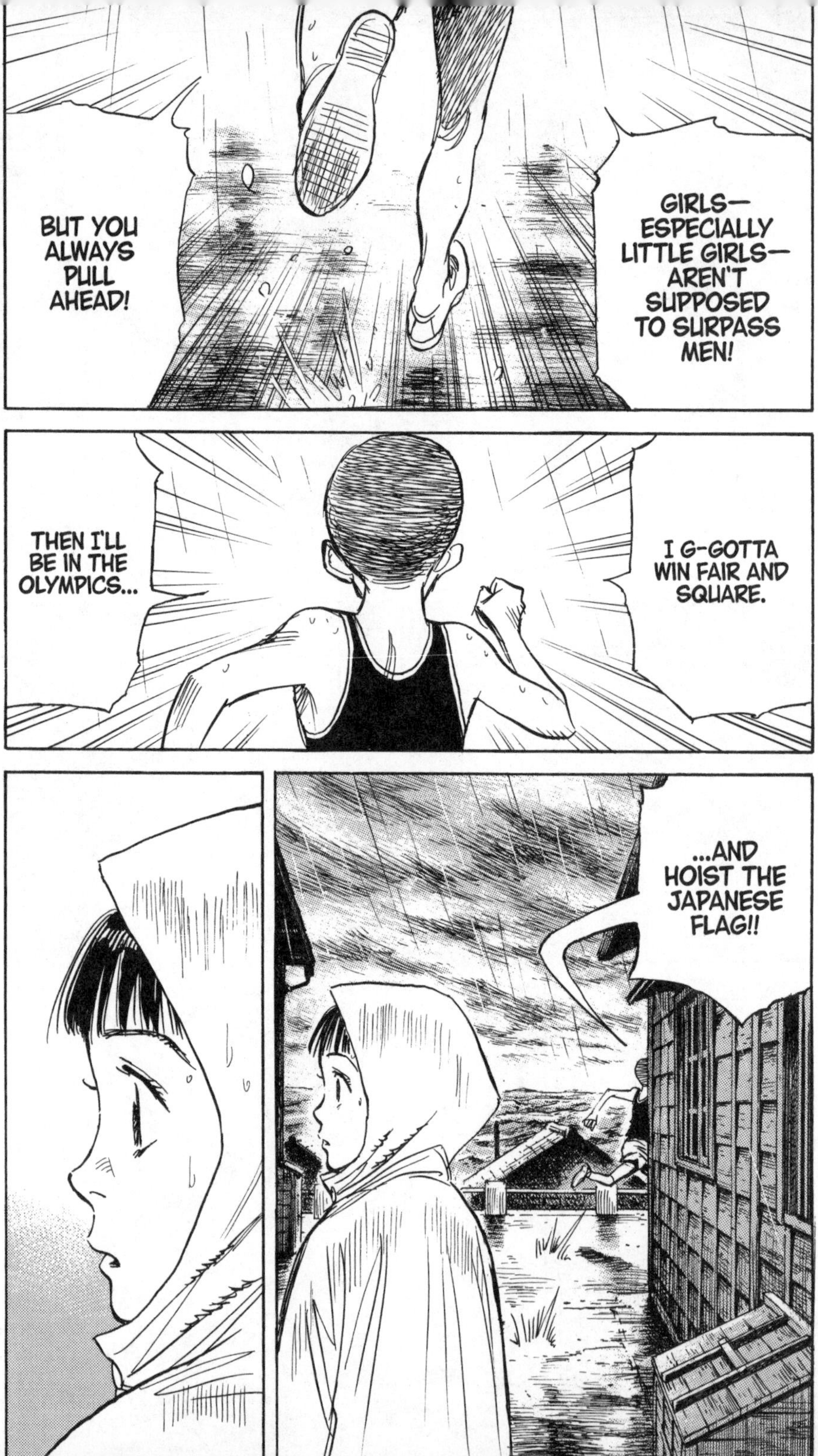
GIRLS—ESPECIALLY LITTLE GIRLS—AREN'T SUPPOSED TO SURPASS MEN!
BUT YOU ALWAYS PULL AHEAD!
I G-GOTTA WIN FAIR AND SQUARE.
THEN I'LL BE IN THE OLYMPICS...
...AND HOIST THE JAPANESE FLAG!!

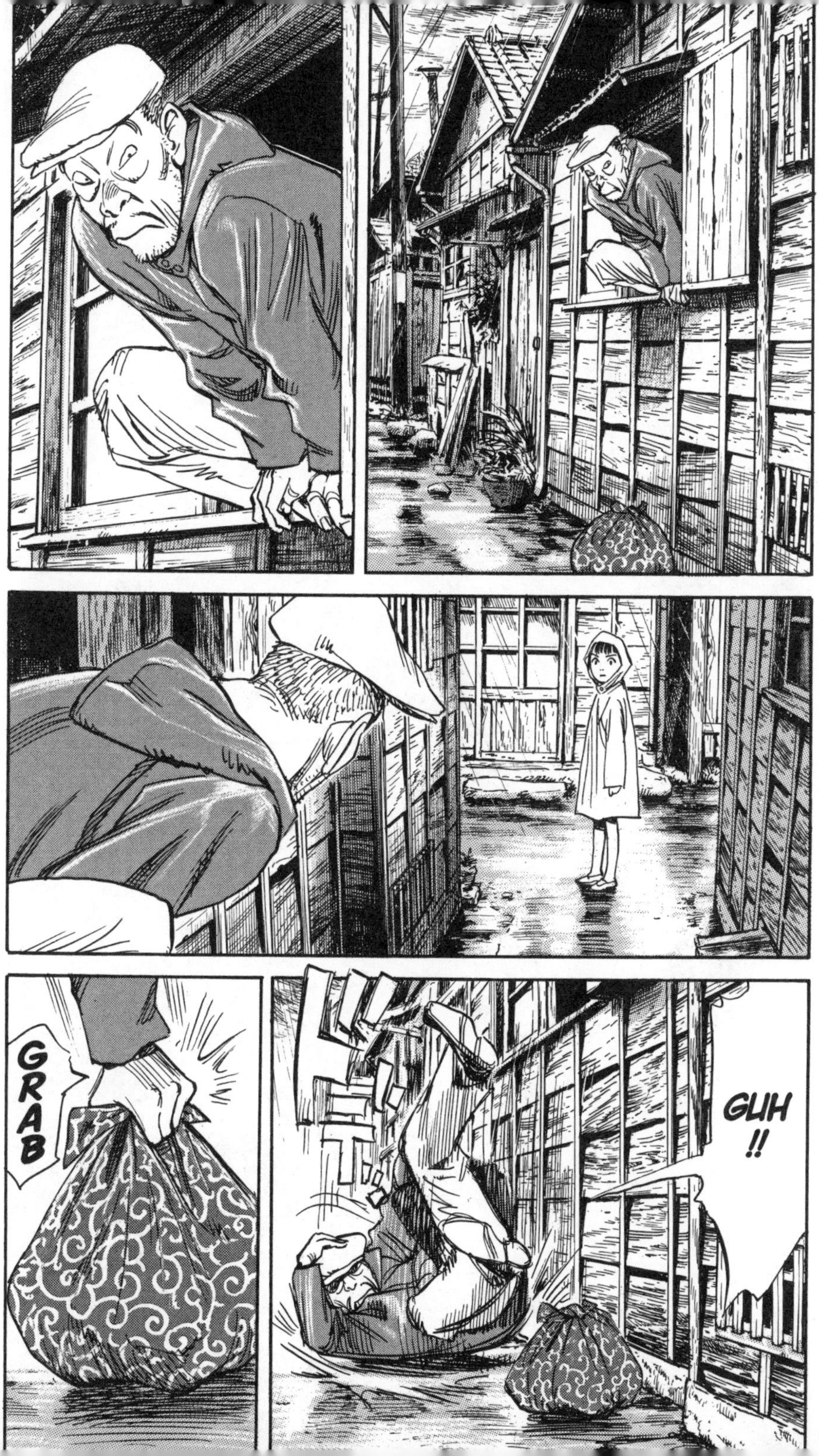
GUH
!!
GRAB

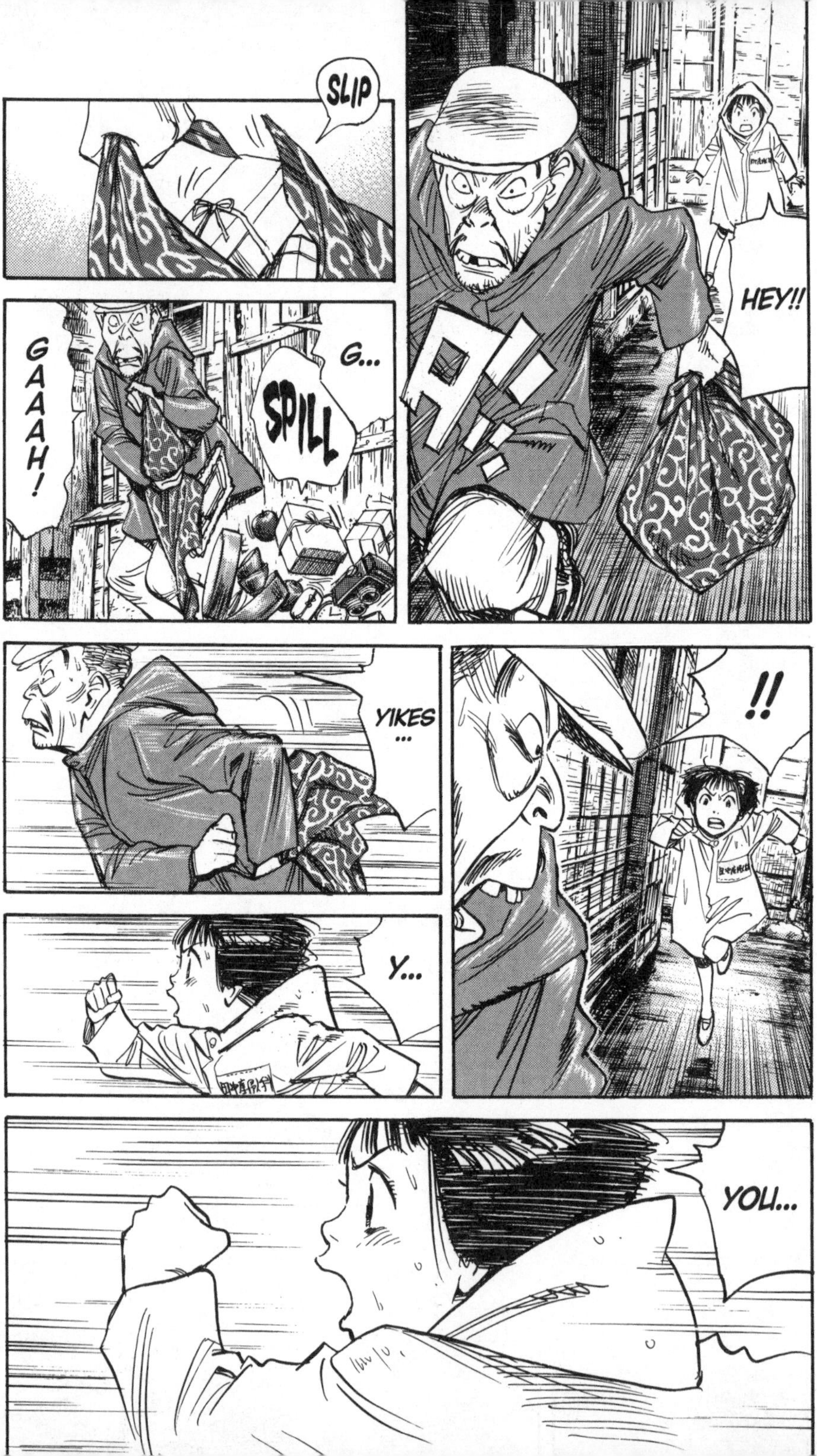
HEY!!
SLIP
G...
SPILL
GAAAAH!
!!
YIKES...
Y...
YOU...

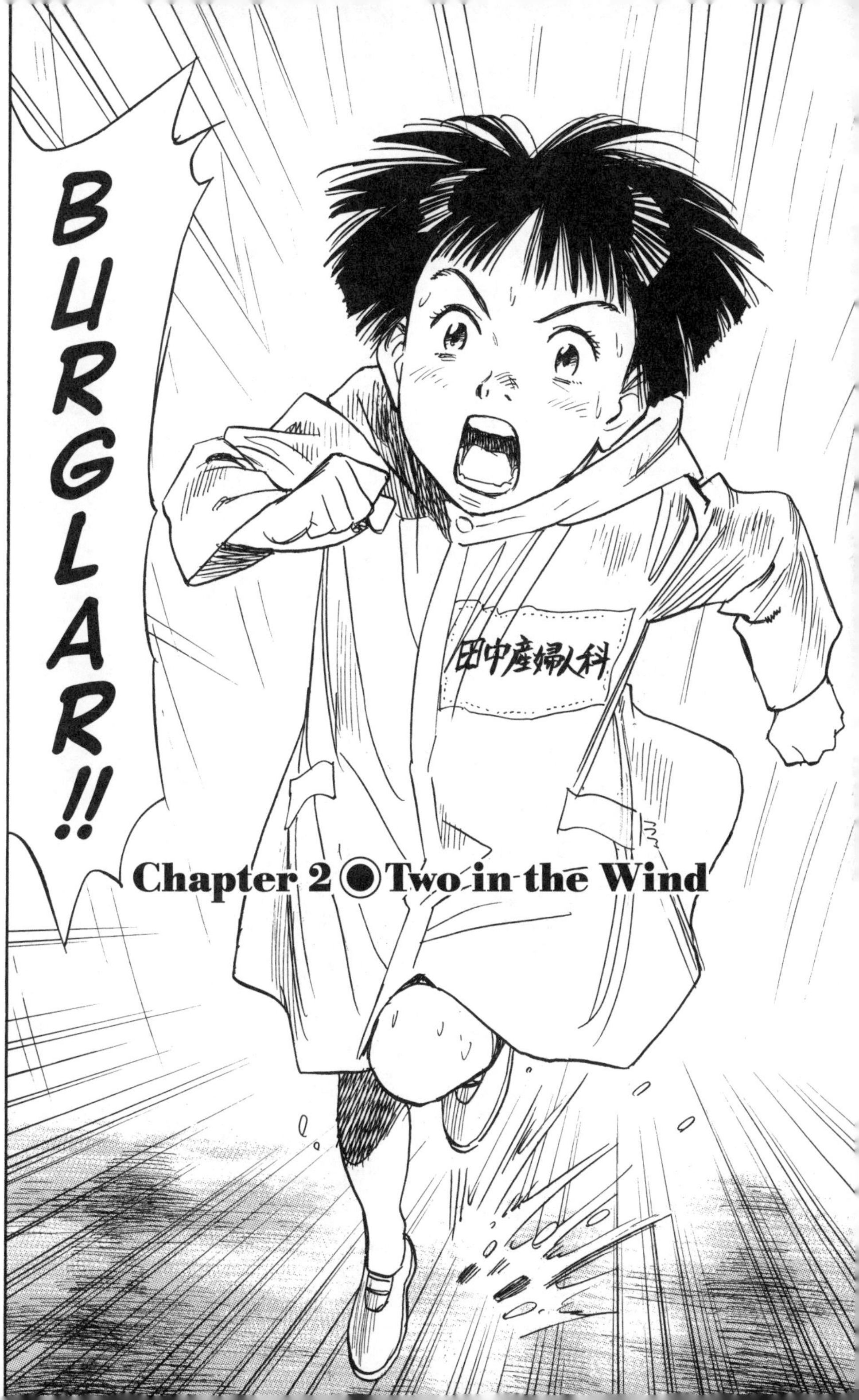
BURGLAR!!
田中産婦人科
Chapter 2 ● Two in the Wind

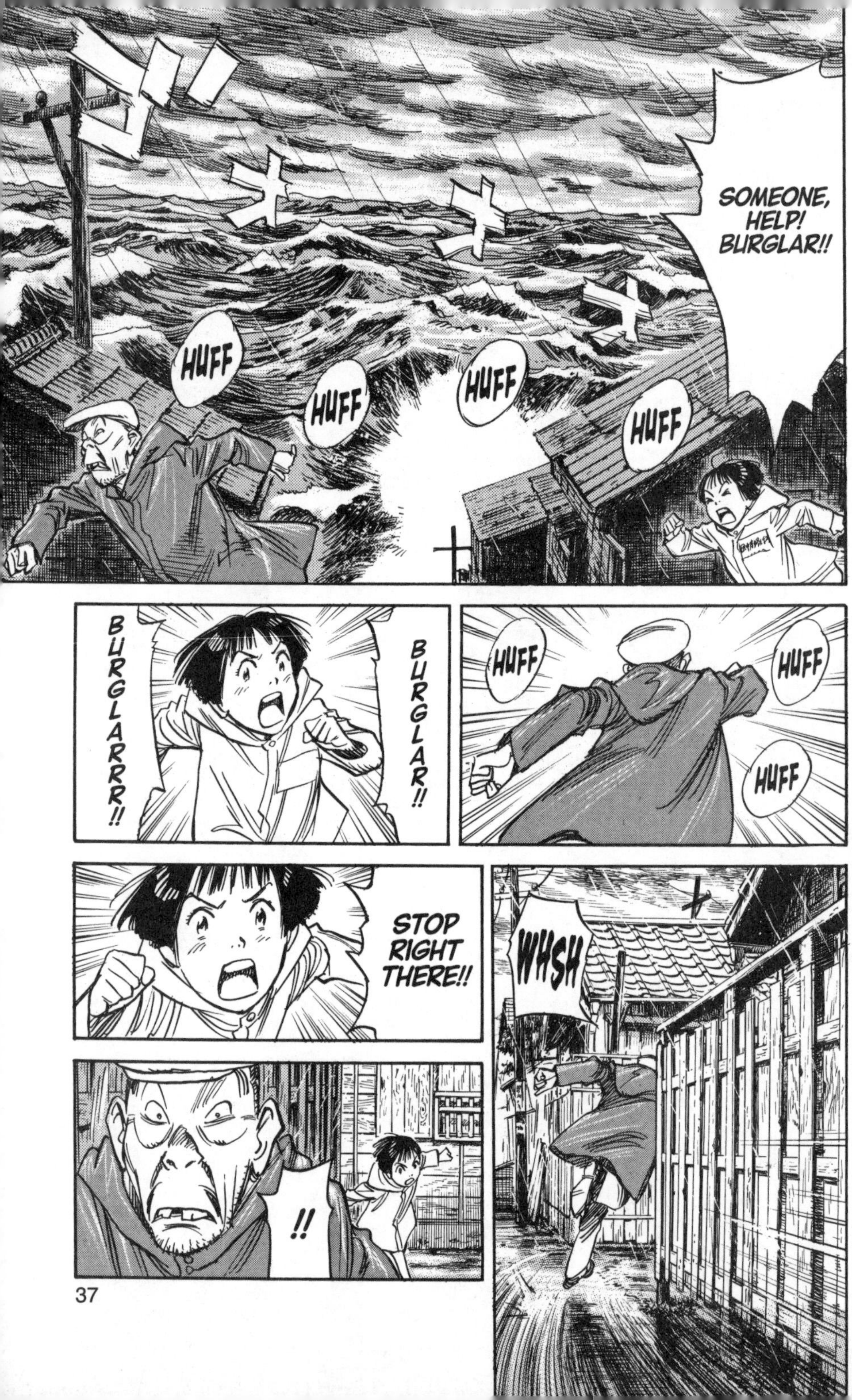
SOMEONE, HELP! BURGLAR!!
HUFF
HUFF
HUFF
HUFF
HUFF
HUFF
HUFF
BURGLAR!!
BURGLARRRR!!
WHSH
STOP RIGHT THERE!!
!!

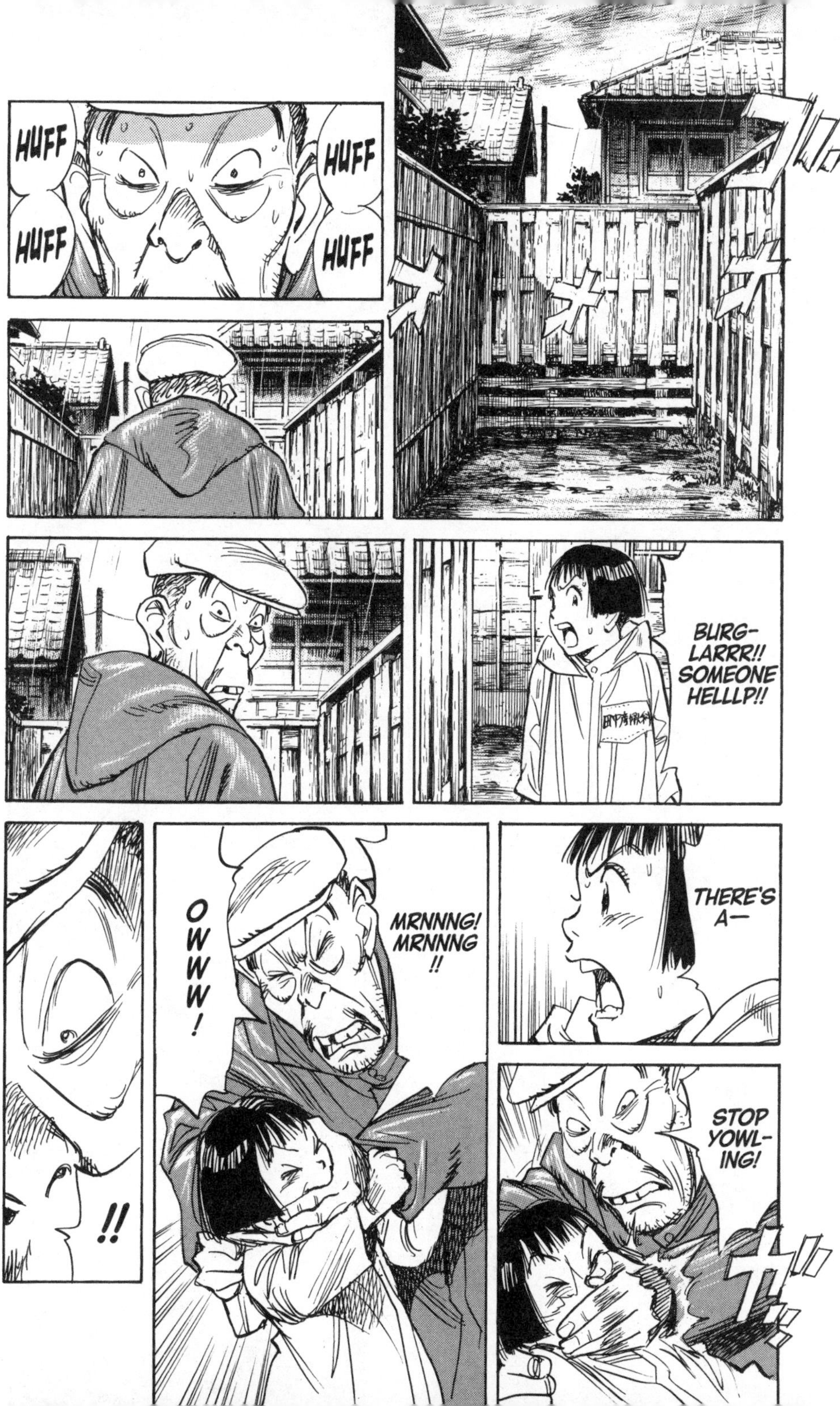
HUFF
HUFF
HUFF
HUFF
BURG-
LARRR!!
SOMEONE
HELLLP!!
THERE'S
A—
STOP
YOWL-
ING!
MRNNNG!
MRNNNG
!!
OWWW!
!!

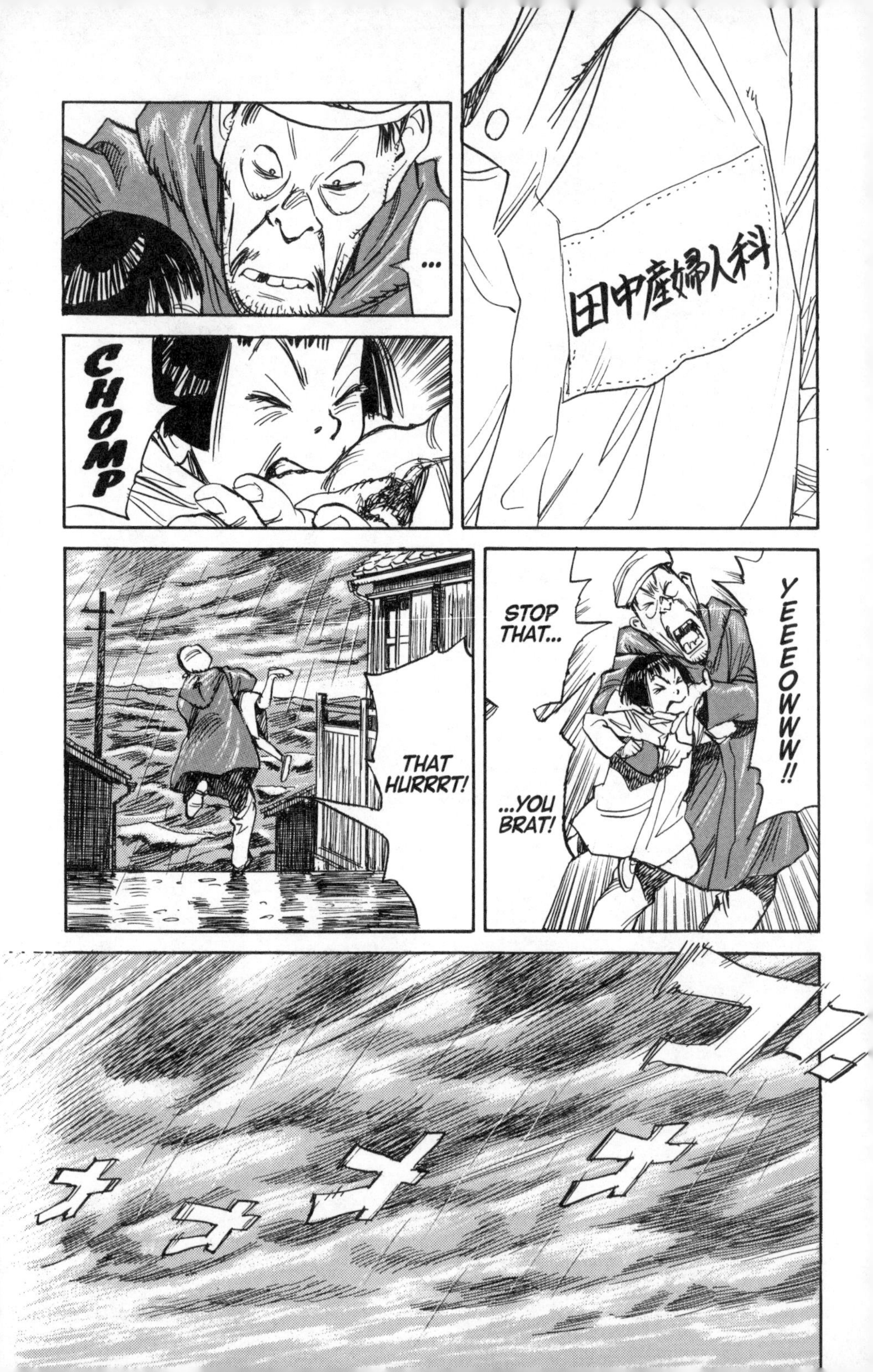
田中産婦人科
...
CHOMP
YEEEOWWW!!
STOP THAT...
...YOU BRAT!
THAT HURRRT!

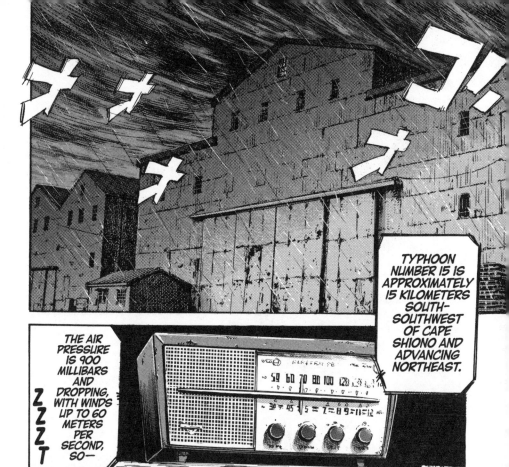

TYPHOON NUMBER 15 IS APPROXIMATELY 15 KILOMETERS SOUTH-SOUTHWEST OF CAPE SHIONO AND ADVANCING NORTHEAST.

THE AIR PRESSURE IS 900 MILLIBARS AND DROPPING, WITH WINDS UP TO 60 METERS PER SECOND, SO—

ZZZT

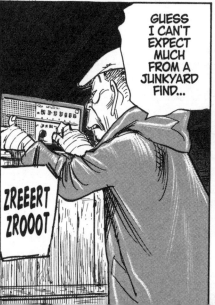

GUESS I CAN'T EXPECT MUCH FROM A JUNKYARD FIND...

ZREEERT ZROOOT

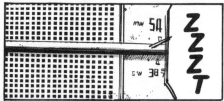

ZZZT

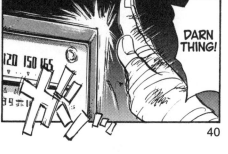

DARN THING!

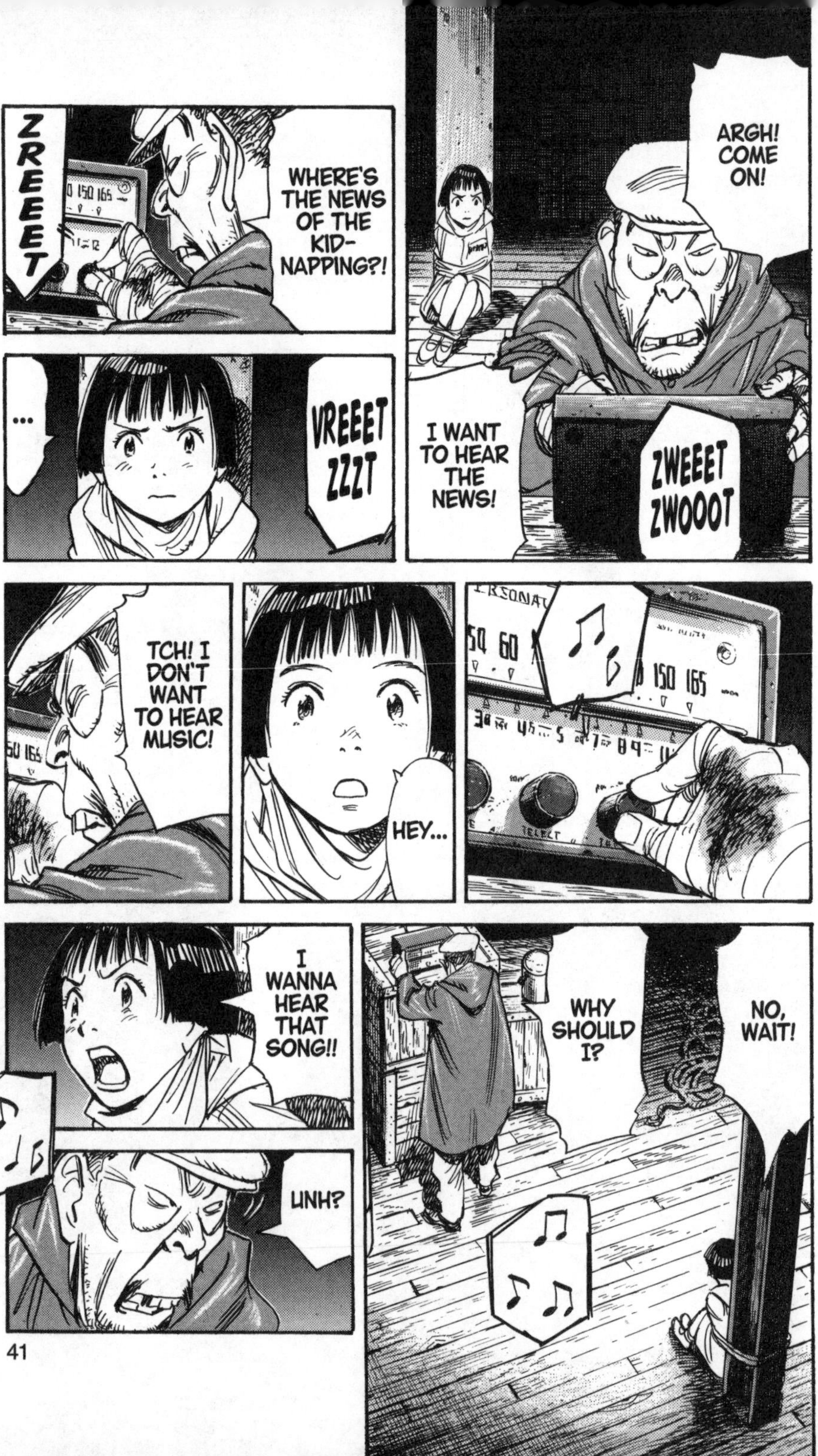
ARGH! COME ON!
ZWEEET ZWOOOT
I WANT TO HEAR THE NEWS!
WHERE'S THE NEWS OF THE KID-NAPPING?!
ZREEET
VREEET ZZZT
...
HEY...
TCH! I DON'T WANT TO HEAR MUSIC!
NO, WAIT!
WHY SHOULD I?
I WANNA HEAR THAT SONG!!
UNH?

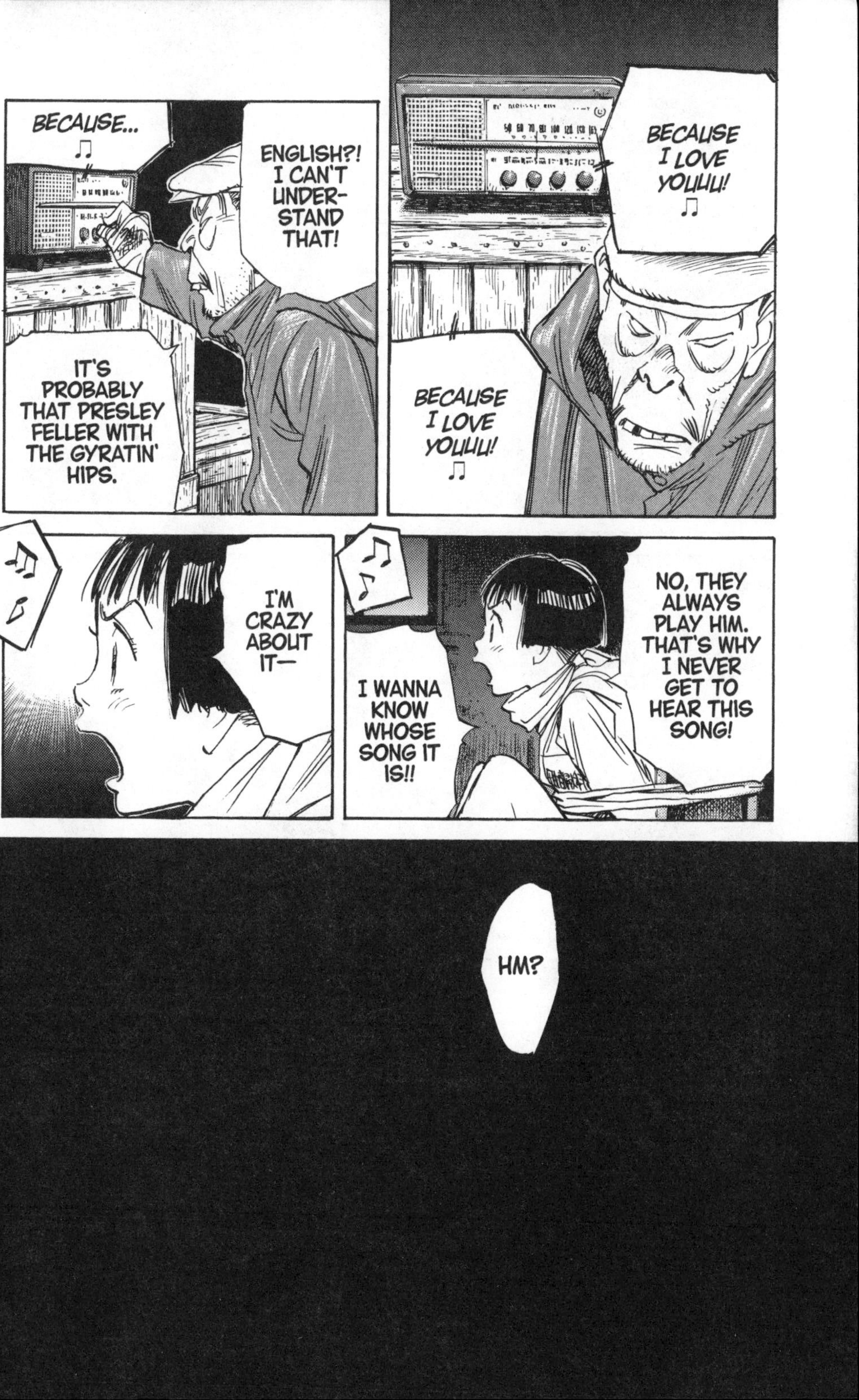
BECAUSE I LOVE YOUUU! ♫
BECAUSE I LOVE YOUUU! ♫
ENGLISH?! I CAN'T UNDER-STAND THAT!
BECAUSE... ♫
IT'S PROBABLY THAT PRESLEY FELLER WITH THE GYRATIN' HIPS.
NO, THEY ALWAYS PLAY HIM. THAT'S WHY I NEVER GET TO HEAR THIS SONG!
I WANNA KNOW WHOSE SONG IT IS!!
I'M CRAZY ABOUT IT—
HM?

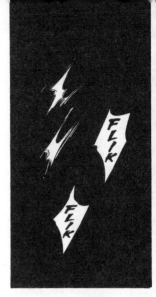

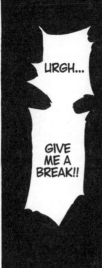

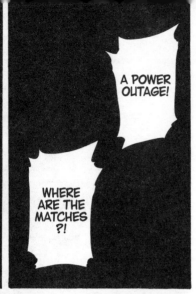

A POWER OUTAGE!
WHERE ARE THE MATCHES ?!
URGH...
GIVE ME A BREAK!!
FLIK
FLIK
FWIK
NOW A CAN-DLE.
I THINK I SWIPED ONE FROM THE FAMILY ALTAR BACK THERE...
YOWCH!
TH-THAT'S HOT!
PHEW ...

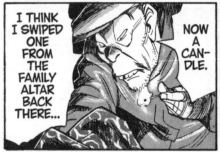

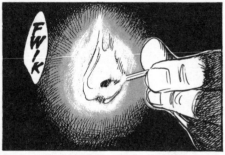

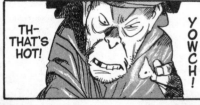

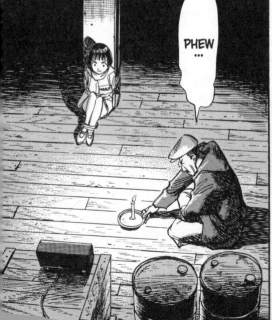

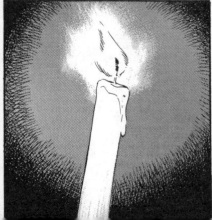

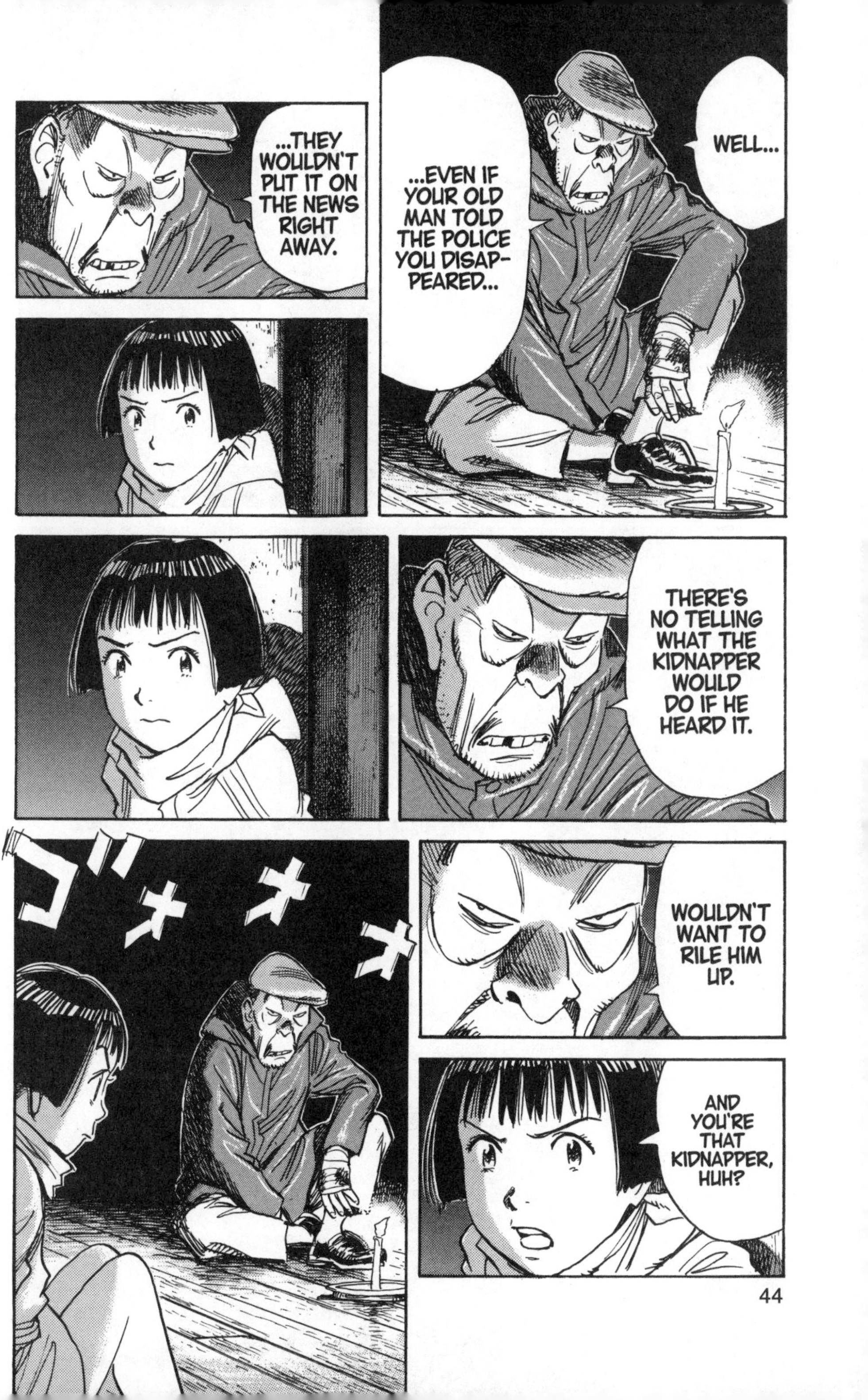
WELL...
...EVEN IF YOUR OLD MAN TOLD THE POLICE YOU DISAPPEARED...
...THEY WOULDN'T PUT IT ON THE NEWS RIGHT AWAY.
THERE'S NO TELLING WHAT THE KIDNAPPER WOULD DO IF HE HEARD IT.
WOULDN'T WANT TO RILE HIM UP.
AND YOU'RE THAT KIDNAPPER, HUH?
ゴオオオ

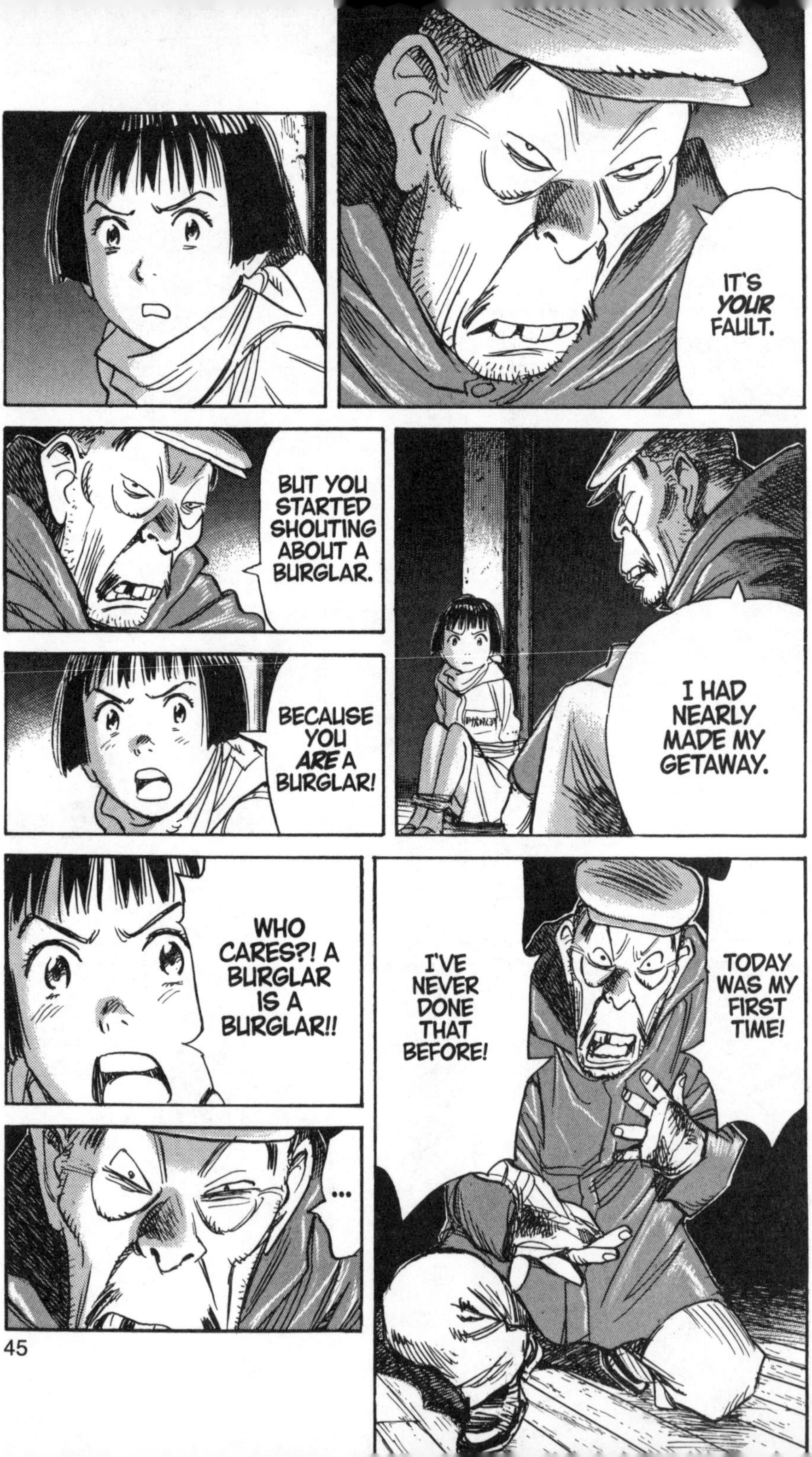
IT'S *YOUR* FAULT.
I HAD NEARLY MADE MY GETAWAY.
BUT YOU STARTED SHOUTING ABOUT A BURGLAR.
BECAUSE YOU *ARE* A BURGLAR!
TODAY WAS MY FIRST TIME!
I'VE NEVER DONE THAT BEFORE!
WHO CARES?! A BURGLAR IS A BURGLAR!!
...

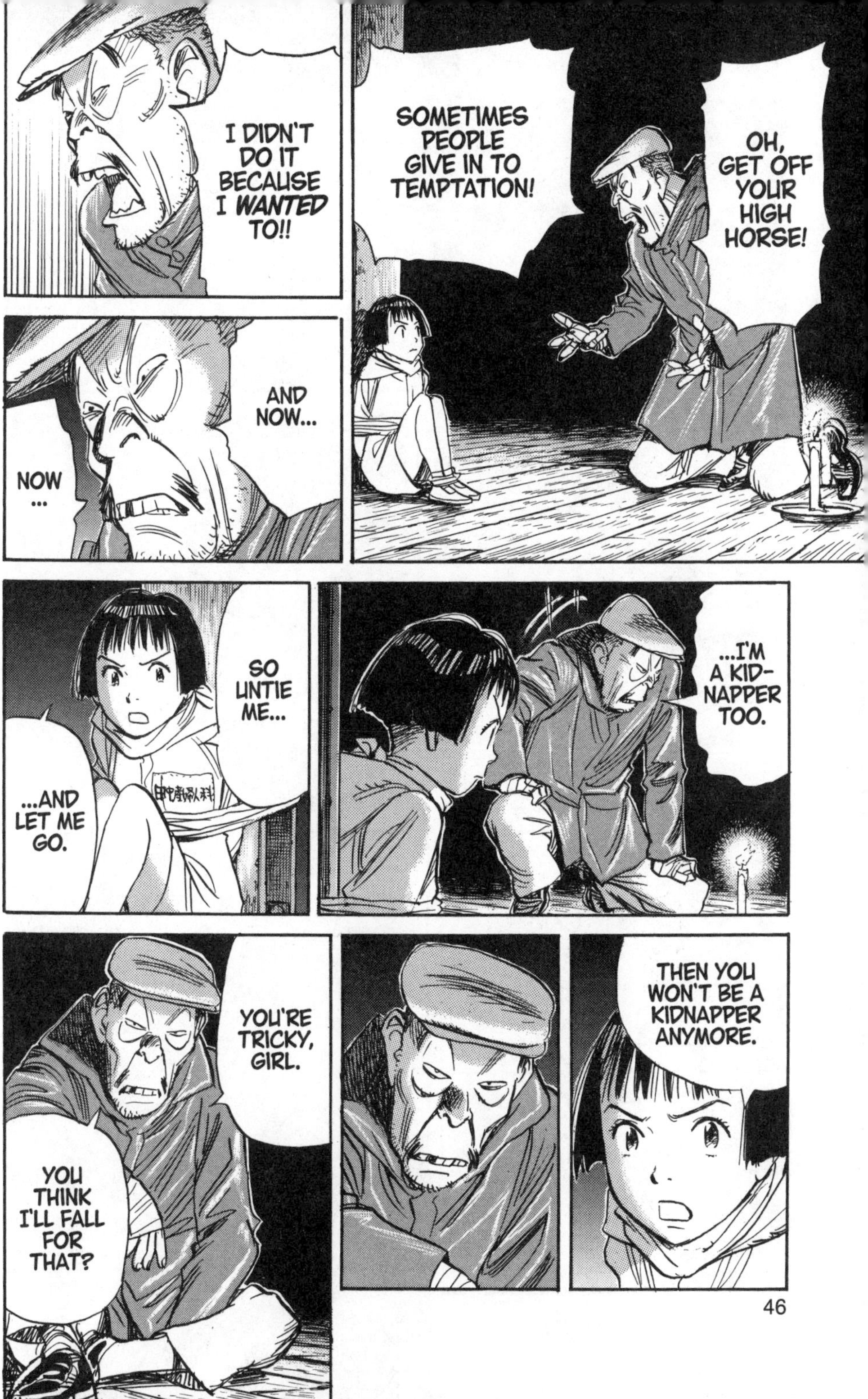
OH, GET OFF YOUR HIGH HORSE!
SOMETIMES PEOPLE GIVE IN TO TEMPTATION!
I DIDN'T DO IT BECAUSE I WANTED TO!!
AND NOW...
NOW ...
...I'M A KID-NAPPER TOO.
SO UNTIE ME...
...AND LET ME GO.
THEN YOU WON'T BE A KIDNAPPER ANYMORE.
YOU'RE TRICKY, GIRL.
YOU THINK I'LL FALL FOR THAT?

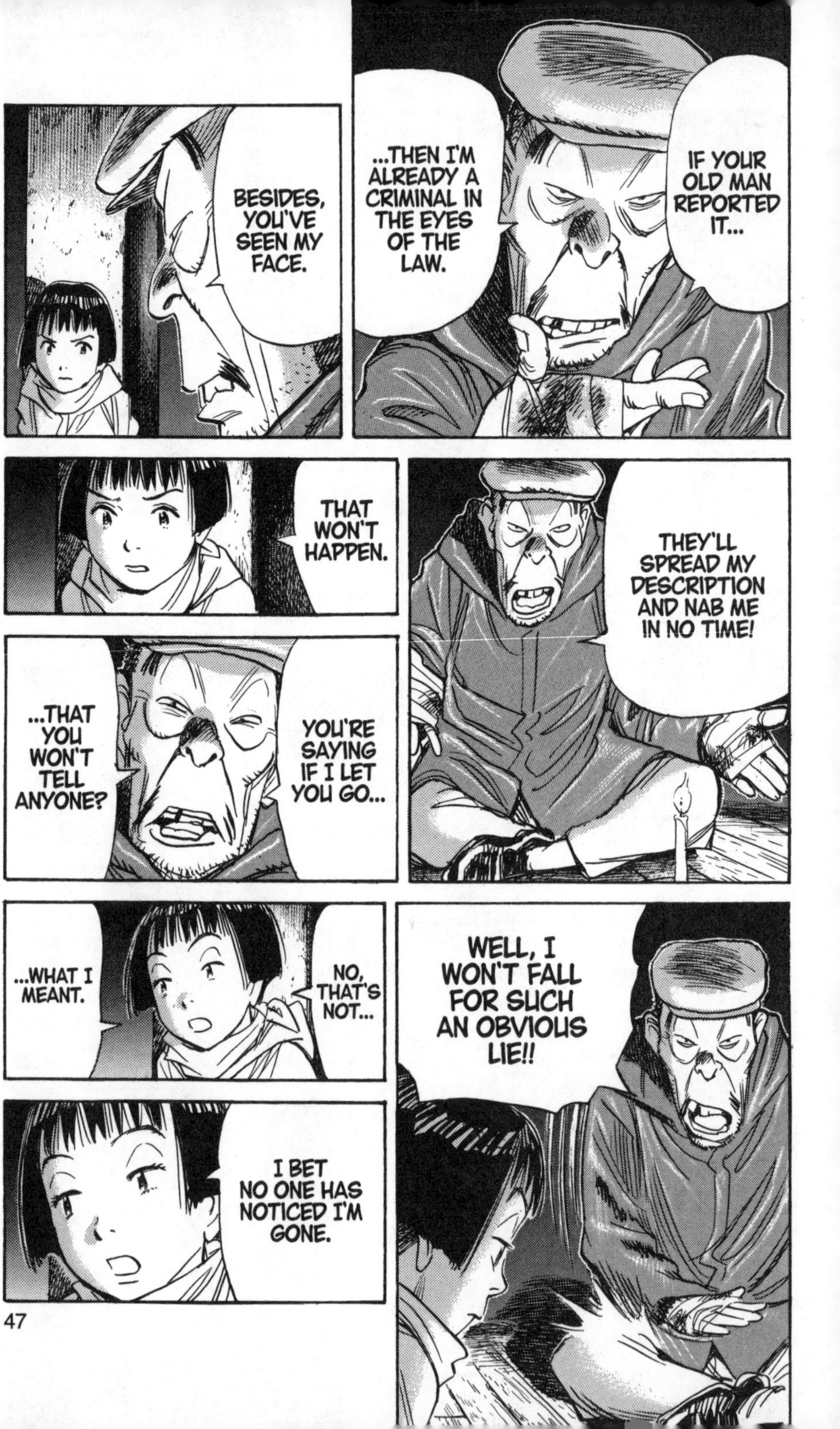
IF YOUR OLD MAN REPORTED IT...
...THEN I'M ALREADY A CRIMINAL IN THE EYES OF THE LAW.
BESIDES, YOU'VE SEEN MY FACE.
THEY'LL SPREAD MY DESCRIPTION AND NAB ME IN NO TIME!
THAT WON'T HAPPEN.
YOU'RE SAYING IF I LET YOU GO...
...THAT YOU WON'T TELL ANYONE?
WELL, I WON'T FALL FOR SUCH AN OBVIOUS LIE!!
NO, THAT'S NOT...
...WHAT I MEANT.
I BET NO ONE HAS NOTICED I'M GONE.

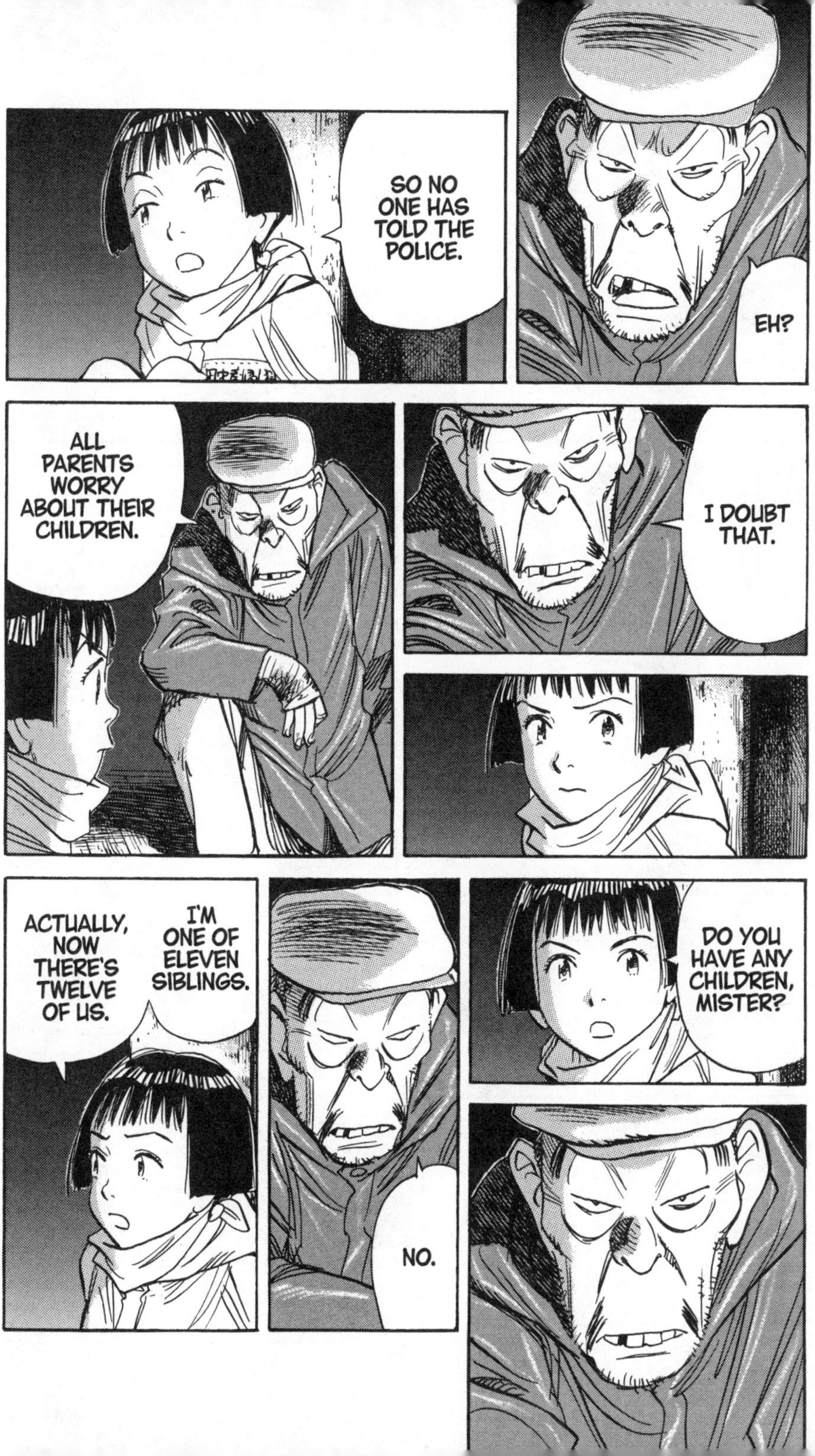
EH?
SO NO ONE HAS TOLD THE POLICE.
I DOUBT THAT.
ALL PARENTS WORRY ABOUT THEIR CHILDREN.
DO YOU HAVE ANY CHILDREN, MISTER?
NO.
I'M ONE OF ELEVEN SIBLINGS.
ACTUALLY, NOW THERE'S TWELVE OF US.

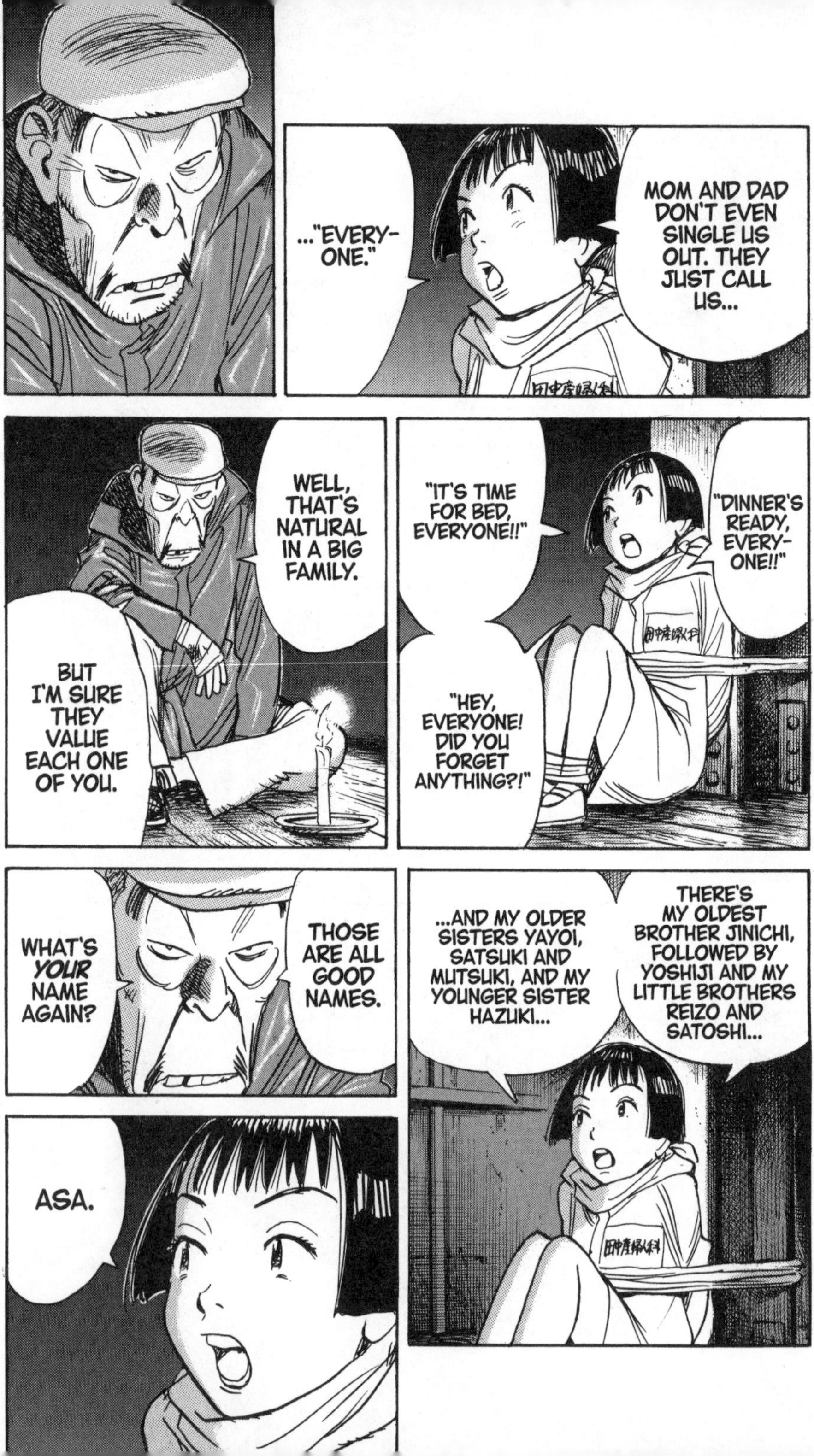
MOM AND DAD DON'T EVEN SINGLE US OUT. THEY JUST CALL US...
..."EVERY-ONE."
"DINNER'S READY, EVERY-ONE!!"
"IT'S TIME FOR BED, EVERYONE!!"
"HEY, EVERYONE! DID YOU FORGET ANYTHING?!"
WELL, THAT'S NATURAL IN A BIG FAMILY.
BUT I'M SURE THEY VALUE EACH ONE OF YOU.
THERE'S MY OLDEST BROTHER JINICHI, FOLLOWED BY YOSHIJI AND MY LITTLE BROTHERS REIZO AND SATOSHI...
...AND MY OLDER SISTERS YAYOI, SATSUKI AND MUTSUKI, AND MY YOUNGER SISTER HAZUKI...
THOSE ARE ALL GOOD NAMES.
WHAT'S *YOUR* NAME AGAIN?
ASA.

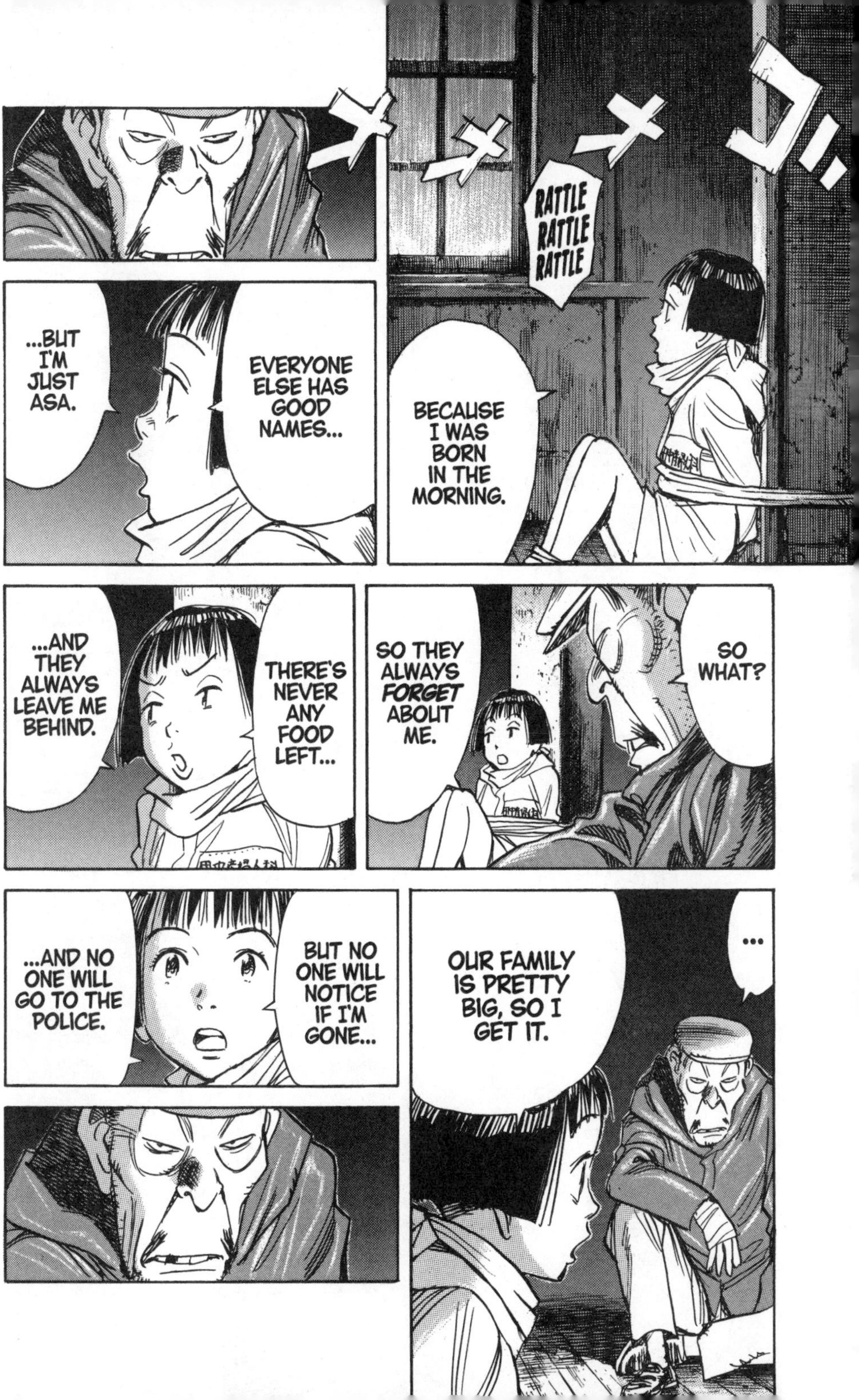
RATTLE RATTLE RATTLE
BECAUSE I WAS BORN IN THE MORNING.
EVERYONE ELSE HAS GOOD NAMES...
...BUT I'M JUST ASA.
SO WHAT?
SO THEY ALWAYS *FORGET* ABOUT ME.
THERE'S NEVER ANY FOOD LEFT...
...AND THEY ALWAYS LEAVE ME BEHIND.
...
OUR FAMILY IS PRETTY BIG, SO I GET IT.
BUT NO ONE WILL NOTICE IF I'M GONE...
...AND NO ONE WILL GO TO THE POLICE.

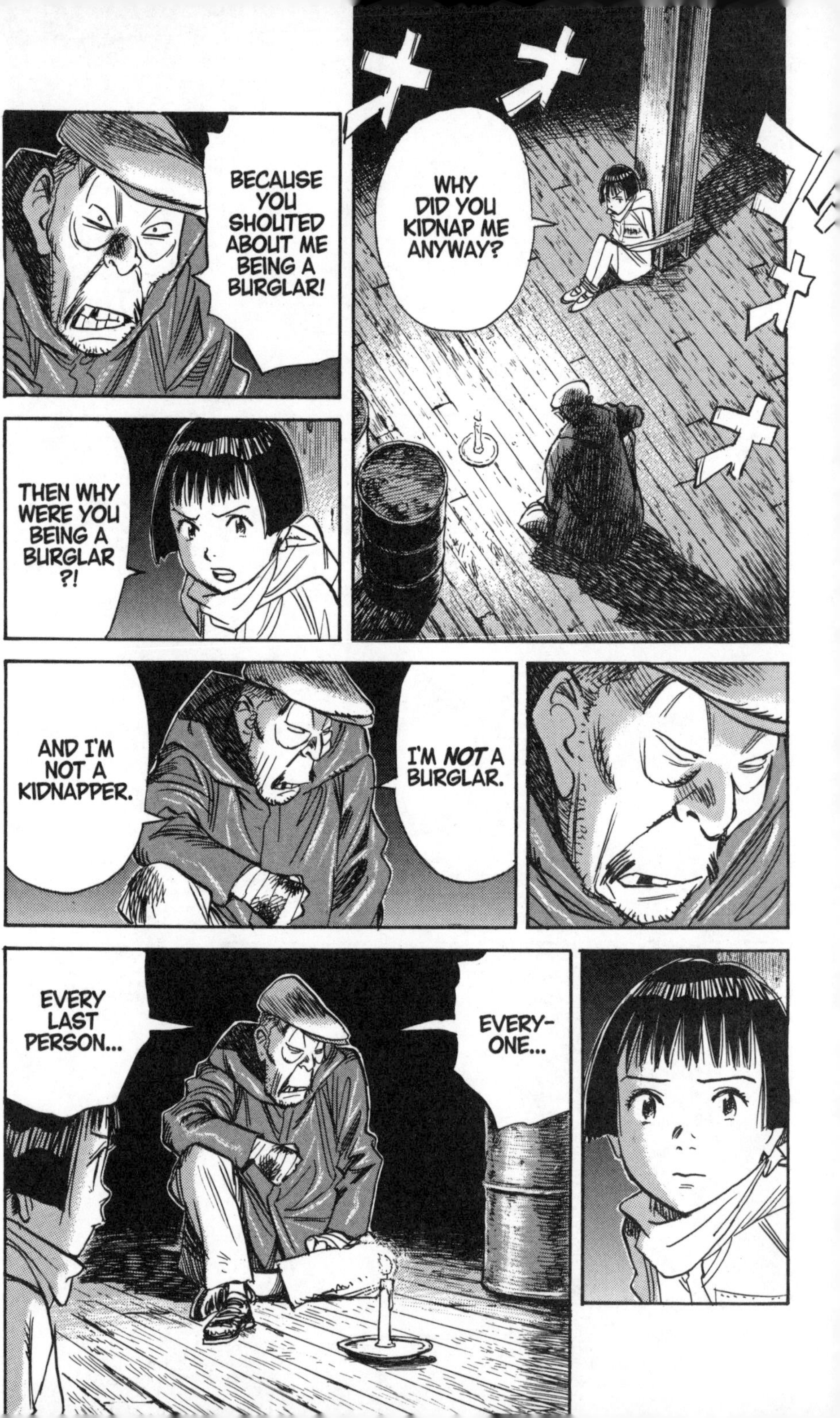
WHY DID YOU KIDNAP ME ANYWAY?
BECAUSE YOU SHOUTED ABOUT ME BEING A BURGLAR!
THEN WHY WERE YOU BEING A BURGLAR ?!
I'M *NOT* A BURGLAR.
AND I'M NOT A KIDNAPPER.
EVERY-ONE...
EVERY LAST PERSON...

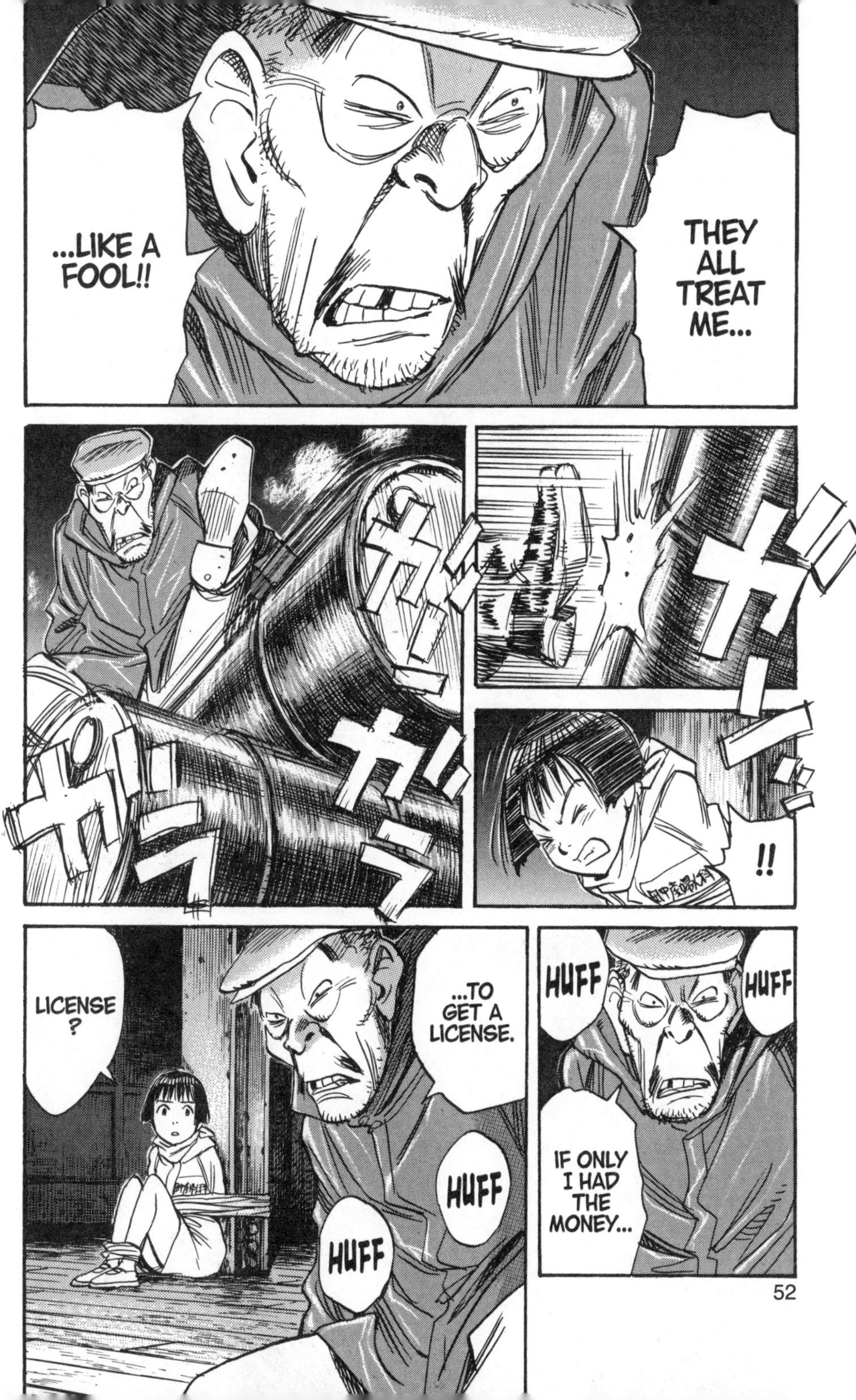
THEY ALL TREAT ME...
...LIKE A FOOL!!
!!
HUFF
HUFF
IF ONLY I HAD THE MONEY...
...TO GET A LICENSE.
LICENSE?
HUFF
HUFF

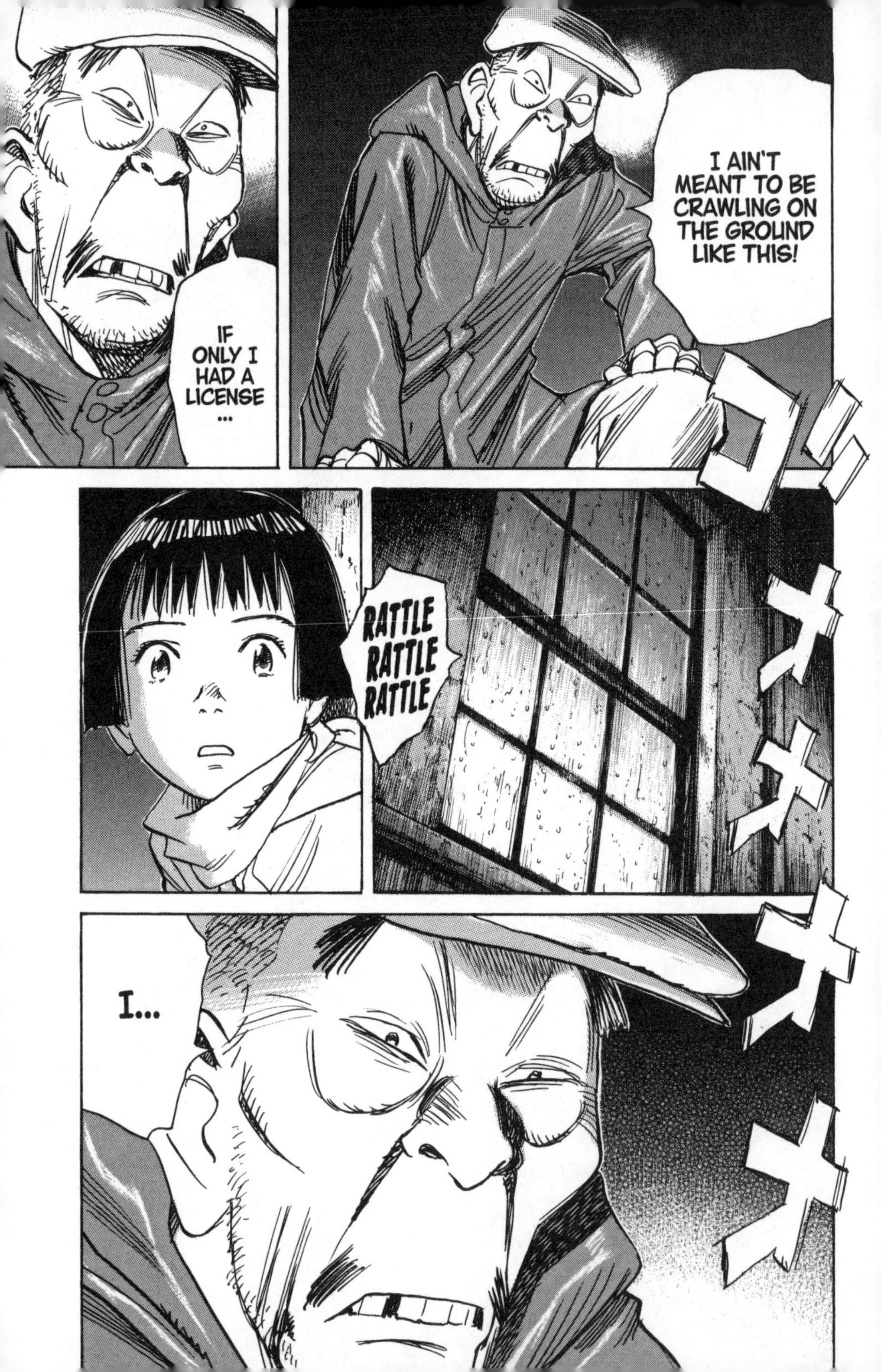
I AIN'T MEANT TO BE CRAWLING ON THE GROUND LIKE THIS!
IF ONLY I HAD A LICENSE ...
RATTLE RATTLE RATTLE
I...

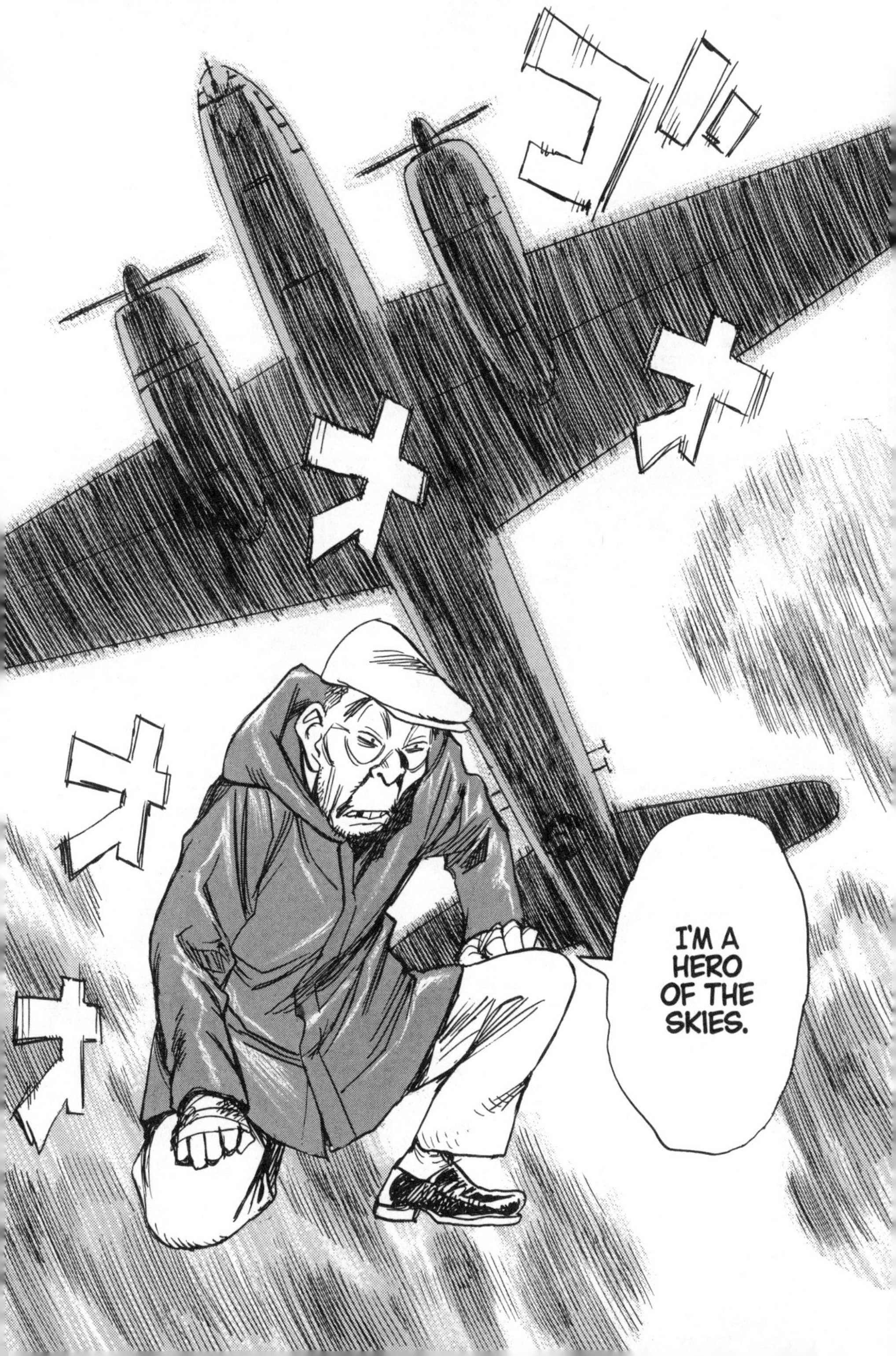
I'M A HERO OF THE SKIES.

Chapter 3 ● Hero of the Skies

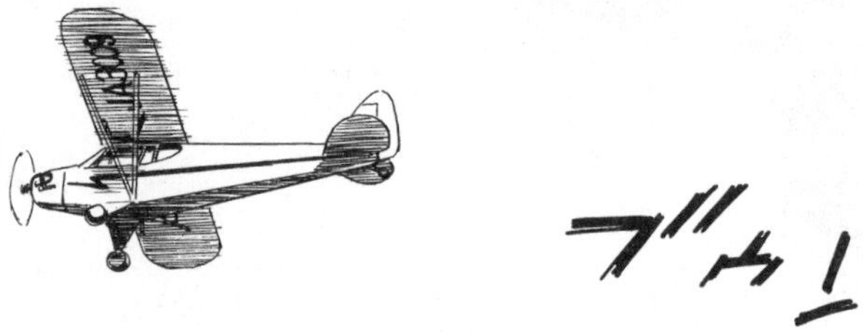
ブォン!

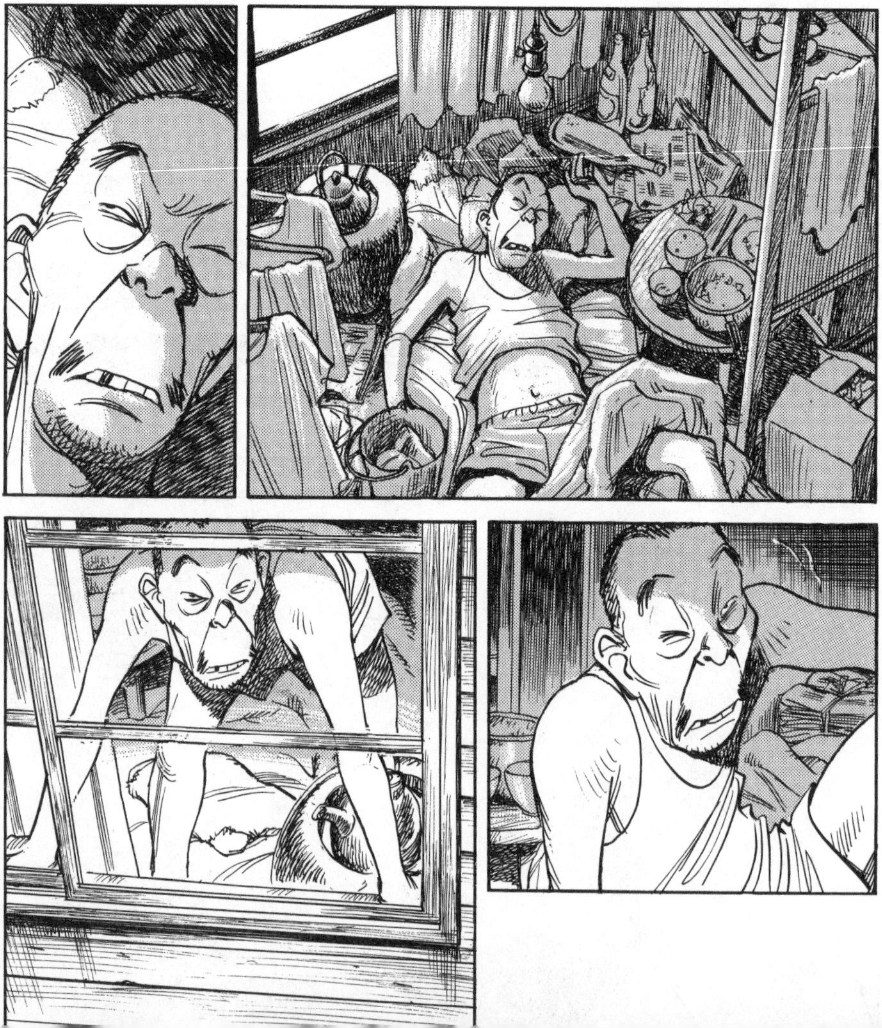

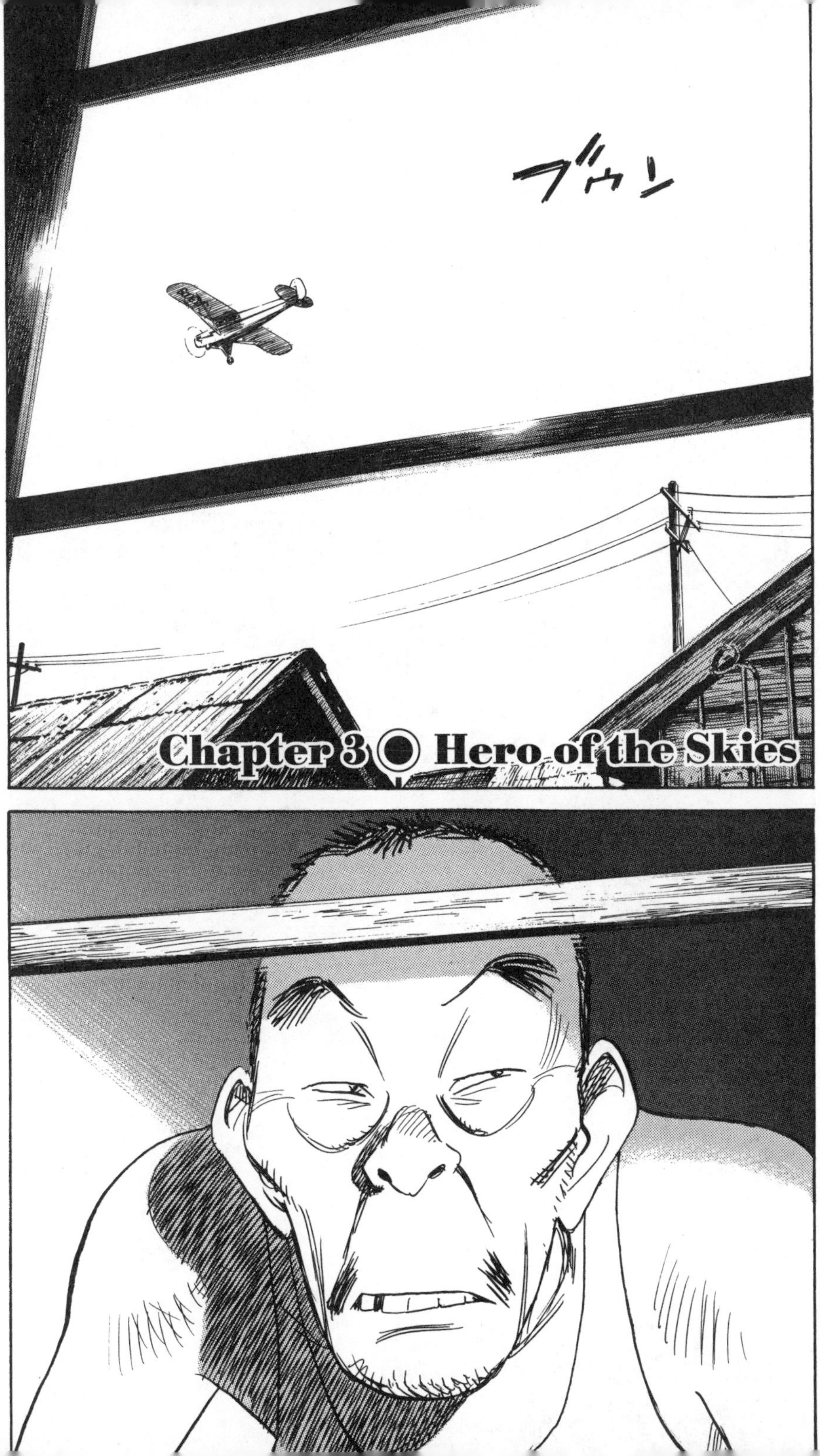
ブゥン
Chapter 3 ● Hero of the Skies

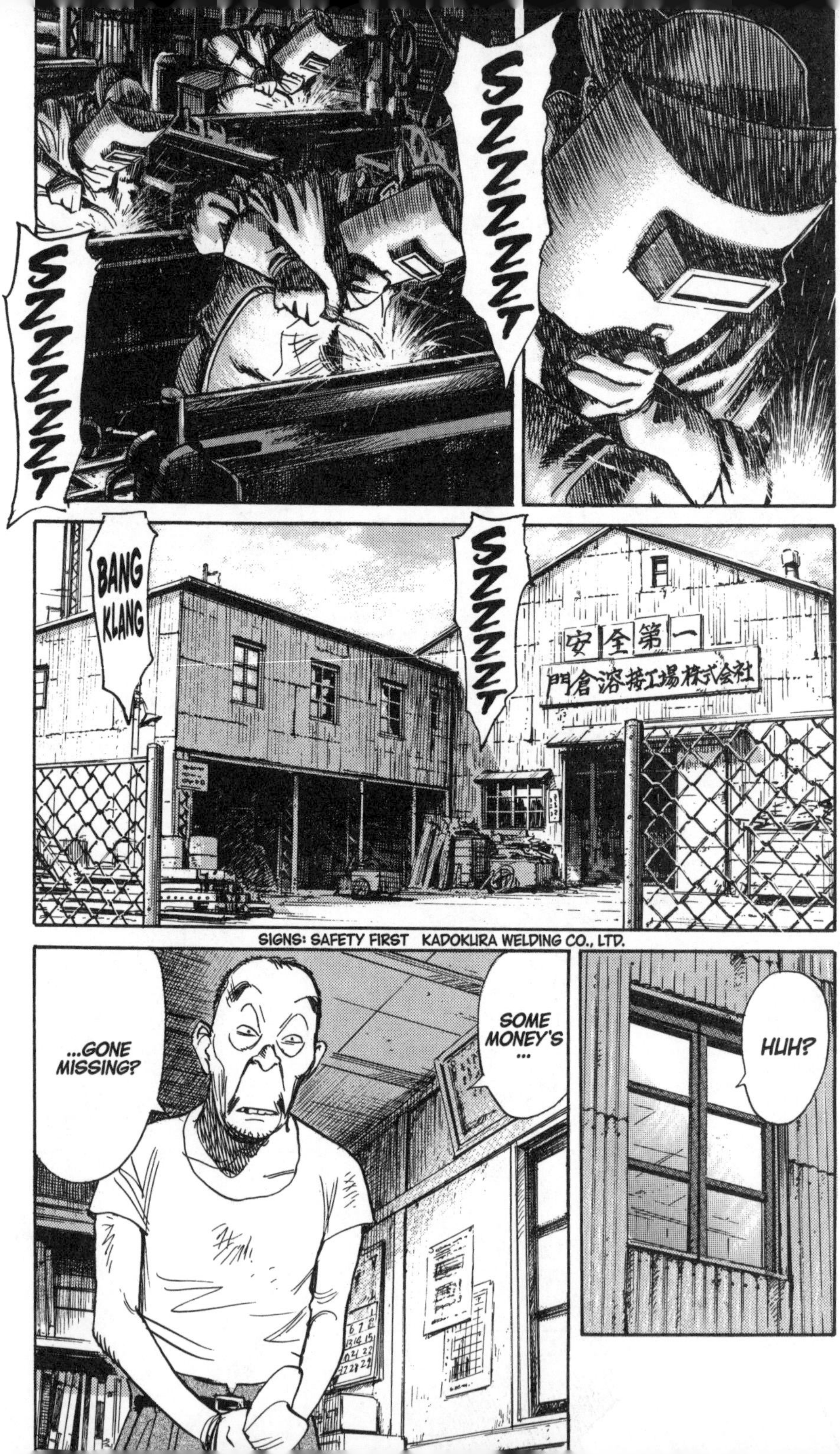
SZZZZZZZZT
SZZZZZZZZT
SZZZZZZT
BANG KLANG
安全第一
門倉溶接工場株式会社
SIGNS: SAFETY FIRST KADOKURA WELDING CO., LTD.
HUH?
SOME MONEY'S ...
...GONE MISSING?

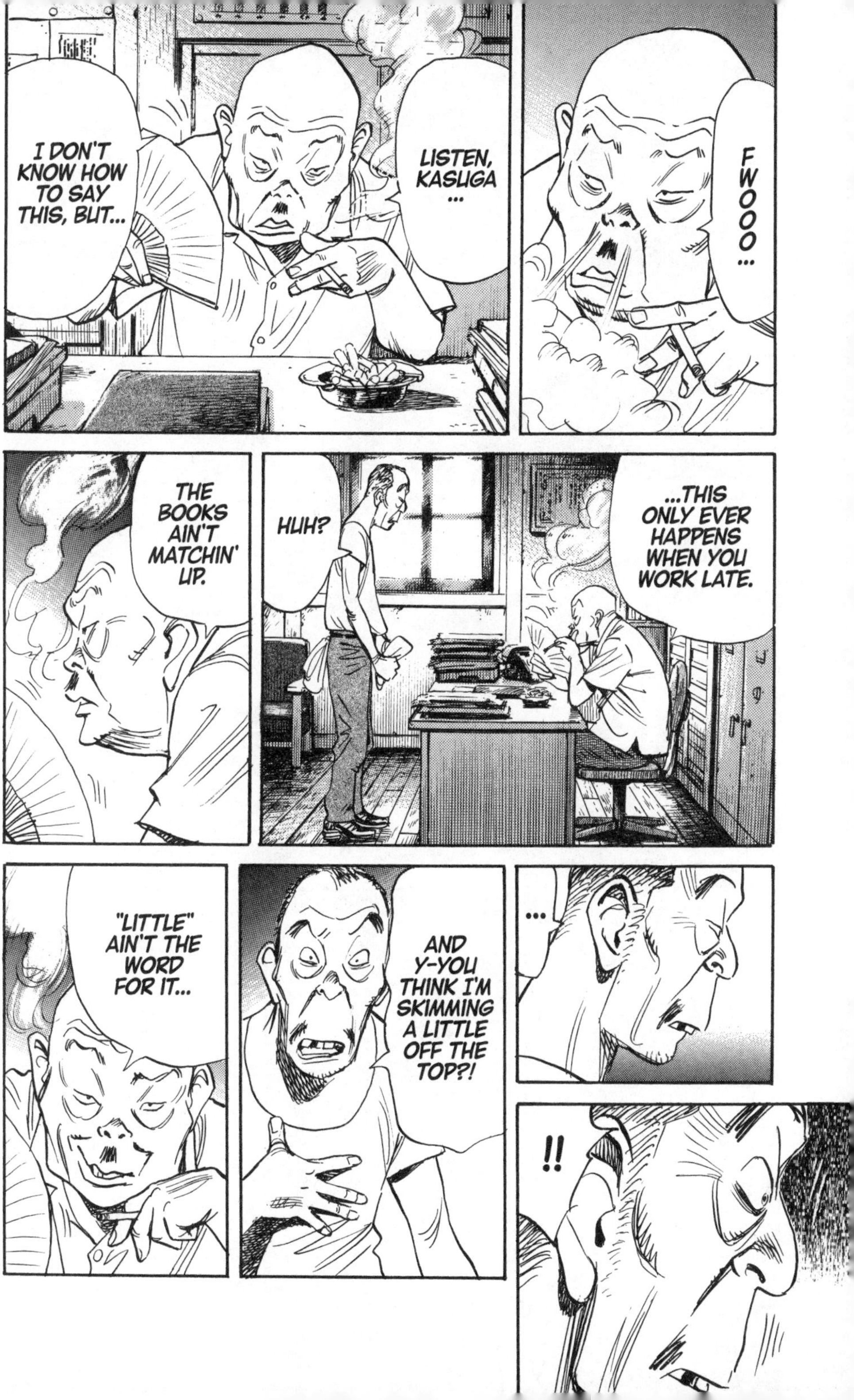
FWOOO...
LISTEN, KASUGA...
I DON'T KNOW HOW TO SAY THIS, BUT...
...THIS ONLY EVER HAPPENS WHEN YOU WORK LATE.
HUH?
THE BOOKS AIN'T MATCHIN' UP.
...
!!
AND Y-YOU THINK I'M SKIMMING A LITTLE OFF THE TOP?!
"LITTLE" AIN'T THE WORD FOR IT...

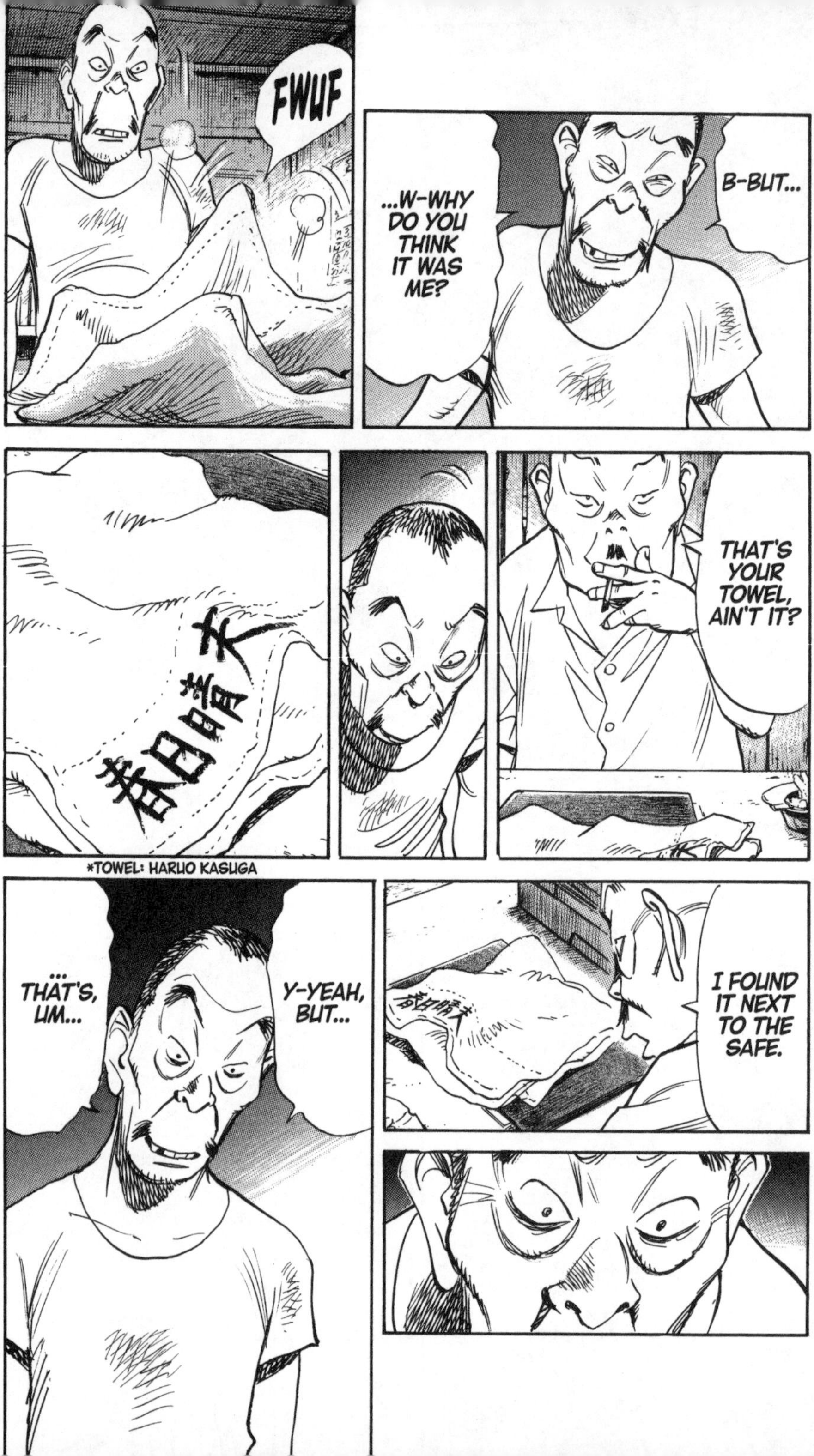
B-BUT...
...W-WHY DO YOU THINK IT WAS ME?
FWUF
THAT'S YOUR TOWEL, AIN'T IT?
*TOWEL: HARUO KASUGA
I FOUND IT NEXT TO THE SAFE.
Y-YEAH, BUT...
... THAT'S, UM...

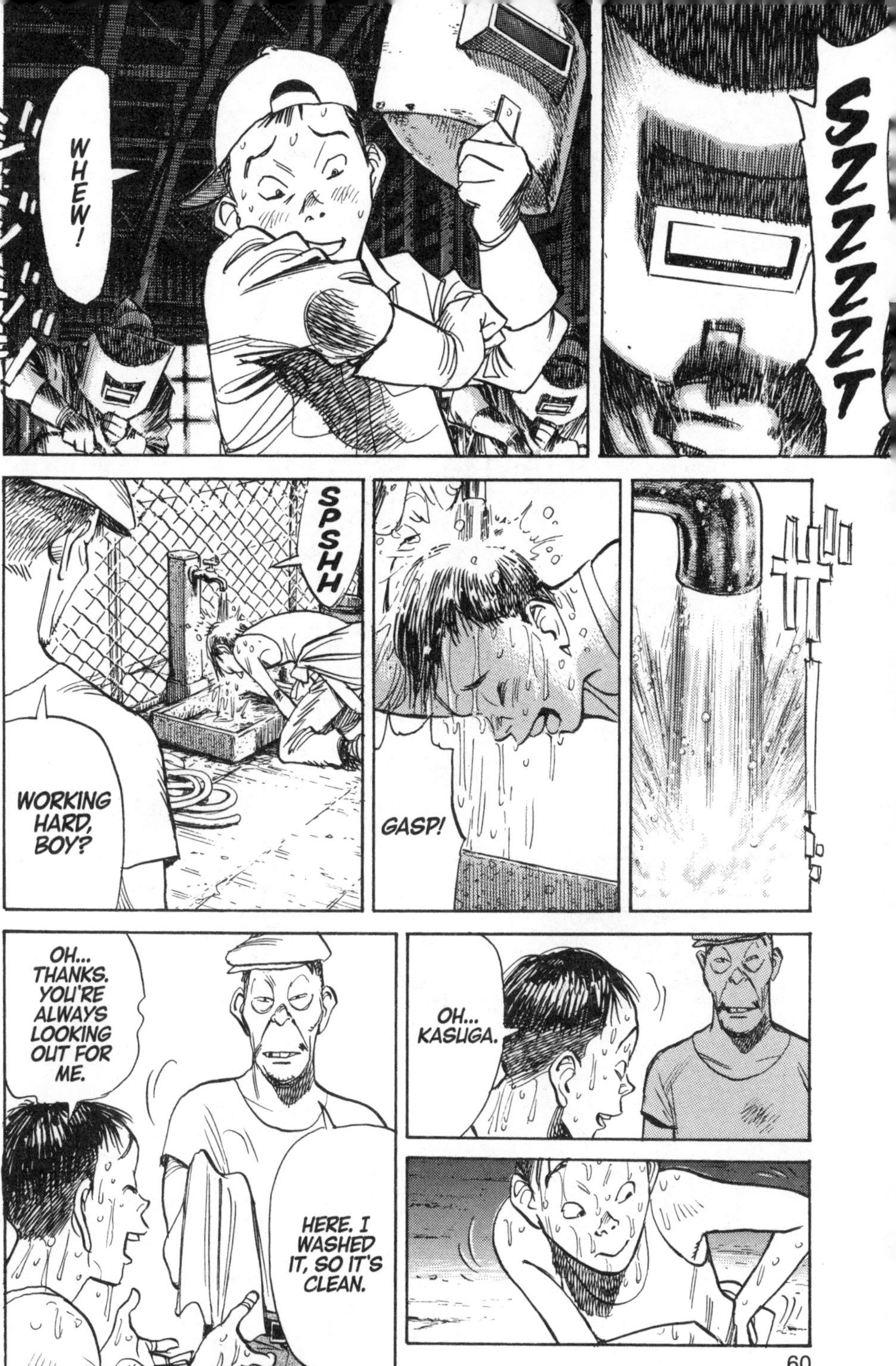
SZZZZZT
WHEW!
SPSHH
GASP!
WORKING HARD, BOY?
OH... KASUGA.
HERE. I WASHED IT, SO IT'S CLEAN.
OH... THANKS. YOU'RE ALWAYS LOOKING OUT FOR ME.

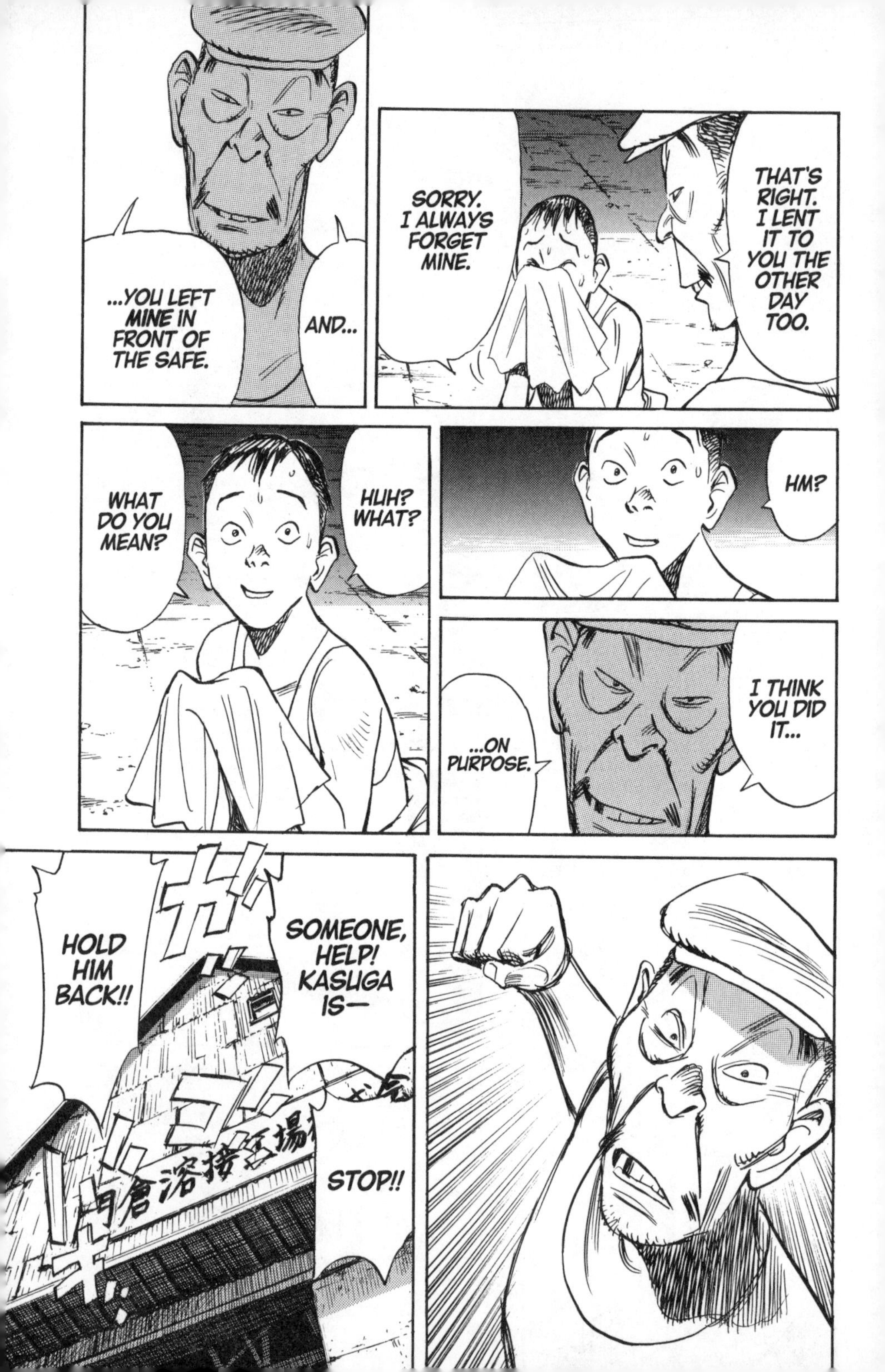

THAT'S RIGHT. I LENT IT TO YOU THE OTHER DAY TOO.
SORRY. I ALWAYS FORGET MINE.
AND...
...YOU LEFT MINE IN FRONT OF THE SAFE.
HM?
I THINK YOU DID IT...
...ON PURPOSE.
HUH? WHAT?
WHAT DO YOU MEAN?
SOMEONE, HELP! KASUGA IS—
HOLD HIM BACK!!
ガッ
ゴッ
STOP!!

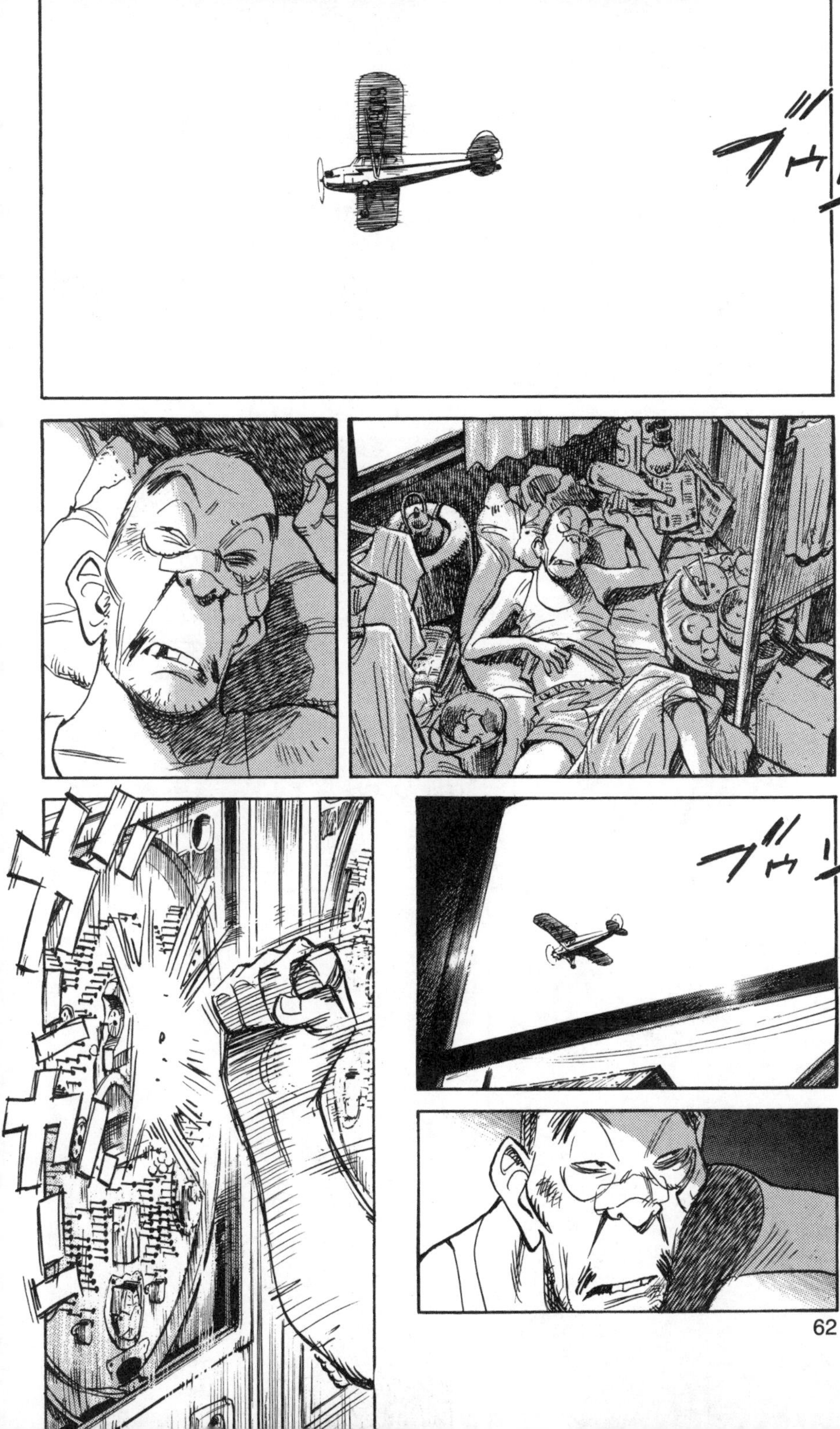
ブゥン
ブゥン
ガッガッ

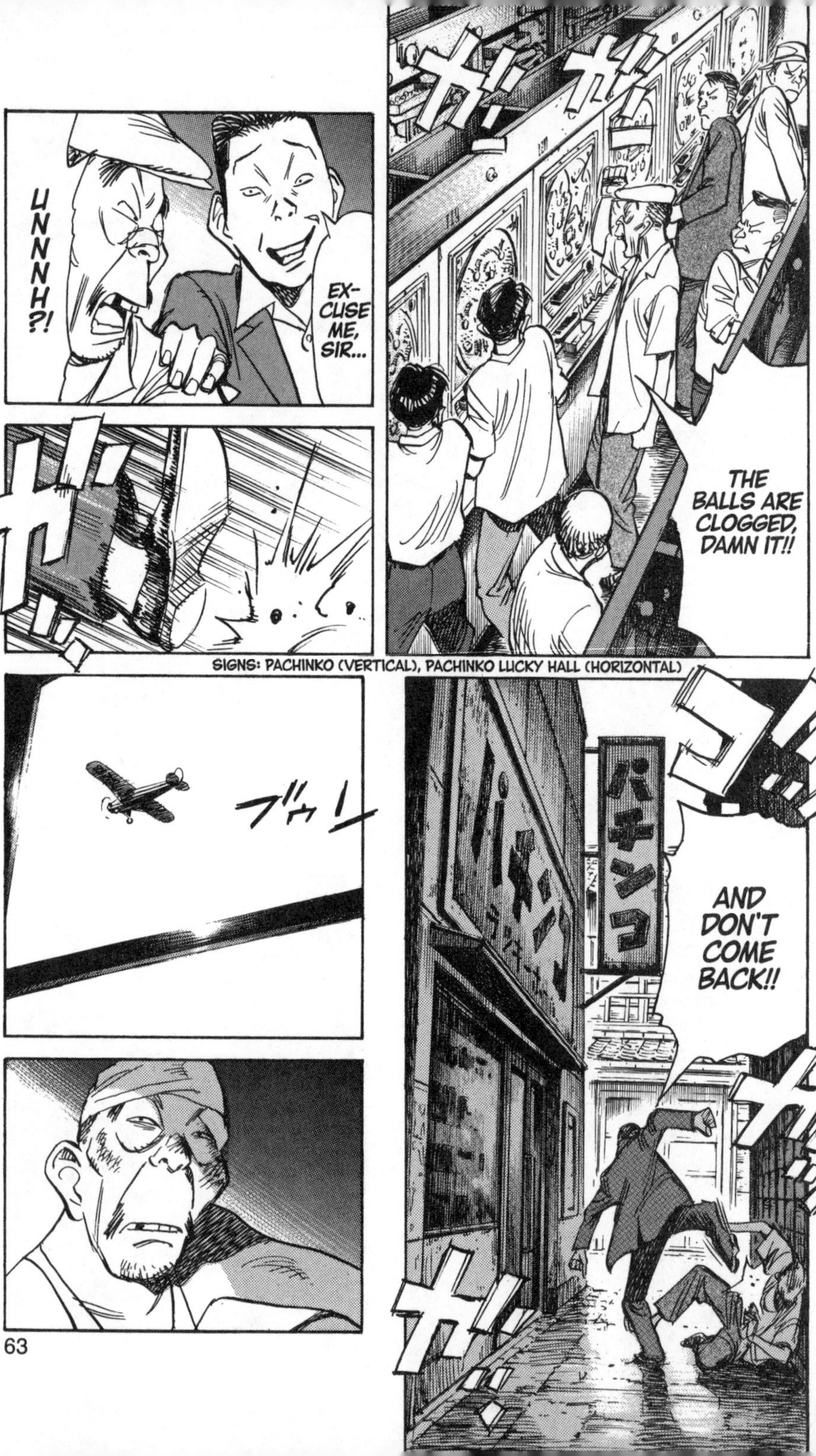
THE BALLS ARE CLOGGED, DAMN IT!!
EX-CUSE ME, SIR...
UNNNNH?!
SIGNS: PACHINKO (VERTICAL), PACHINKO LUCKY HALL (HORIZONTAL)
パチンコ
AND DON'T COME BACK!!

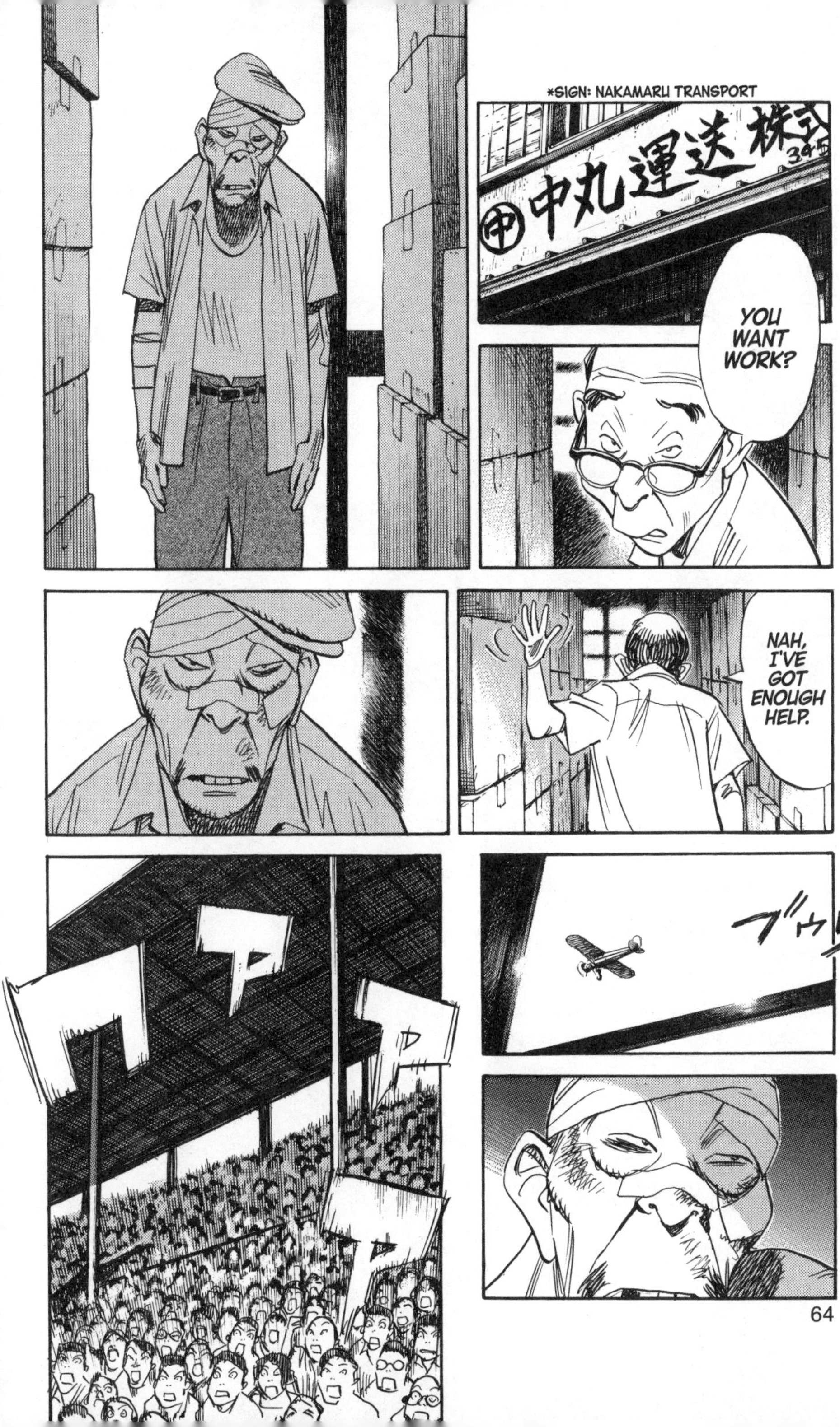
*SIGN: NAKAMARU TRANSPORT
中丸運送 株式
YOU WANT WORK?
NAH, I'VE GOT ENOUGH HELP.
ブゥン

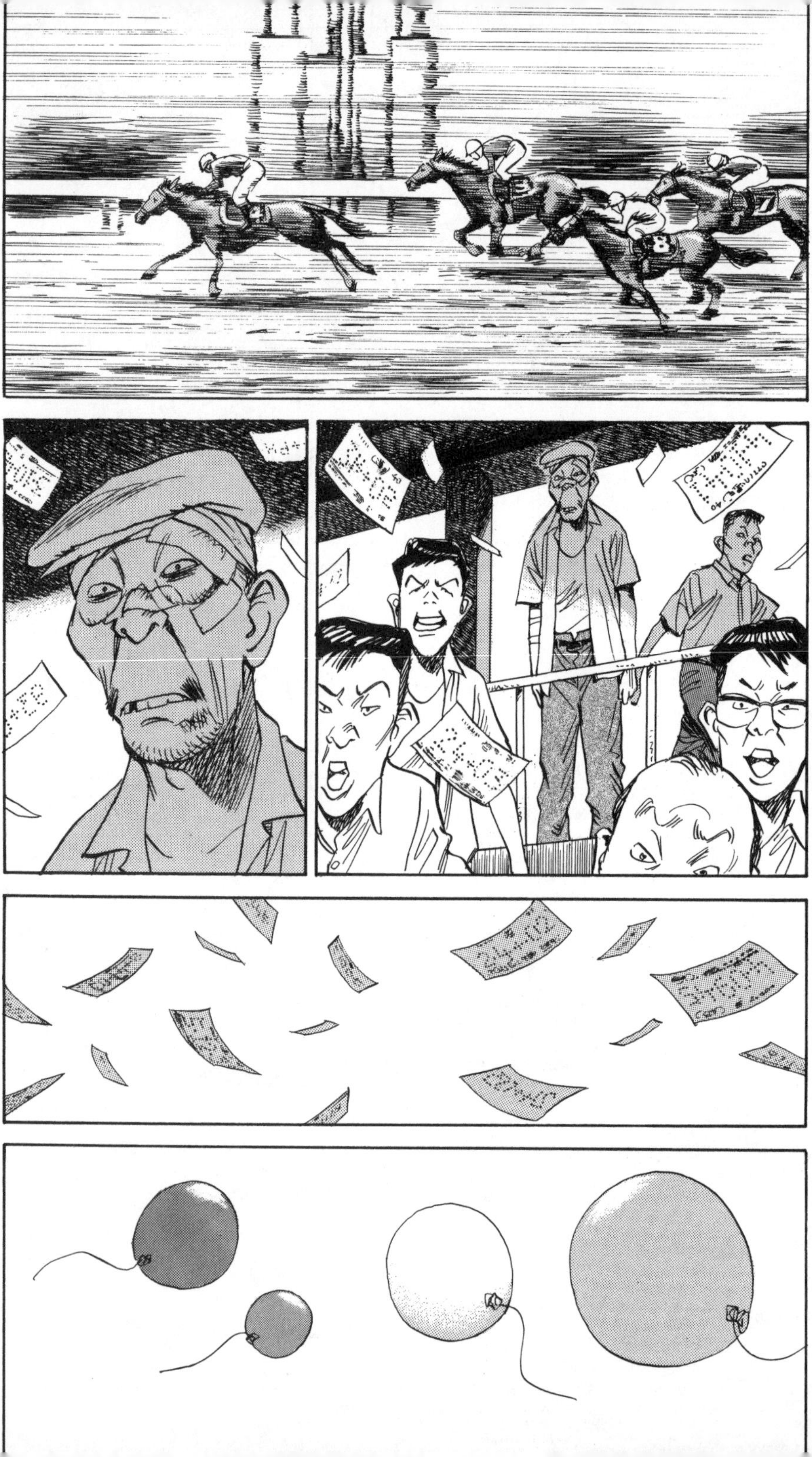

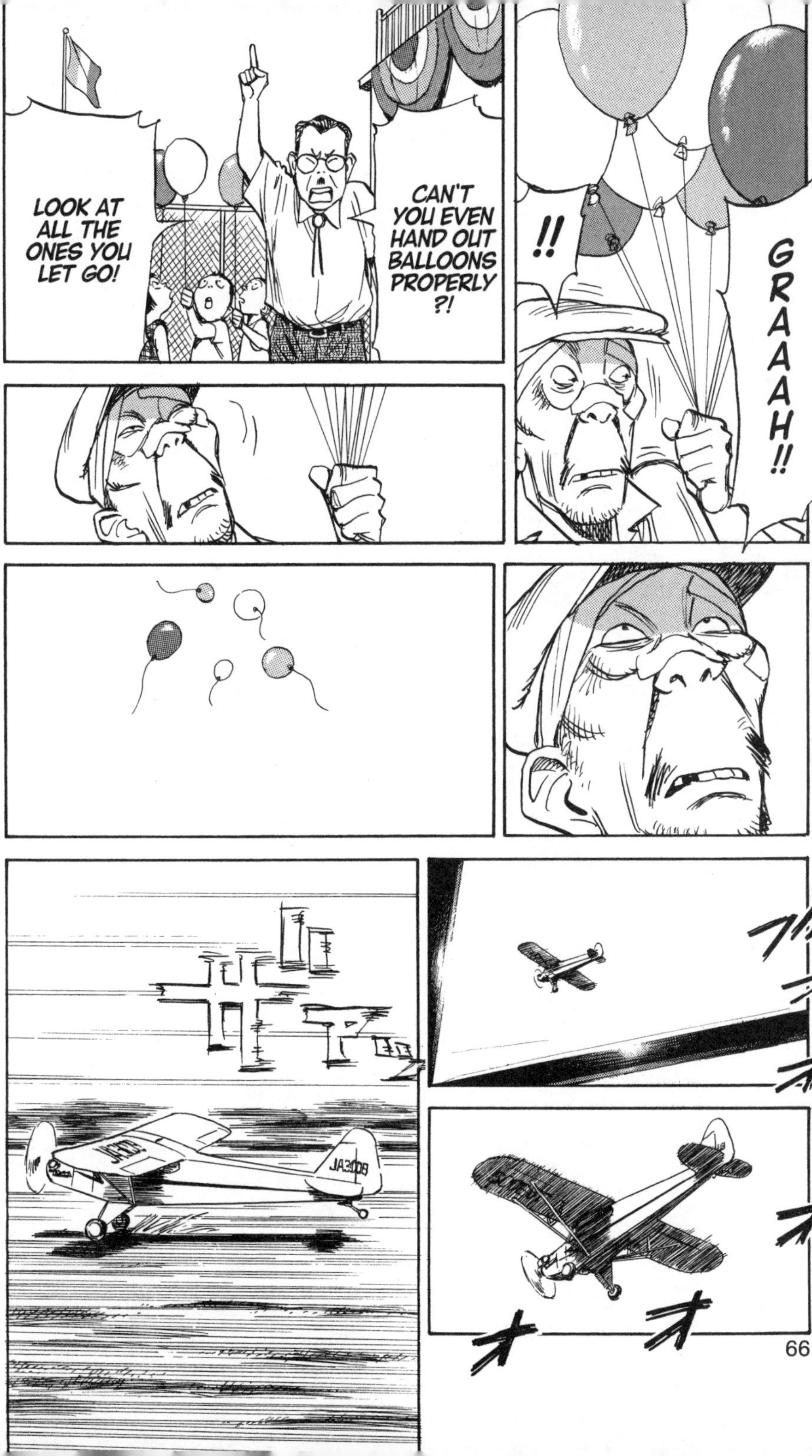

!!
GRAAAAH!!
CAN'T YOU EVEN HAND OUT BALLOONS PROPERLY ?!
LOOK AT ALL THE ONES YOU LET GO!
ブオオオ
オオオ

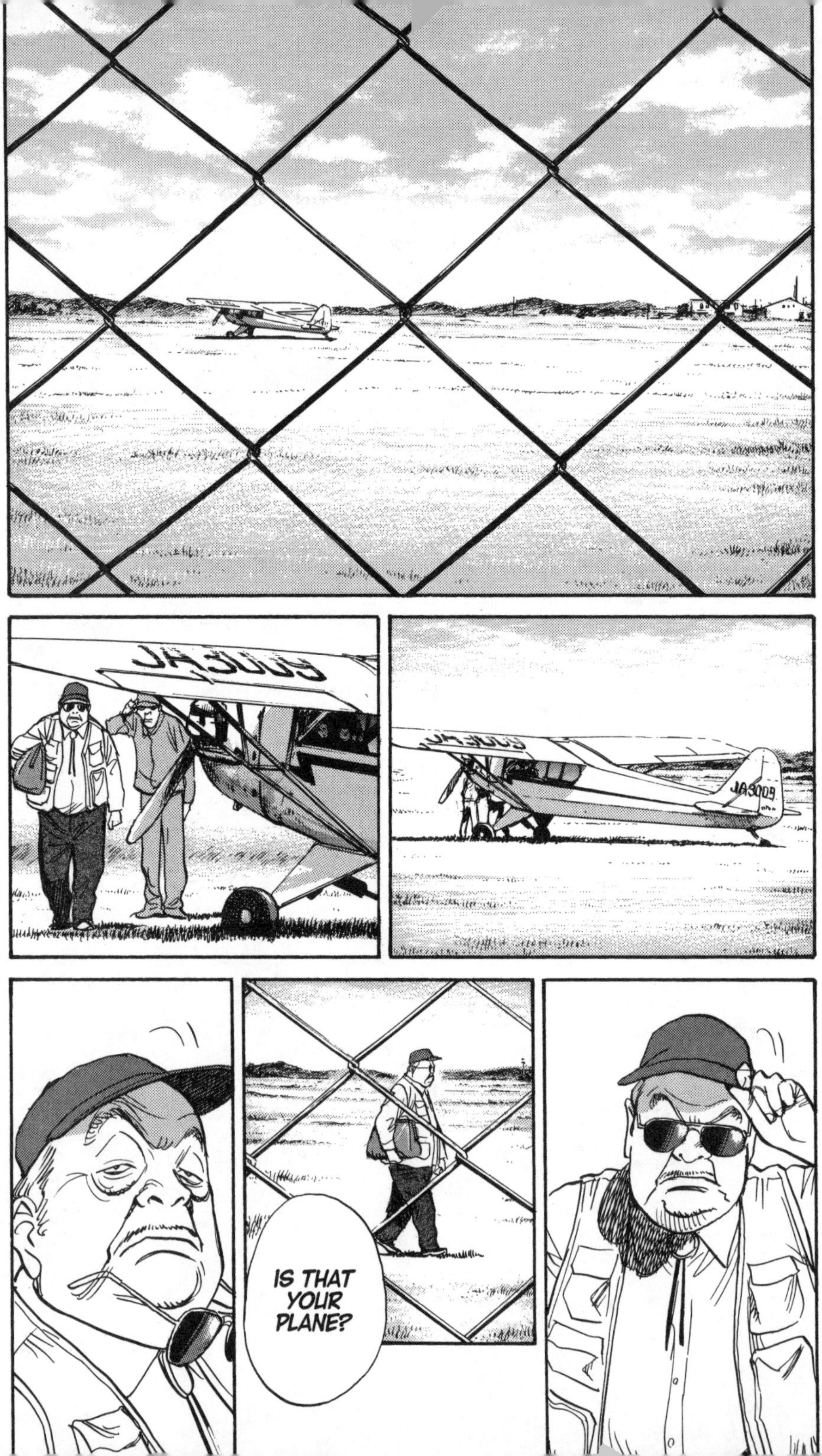
JA3009
JA3009
IS THAT YOUR PLANE?

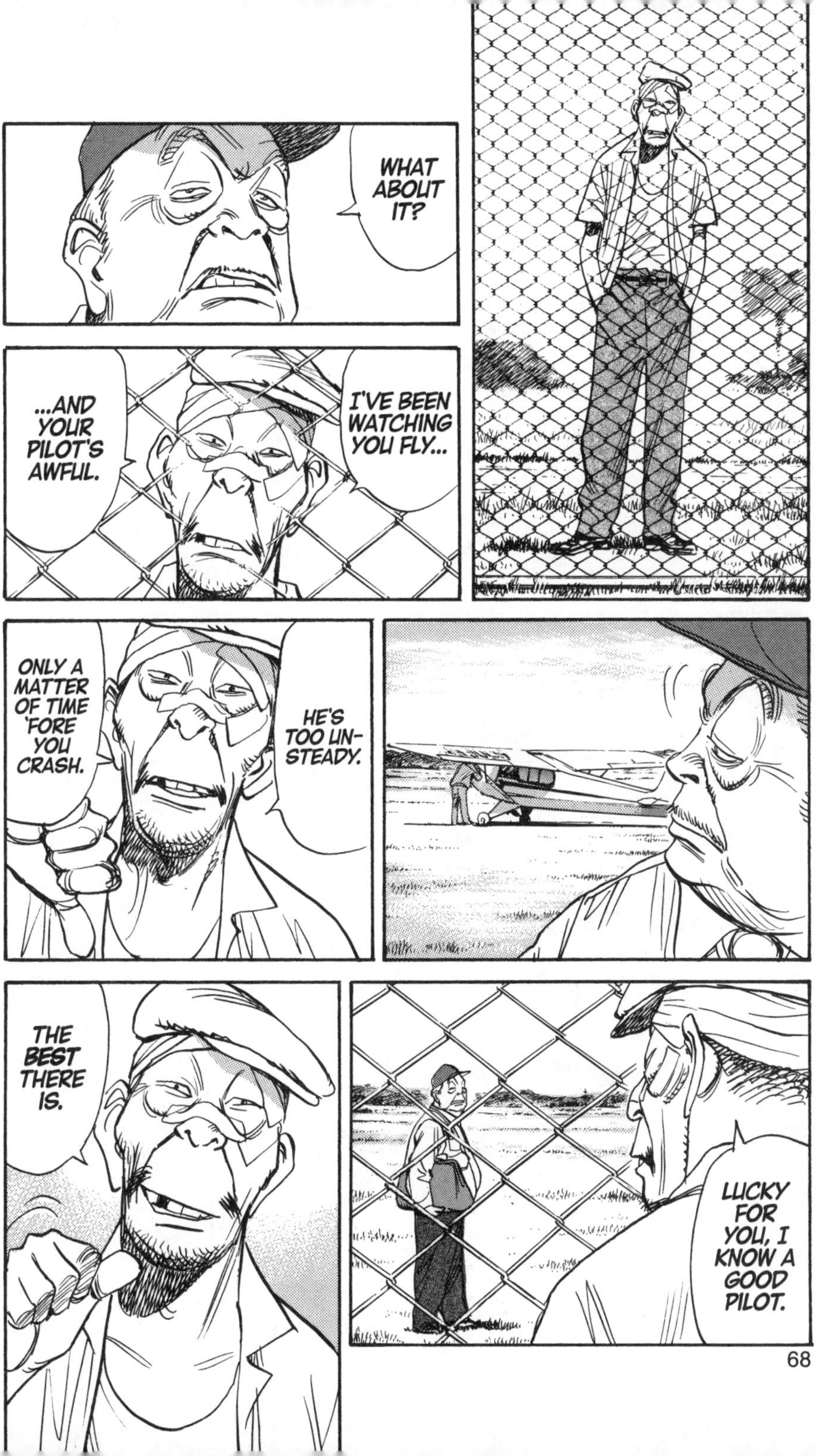
WHAT ABOUT IT?
I'VE BEEN WATCHING YOU FLY...
...AND YOUR PILOT'S AWFUL.
HE'S TOO UN-STEADY.
ONLY A MATTER OF TIME 'FORE YOU CRASH.
LUCKY FOR YOU, I KNOW A GOOD PILOT.
THE BEST THERE IS.

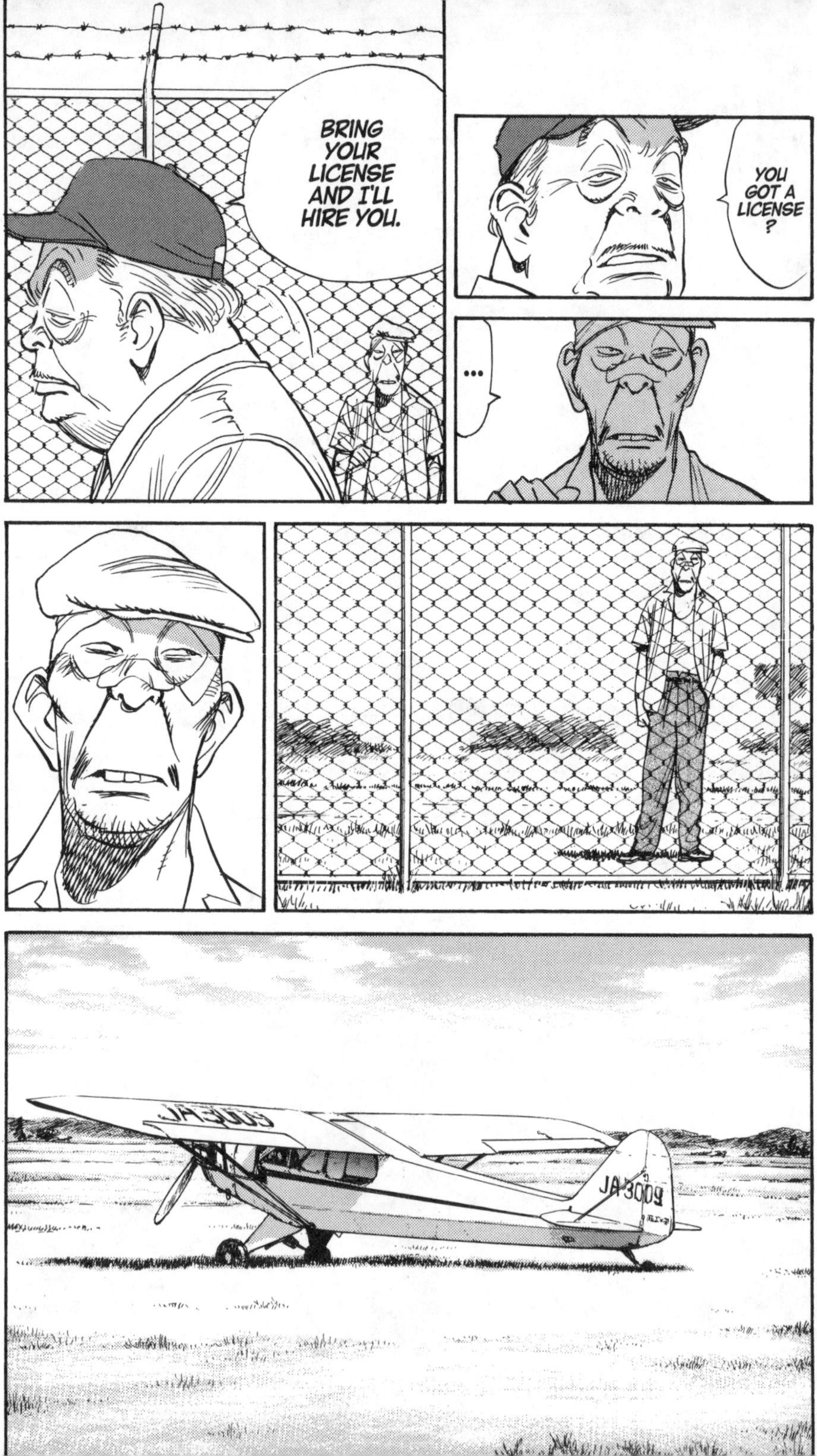
YOU GOT A LICENSE?
...
BRING YOUR LICENSE AND I'LL HIRE YOU.
JA3009

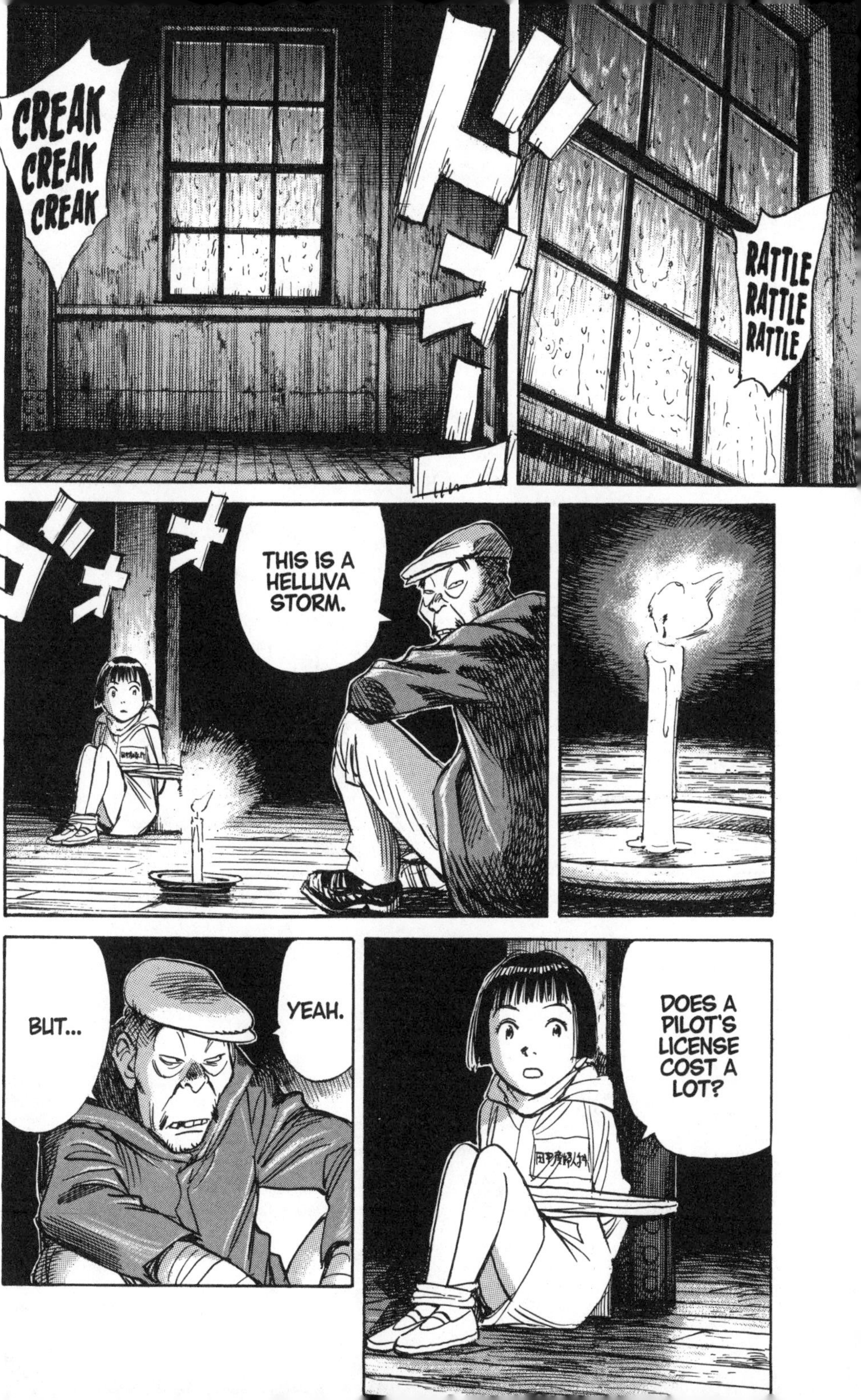
RATTLE RATTLE RATTLE
CREAK CREAK CREAK
THIS IS A HELLUVA STORM.
DOES A PILOT'S LICENSE COST A LOT?
YEAH.
BUT...

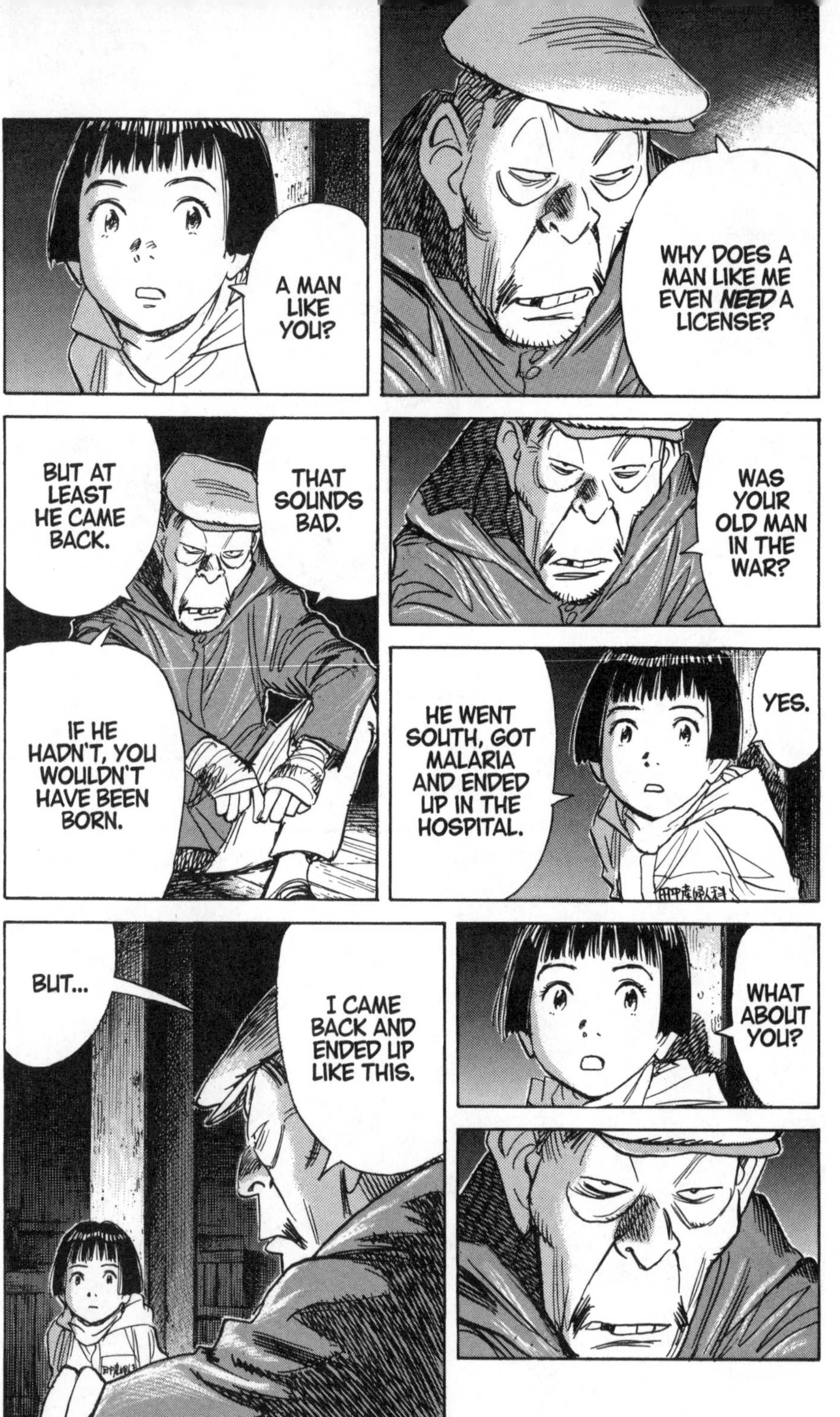
WHY DOES A MAN LIKE ME EVEN NEED A LICENSE?
A MAN LIKE YOU?
WAS YOUR OLD MAN IN THE WAR?
YES.
HE WENT SOUTH, GOT MALARIA AND ENDED UP IN THE HOSPITAL.
田中産婦人科
THAT SOUNDS BAD.
BUT AT LEAST HE CAME BACK.
IF HE HADN'T, YOU WOULDN'T HAVE BEEN BORN.
WHAT ABOUT YOU?
I CAME BACK AND ENDED UP LIKE THIS.
BUT...

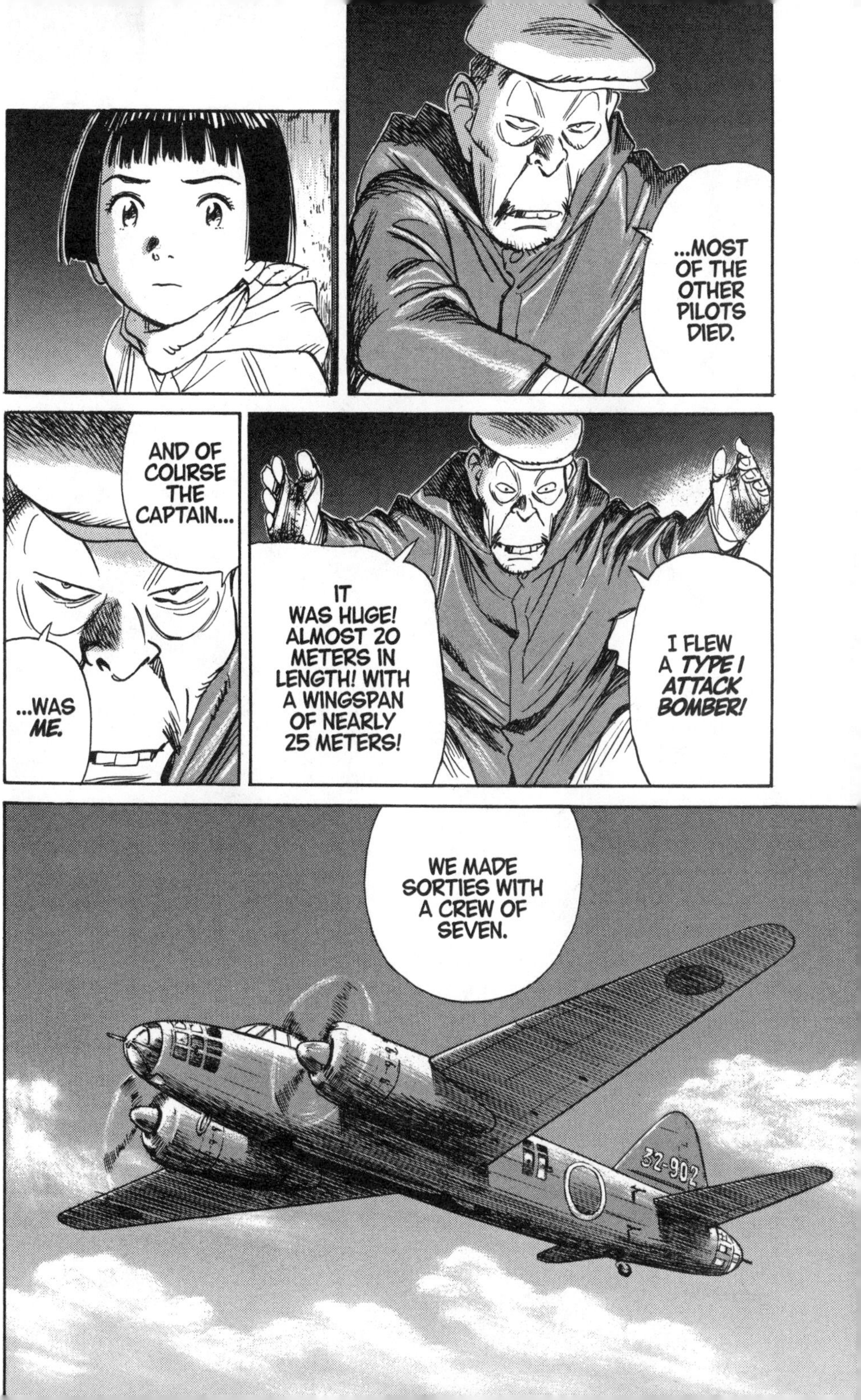
...MOST OF THE OTHER PILOTS DIED.
I FLEW A *TYPE I ATTACK BOMBER!*
IT WAS HUGE! ALMOST 20 METERS IN LENGTH! WITH A WINGSPAN OF NEARLY 25 METERS!
AND OF COURSE THE CAPTAIN...
...WAS *ME.*
WE MADE SORTIES WITH A CREW OF SEVEN.
32-902

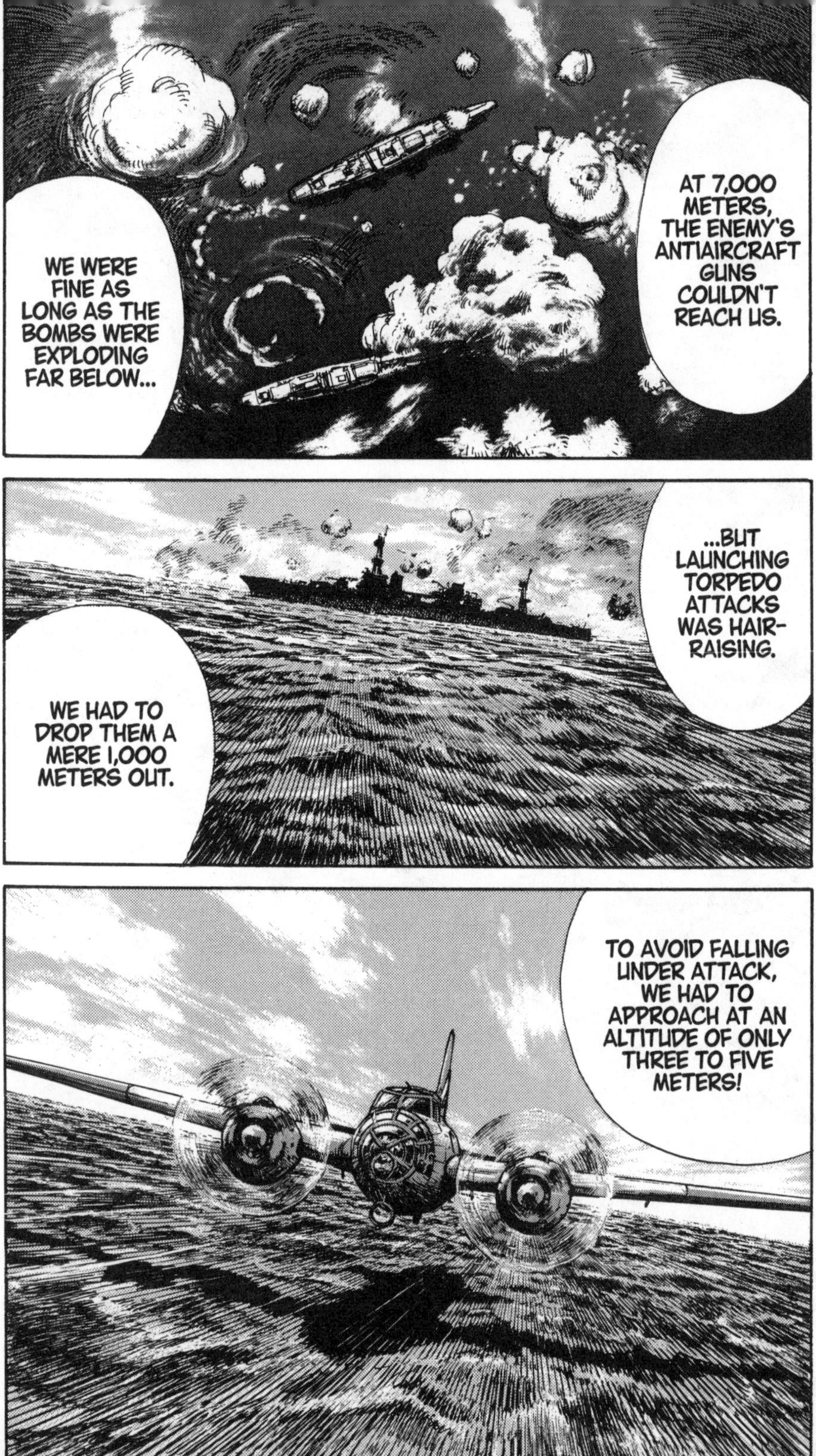
AT 7,000 METERS, THE ENEMY'S ANTIAIRCRAFT GUNS COULDN'T REACH US.
WE WERE FINE AS LONG AS THE BOMBS WERE EXPLODING FAR BELOW...
...BUT LAUNCHING TORPEDO ATTACKS WAS HAIR-RAISING.
WE HAD TO DROP THEM A MERE 1,000 METERS OUT.
TO AVOID FALLING UNDER ATTACK, WE HAD TO APPROACH AT AN ALTITUDE OF ONLY THREE TO FIVE METERS!

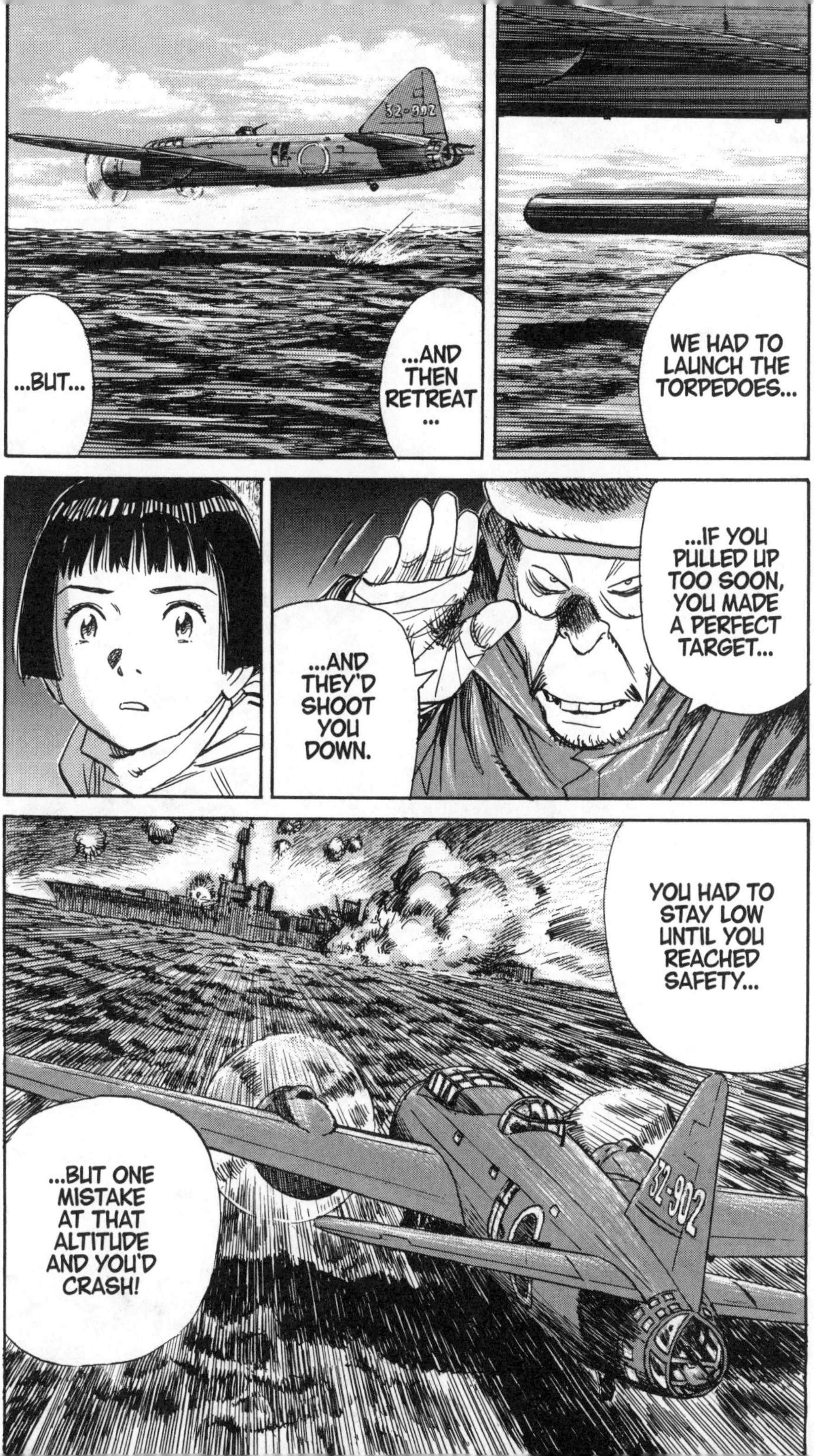
WE HAD TO LAUNCH THE TORPEDOES...
...AND THEN RETREAT ...
...BUT...
...IF YOU PULLED UP TOO SOON, YOU MADE A PERFECT TARGET...
...AND THEY'D SHOOT YOU DOWN.
YOU HAD TO STAY LOW UNTIL YOU REACHED SAFETY...
...BUT ONE MISTAKE AT THAT ALTITUDE AND YOU'D CRASH!

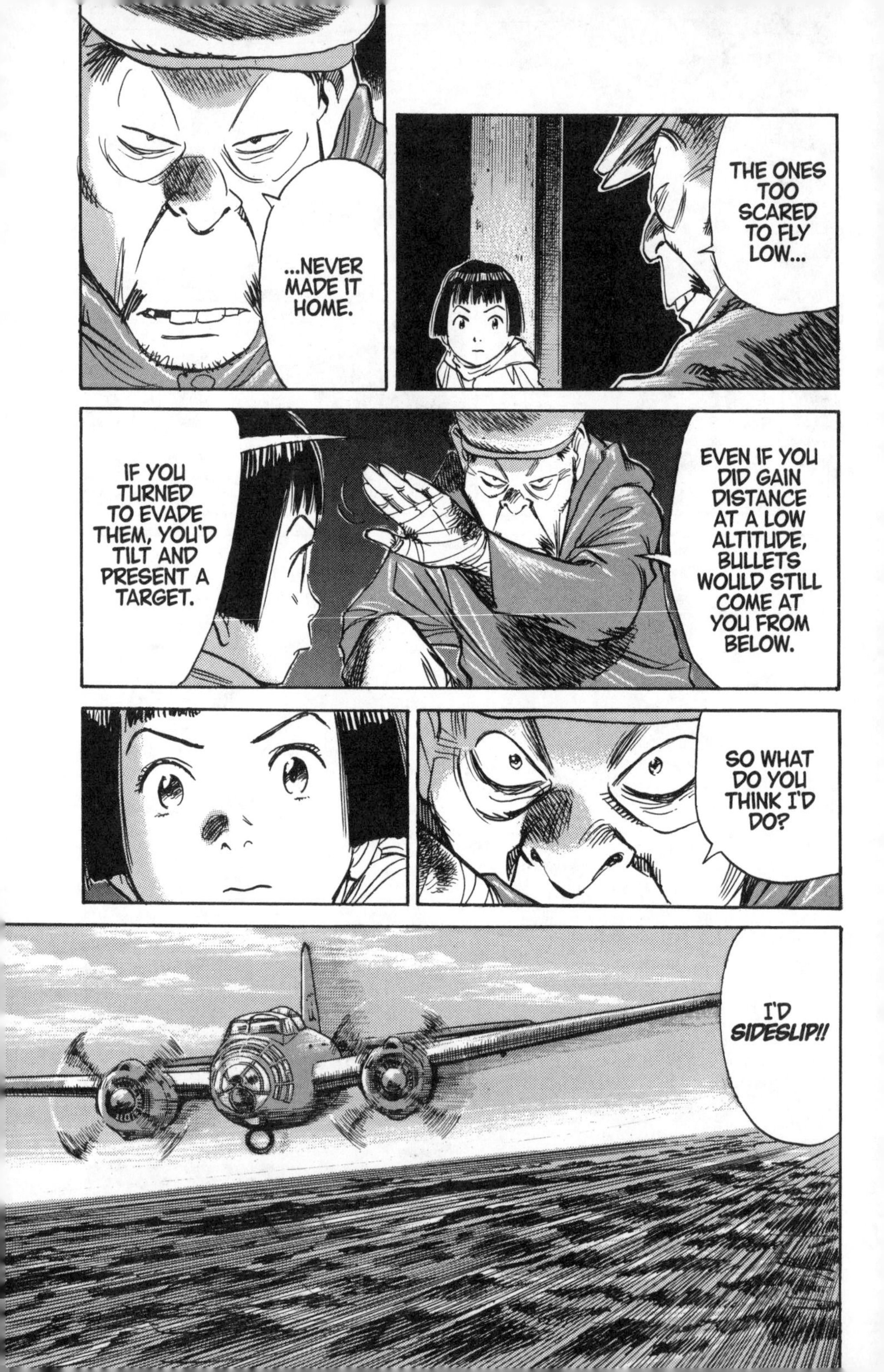
THE ONES TOO SCARED TO FLY LOW...
...NEVER MADE IT HOME.
EVEN IF YOU DID GAIN DISTANCE AT A LOW ALTITUDE, BULLETS WOULD STILL COME AT YOU FROM BELOW.
IF YOU TURNED TO EVADE THEM, YOU'D TILT AND PRESENT A TARGET.
SO WHAT DO YOU THINK I'D DO?
I'D *SIDESLIP!!*

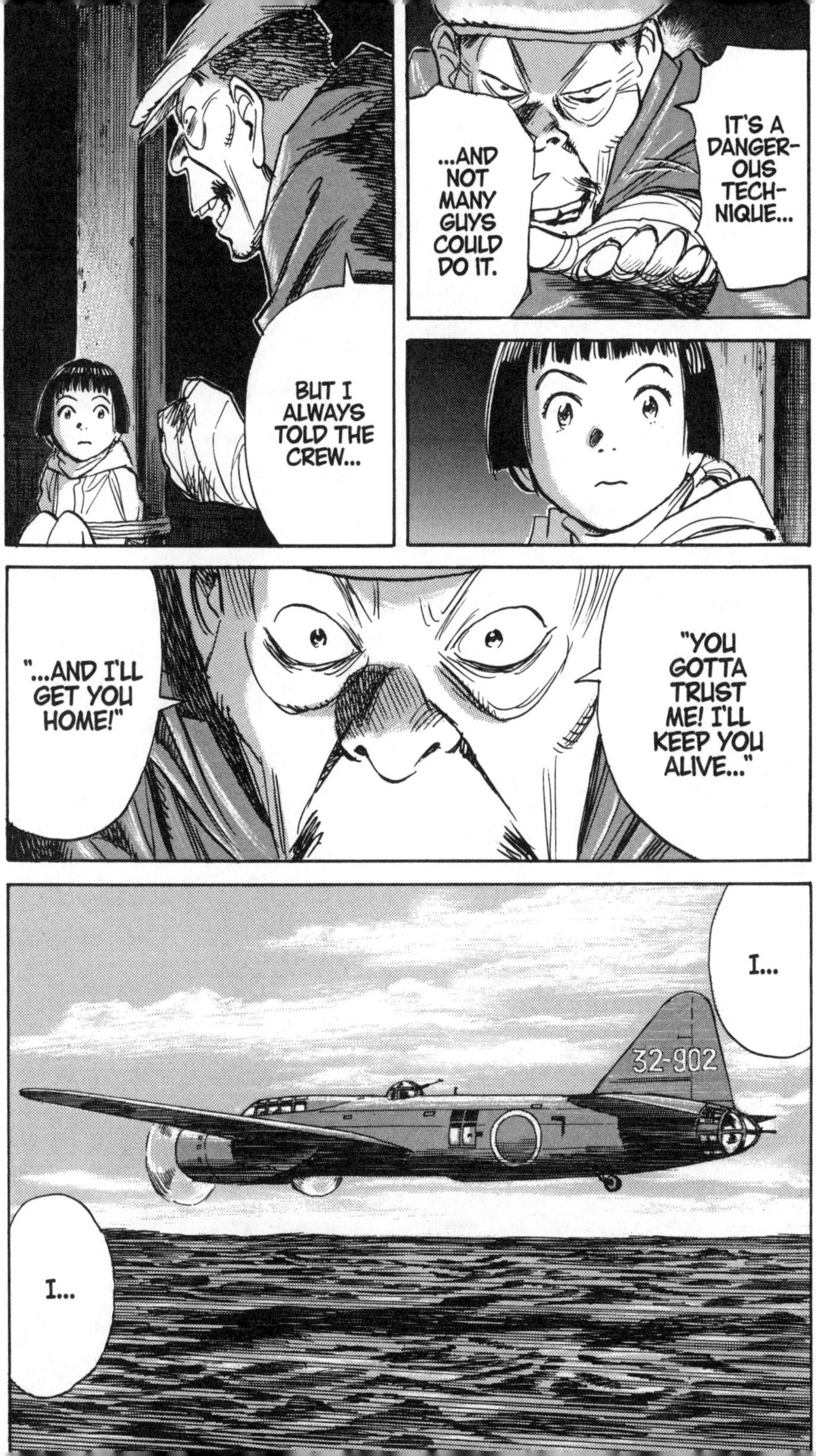
IT'S A DANGEROUS TECHNIQUE...
...AND NOT MANY GUYS COULD DO IT.
BUT I ALWAYS TOLD THE CREW...
"YOU GOTTA TRUST ME! I'LL KEEP YOU ALIVE..."
"...AND I'LL GET YOU HOME!"
I...
32-902
I...

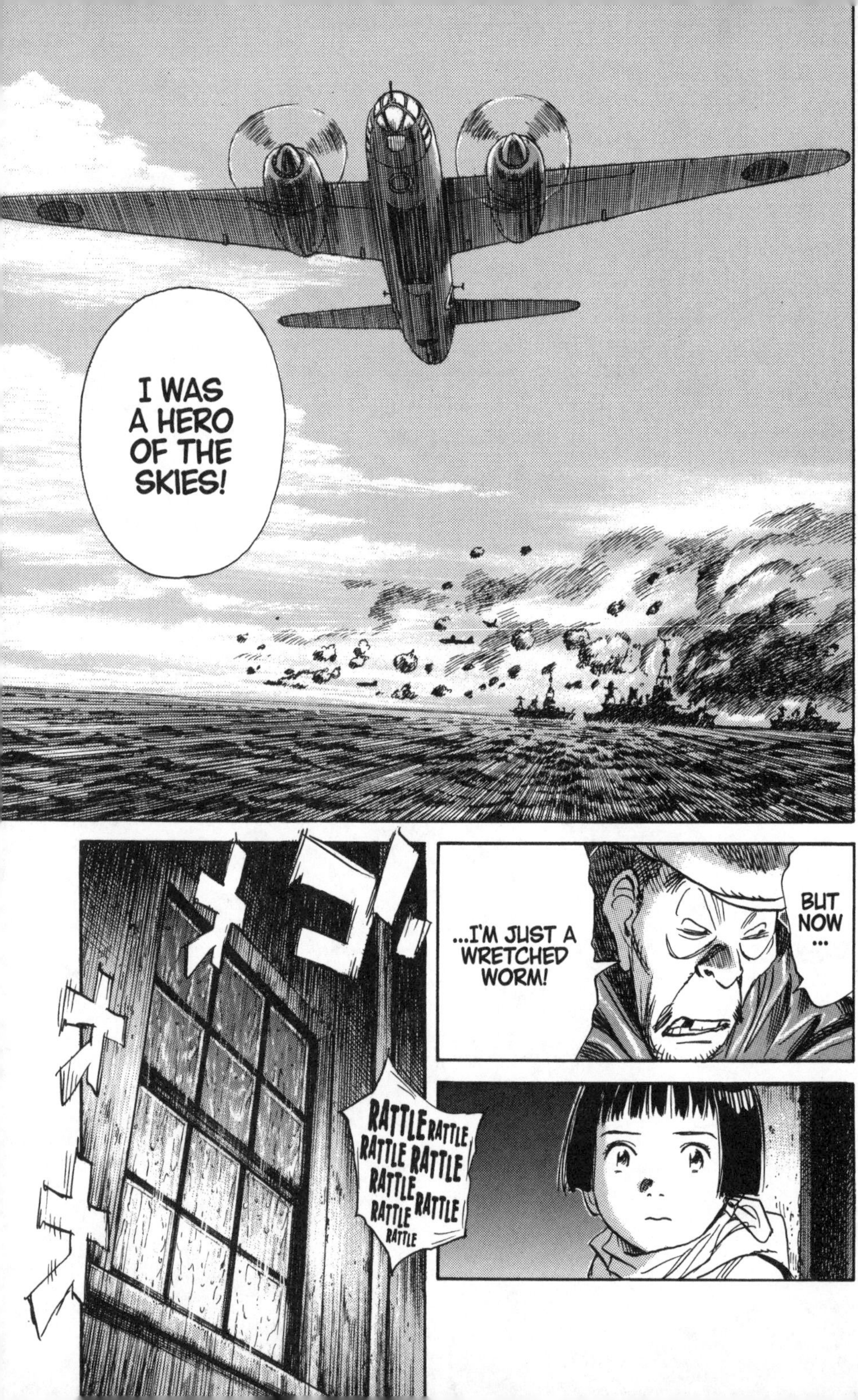
I WAS A HERO OF THE SKIES!
BUT NOW...
...I'M JUST A WRETCHED WORM!
RATTLE RATTLE RATTLE RATTLE RATTLE RATTLE RATTLE RATTLE

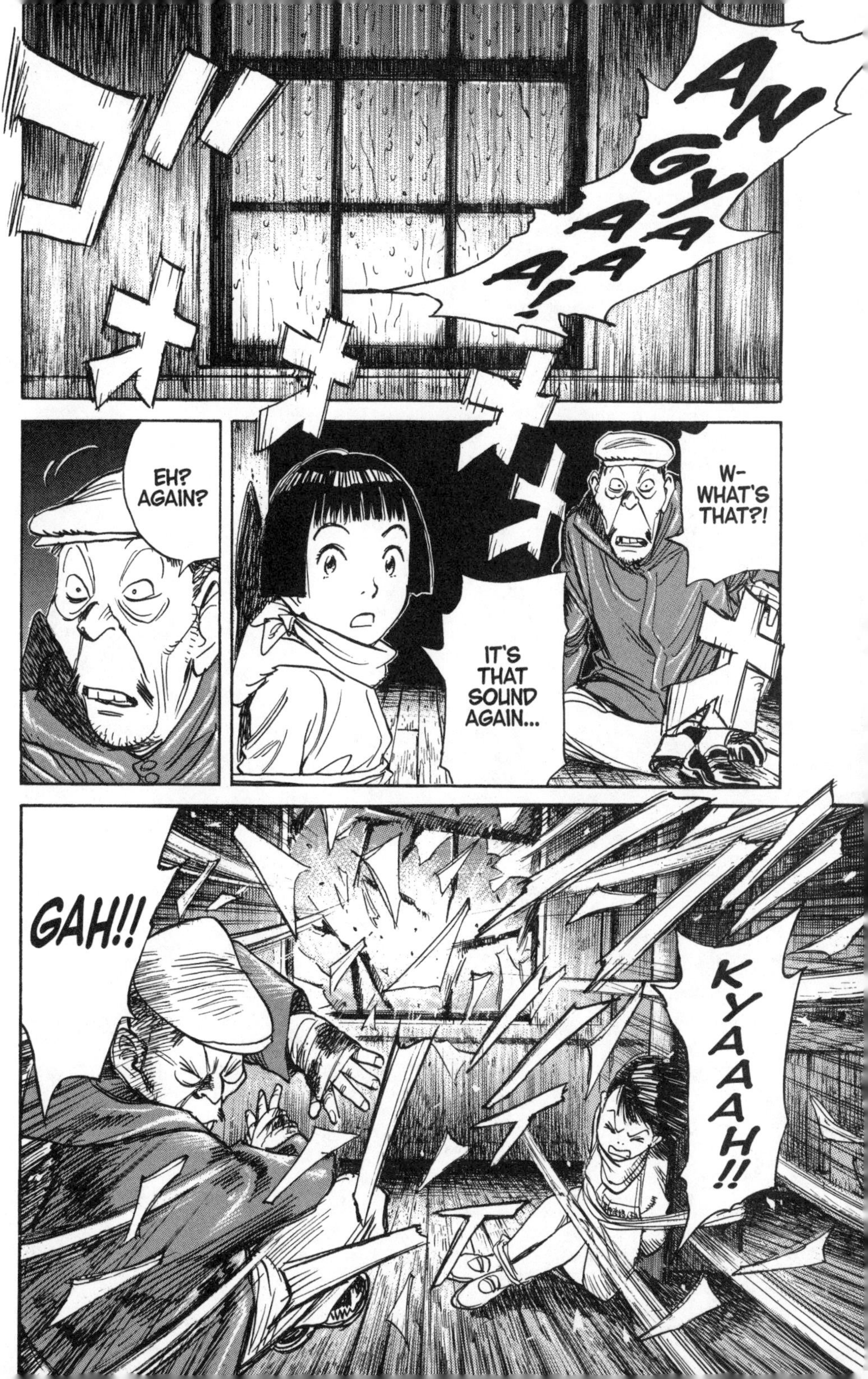

ANGYAAAA!
W-WHAT'S THAT?!
IT'S THAT SOUND AGAIN...
EH? AGAIN?
KYAAAAH!!
GAH!!

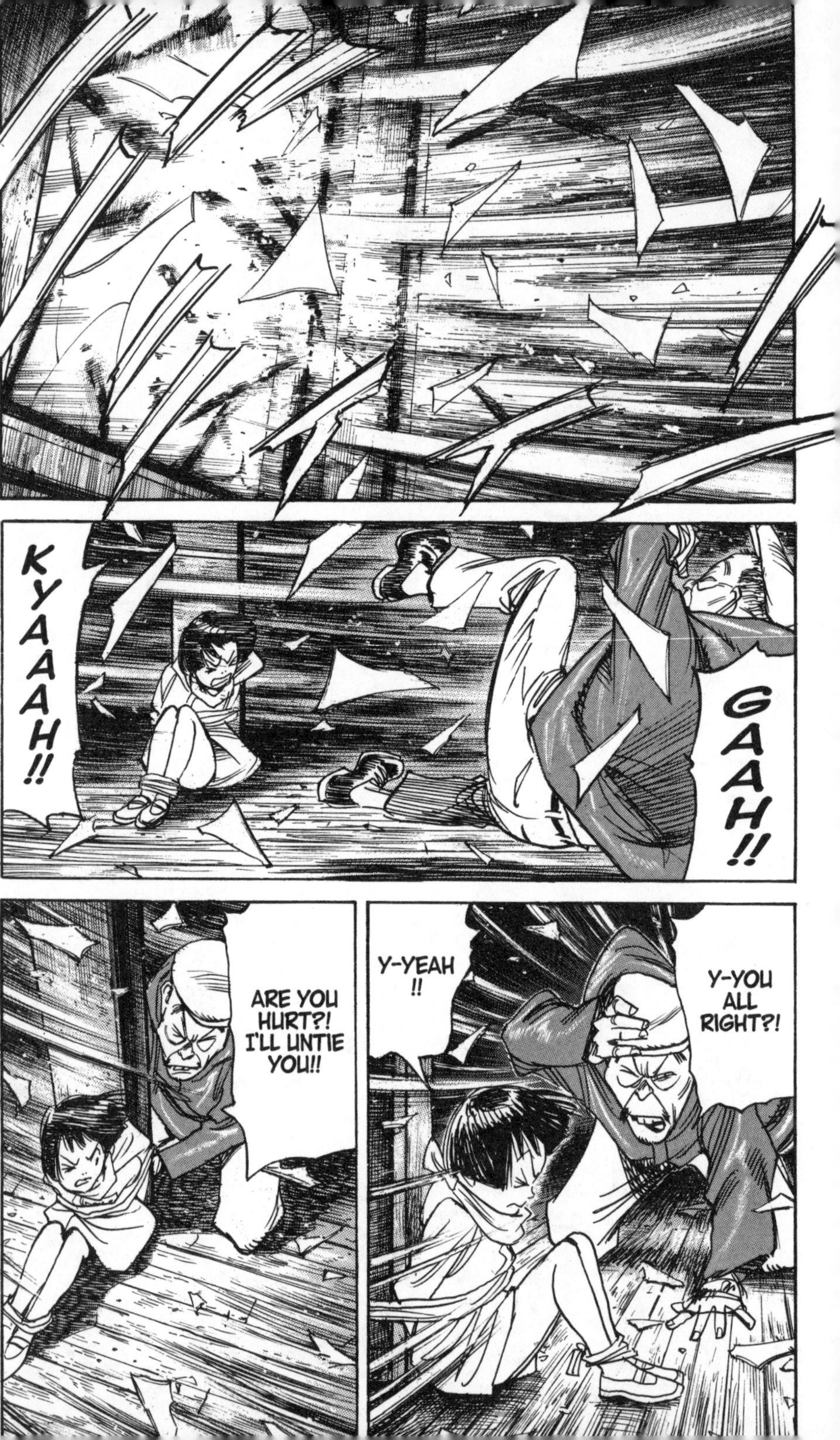
GAAAH!!
KYAAAAH!!
Y-YOU ALL RIGHT?!
Y-YEAH !!
ARE YOU HURT?! I'LL UNTIE YOU!!

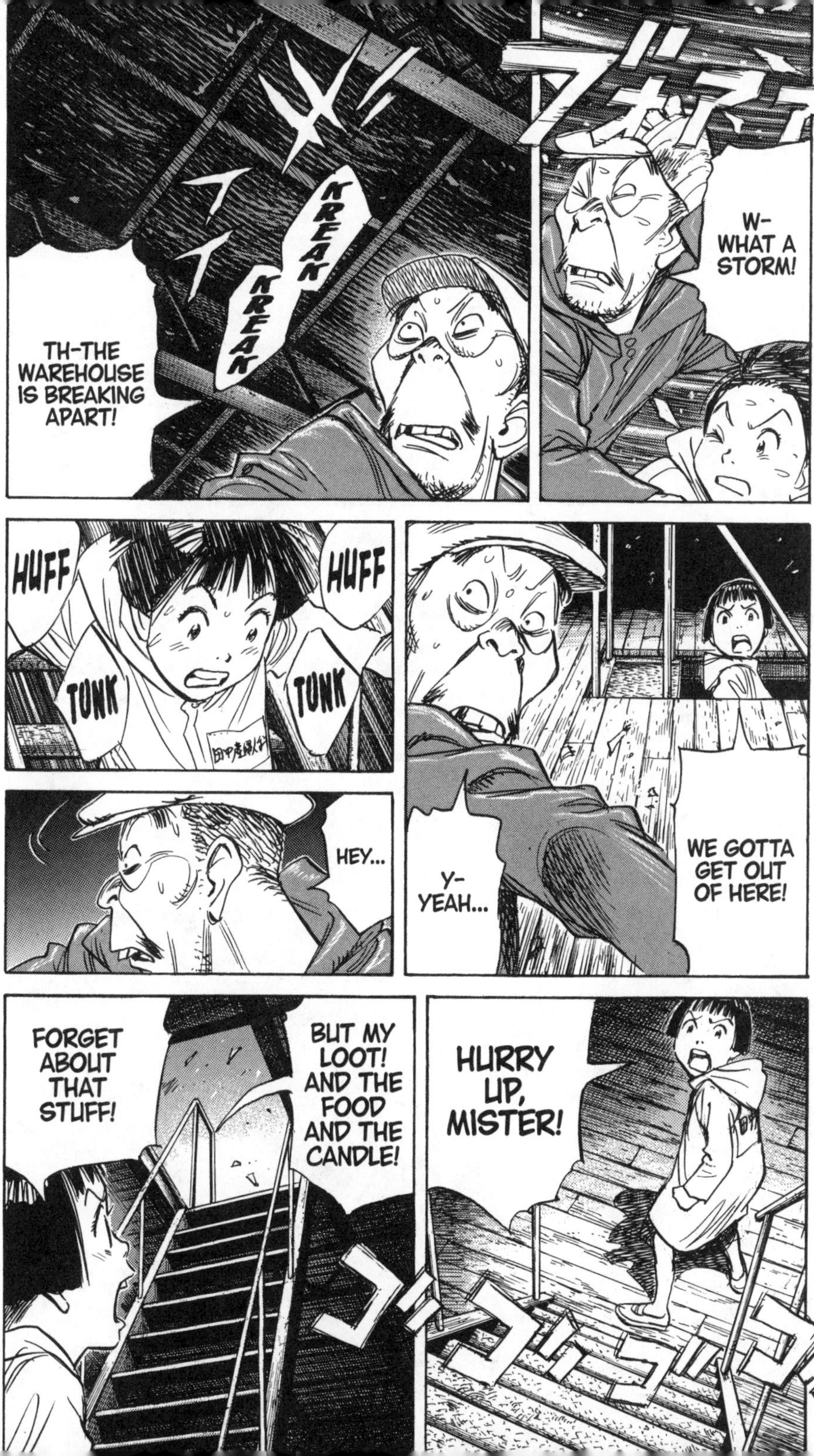
W-
WHAT A STORM!
KREAK
KREAK
TH-THE WAREHOUSE IS BREAKING APART!
WE GOTTA GET OUT OF HERE!
Y-
YEAH...
HUFF
HUFF
TUNK
TUNK
HEY...
HURRY UP, MISTER!
BUT MY LOOT! AND THE FOOD AND THE CANDLE!
FORGET ABOUT THAT STUFF!

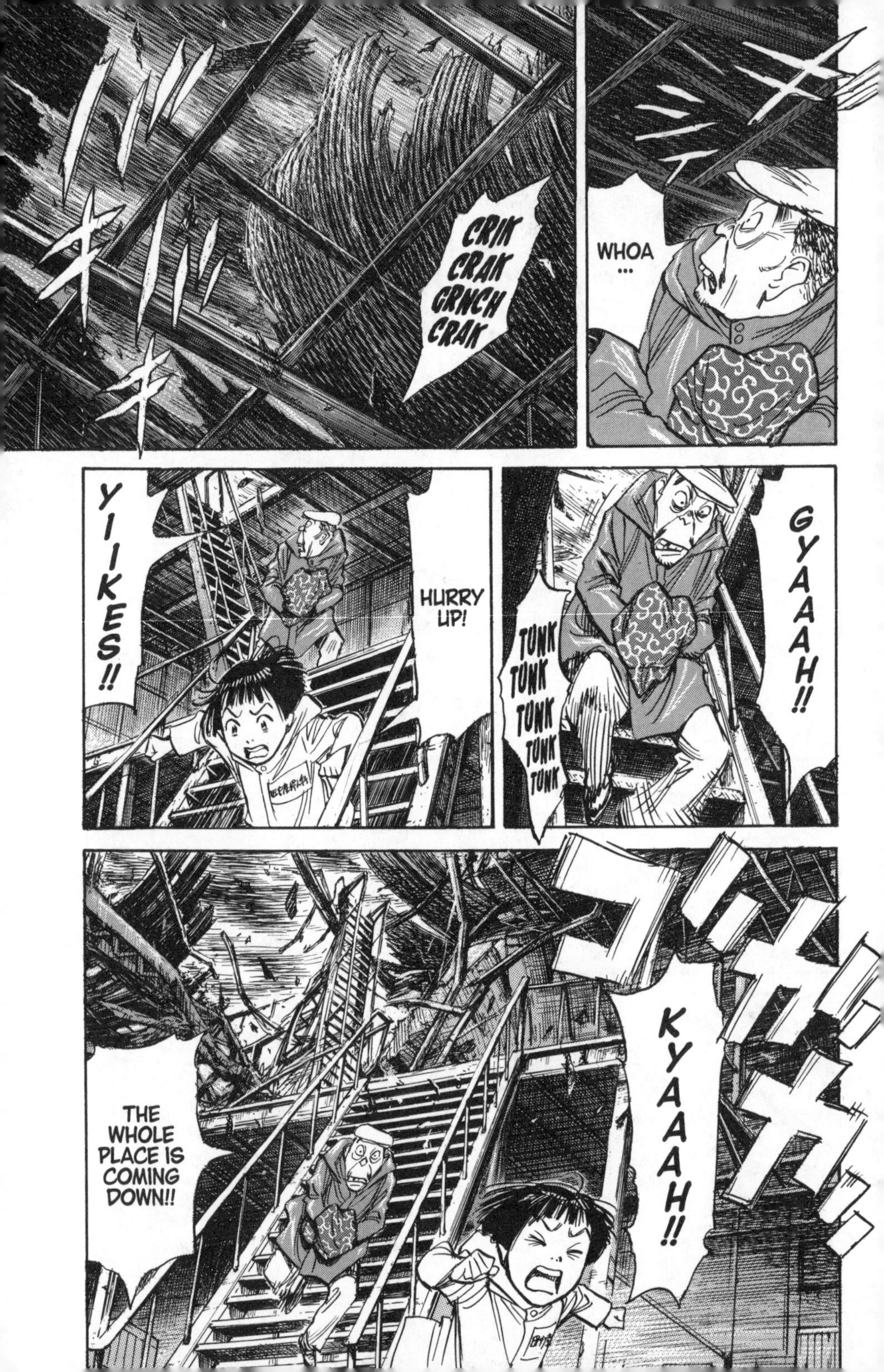
WHOA
...
CRIK
CRAK
GRNCH
CRAK
GYAAAAH!!
TUNK
TUNK
TUNK
TUNK
TUNK
HURRY UP!
YIIKES!!
KYAAAAH!!
THE WHOLE PLACE IS COMING DOWN!!

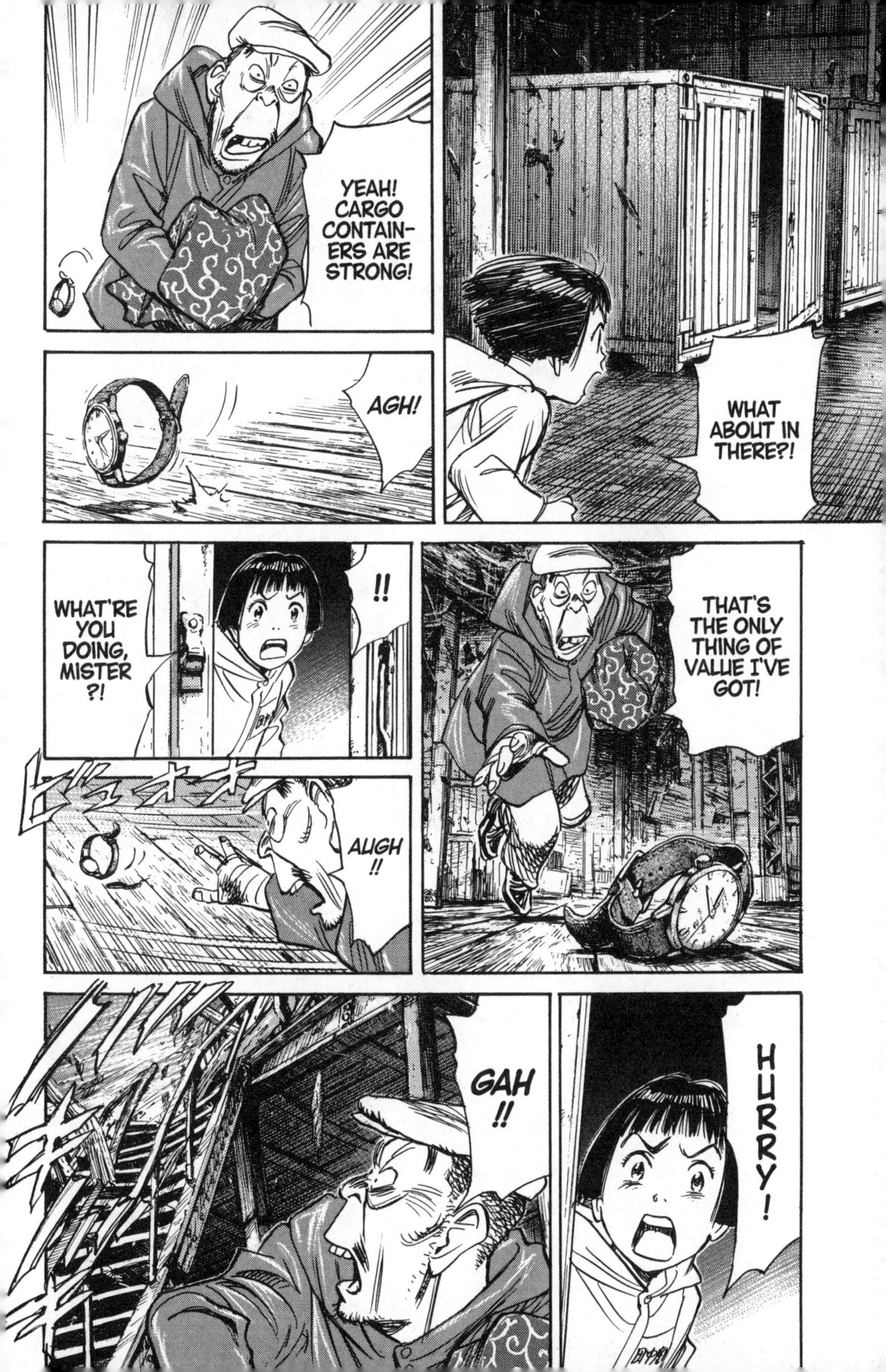
WHAT ABOUT IN THERE?!
YEAH! CARGO CONTAINERS ARE STRONG!
AGH!
THAT'S THE ONLY THING OF VALUE I'VE GOT!
!!
WHAT'RE YOU DOING, MISTER?!
AUGH!!
HURRY!
GAH!!

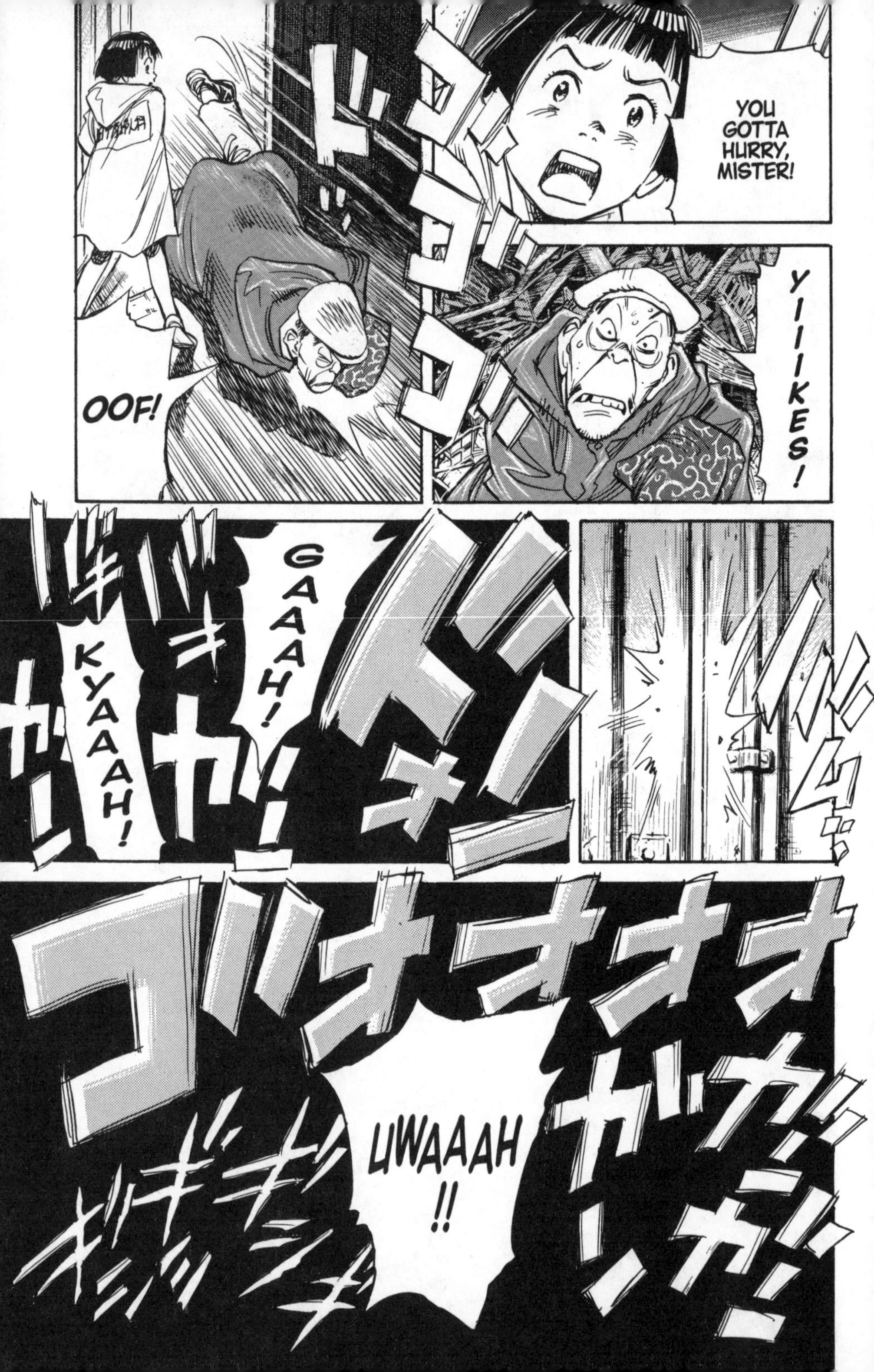
YOU GOTTA HURRY, MISTER!
YIIIIKES!
OOF!
GAAAAH!
KYAAAAH!
UWAAAH !!

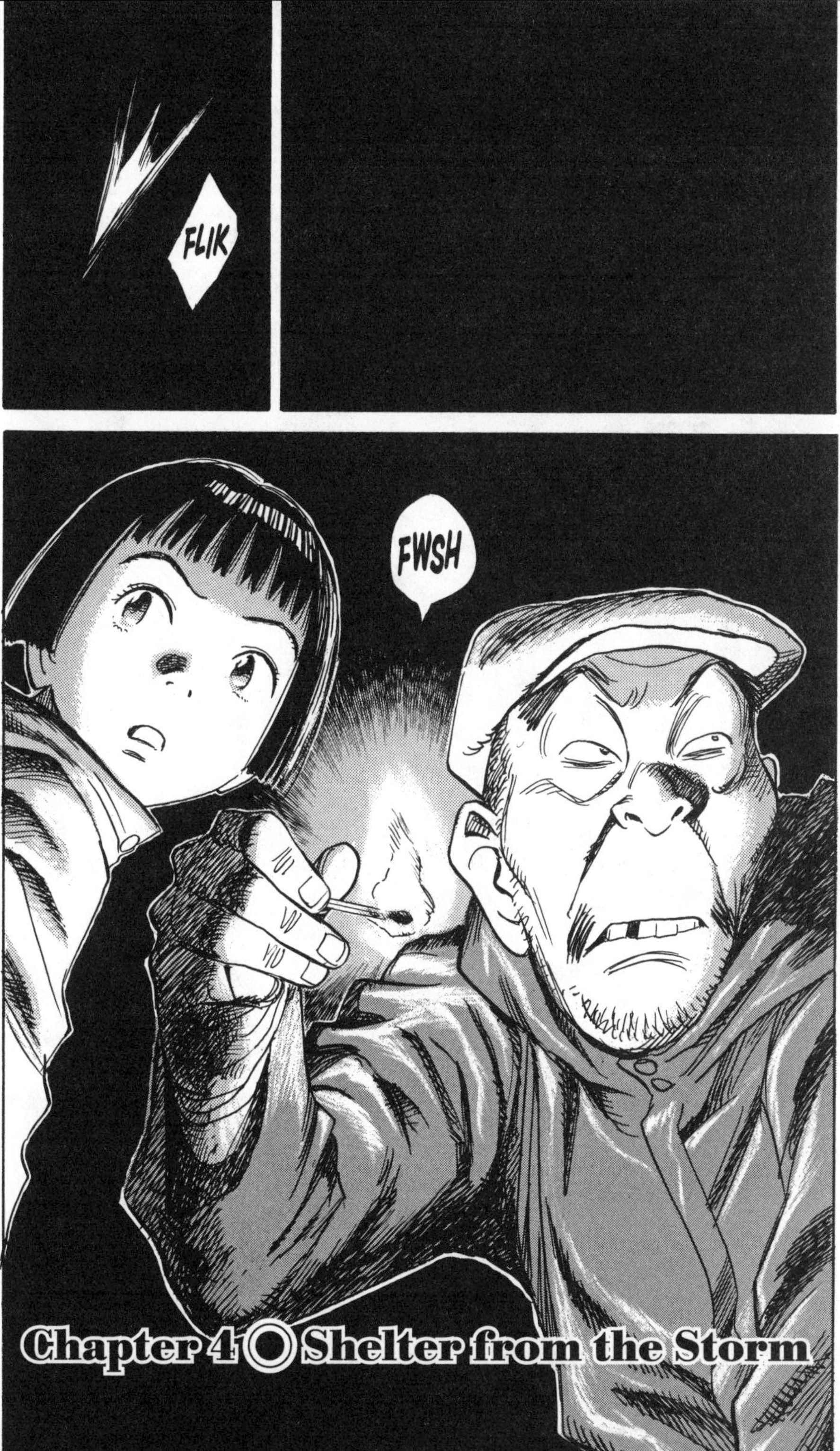
FLIK
FWSH

Chapter 4 ◯ Shelter from the Storm

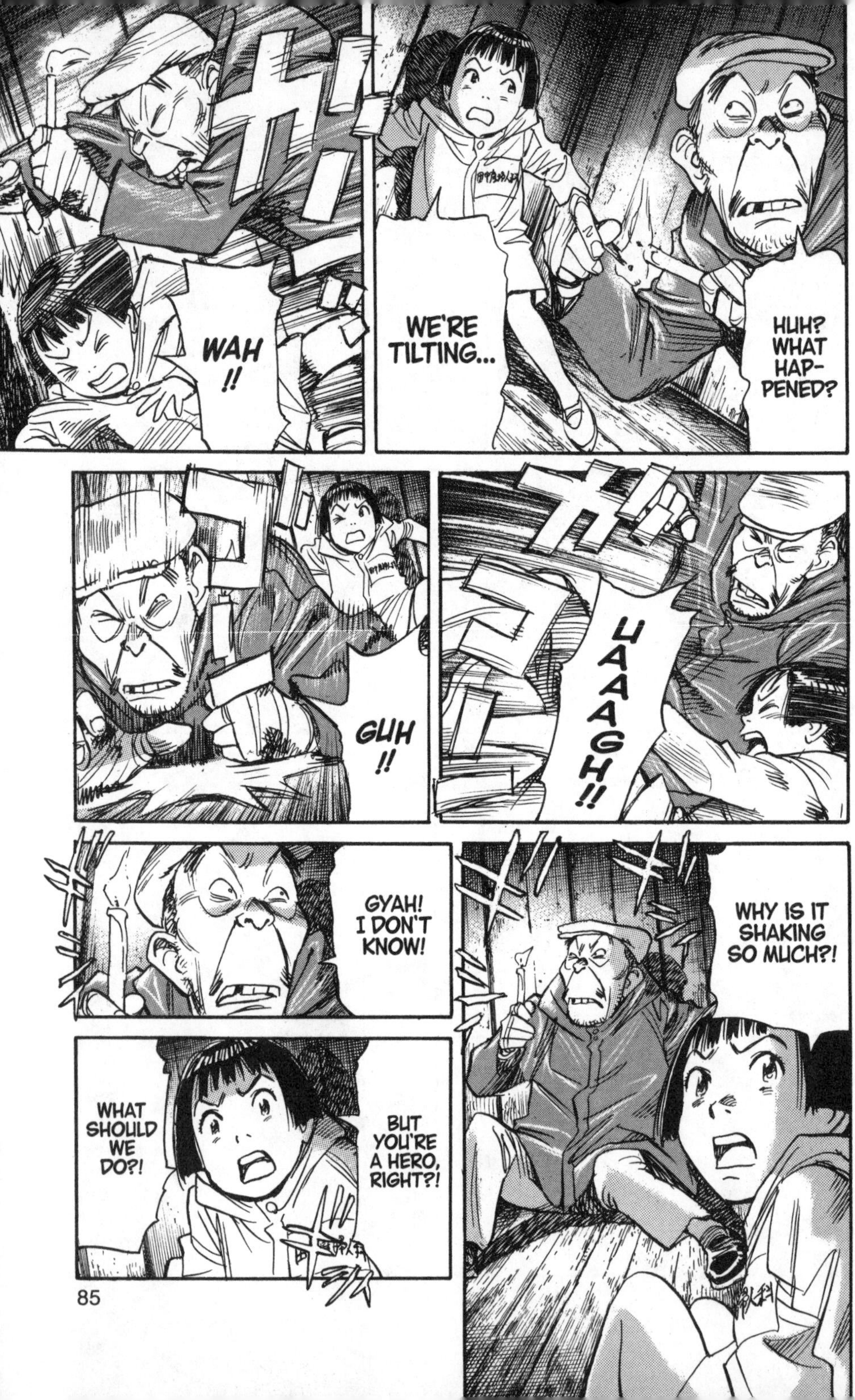
HUH? WHAT HAP-PENED?
WE'RE TILTING...
WAH !!
UAAAAGH!!
GUH !!
WHY IS IT SHAKING SO MUCH?!
GYAH! I DON'T KNOW!
BUT YOU'RE A HERO, RIGHT?!
WHAT SHOULD WE DO?!

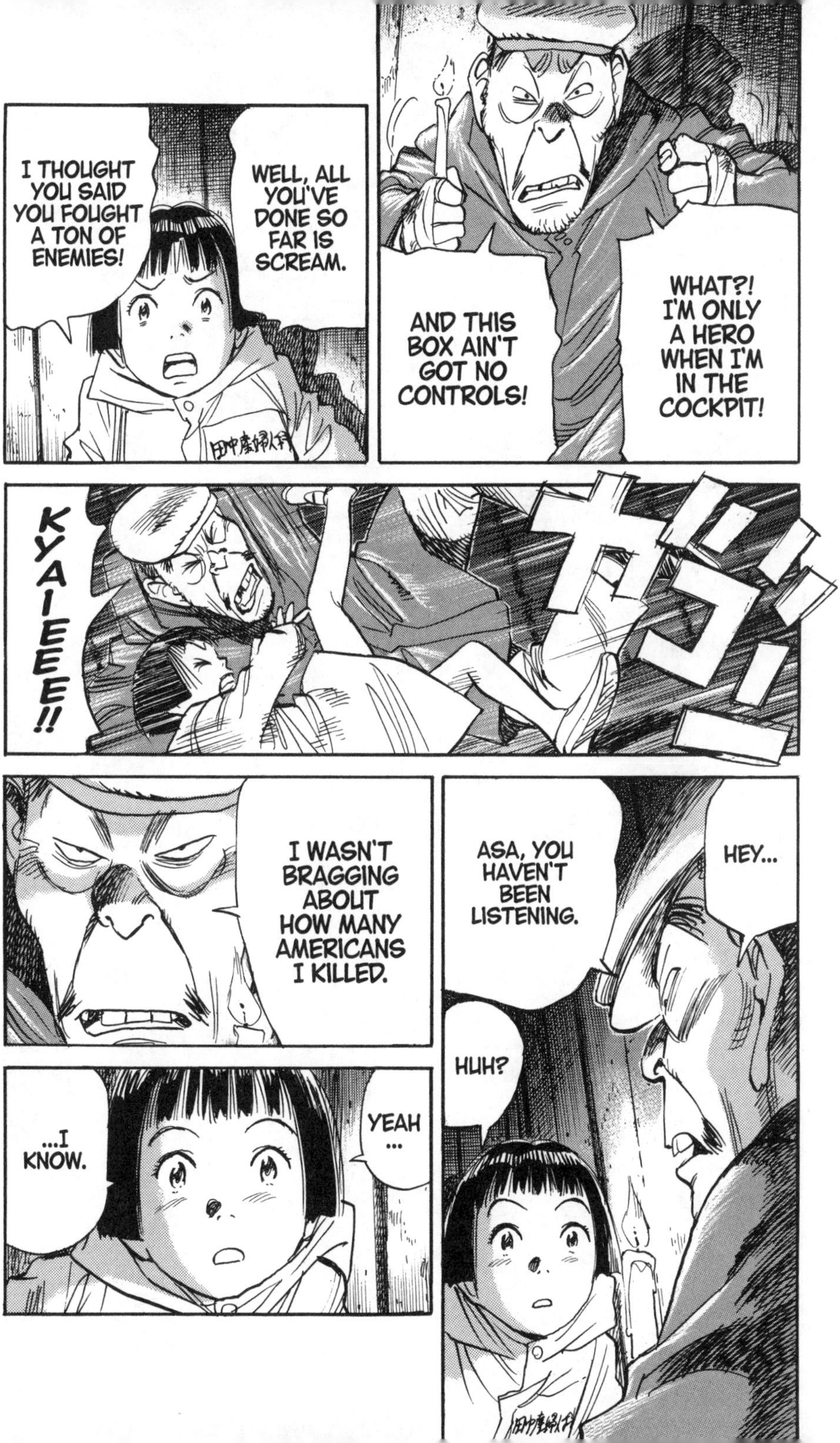
WHAT?! I'M ONLY A HERO WHEN I'M IN THE COCKPIT!
AND THIS BOX AIN'T GOT NO CONTROLS!
WELL, ALL YOU'VE DONE SO FAR IS SCREAM.
I THOUGHT YOU SAID YOU FOUGHT A TON OF ENEMIES!
KYAIEEEE!!
HEY...
ASA, YOU HAVEN'T BEEN LISTENING.
HUH?
I WASN'T BRAGGING ABOUT HOW MANY AMERICANS I KILLED.
YEAH ...
...I KNOW.

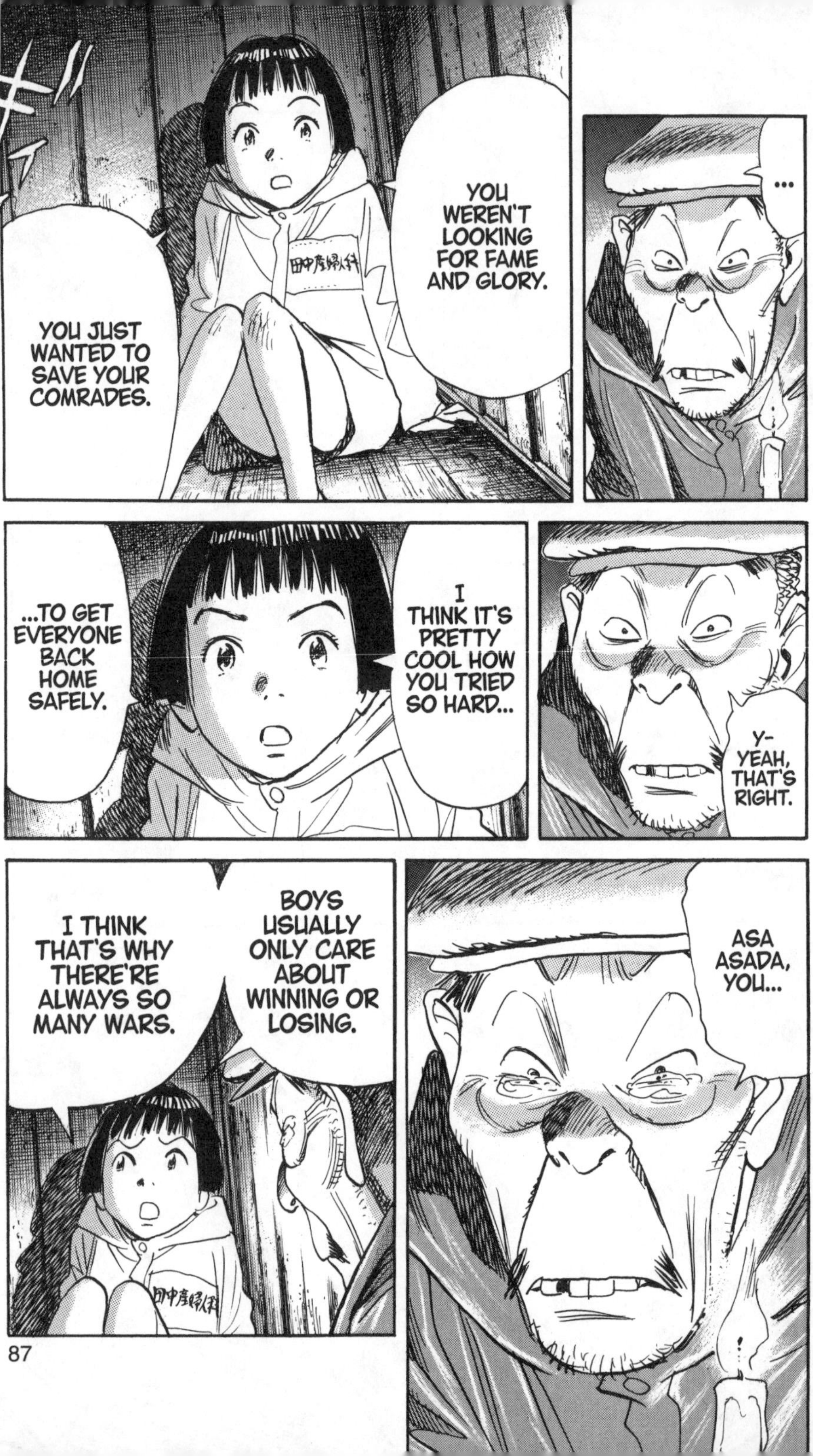
...
YOU WEREN'T LOOKING FOR FAME AND GLORY.
ギリィ
田中産婦人科
YOU JUST WANTED TO SAVE YOUR COMRADES.
Y-YEAH, THAT'S RIGHT.
I THINK IT'S PRETTY COOL HOW YOU TRIED SO HARD...
...TO GET EVERYONE BACK HOME SAFELY.
ASA ASADA, YOU...
BOYS USUALLY ONLY CARE ABOUT WINNING OR LOSING.
I THINK THAT'S WHY THERE'RE ALWAYS SO MANY WARS.
田中産婦人科

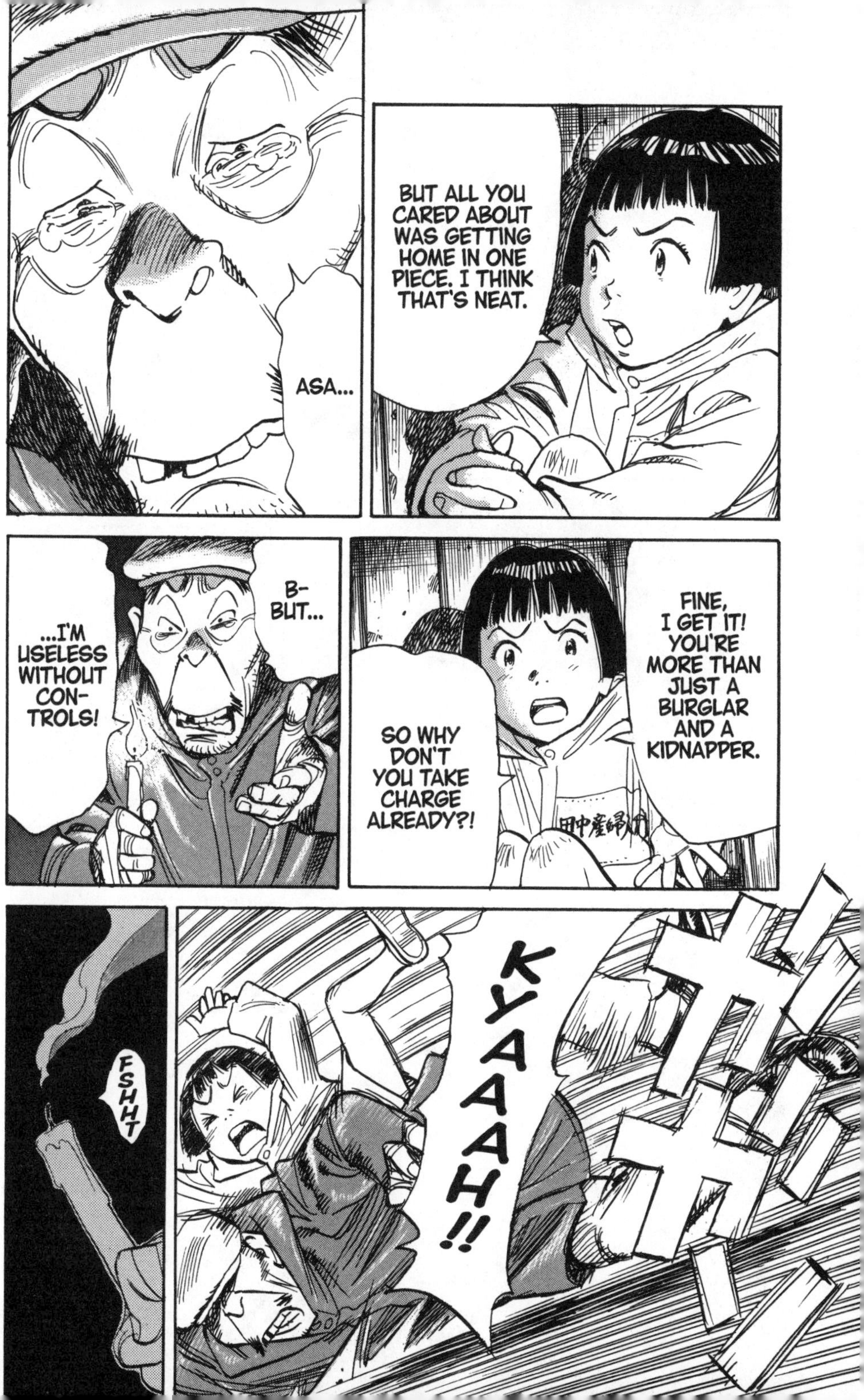
BUT ALL YOU CARED ABOUT WAS GETTING HOME IN ONE PIECE. I THINK THAT'S NEAT.
ASA...
FINE, I GET IT! YOU'RE MORE THAN JUST A BURGLAR AND A KIDNAPPER.
SO WHY DON'T YOU TAKE CHARGE ALREADY?!
B-BUT...
...I'M USELESS WITHOUT CON-TROLS!
KYAAAAH!!
FSHHT

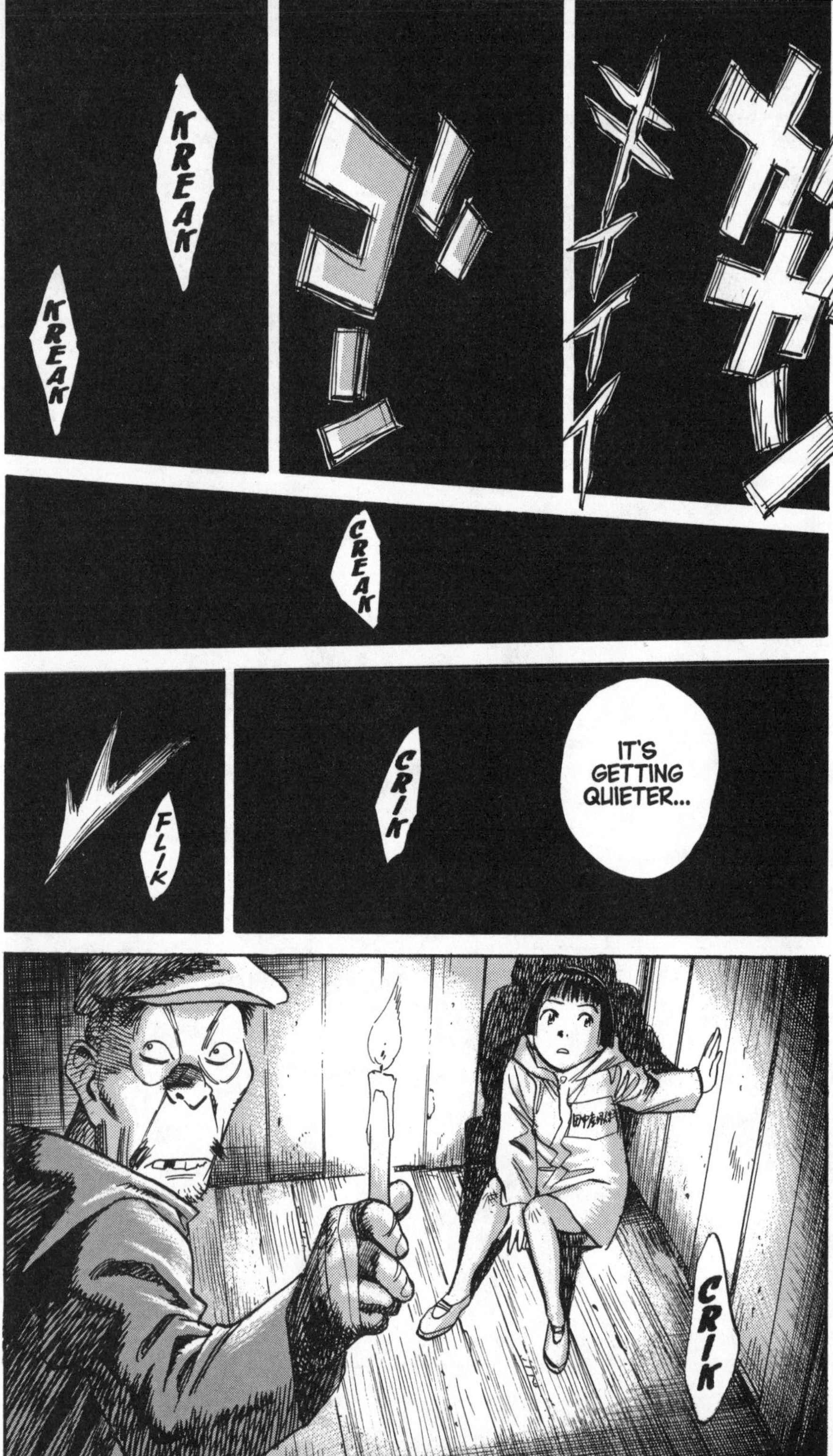
KREAK
KREAK
CREAK
IT'S GETTING QUIETER...
CRIK
FLIK
CRIK

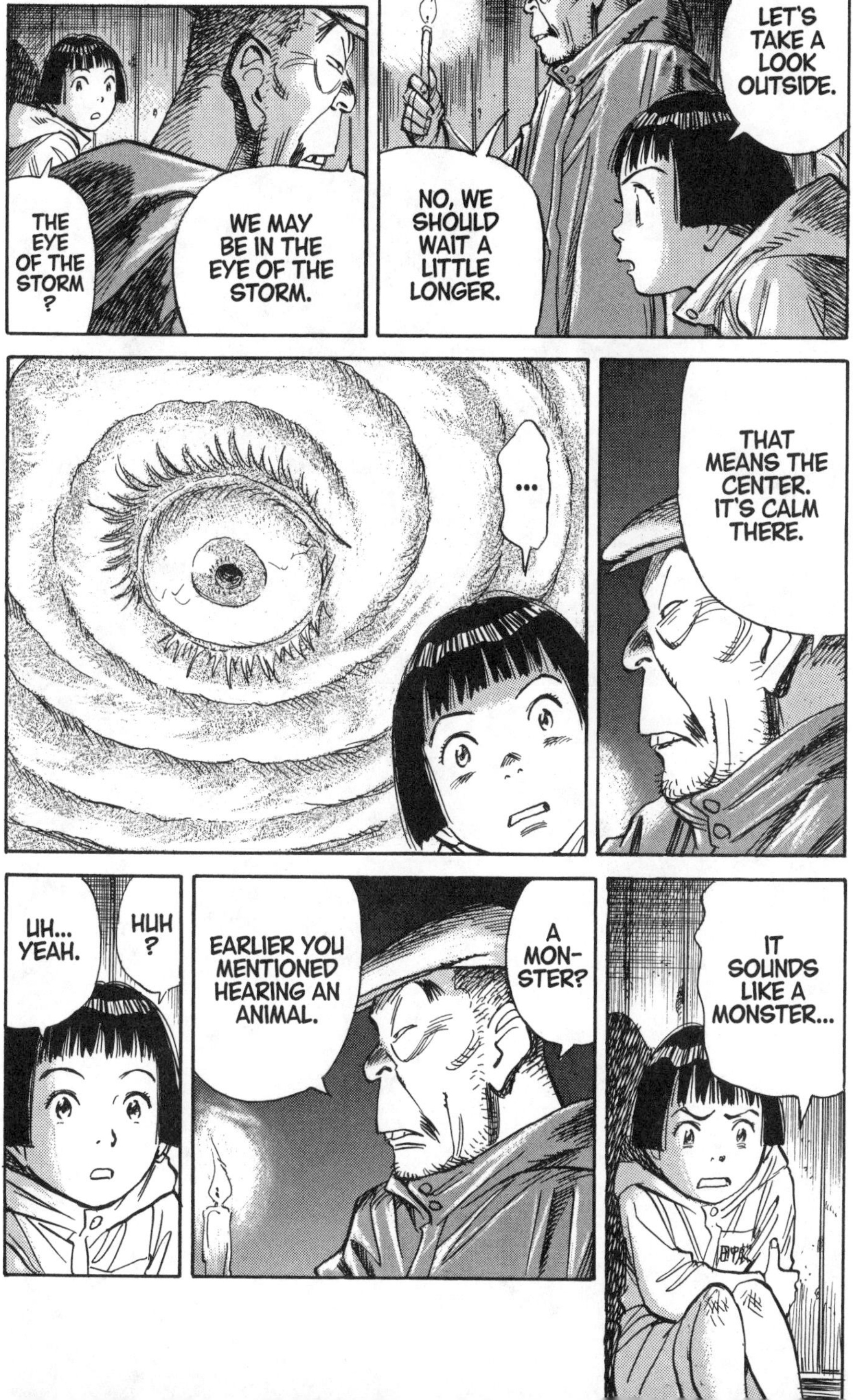
LET'S TAKE A LOOK OUTSIDE.
NO, WE SHOULD WAIT A LITTLE LONGER.
WE MAY BE IN THE EYE OF THE STORM.
THE EYE OF THE STORM?
THAT MEANS THE CENTER. IT'S CALM THERE.
...
IT SOUNDS LIKE A MONSTER...
A MONSTER?
EARLIER YOU MENTIONED HEARING AN ANIMAL.
HUH?
UH... YEAH.

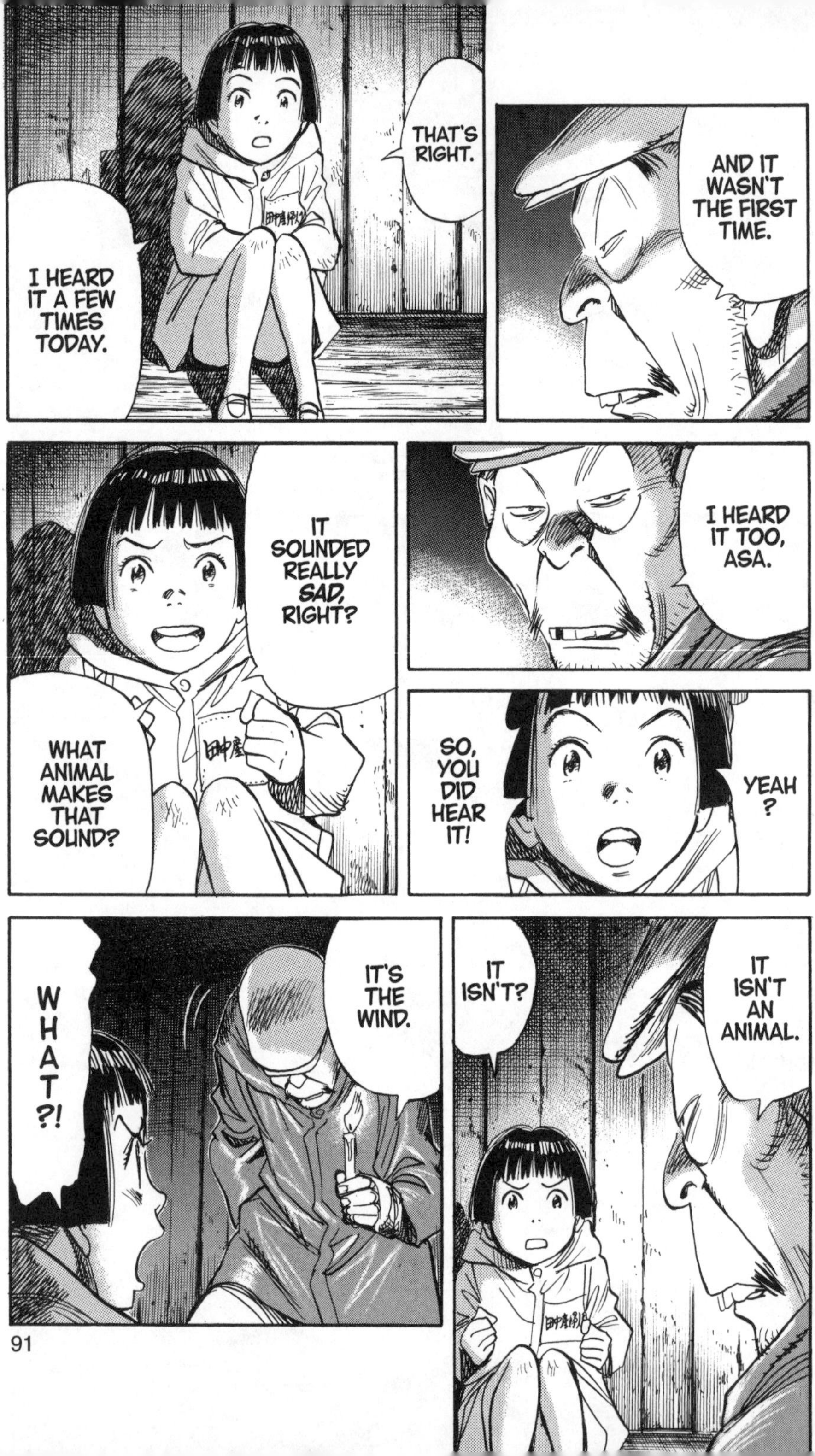
AND IT WASN'T THE FIRST TIME.
THAT'S RIGHT.
I HEARD IT A FEW TIMES TODAY.
I HEARD IT TOO, ASA.
YEAH?
SO, YOU DID HEAR IT!
IT SOUNDED REALLY SAD, RIGHT?
WHAT ANIMAL MAKES THAT SOUND?
IT ISN'T AN ANIMAL.
IT ISN'T?
IT'S THE WIND.
WHAT?!

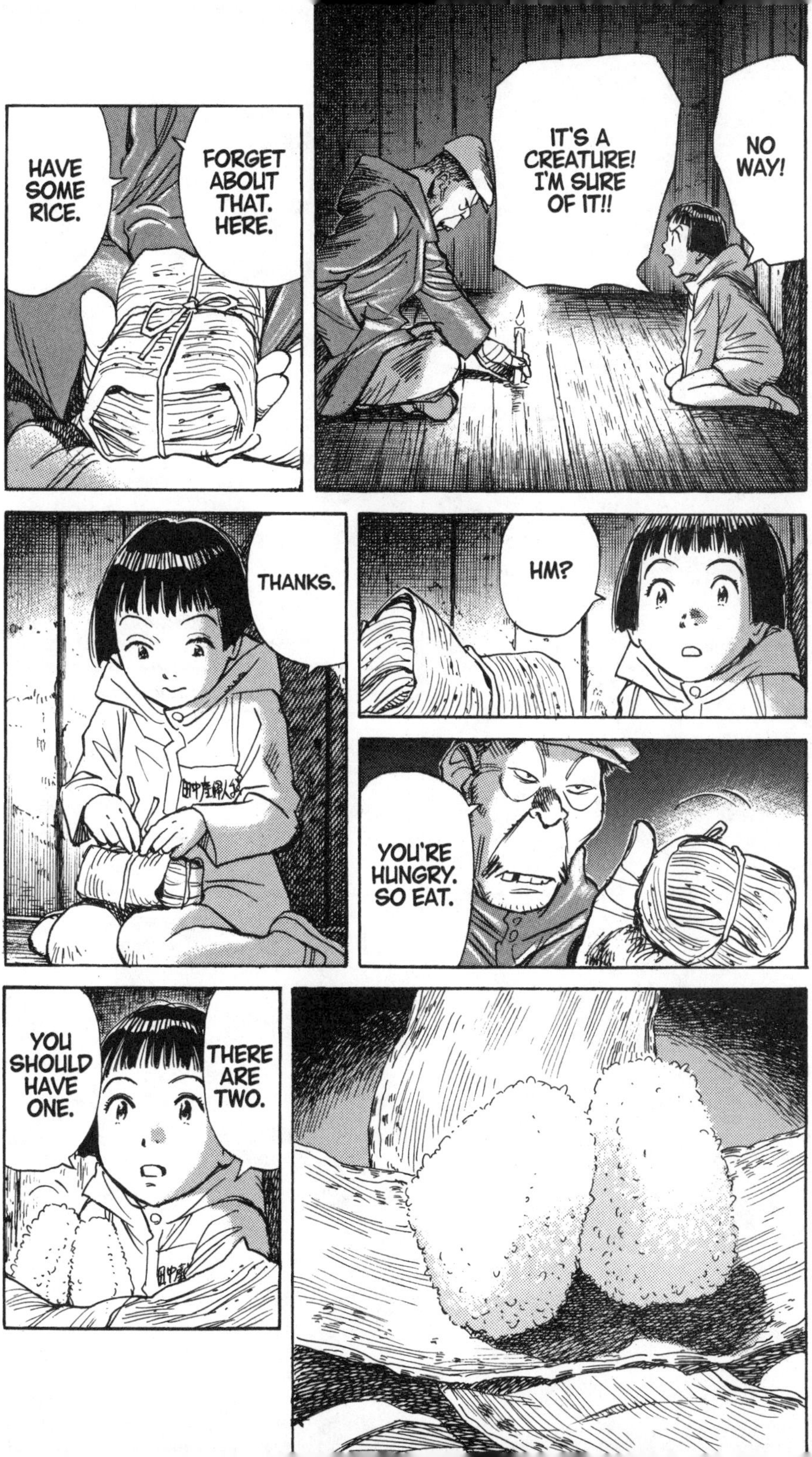
NO WAY!
IT'S A CREATURE! I'M SURE OF IT!!
FORGET ABOUT THAT. HERE.
HAVE SOME RICE.
HM?
YOU'RE HUNGRY. SO EAT.
THANKS.
THERE ARE TWO.
YOU SHOULD HAVE ONE.

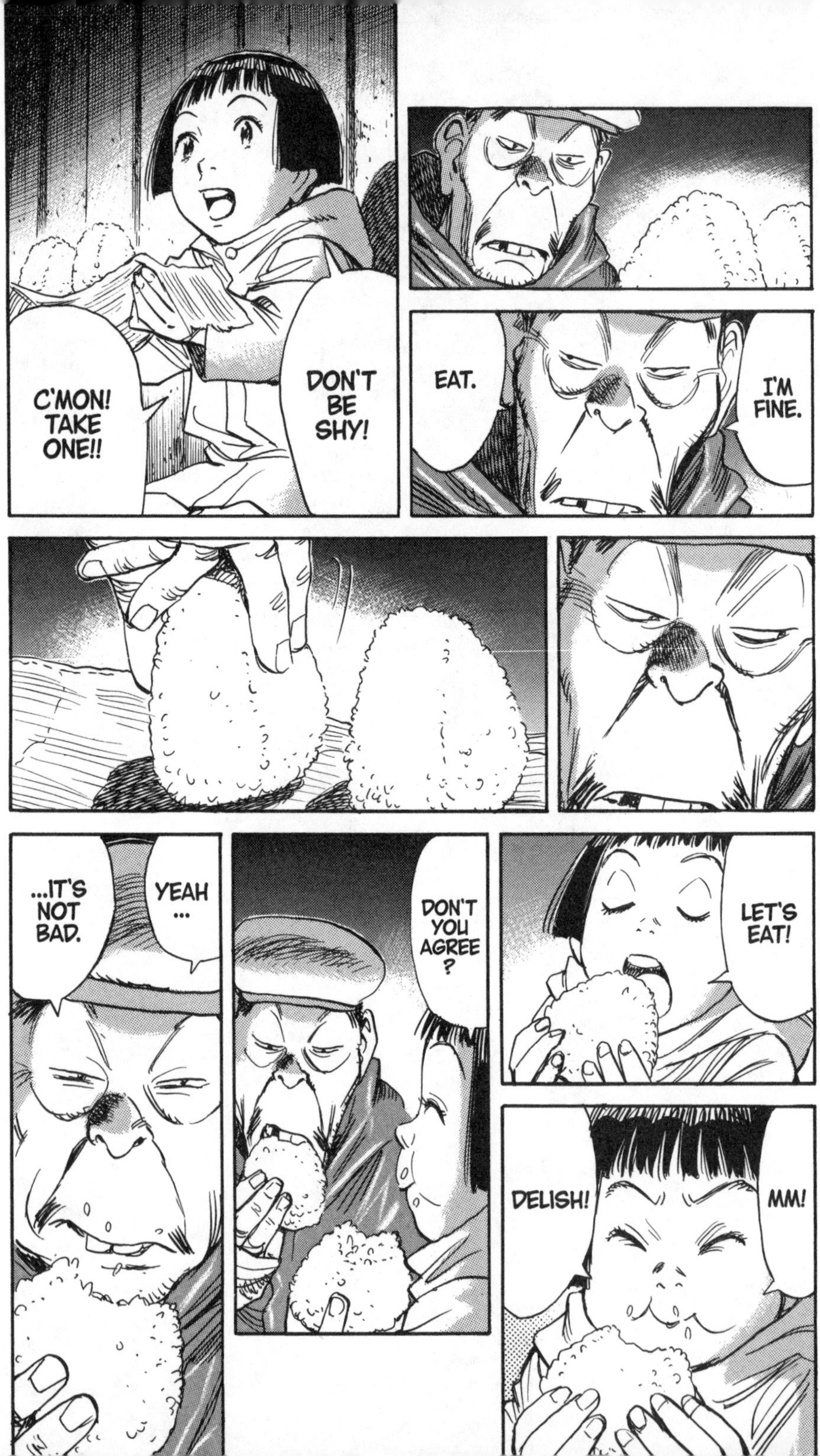
I'M FINE.
EAT.
DON'T BE SHY!
C'MON! TAKE ONE!!
LET'S EAT!
MM!
DELISH!
DON'T YOU AGREE?
YEAH...
...IT'S NOT BAD.

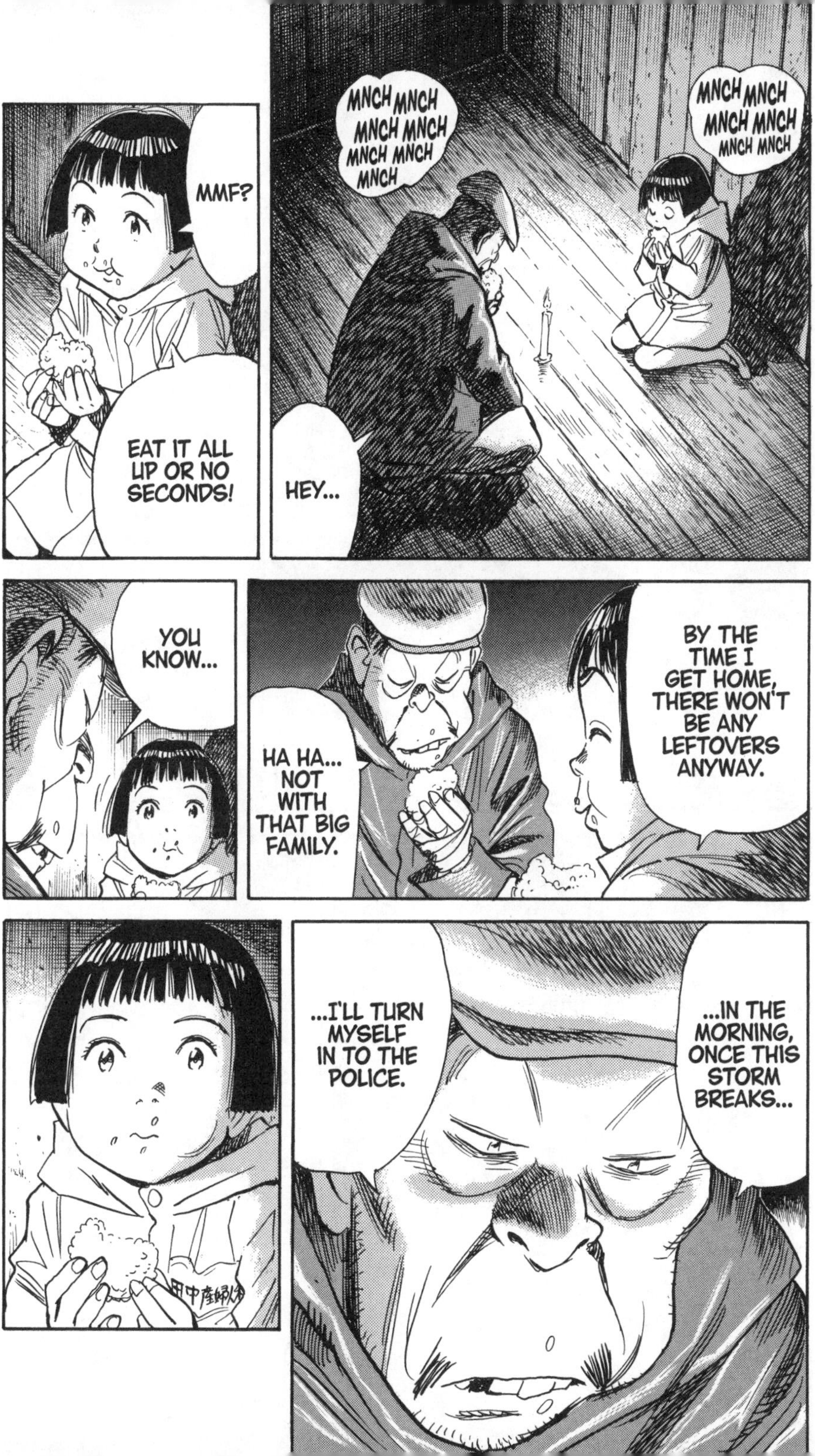
MNCH MNCH MNCH MNCH MNCH MNCH
MNCH MNCH MNCH MNCH MNCH MNCH MNCH
HEY...
MMF?
EAT IT ALL UP OR NO SECONDS!
BY THE TIME I GET HOME, THERE WON'T BE ANY LEFTOVERS ANYWAY.
HA HA... NOT WITH THAT BIG FAMILY.
YOU KNOW...
...IN THE MORNING, ONCE THIS STORM BREAKS...
...I'LL TURN MYSELF IN TO THE POLICE.

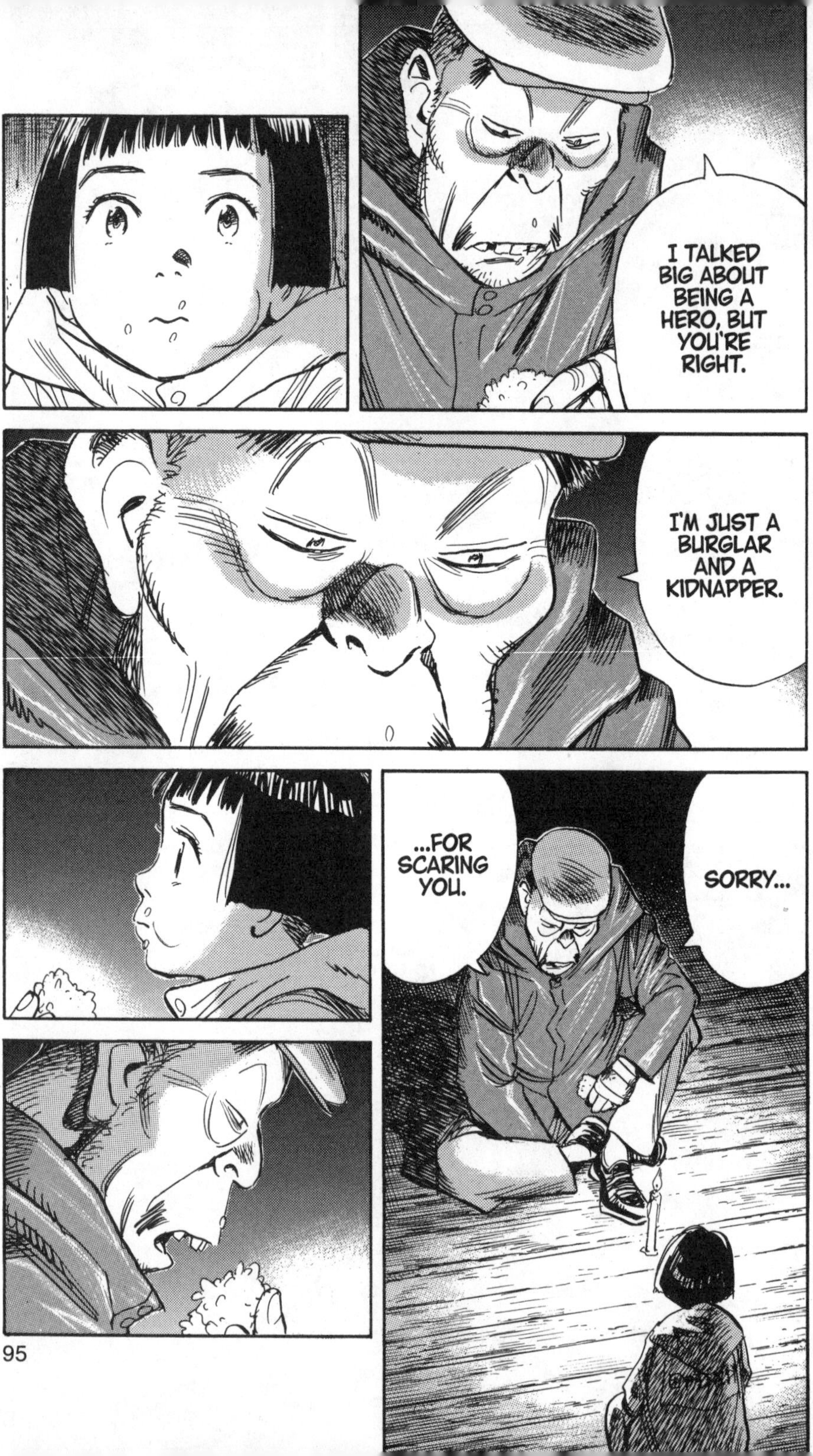
I TALKED BIG ABOUT BEING A HERO, BUT YOU'RE RIGHT.
I'M JUST A BURGLAR AND A KIDNAPPER.
SORRY...
...FOR SCARING YOU.

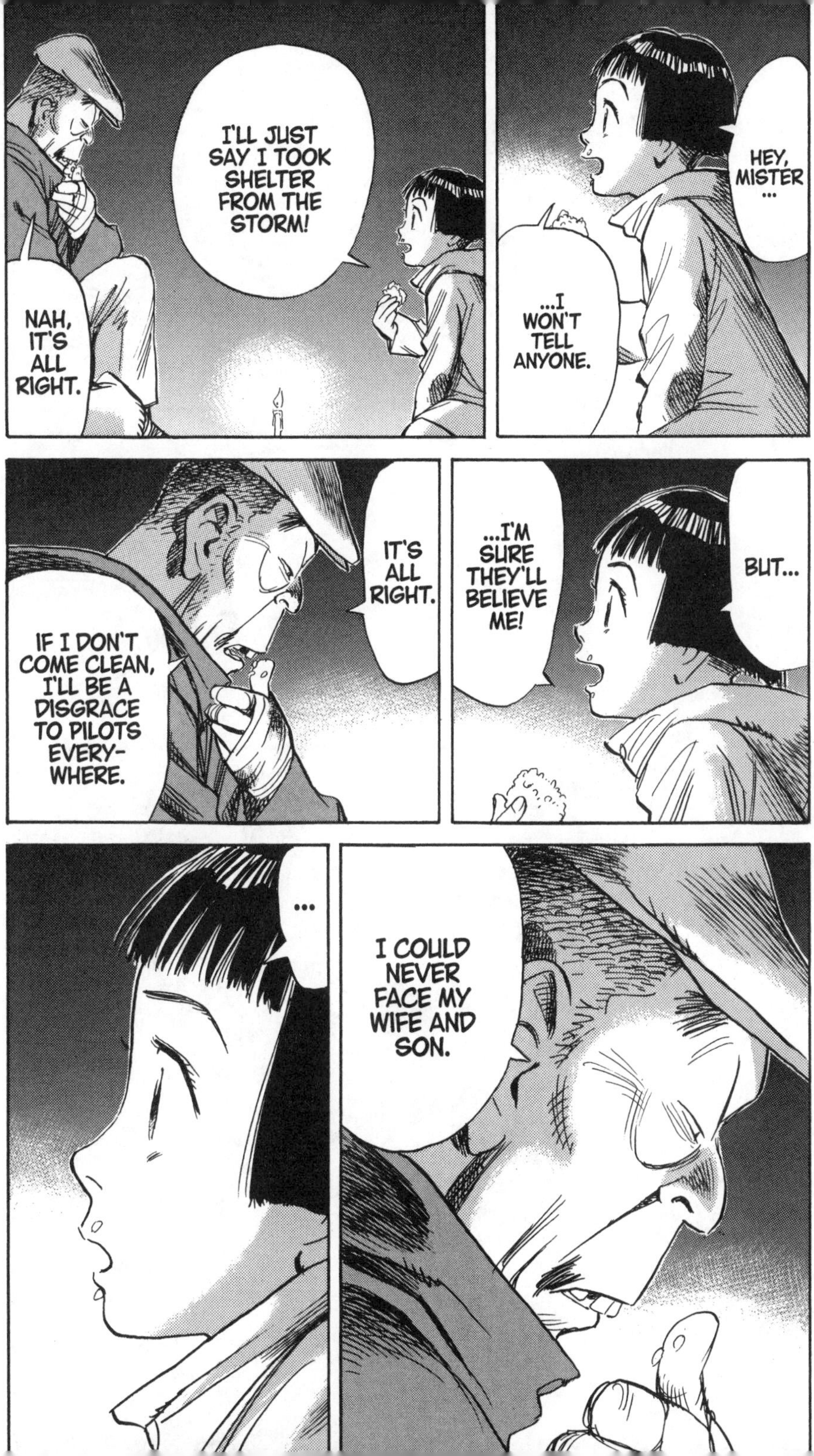
HEY, MISTER ...
...I WON'T TELL ANYONE.
I'LL JUST SAY I TOOK SHELTER FROM THE STORM!
NAH, IT'S ALL RIGHT.
BUT...
...I'M SURE THEY'LL BELIEVE ME!
IT'S ALL RIGHT.
IF I DON'T COME CLEAN, I'LL BE A DISGRACE TO PILOTS EVERY-WHERE.
I COULD NEVER FACE MY WIFE AND SON.
...

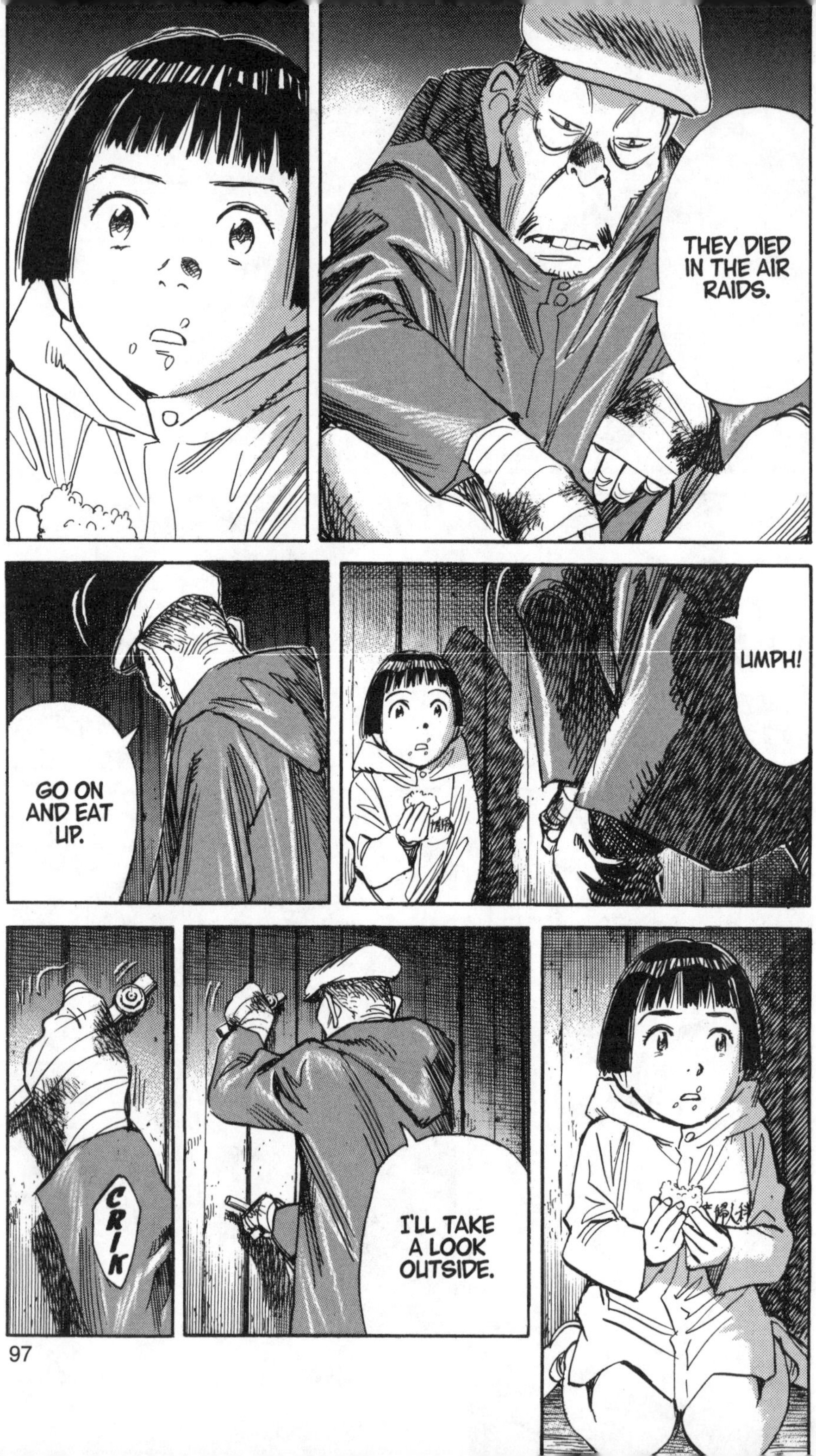
THEY DIED IN THE AIR RAIDS.
UMPH!
GO ON AND EAT UP.
I'LL TAKE A LOOK OUTSIDE.
CRIK

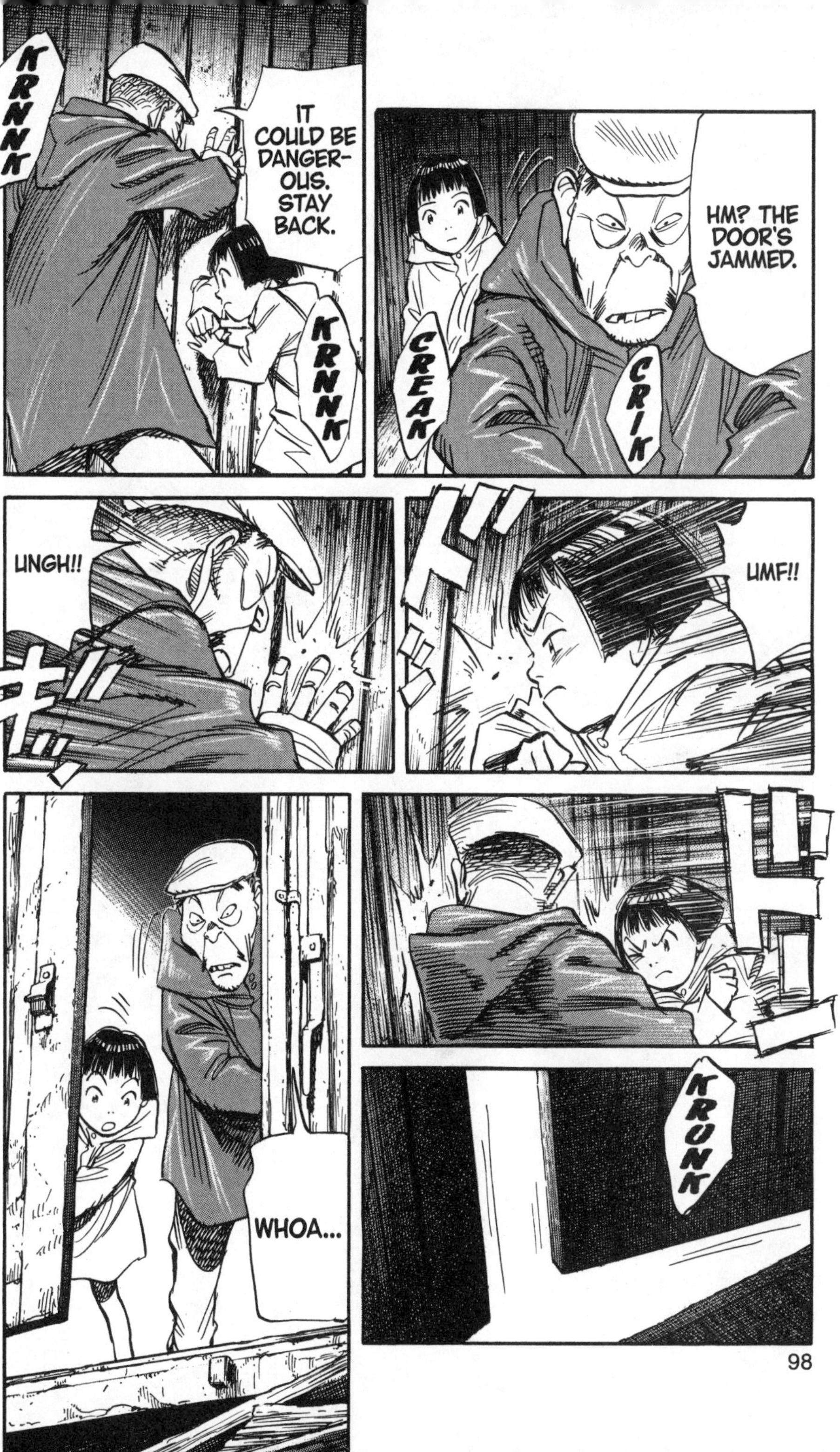
HM? THE DOOR'S JAMMED.
CRIK
CREAK
IT COULD BE DANGER-OUS. STAY BACK.
KRNNK
KRNNK
UMF!!
UNGH!!
KRUNK
WHOA...

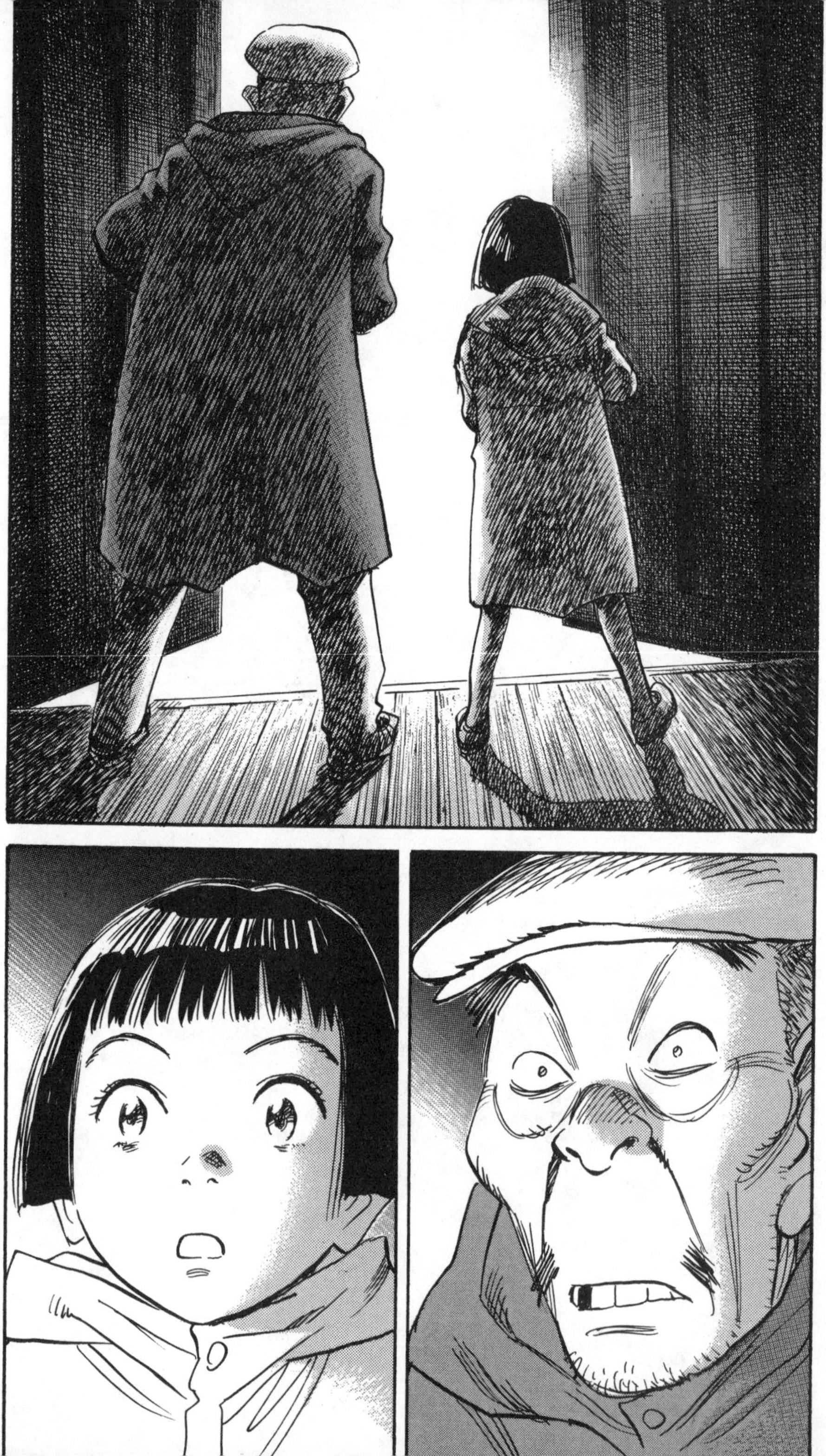

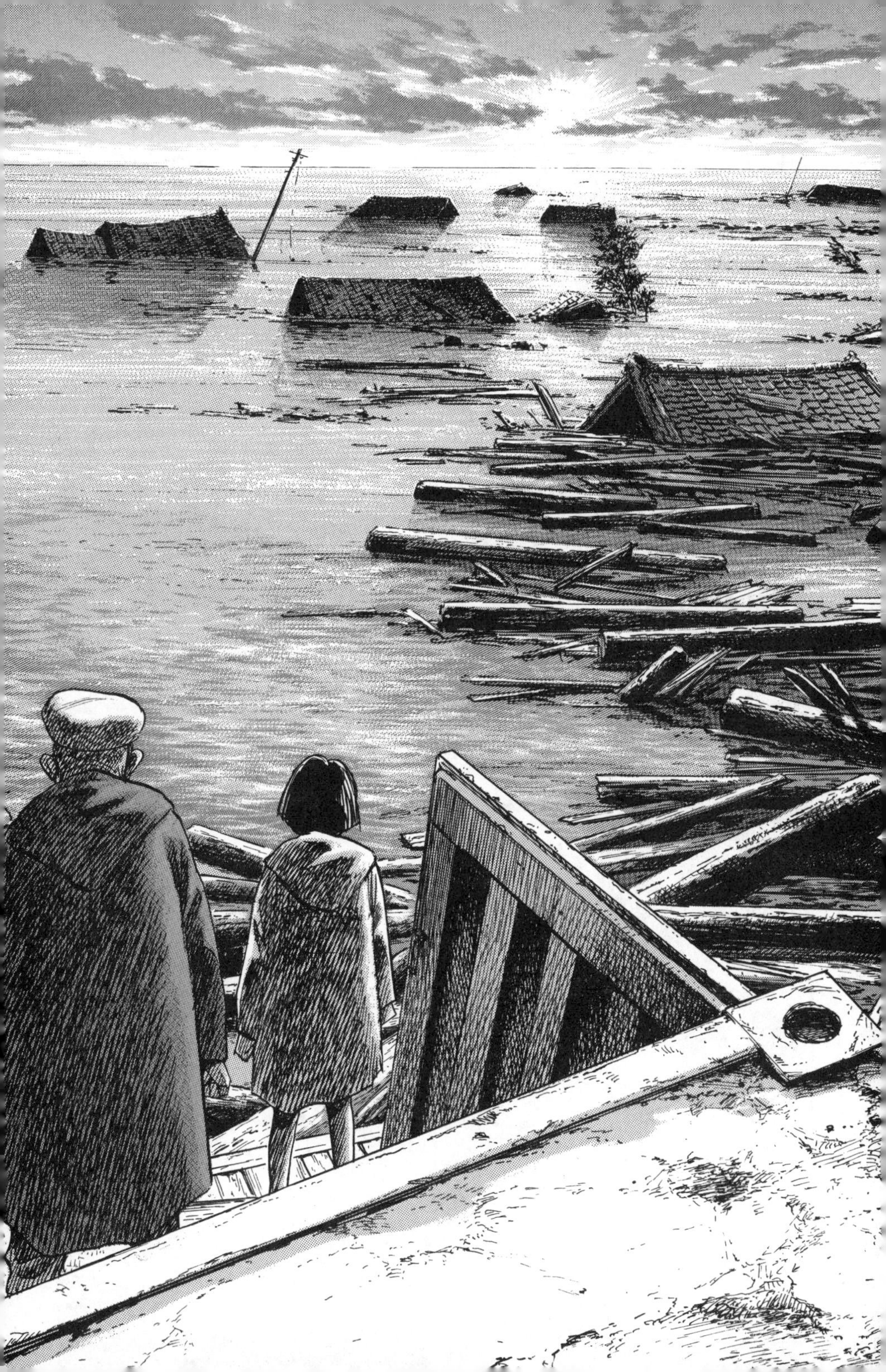

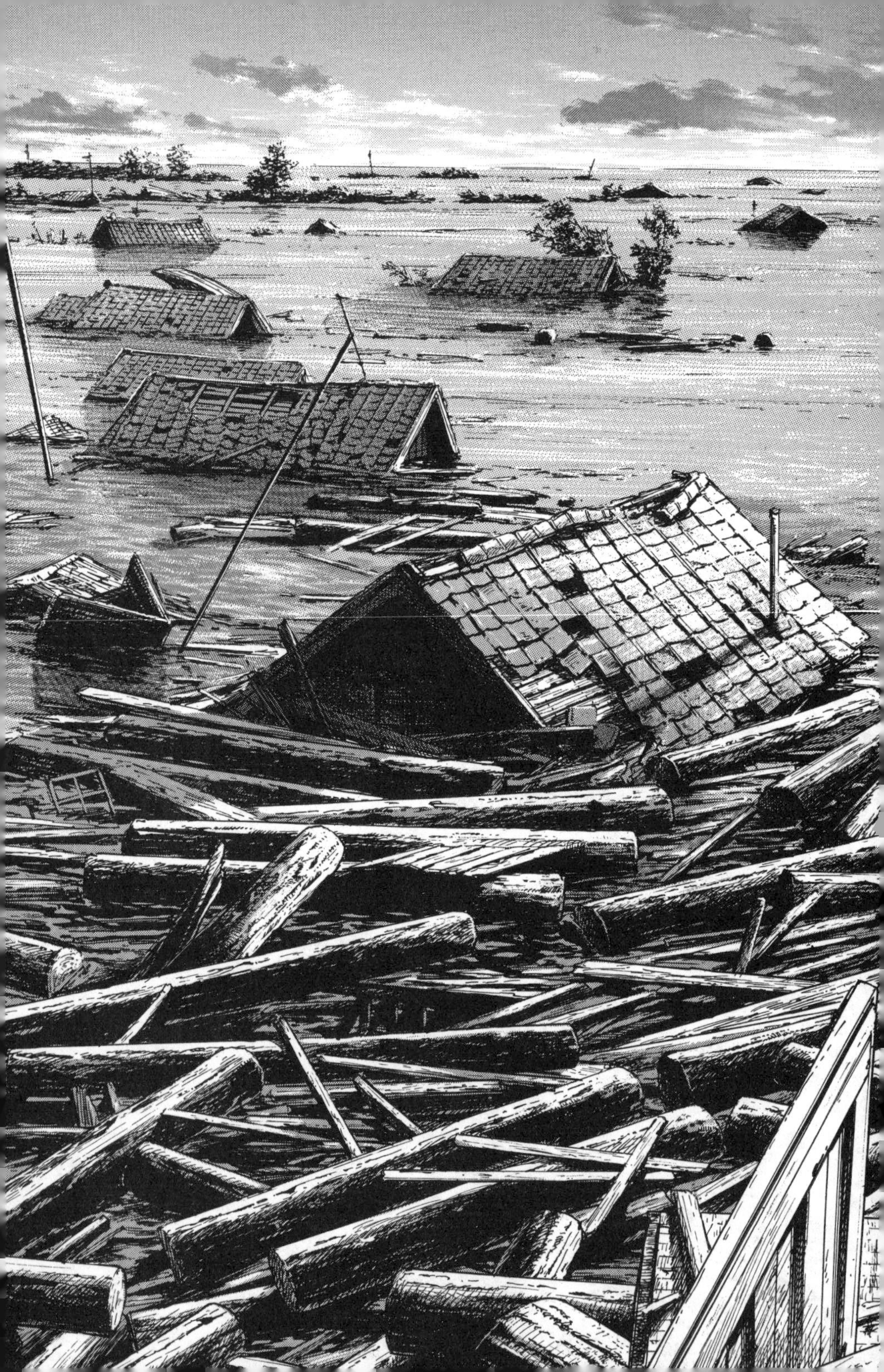

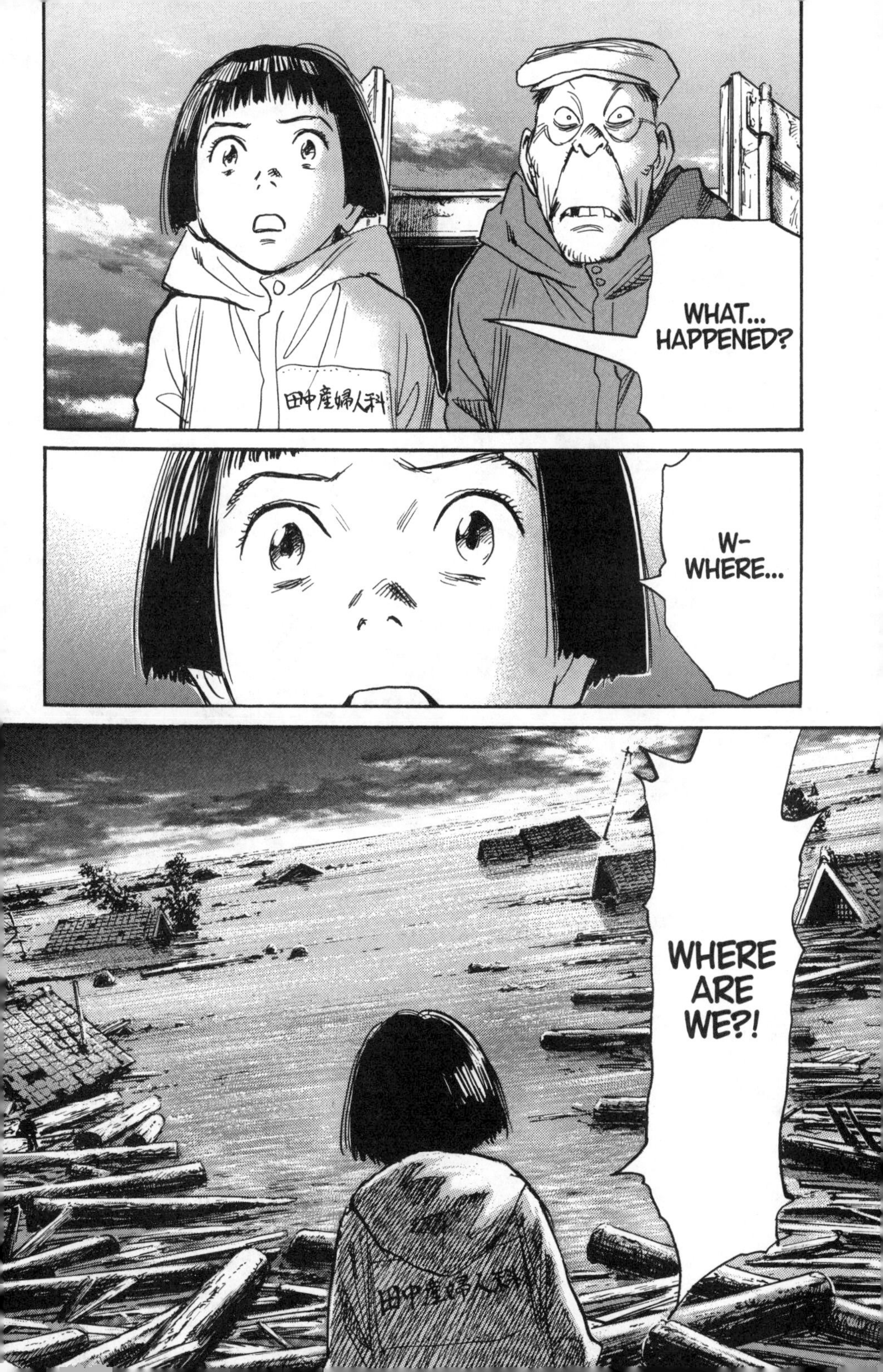
WHAT... HAPPENED?
田中産婦人科
W- WHERE...
WHERE ARE WE?!
田中産婦人科

Chapter 5 ● The Flood

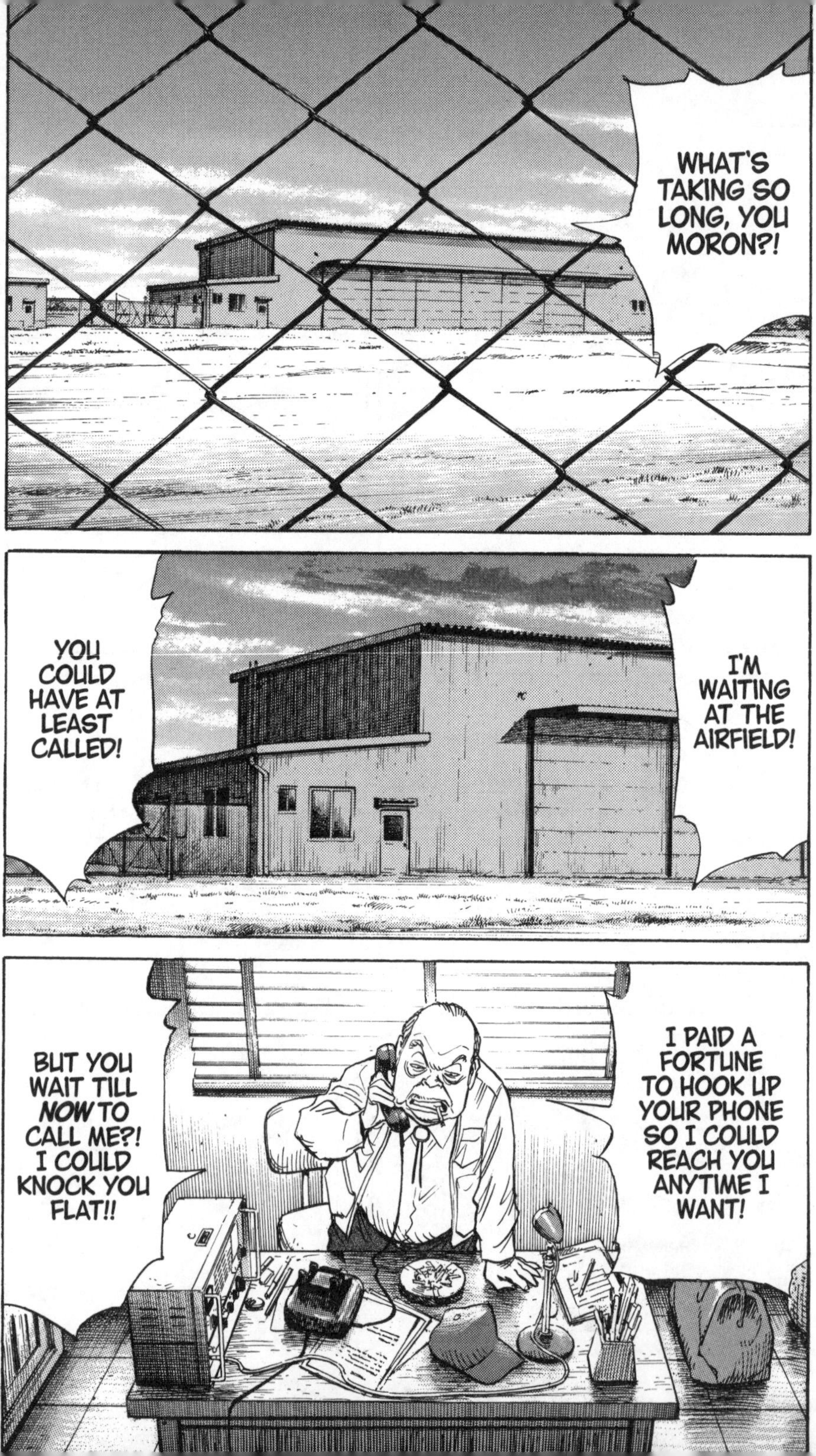
WHAT'S TAKING SO LONG, YOU MORON?!
I'M WAITING AT THE AIRFIELD!
YOU COULD HAVE AT LEAST CALLED!
I PAID A FORTUNE TO HOOK UP YOUR PHONE SO I COULD REACH YOU ANYTIME I WANT!
BUT YOU WAIT TILL *NOW* TO CALL ME?! I COULD KNOCK YOU FLAT!!

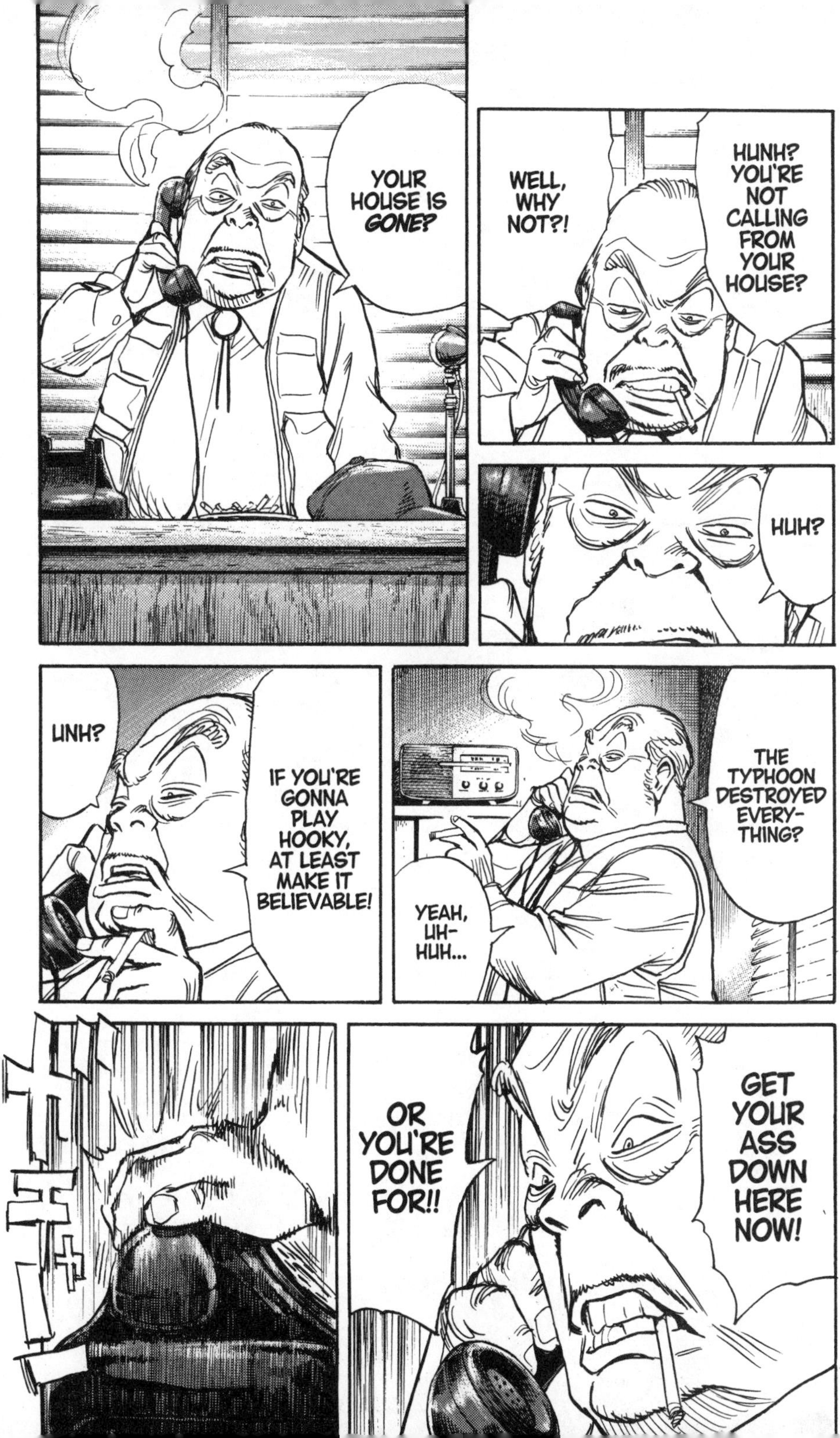
HUNH? YOU'RE NOT CALLING FROM YOUR HOUSE?
WELL, WHY NOT?!
HUH?
YOUR HOUSE IS GONE?
THE TYPHOON DESTROYED EVERY-THING?
YEAH, UH-HUH...
UNH?
IF YOU'RE GONNA PLAY HOOKY, AT LEAST MAKE IT BELIEVABLE!
GET YOUR ASS DOWN HERE NOW!
OR YOU'RE DONE FOR!!

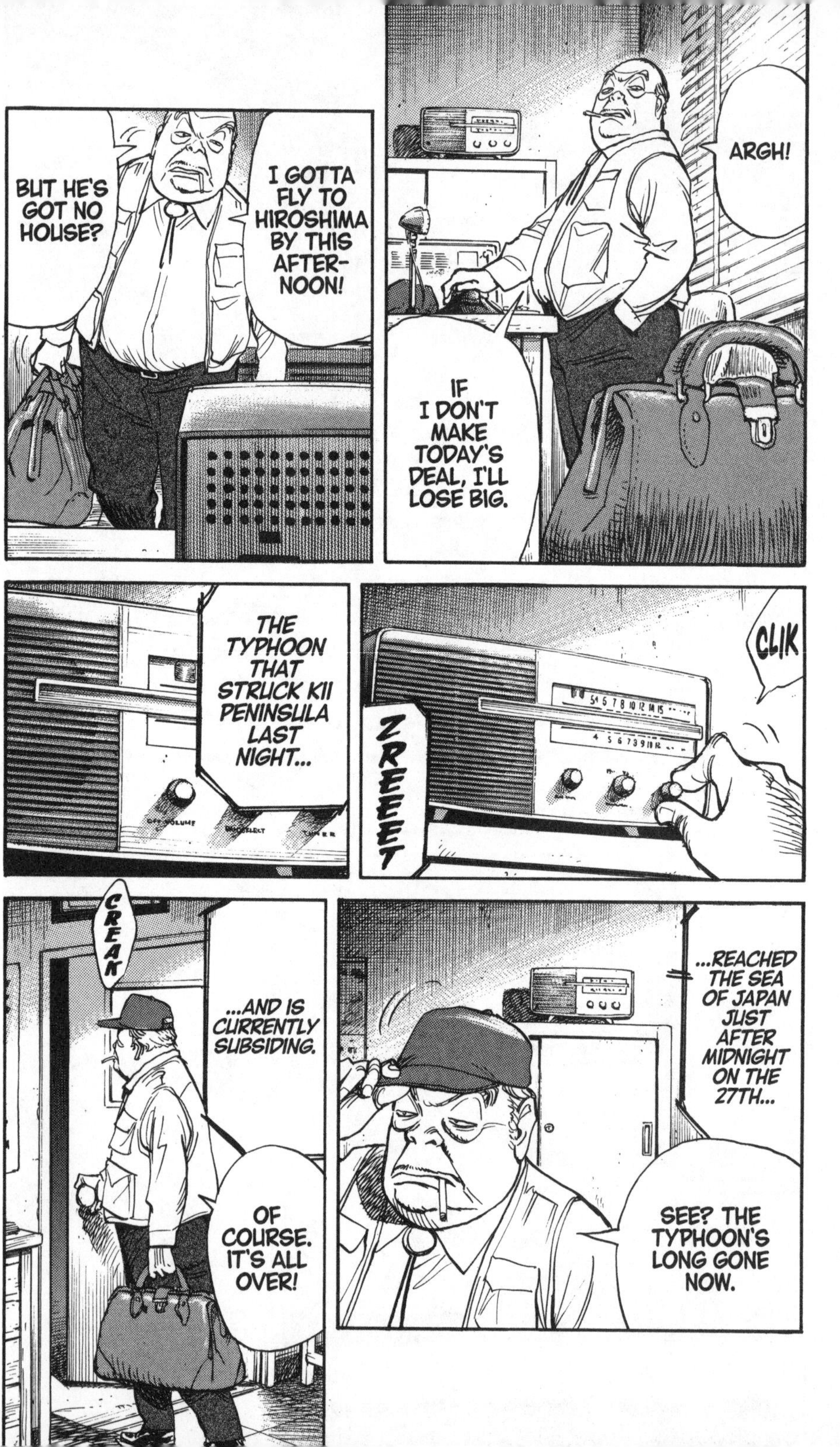
ARGH!
IF I DON'T MAKE TODAY'S DEAL, I'LL LOSE BIG.
I GOTTA FLY TO HIROSHIMA BY THIS AFTERNOON!
BUT HE'S GOT NO HOUSE?
CLIK
ZREEEET
THE TYPHOON THAT STRUCK KII PENINSULA LAST NIGHT...
...REACHED THE SEA OF JAPAN JUST AFTER MIDNIGHT ON THE 27TH...
SEE? THE TYPHOON'S LONG GONE NOW.
CREAK
...AND IS CURRENTLY SUBSIDING.
OF COURSE. IT'S ALL OVER!

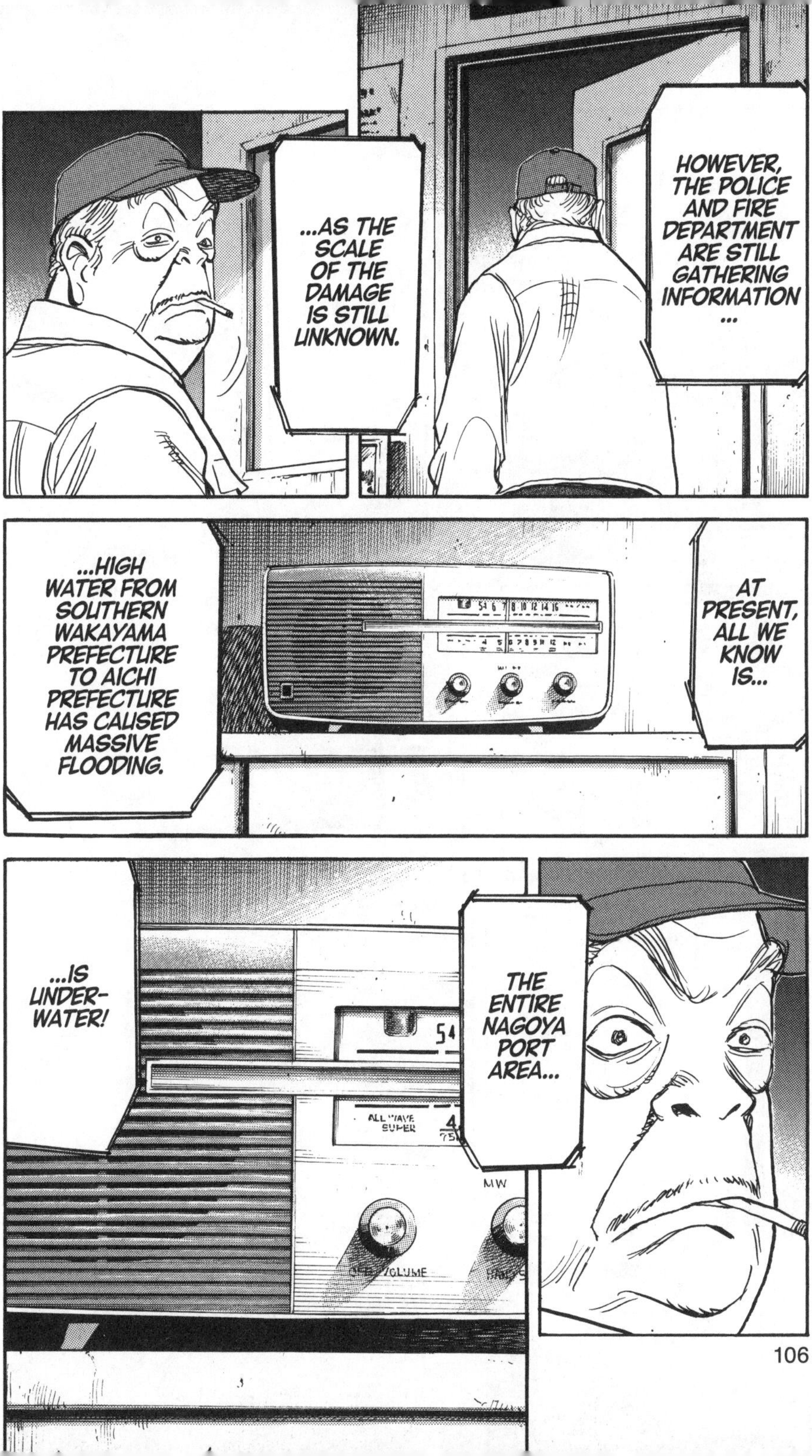
HOWEVER, THE POLICE AND FIRE DEPARTMENT ARE STILL GATHERING INFORMATION...
...AS THE SCALE OF THE DAMAGE IS STILL UNKNOWN.
AT PRESENT, ALL WE KNOW IS...
...HIGH WATER FROM SOUTHERN WAKAYAMA PREFECTURE TO AICHI PREFECTURE HAS CAUSED MASSIVE FLOODING.
THE ENTIRE NAGOYA PORT AREA...
...IS UNDER-WATER!
ALL WAVE SUPER
MW
VOLUME

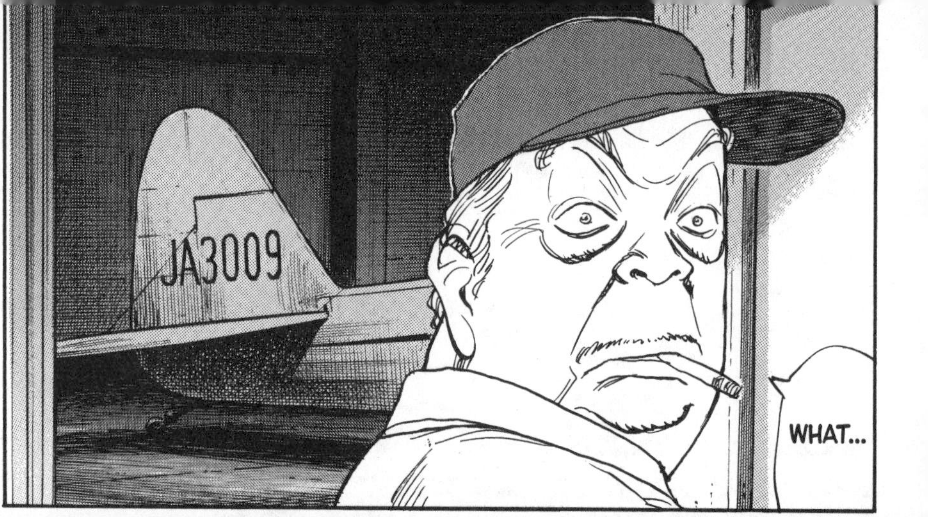
JA3009
WHAT...

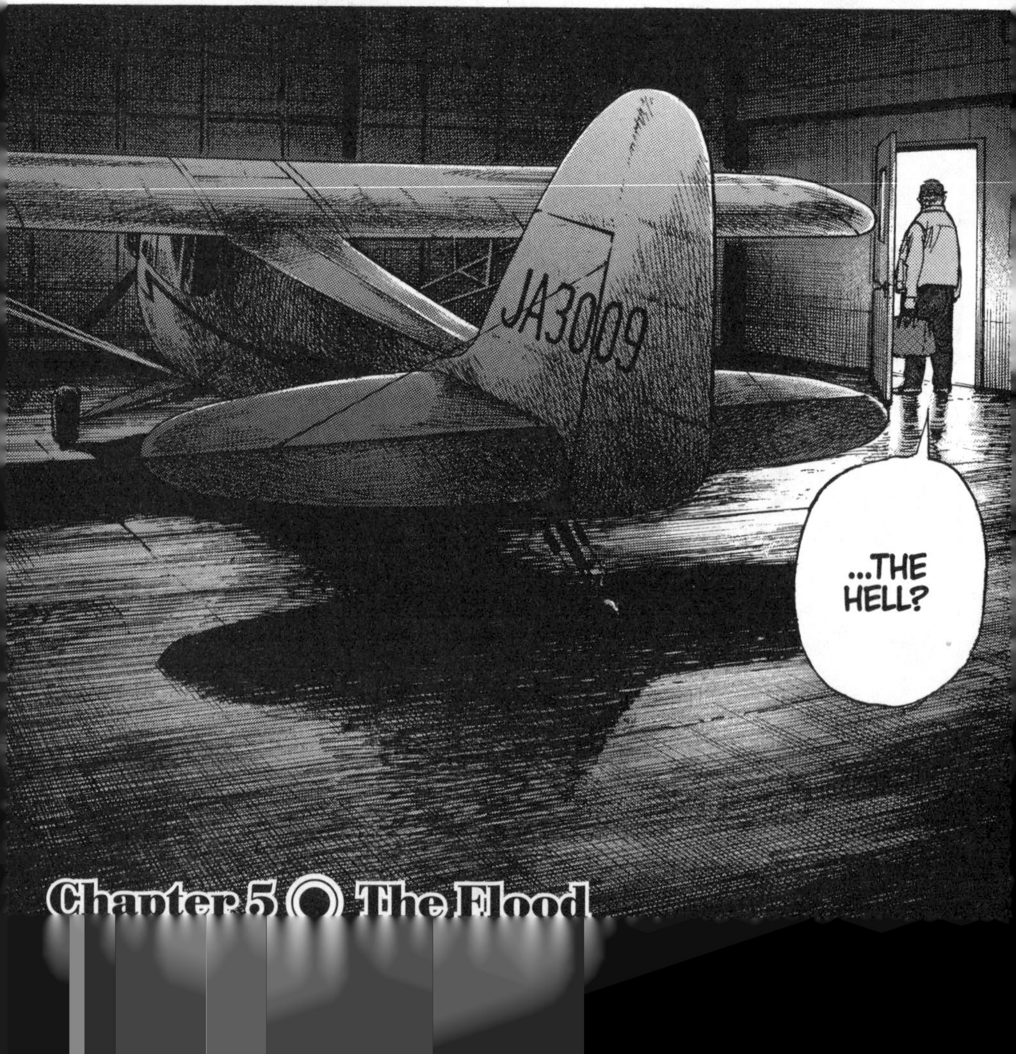
JA3009
...THE HELL?

Chapter 5 ○ The Flood

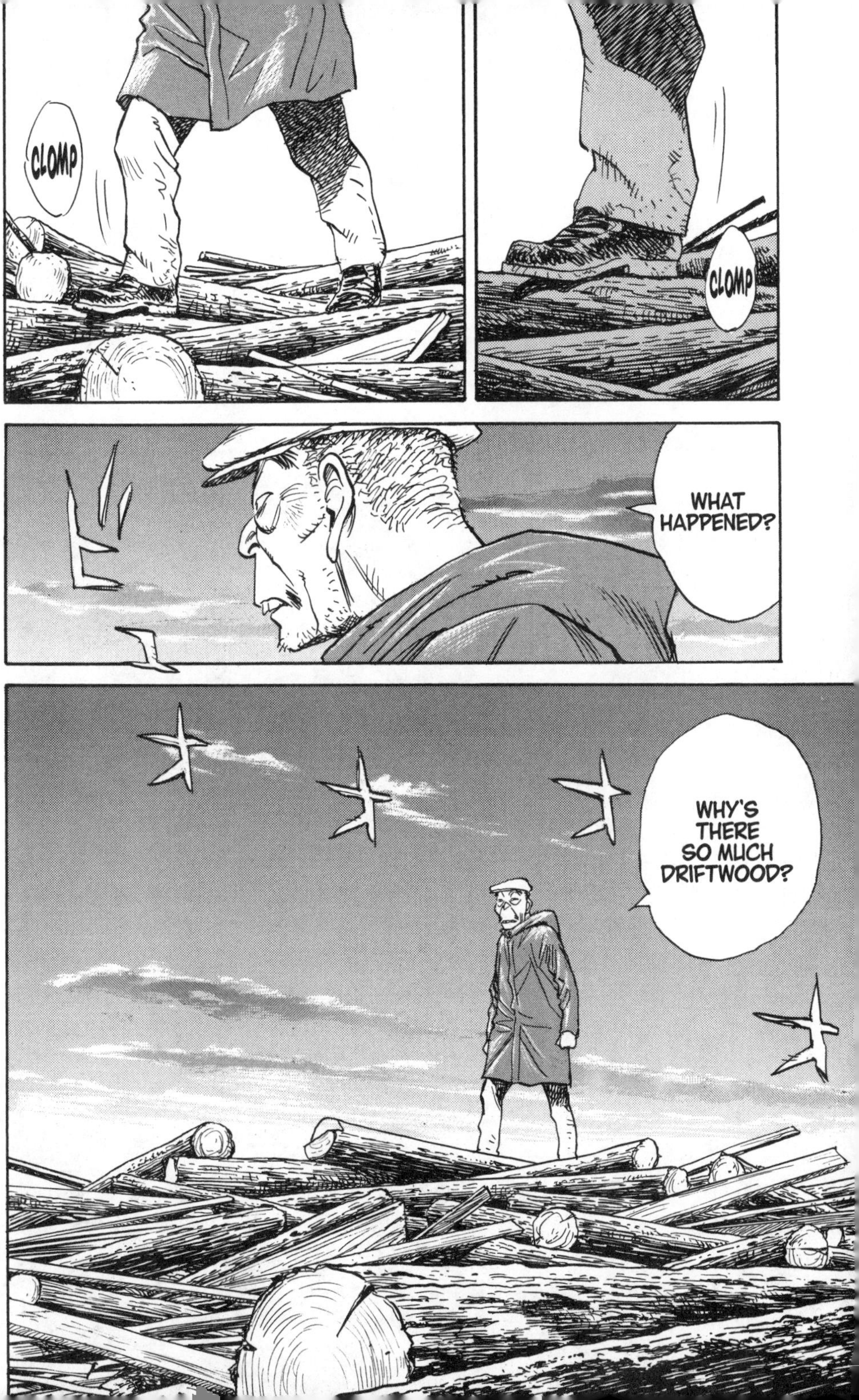

CLOMP
CLOMP
WHAT HAPPENED?
WHY'S THERE SO MUCH DRIFTWOOD?

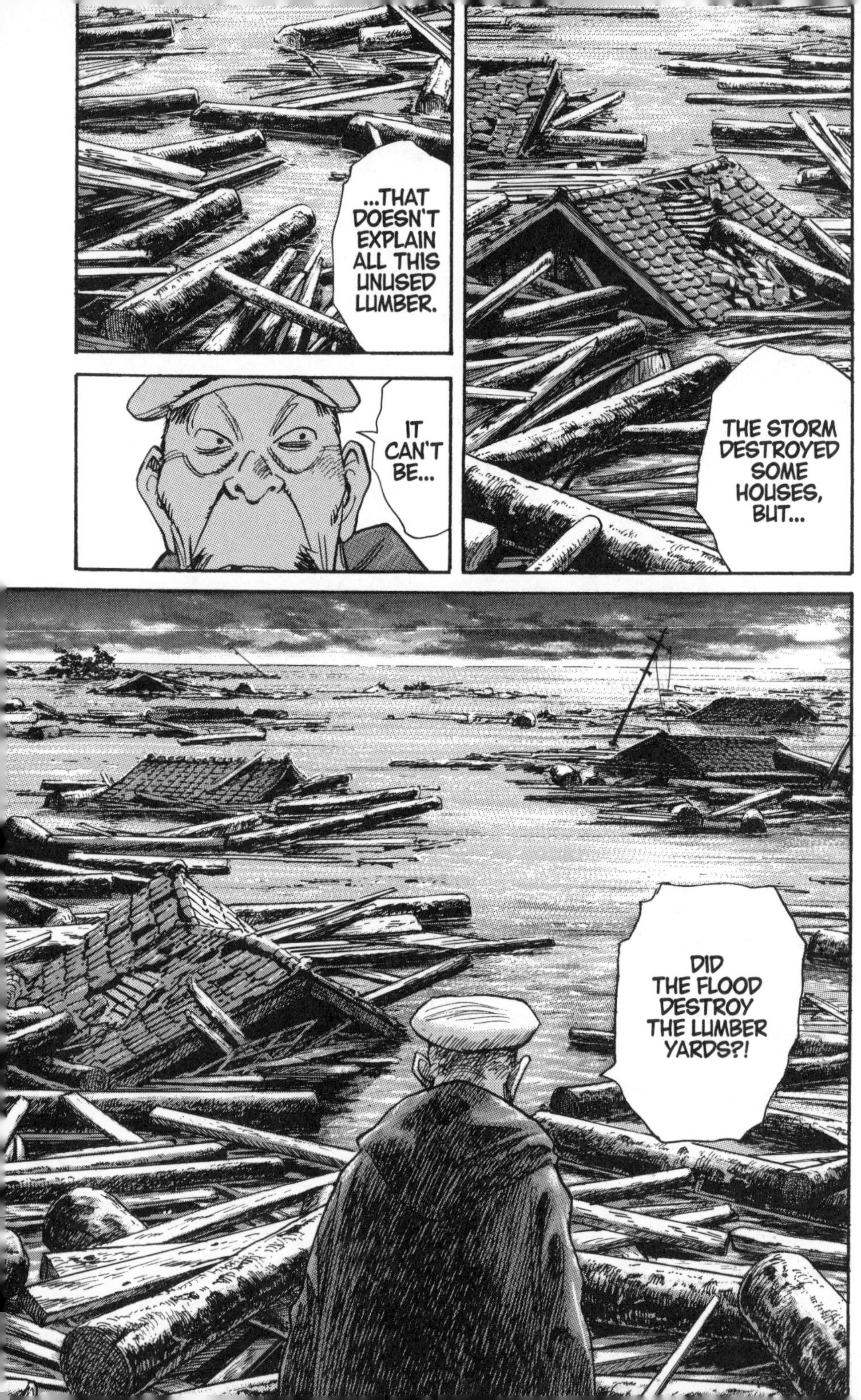
THE STORM DESTROYED SOME HOUSES, BUT...
...THAT DOESN'T EXPLAIN ALL THIS UNUSED LUMBER.
IT CAN'T BE...
DID THE FLOOD DESTROY THE LUMBER YARDS?!

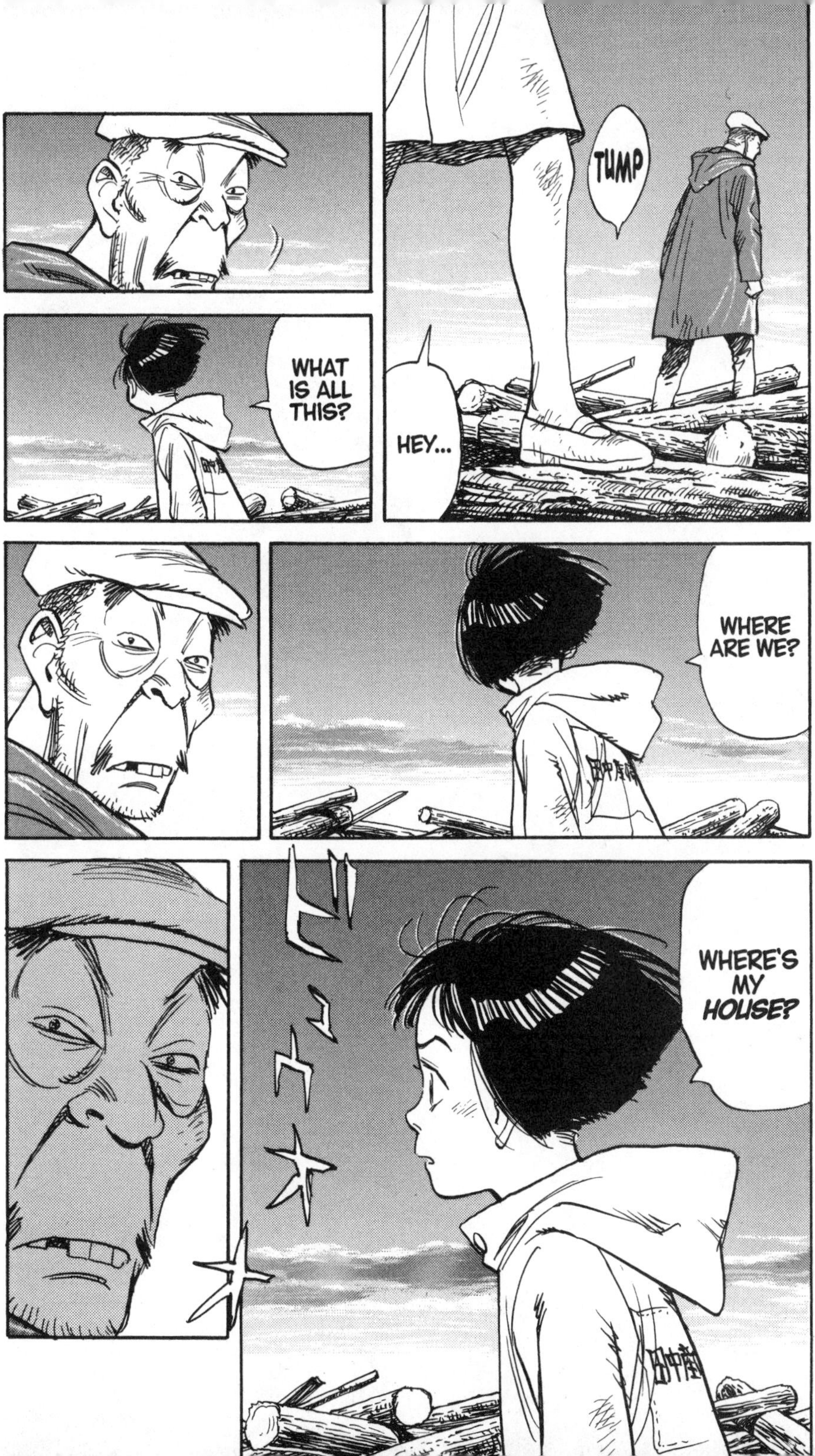
TUMP
HEY...
WHAT IS ALL THIS?
WHERE ARE WE?
WHERE'S MY *HOUSE?*

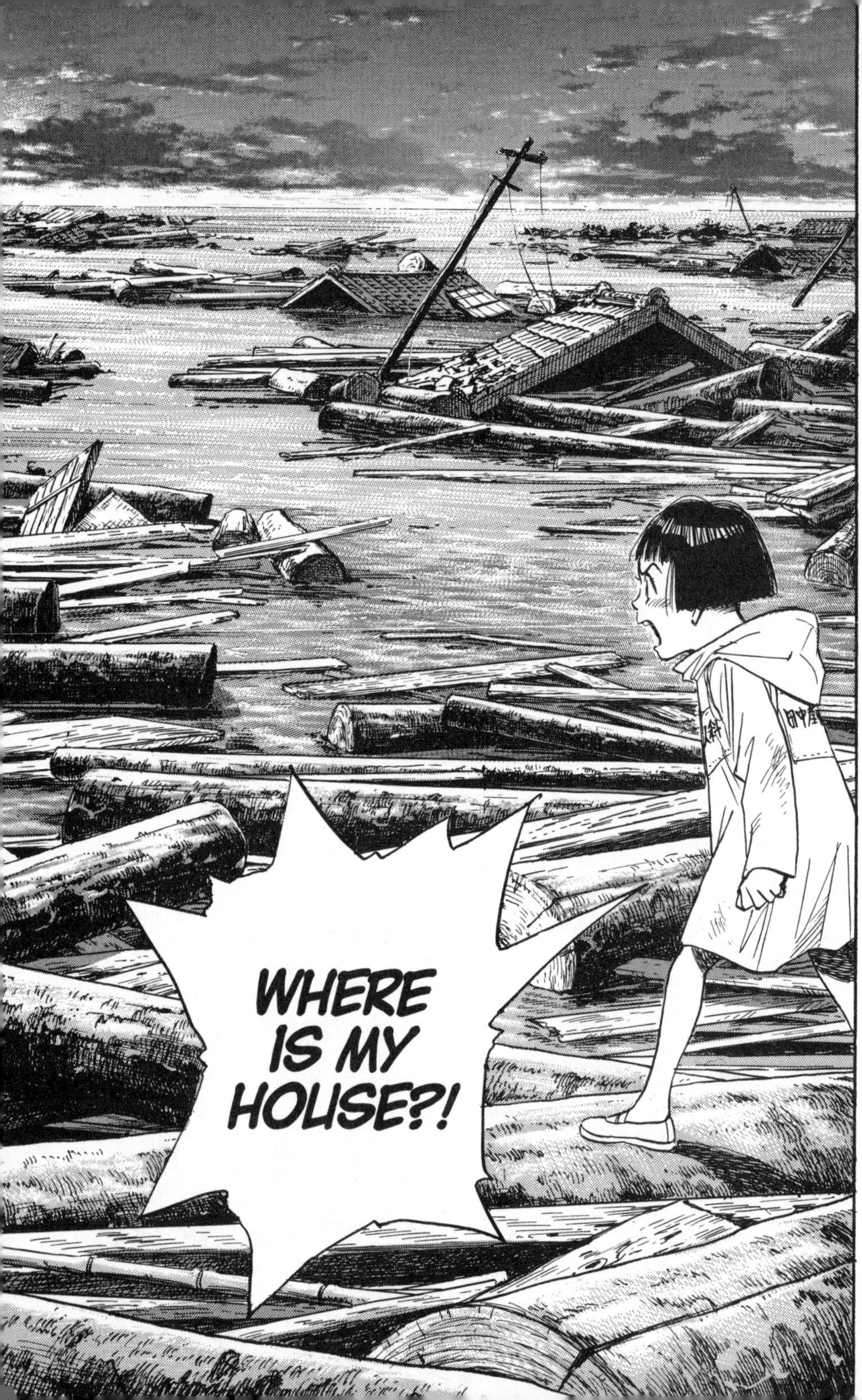
WHERE IS MY HOUSE?!

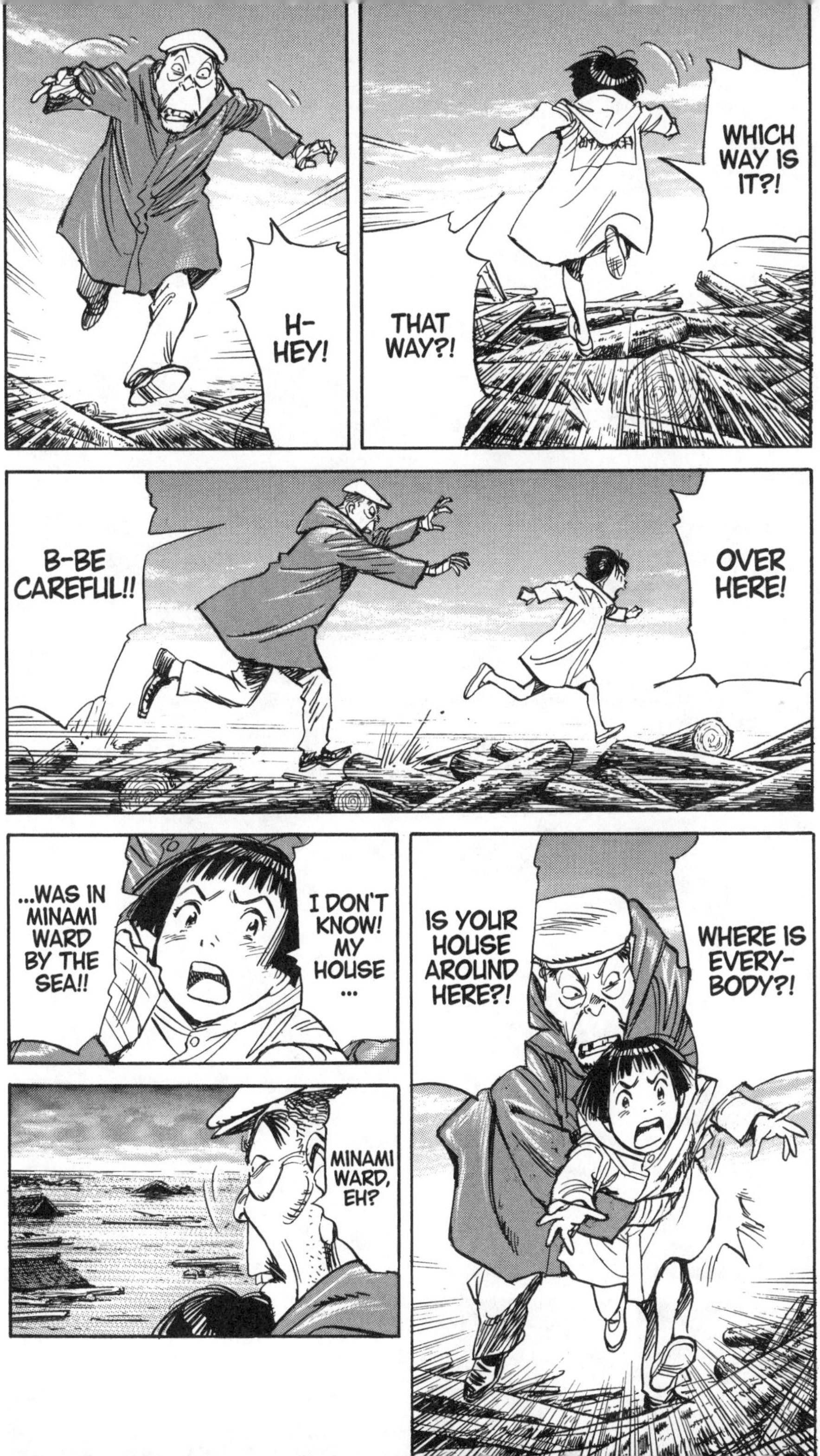
WHICH WAY IS IT?!
THAT WAY?!
H-HEY!
OVER HERE!
B-BE CAREFUL!!
WHERE IS EVERYBODY?!
IS YOUR HOUSE AROUND HERE?!
I DON'T KNOW! MY HOUSE ...
...WAS IN MINAMI WARD BY THE SEA!!
MINAMI WARD, EH?

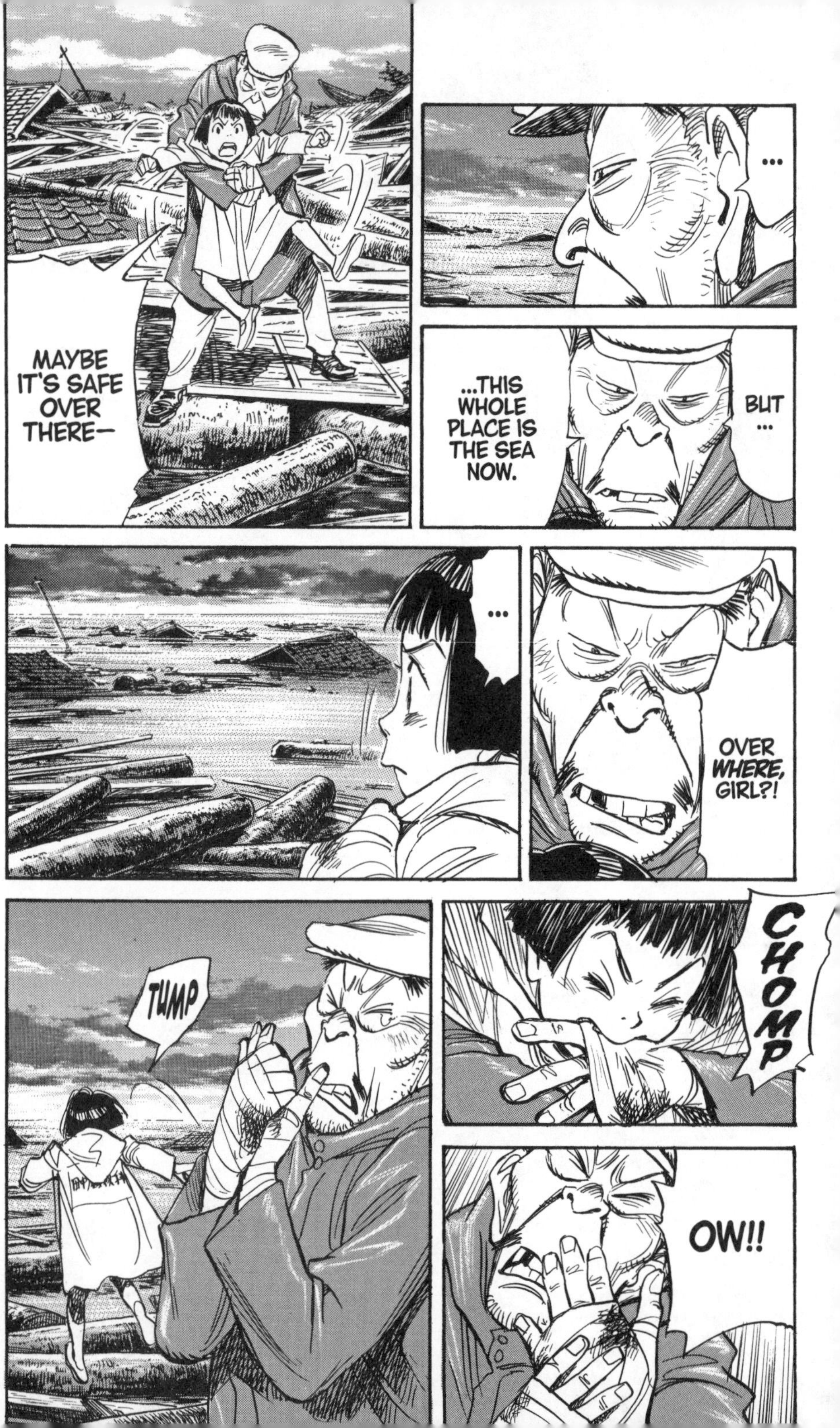
...
BUT ...
...THIS WHOLE PLACE IS THE SEA NOW.
MAYBE IT'S SAFE OVER THERE—
OVER WHERE, GIRL?!
...
CHOMP
OW!!
TUMP

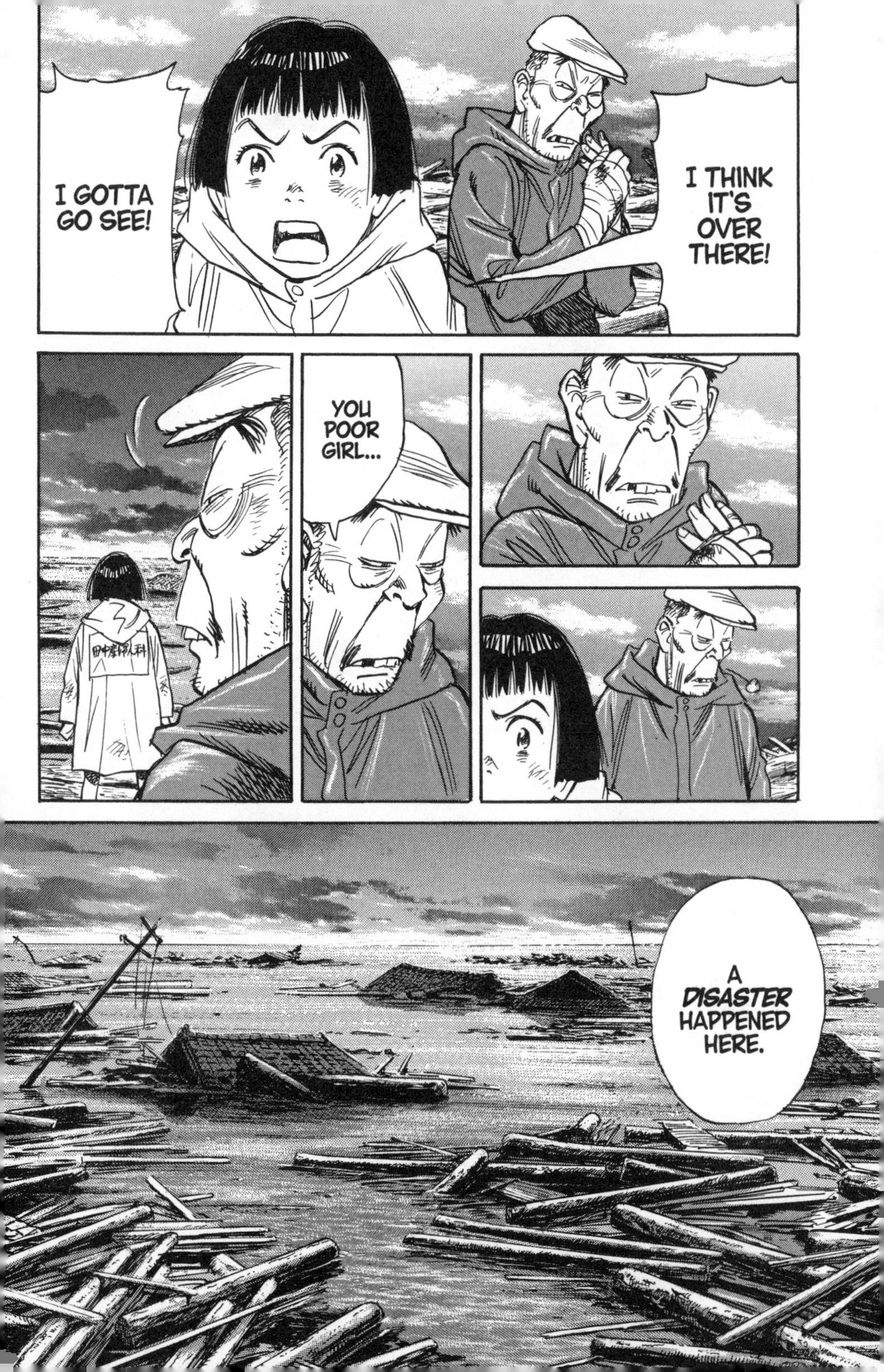
I THINK IT'S OVER THERE!
I GOTTA GO SEE!
YOU POOR GIRL...
A *DISASTER* HAPPENED HERE.

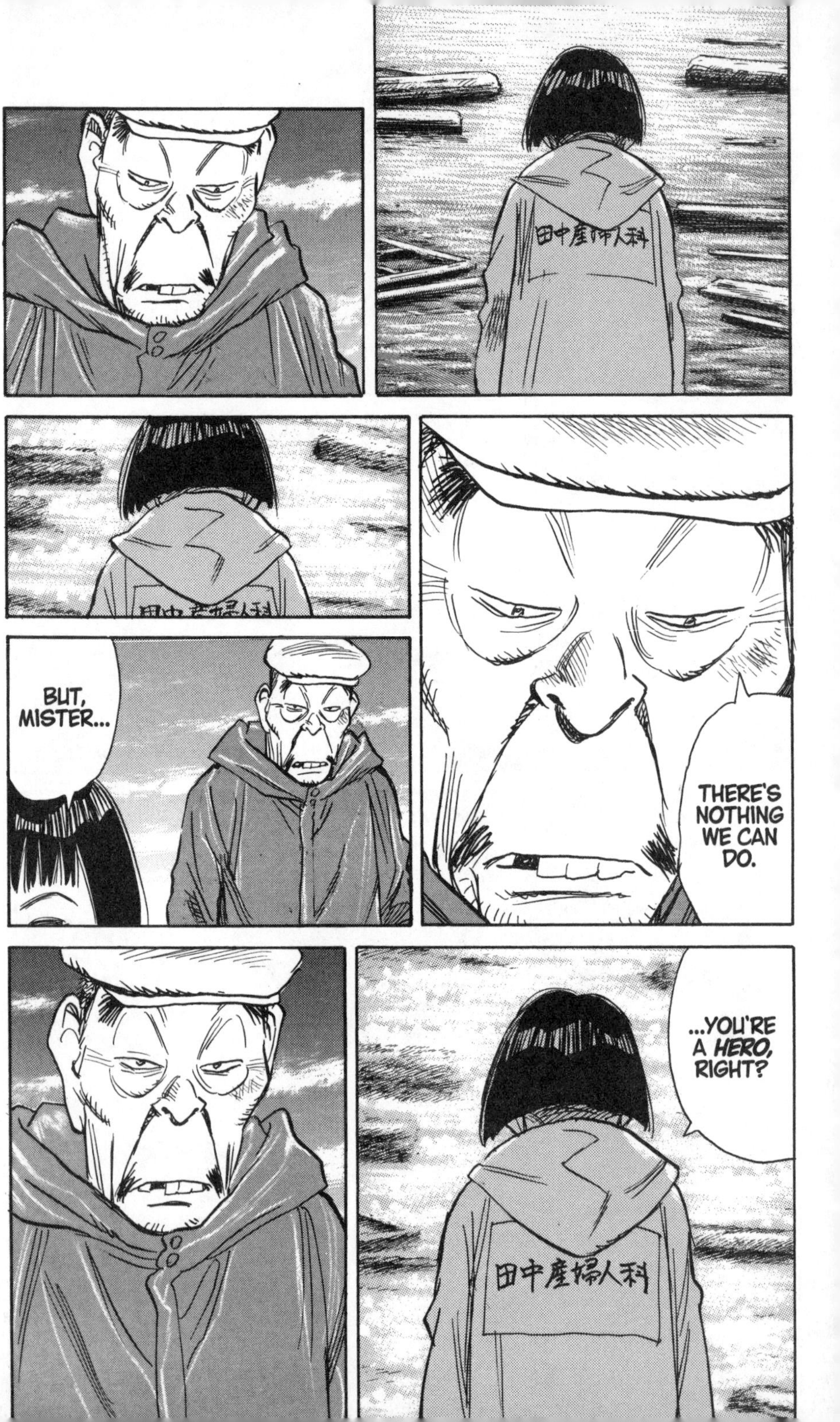
THERE'S NOTHING WE CAN DO.
BUT, MISTER...
...YOU'RE A *HERO*, RIGHT?
田中産婦人科

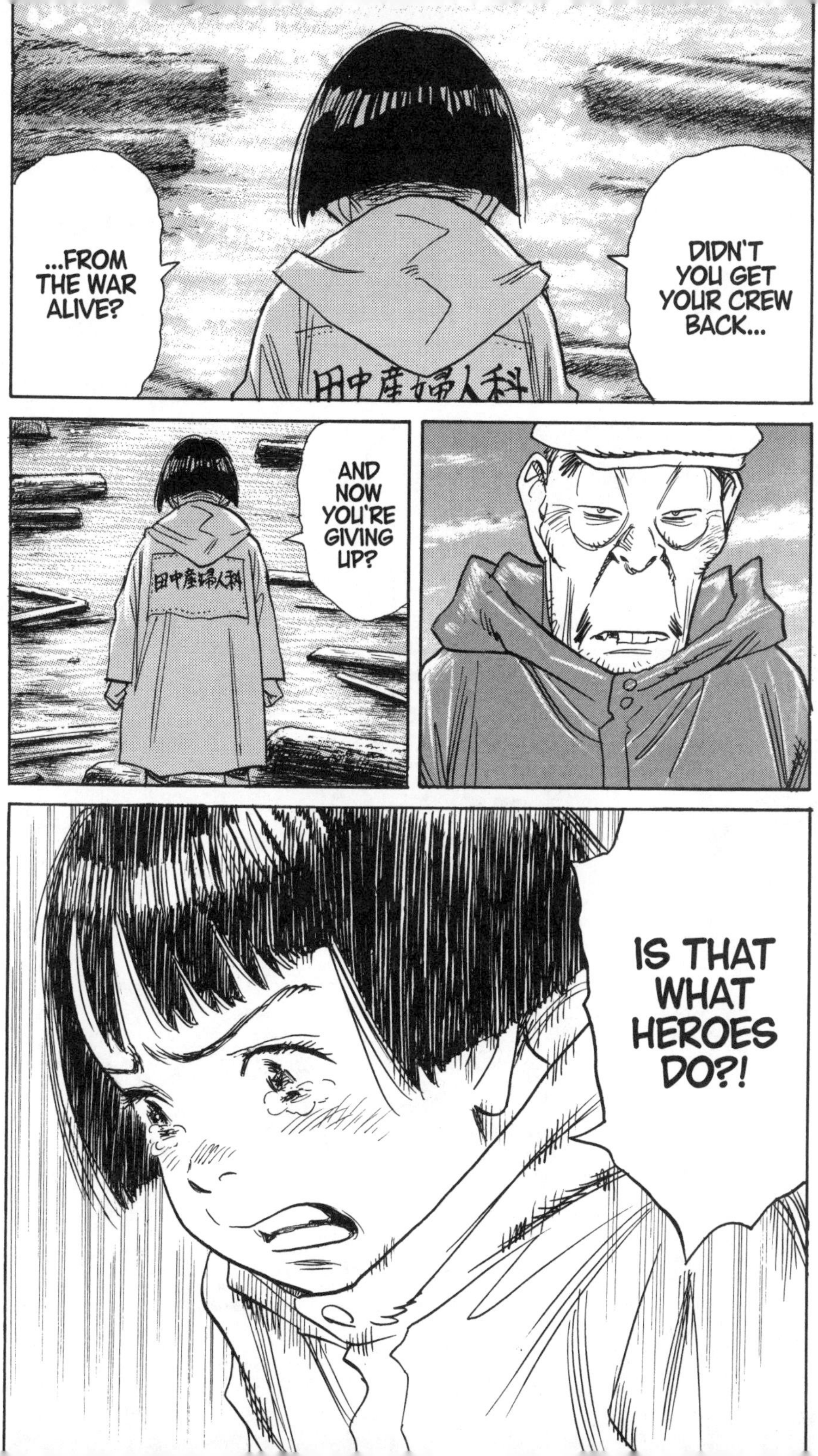
DIDN'T YOU GET YOUR CREW BACK...
...FROM THE WAR ALIVE?
田中産婦人科
AND NOW YOU'RE GIVING UP?
IS THAT WHAT HEROES DO?!

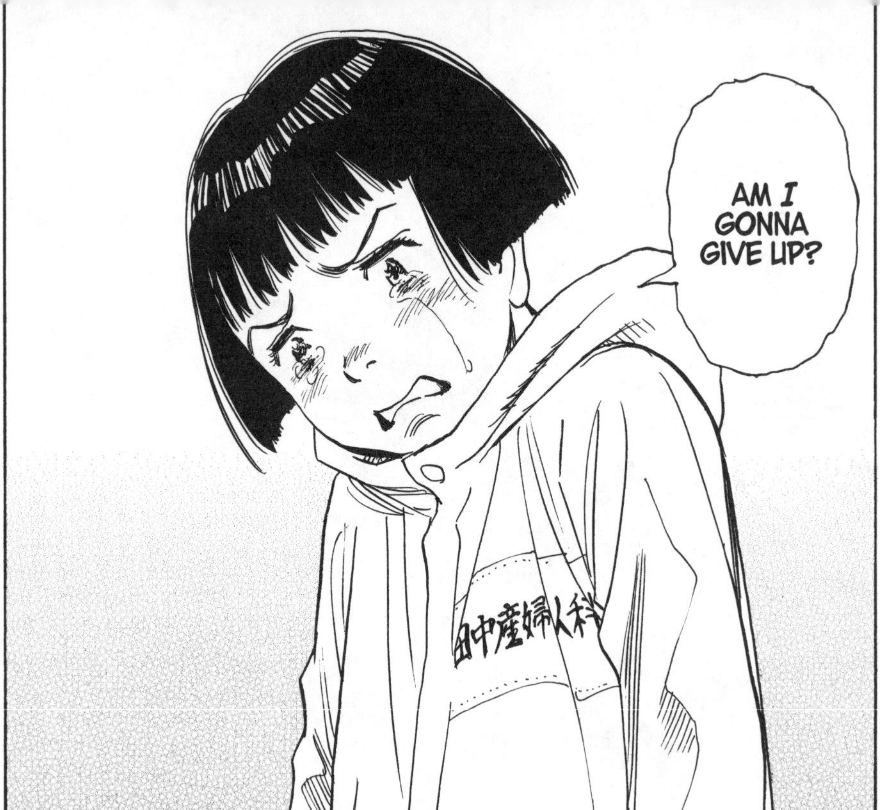
AM I GONNA GIVE UP?
中産婦人科
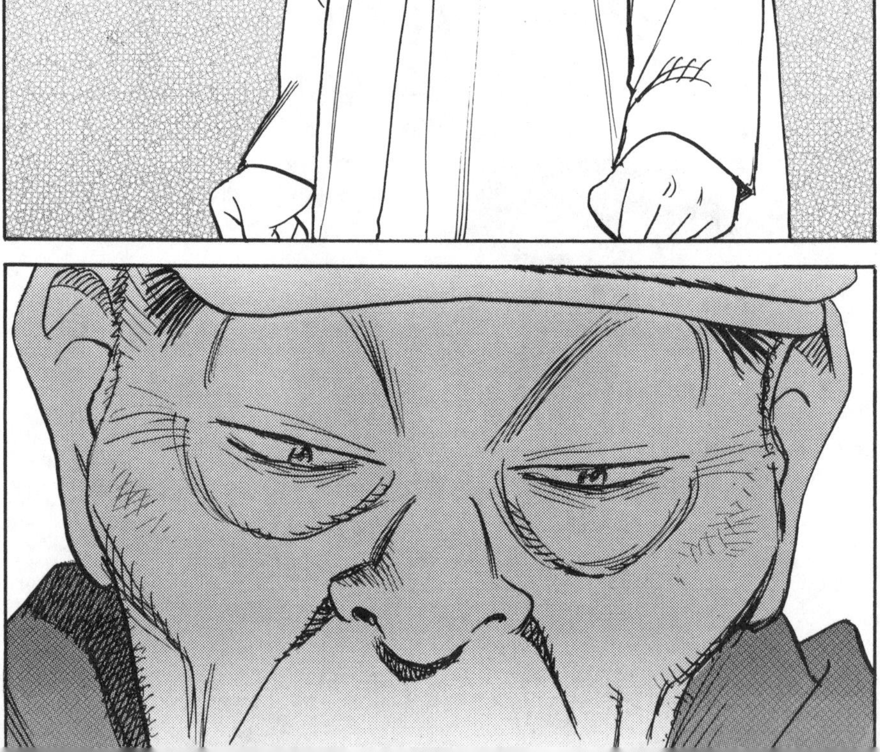

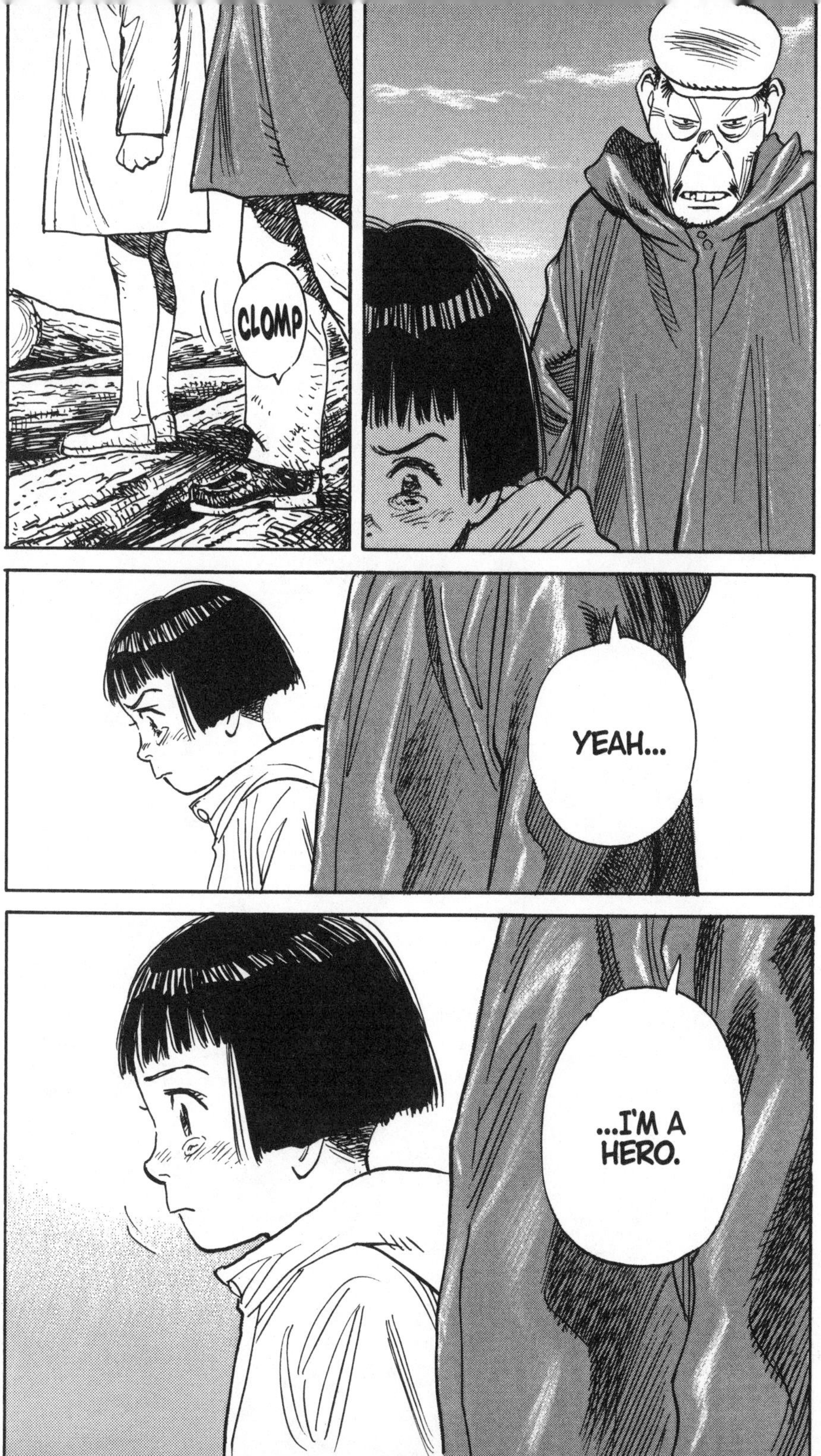
CLOMP
YEAH...
...I'M A HERO.

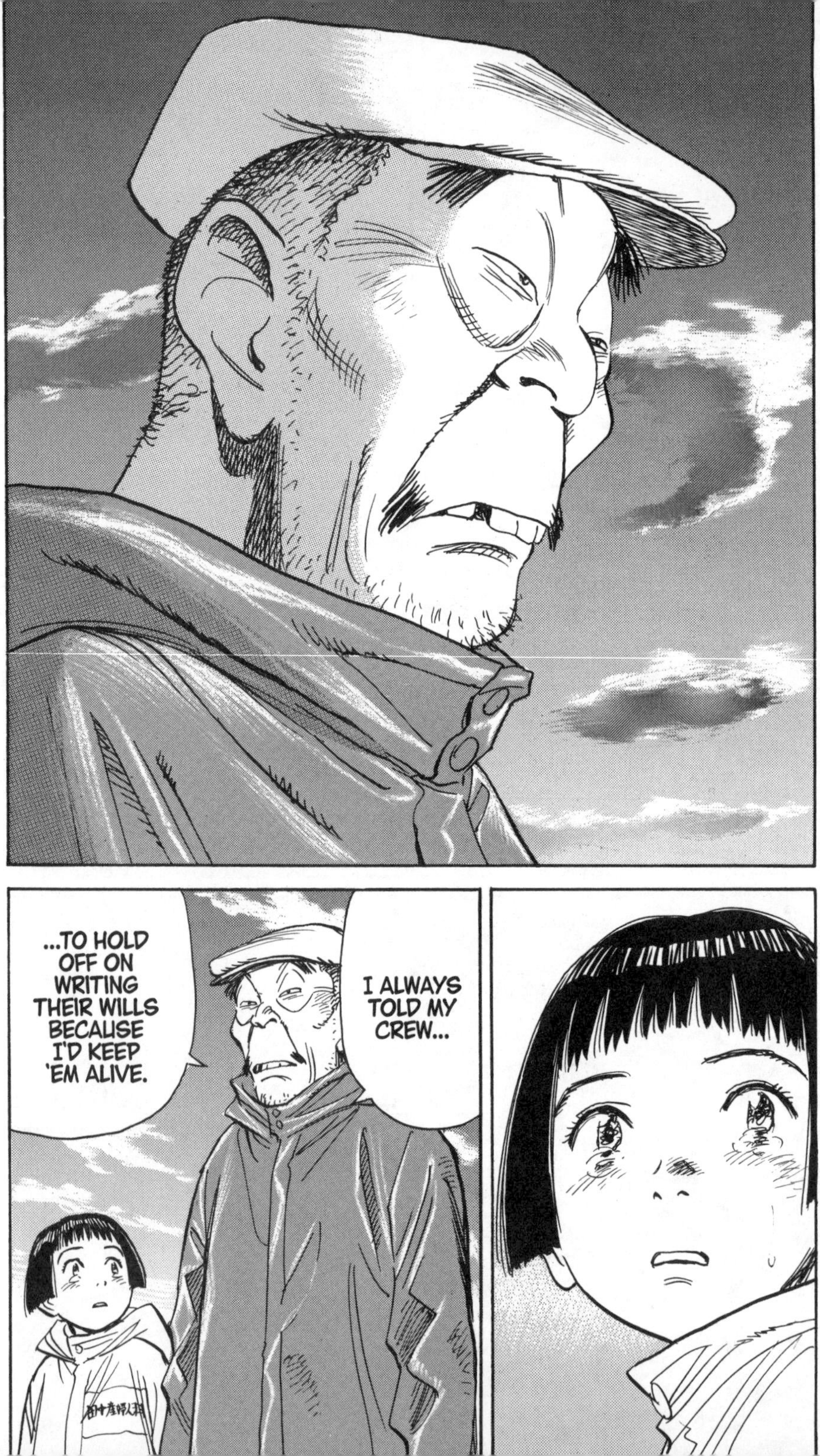
I ALWAYS TOLD MY CREW...
...TO HOLD OFF ON WRITING THEIR WILLS BECAUSE I'D KEEP 'EM ALIVE.

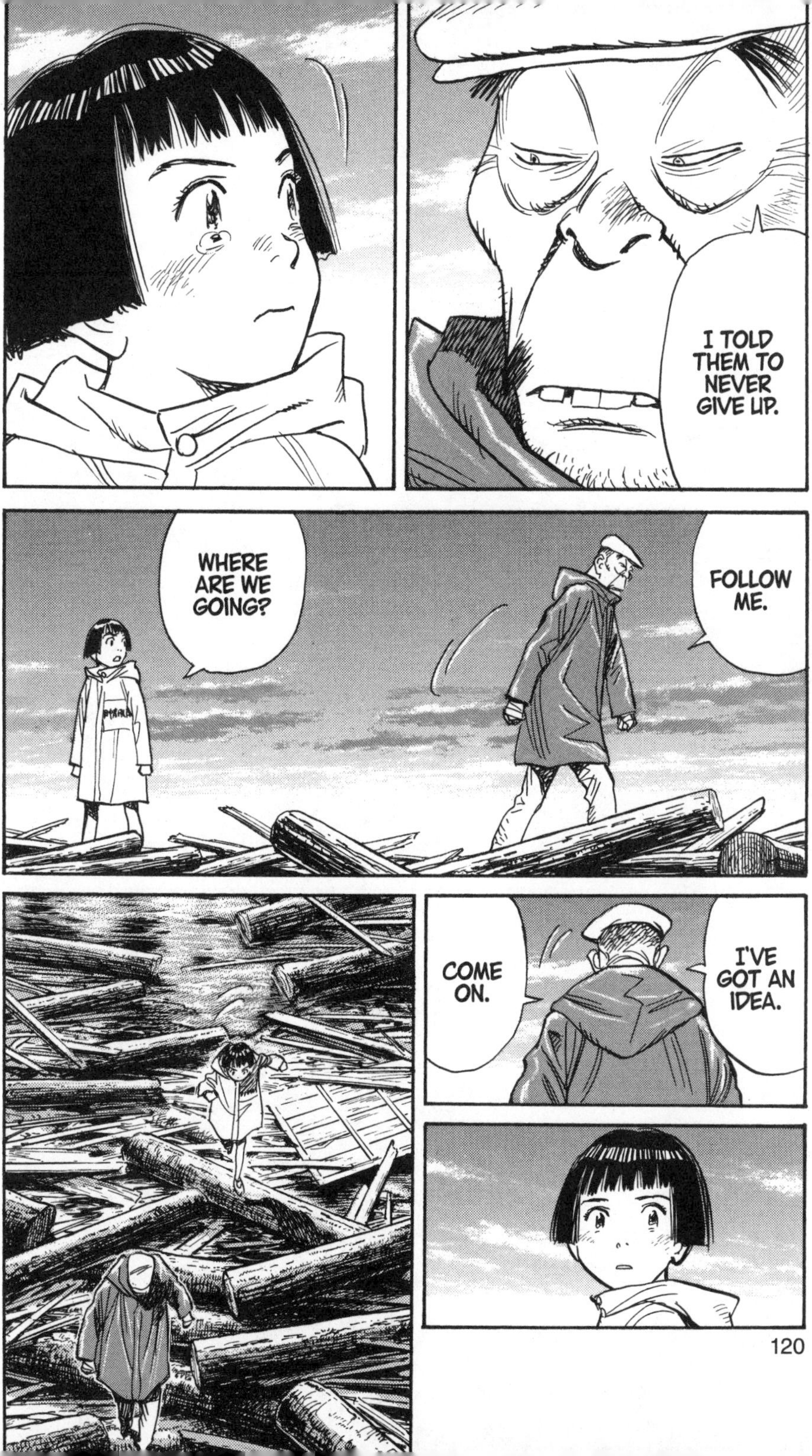
I TOLD THEM TO NEVER GIVE UP.
FOLLOW ME.
WHERE ARE WE GOING?
I'VE GOT AN IDEA.
COME ON.

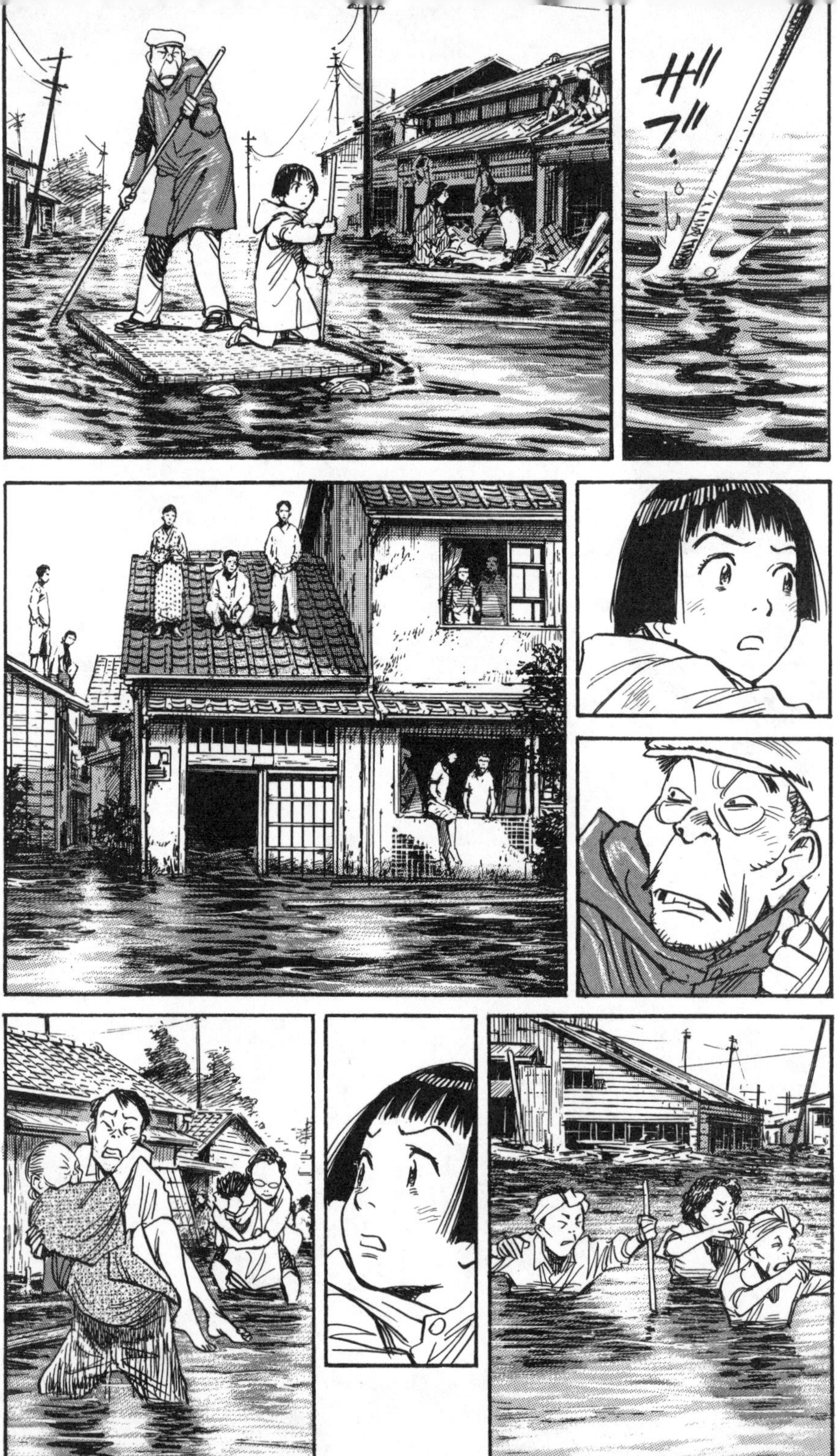
ザブ…

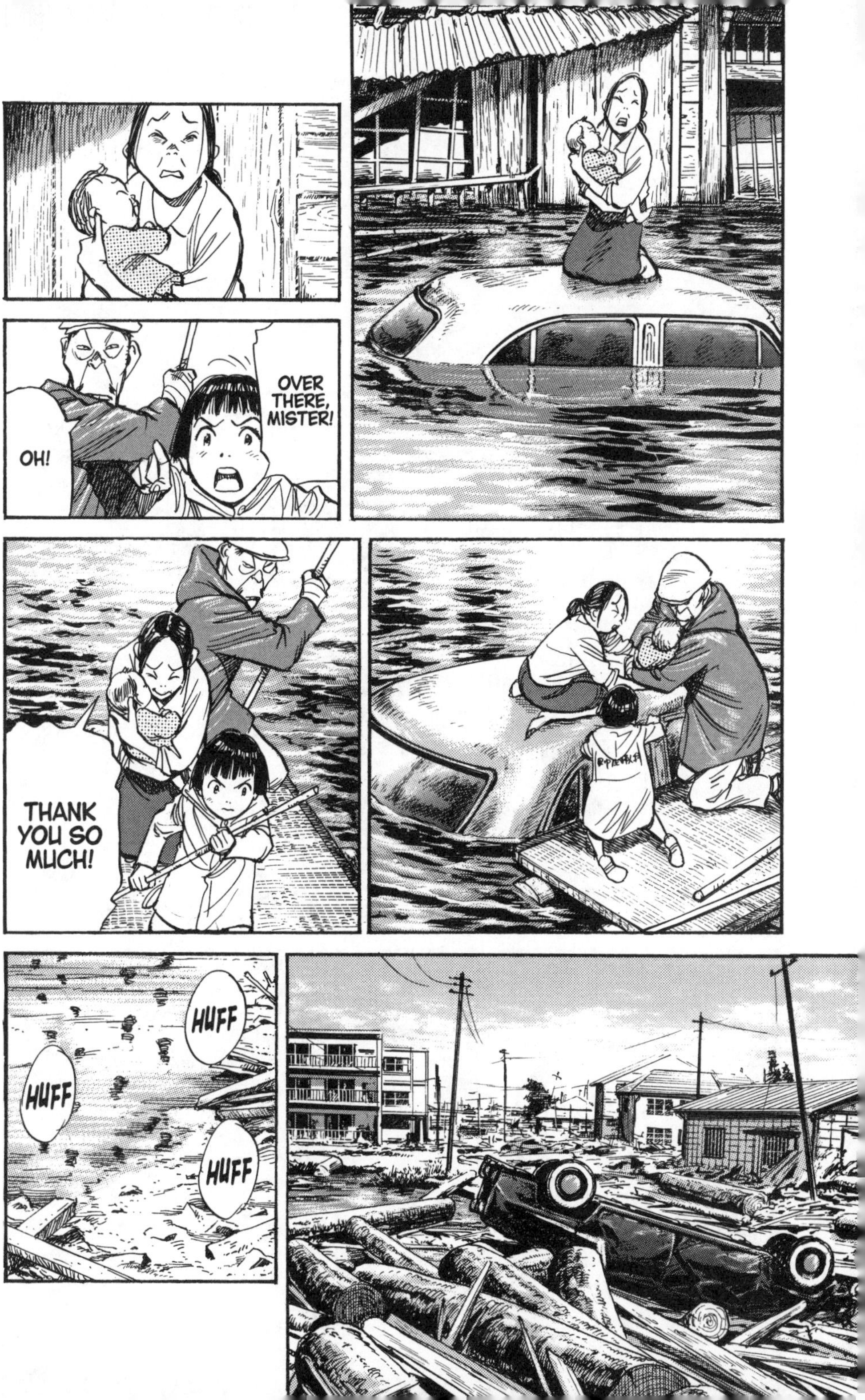
OVER THERE, MISTER!
OH!
THANK YOU SO MUCH!
HUFF
HUFF
HUFF

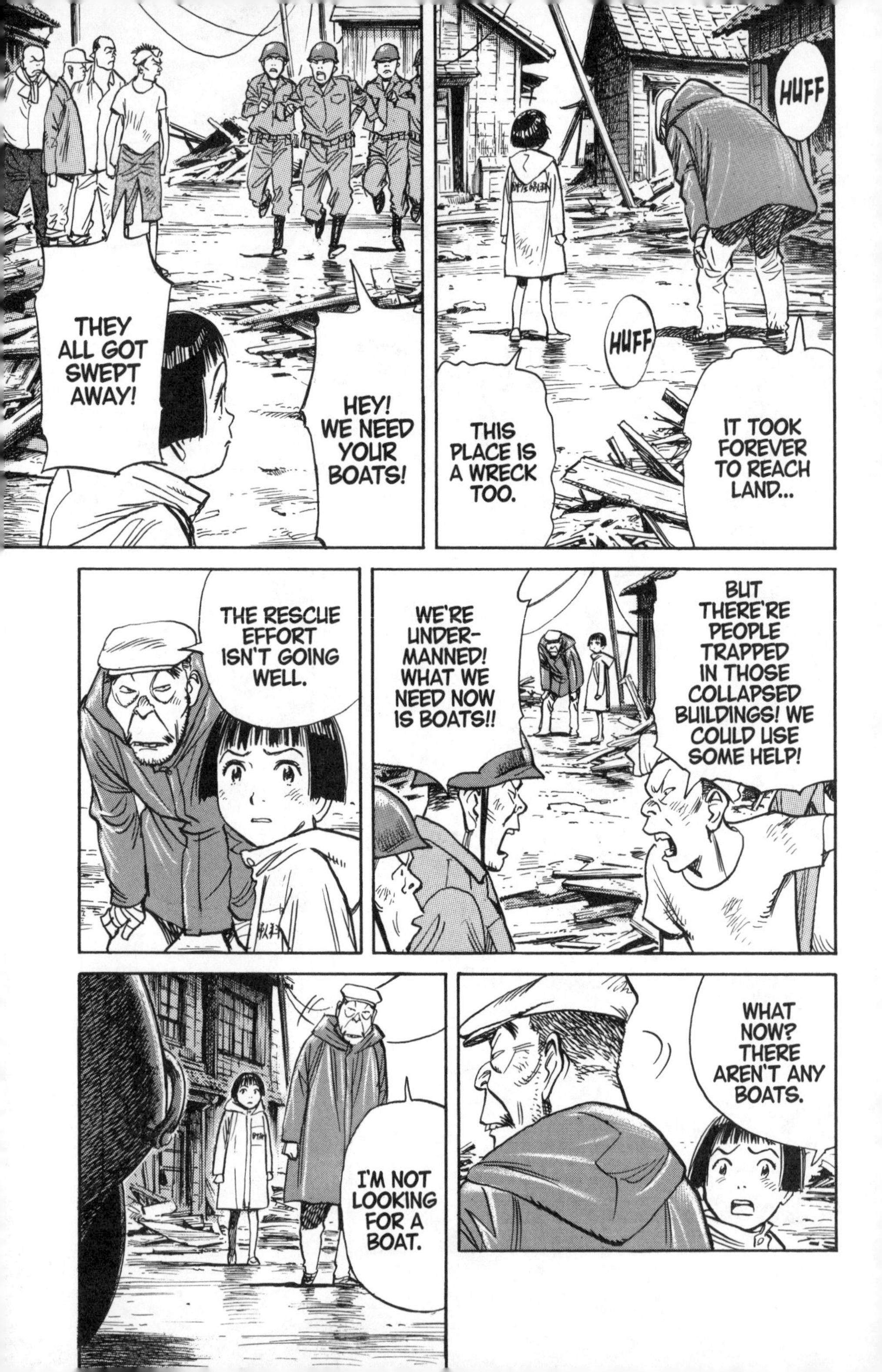
HUFF
HUFF
IT TOOK FOREVER TO REACH LAND...
THIS PLACE IS A WRECK TOO.
HEY! WE NEED YOUR BOATS!
THEY ALL GOT SWEPT AWAY!
BUT THERE'RE PEOPLE TRAPPED IN THOSE COLLAPSED BUILDINGS! WE COULD USE SOME HELP!
WE'RE UNDER-MANNED! WHAT WE NEED NOW IS BOATS!!
THE RESCUE EFFORT ISN'T GOING WELL.
WHAT NOW? THERE AREN'T ANY BOATS.
I'M NOT LOOKING FOR A BOAT.

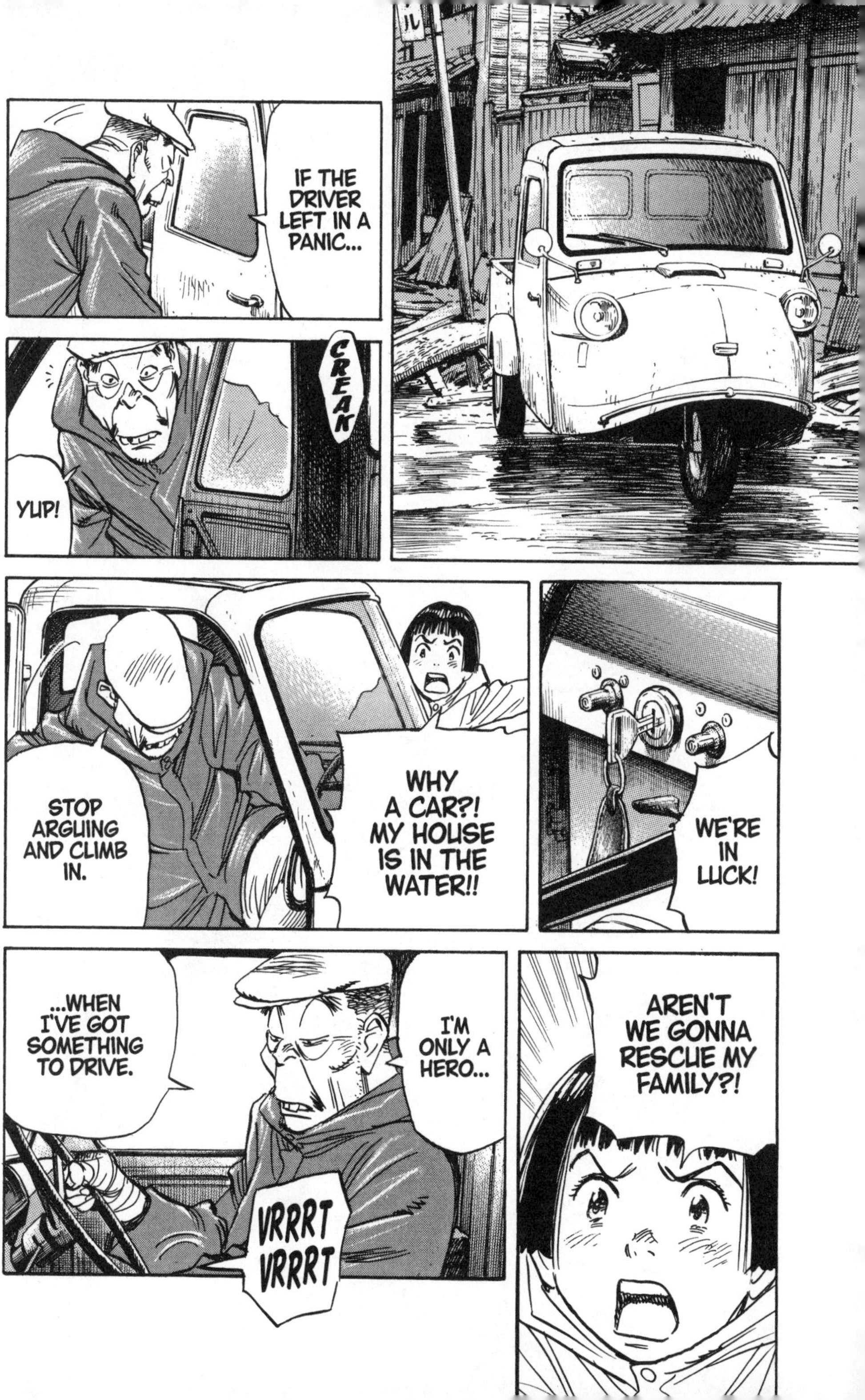
ル
IF THE DRIVER LEFT IN A PANIC...
CREAK
YUP!
WE'RE IN LUCK!
WHY A CAR?! MY HOUSE IS IN THE WATER!!
STOP ARGUING AND CLIMB IN.
AREN'T WE GONNA RESCUE MY FAMILY?!
I'M ONLY A HERO...
...WHEN I'VE GOT SOMETHING TO DRIVE.
VRRRT VRRRT

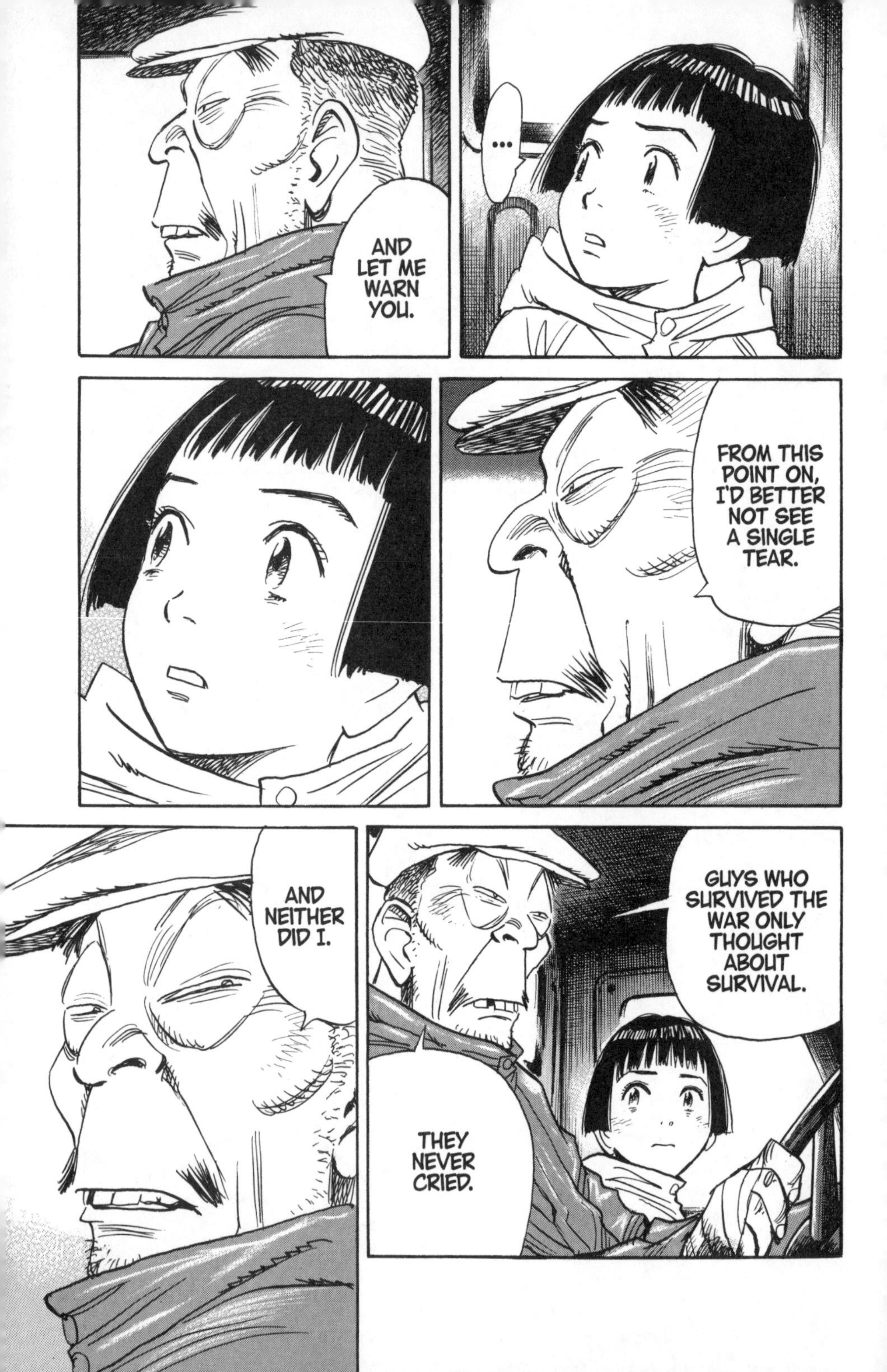
...
AND LET ME WARN YOU.
FROM THIS POINT ON, I'D BETTER NOT SEE A SINGLE TEAR.
GUYS WHO SURVIVED THE WAR ONLY THOUGHT ABOUT SURVIVAL.
THEY NEVER CRIED.
AND NEITHER DID I.

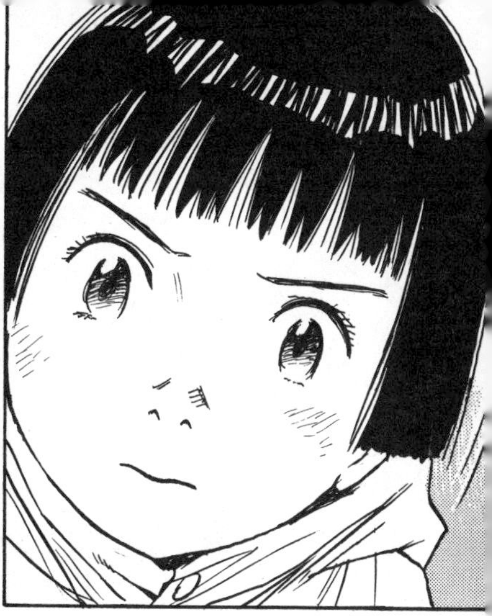

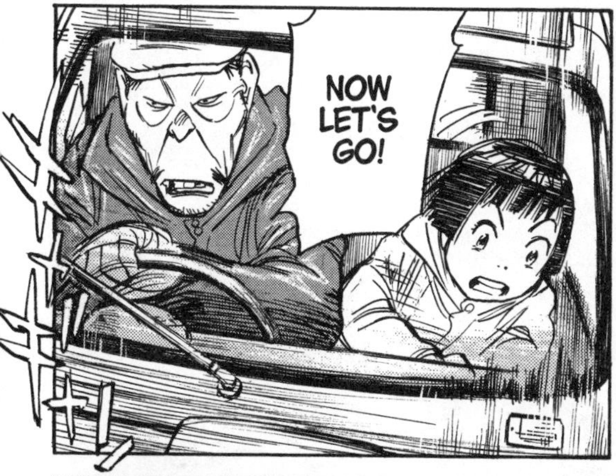
NOW LET'S GO!

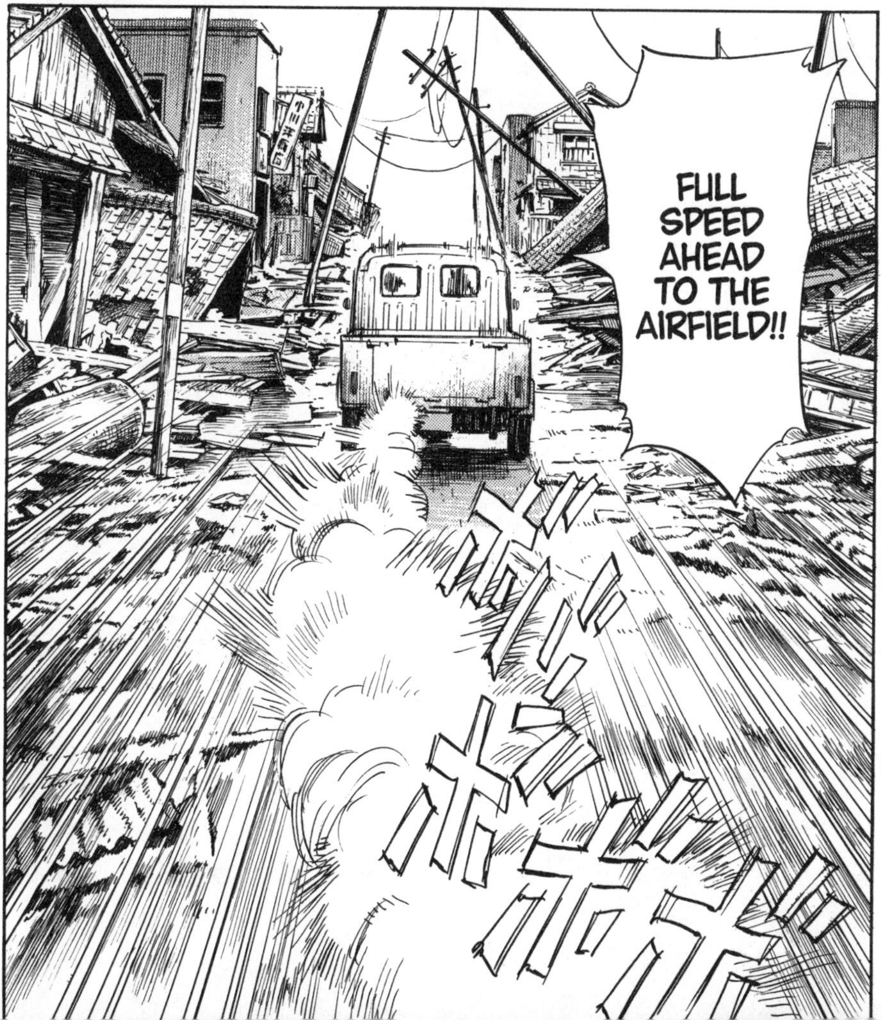
FULL SPEED AHEAD TO THE AIRFIELD!!

Chapter 6 ● Diner Kinuyo

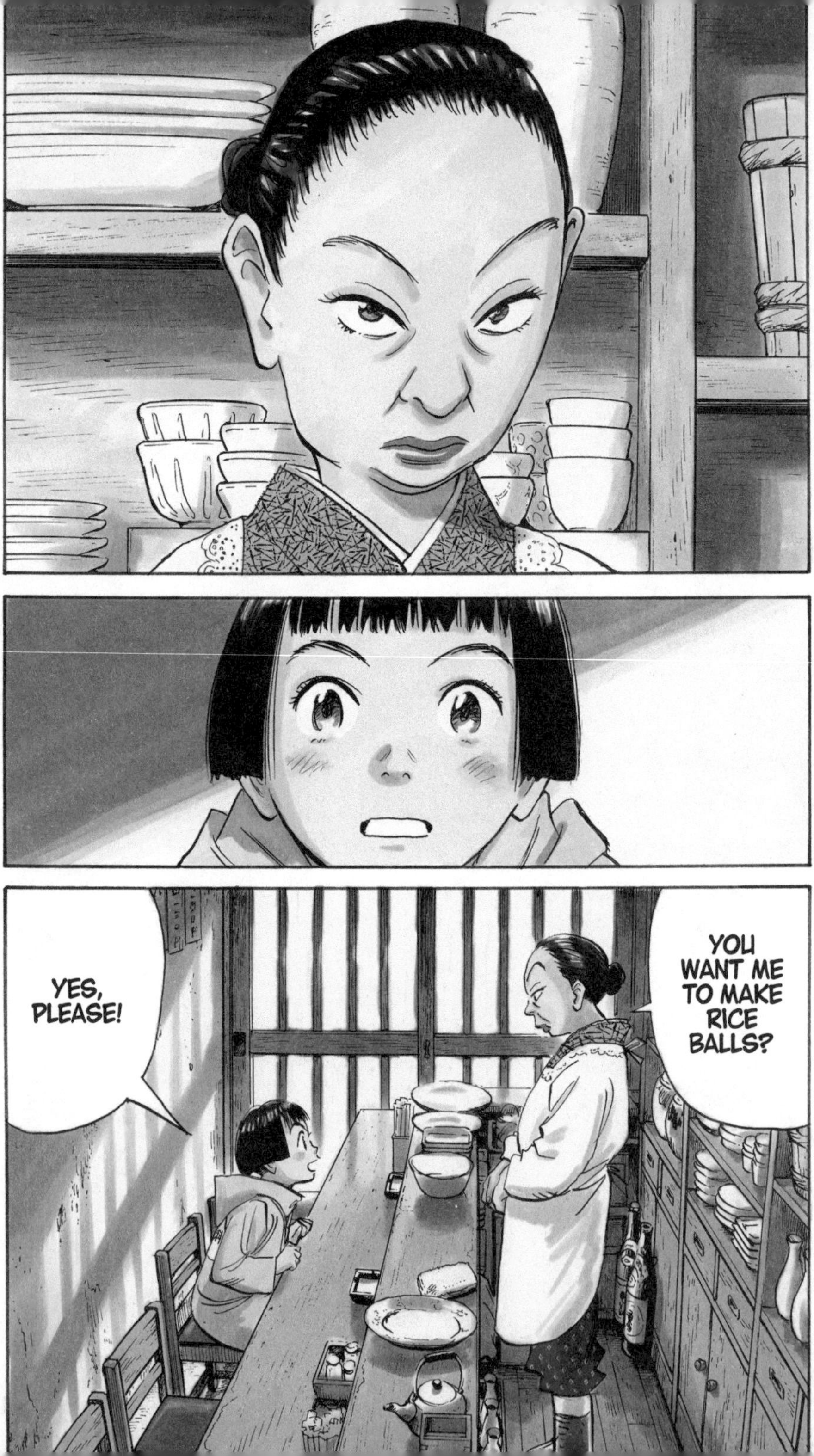
YOU WANT ME TO MAKE RICE BALLS?
YES, PLEASE!

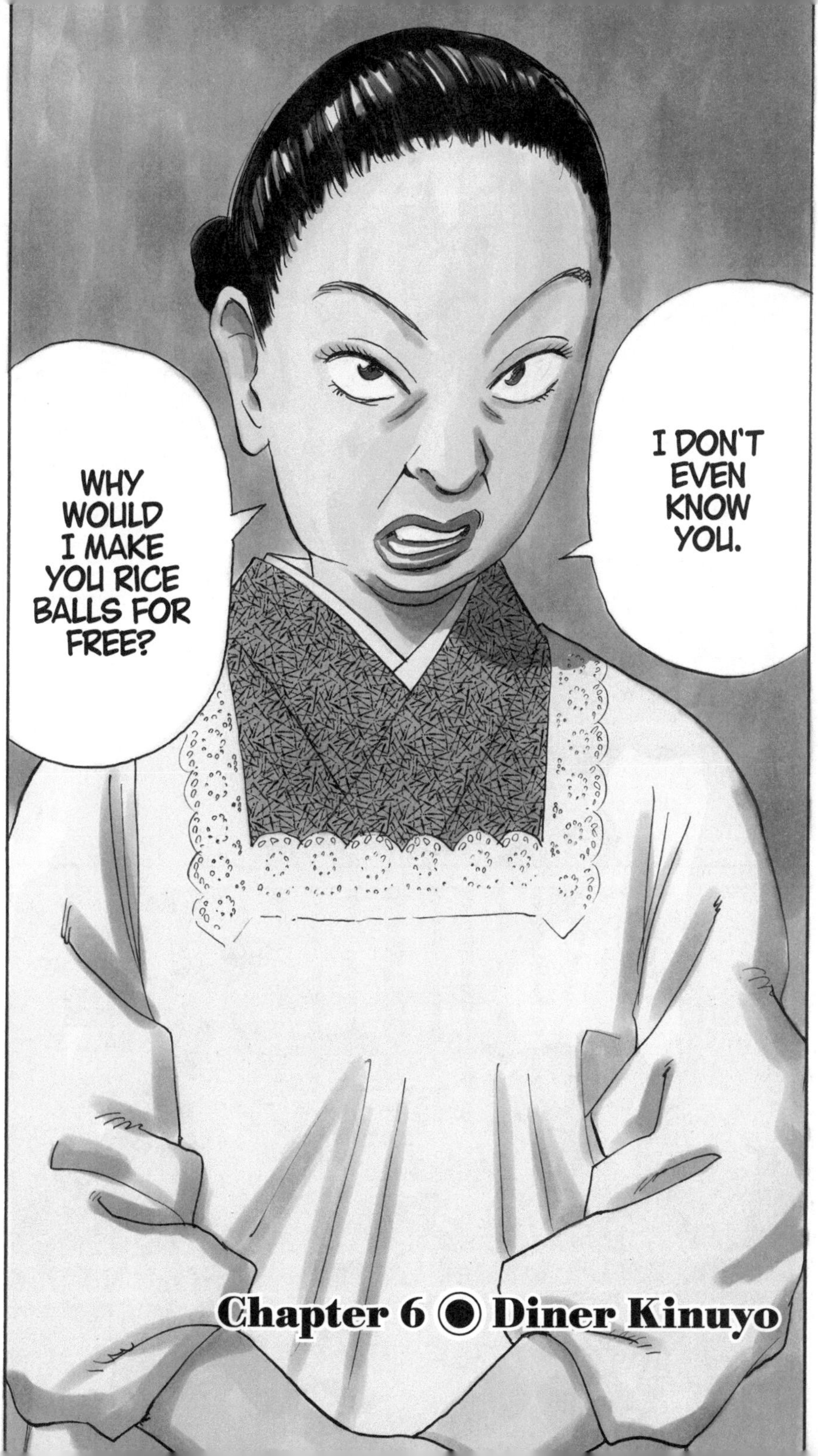
I DON'T EVEN KNOW YOU.
WHY WOULD I MAKE YOU RICE BALLS FOR FREE?

Chapter 6 ◉ Diner Kinuyo

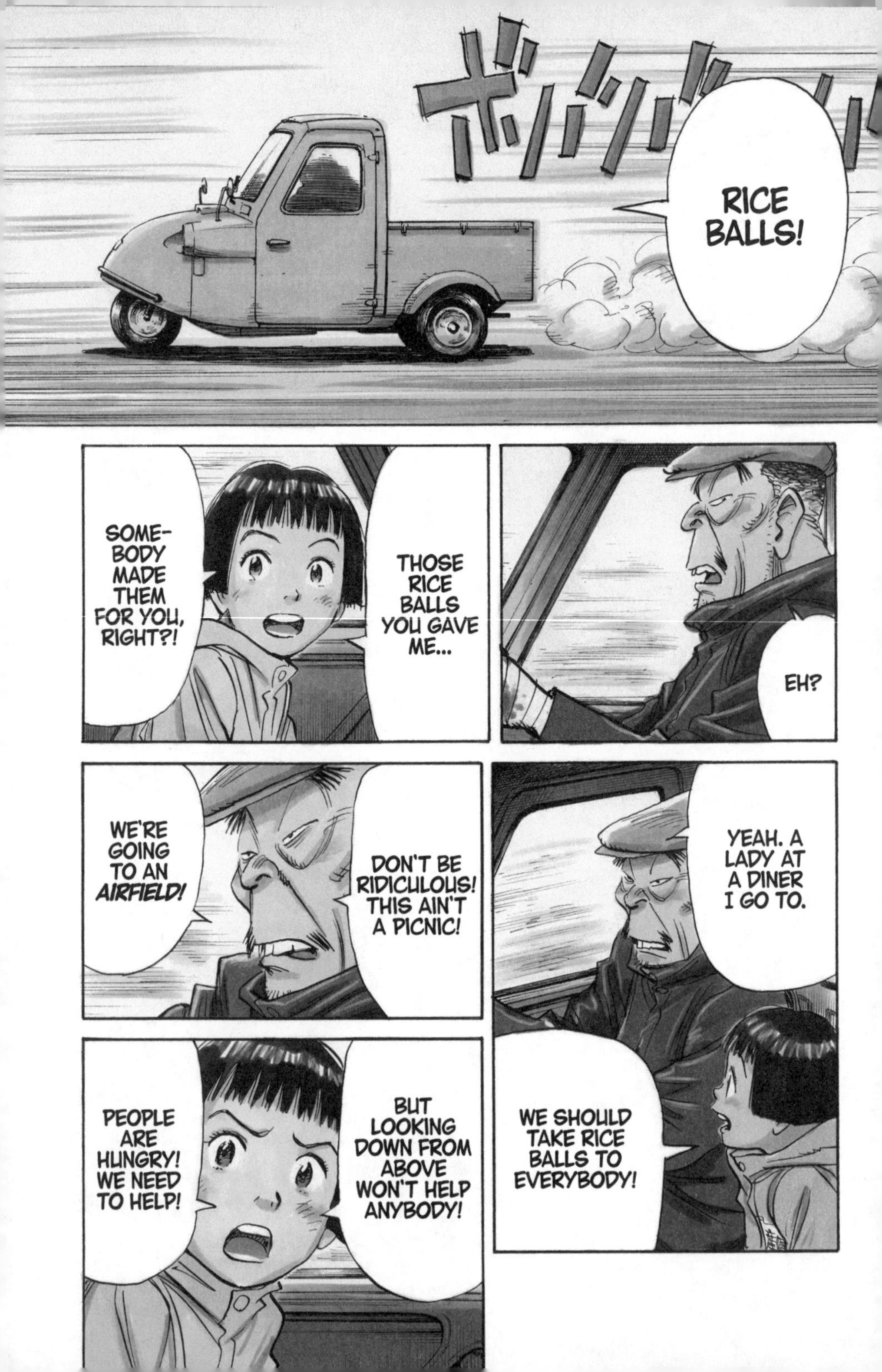
RICE BALLS!
EH?
THOSE RICE BALLS YOU GAVE ME...
SOME-BODY MADE THEM FOR YOU, RIGHT?!
YEAH. A LADY AT A DINER I GO TO.
WE SHOULD TAKE RICE BALLS TO EVERYBODY!
DON'T BE RIDICULOUS! THIS AIN'T A PICNIC!
WE'RE GOING TO AN *AIRFIELD!*
BUT LOOKING DOWN FROM ABOVE WON'T HELP ANYBODY!
PEOPLE ARE HUNGRY! WE NEED TO HELP!

ASADORA!

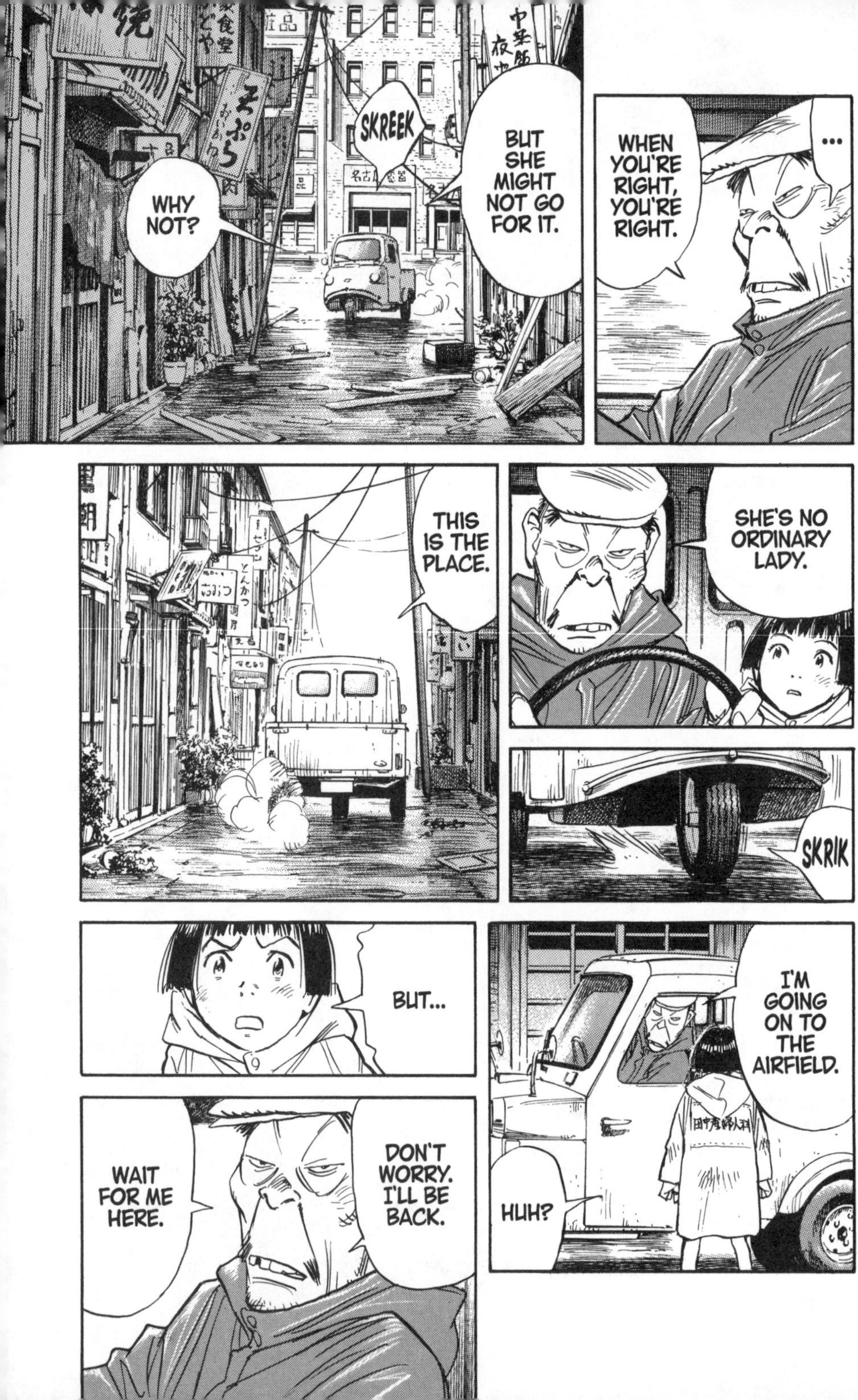
...
WHEN YOU'RE RIGHT, YOU'RE RIGHT.
BUT SHE MIGHT NOT GO FOR IT.
SKREEK
WHY NOT?
SHE'S NO ORDINARY LADY.
SKRIK
THIS IS THE PLACE.
I'M GOING ON TO THE AIRFIELD.
HUH?
BUT...
DON'T WORRY. I'LL BE BACK.
WAIT FOR ME HERE.

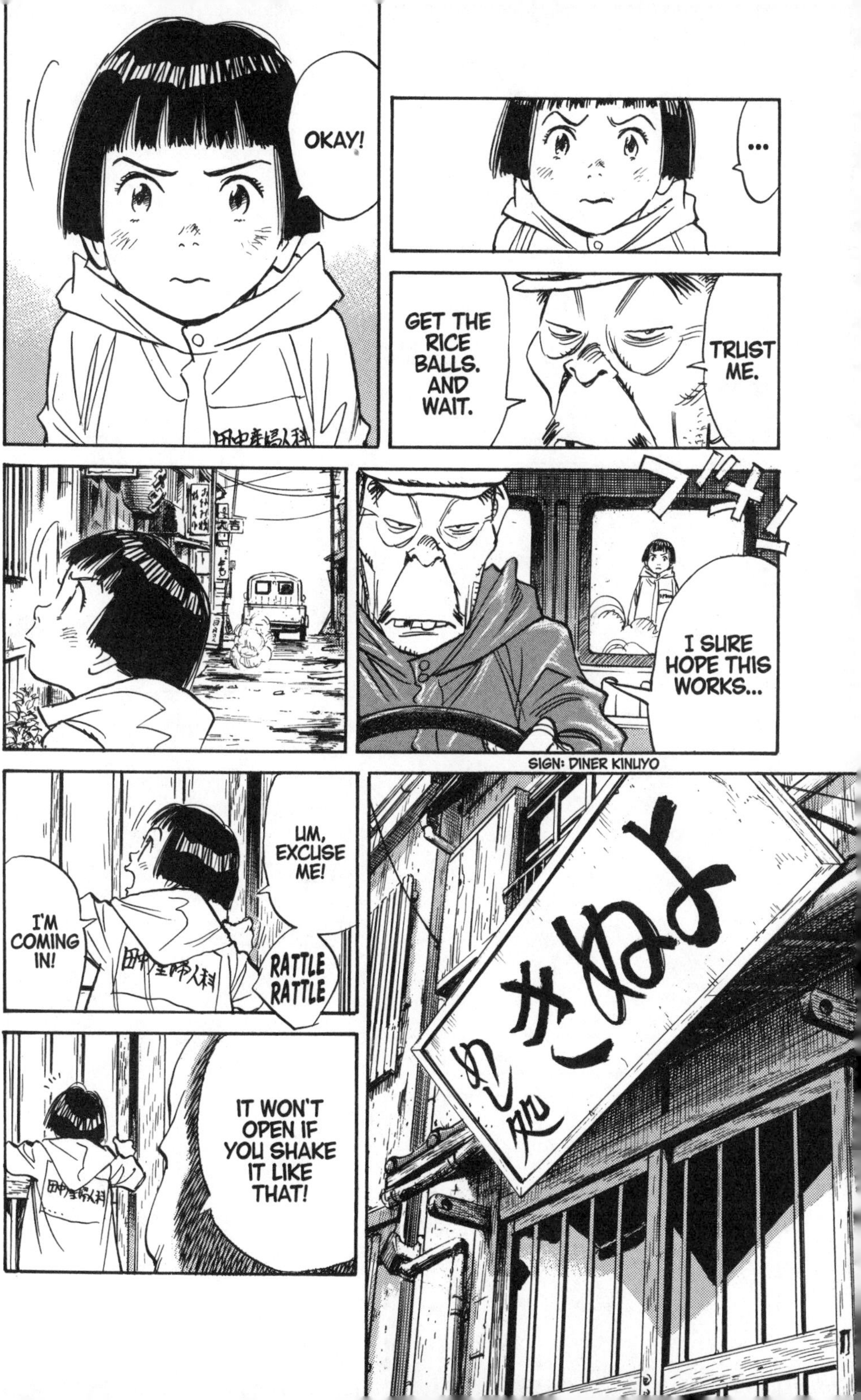
...
TRUST ME.
GET THE RICE BALLS. AND WAIT.
OKAY!
I SURE HOPE THIS WORKS...
SIGN: DINER KINUYO
めし処 きぬよ
UM, EXCUSE ME!
RATTLE RATTLE
I'M COMING IN!
IT WON'T OPEN IF YOU SHAKE IT LIKE THAT!

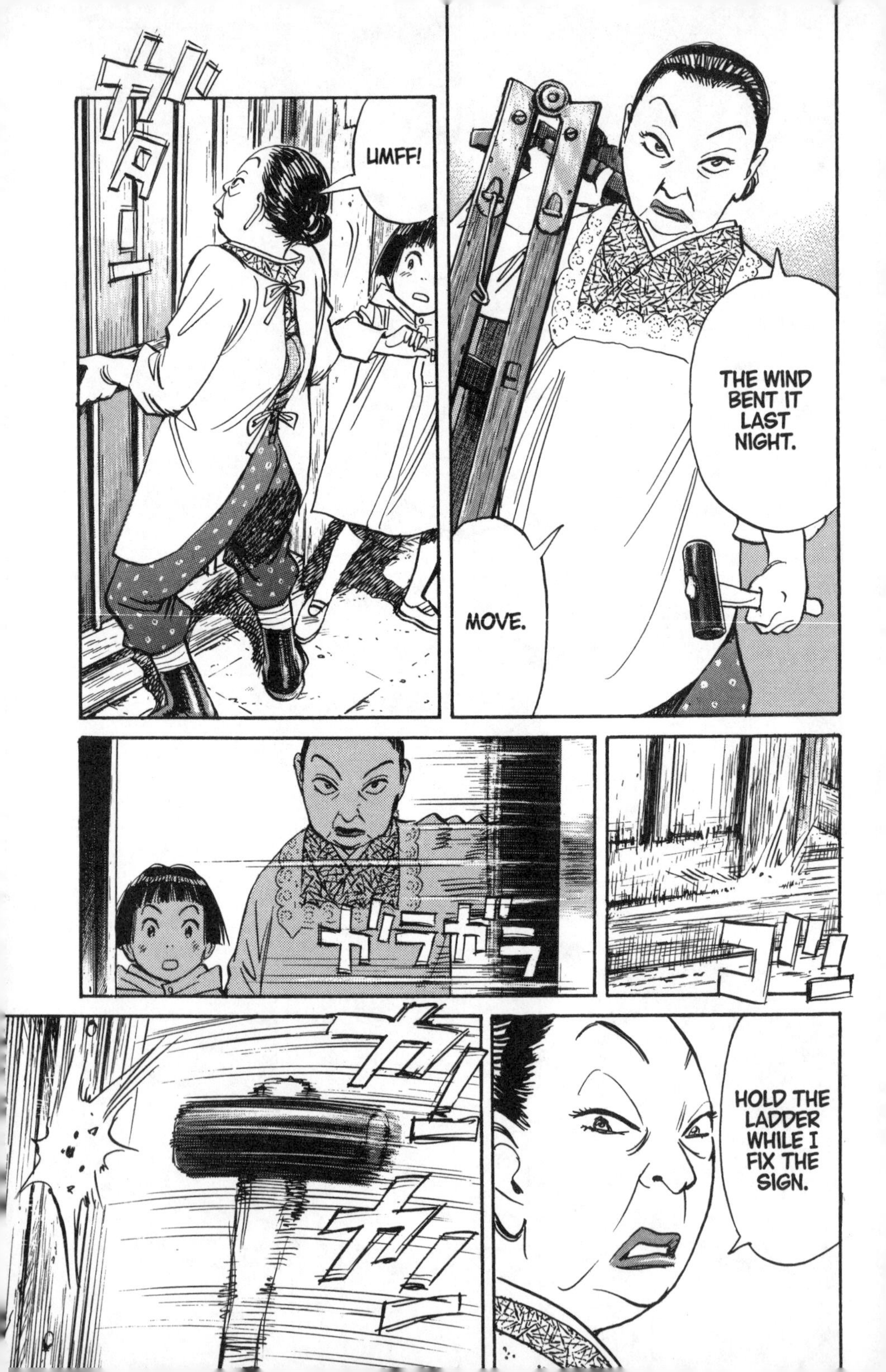
THE WIND BENT IT LAST NIGHT.
MOVE.
UMFF!
HOLD THE LADDER WHILE I FIX THE SIGN.

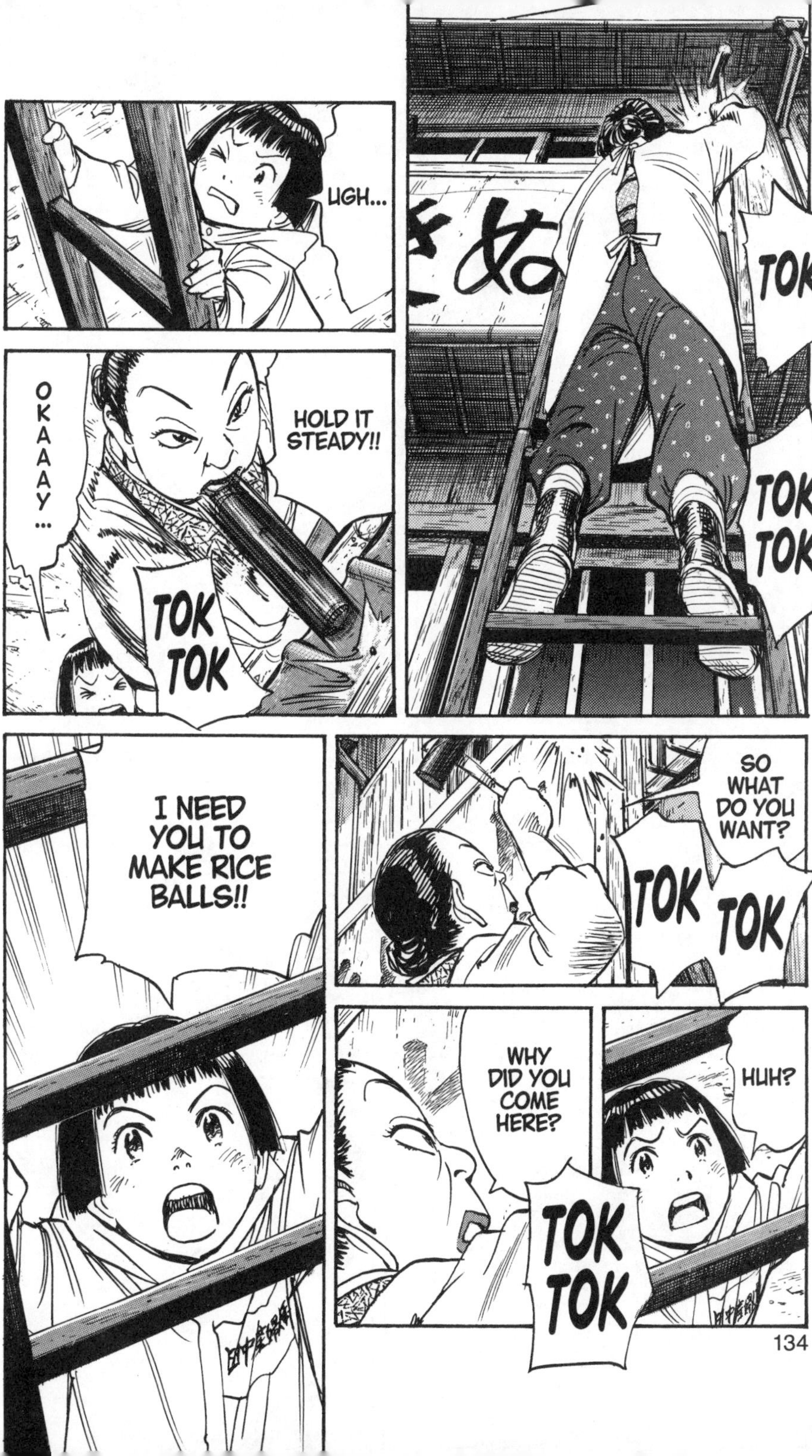
TOK
TOK TOK
UGH...
HOLD IT STEADY!!
OKAAAAY...
TOK TOK
SO WHAT DO YOU WANT?
TOK TOK
HUH?
WHY DID YOU COME HERE?
TOK TOK
I NEED YOU TO MAKE RICE BALLS!!

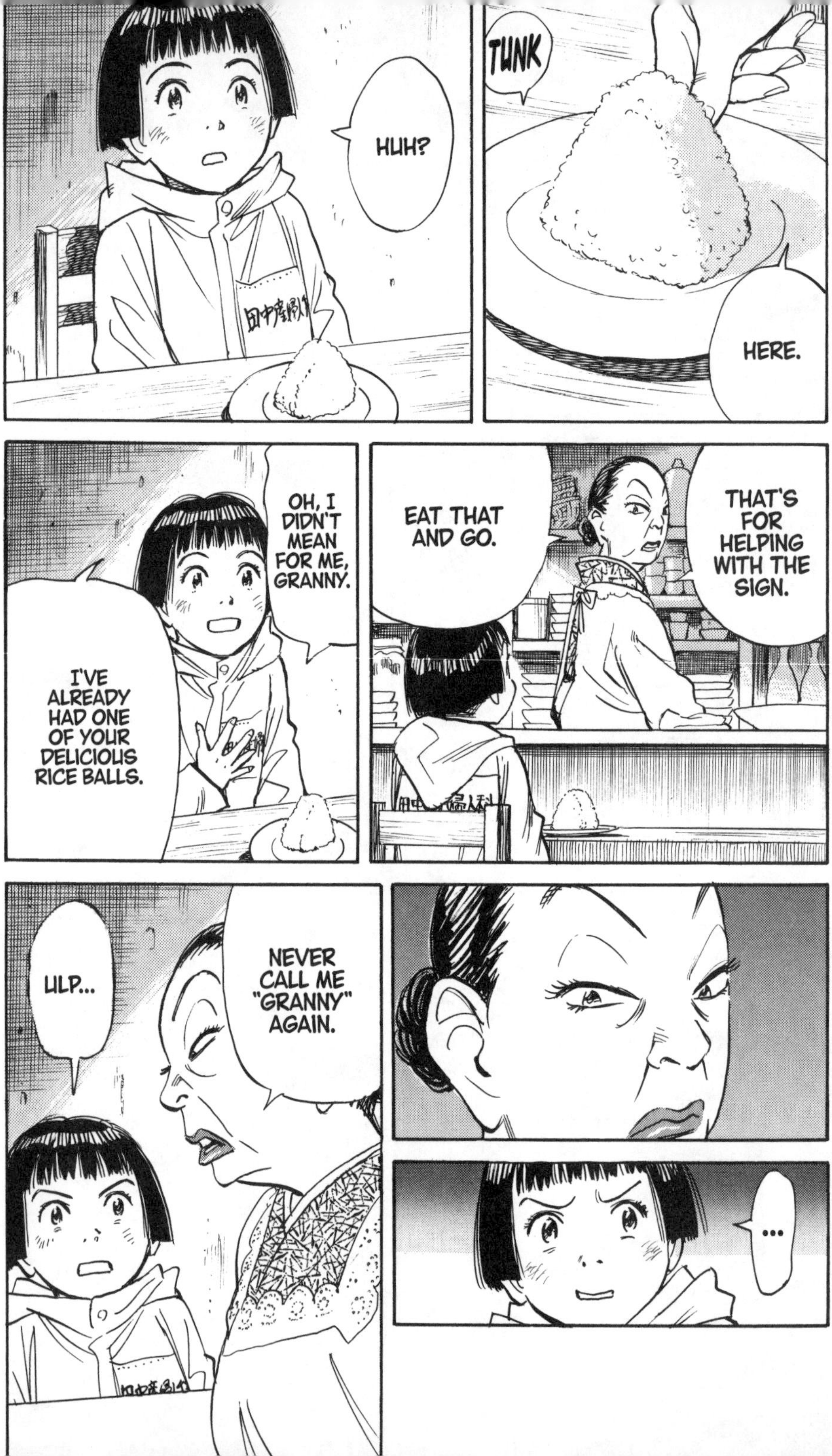
TUNK
HERE.
HUH?
THAT'S FOR HELPING WITH THE SIGN.
EAT THAT AND GO.
OH, I DIDN'T MEAN FOR ME, GRANNY.
I'VE ALREADY HAD ONE OF YOUR DELICIOUS RICE BALLS.
...
NEVER CALL ME "GRANNY" AGAIN.
ULP...

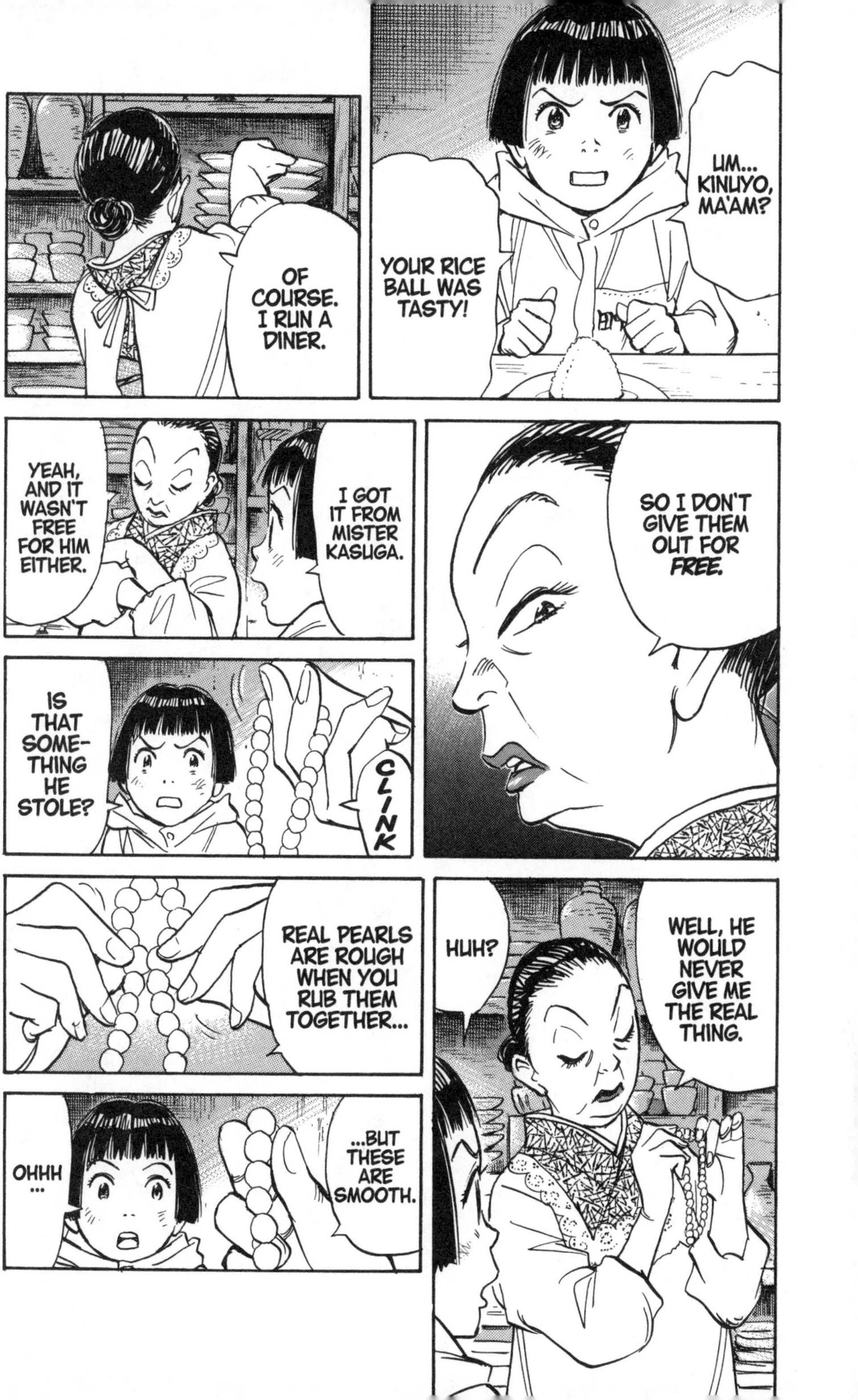
UM... KINUYO, MA'AM?
YOUR RICE BALL WAS TASTY!
OF COURSE. I RUN A DINER.
SO I DON'T GIVE THEM OUT FOR *FREE.*
I GOT IT FROM MISTER KASUGA.
YEAH, AND IT WASN'T FREE FOR HIM EITHER.
CLINK
IS THAT SOMETHING HE STOLE?
WELL, HE WOULD NEVER GIVE ME THE REAL THING.
HUH?
REAL PEARLS ARE ROUGH WHEN YOU RUB THEM TOGETHER...
...BUT THESE ARE SMOOTH.
OHHH ...

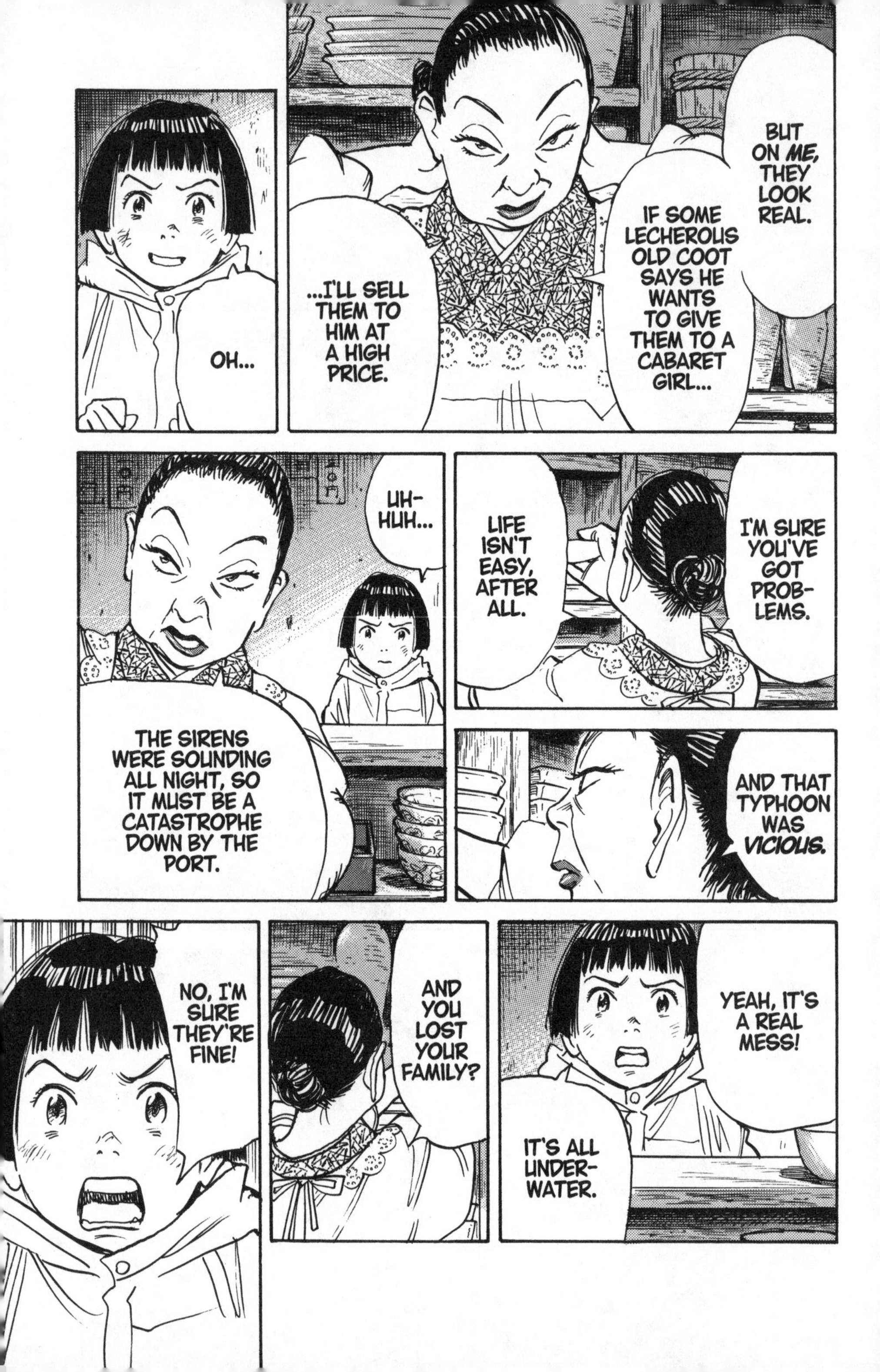
BUT ON *ME*, THEY LOOK REAL.
IF SOME LECHEROUS OLD COOT SAYS HE WANTS TO GIVE THEM TO A CABARET GIRL...
...I'LL SELL THEM TO HIM AT A HIGH PRICE.
OH...
I'M SURE YOU'VE GOT PROB-LEMS.
LIFE ISN'T EASY, AFTER ALL.
AND THAT TYPHOON WAS *VICIOUS*.
UH-HUH...
THE SIRENS WERE SOUNDING ALL NIGHT, SO IT MUST BE A CATASTROPHE DOWN BY THE PORT.
YEAH, IT'S A REAL MESS!
IT'S ALL UNDER-WATER.
AND YOU LOST YOUR FAMILY?
NO, I'M SURE THEY'RE FINE!

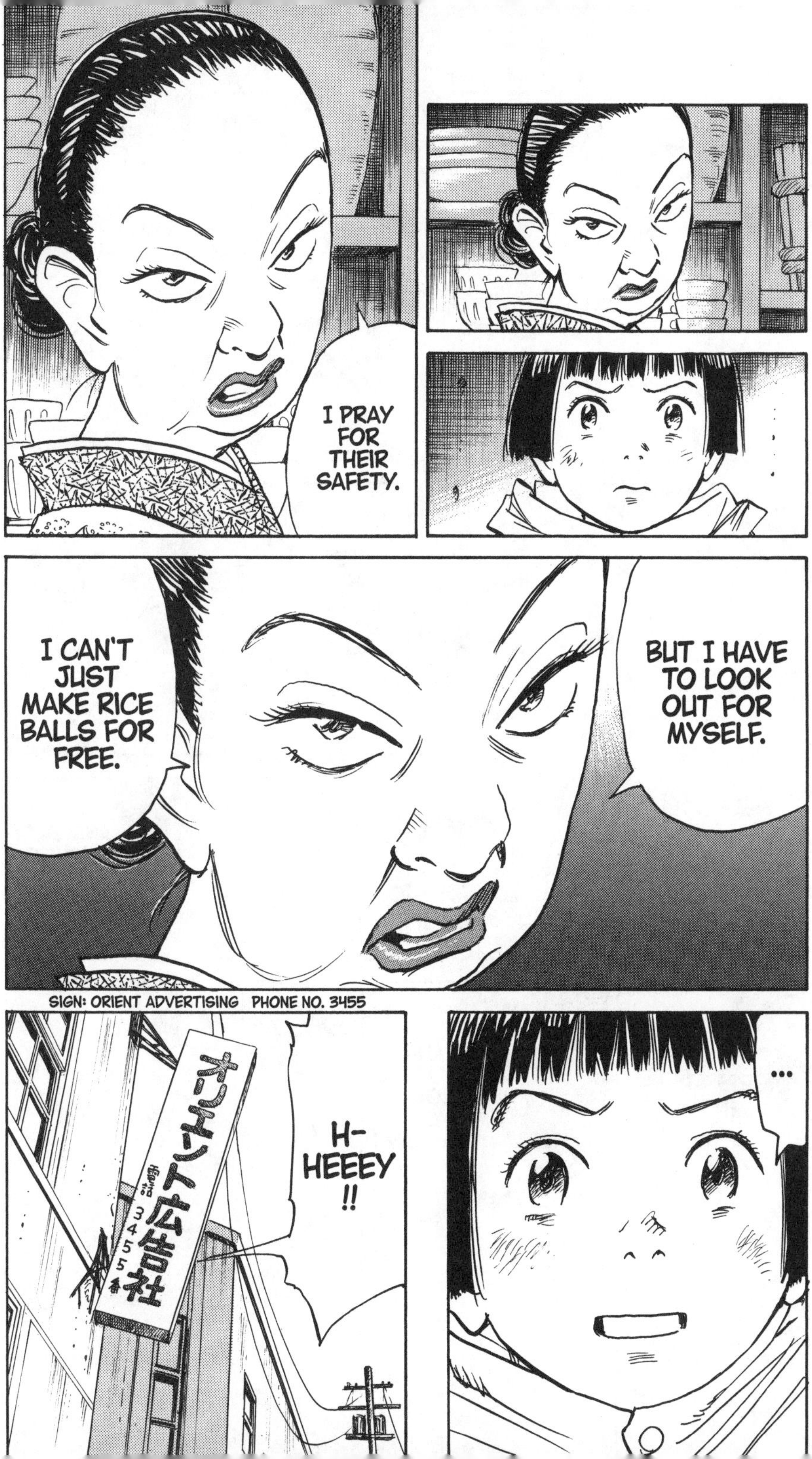
I PRAY FOR THEIR SAFETY.
BUT I HAVE TO LOOK OUT FOR MYSELF.
I CAN'T JUST MAKE RICE BALLS FOR FREE.
...
SIGN: ORIENT ADVERTISING PHONE NO. 3455
H-HEEEY!!
オリエント広告社
電話3455番

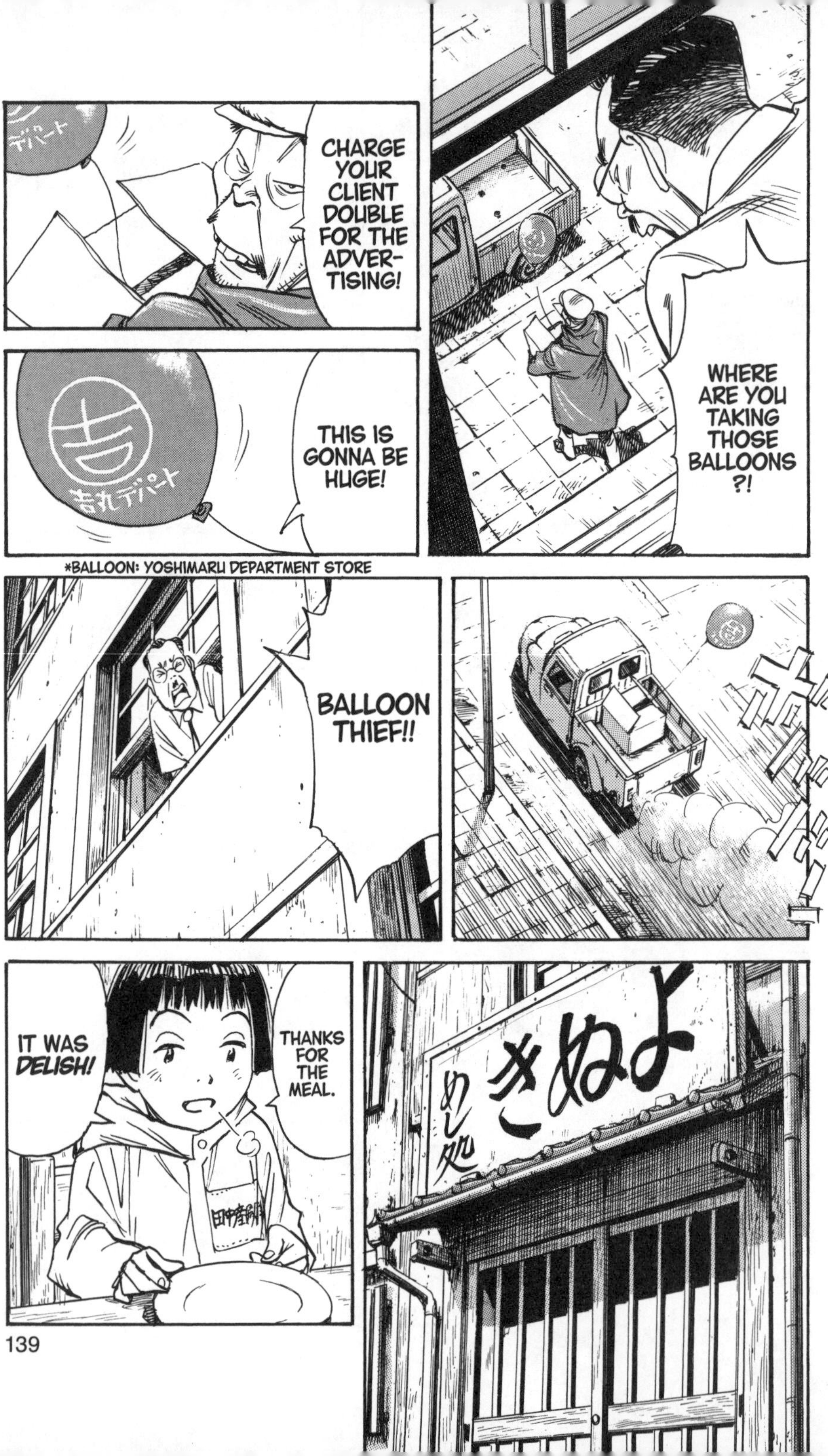
WHERE ARE YOU TAKING THOSE BALLOONS?!
CHARGE YOUR CLIENT DOUBLE FOR THE ADVER-TISING!
THIS IS GONNA BE HUGE!
吉丸デパート
*BALLOON: YOSHIMARU DEPARTMENT STORE
BALLOON THIEF!!
めし処 きぬよ
THANKS FOR THE MEAL.
IT WAS *DELISH!*

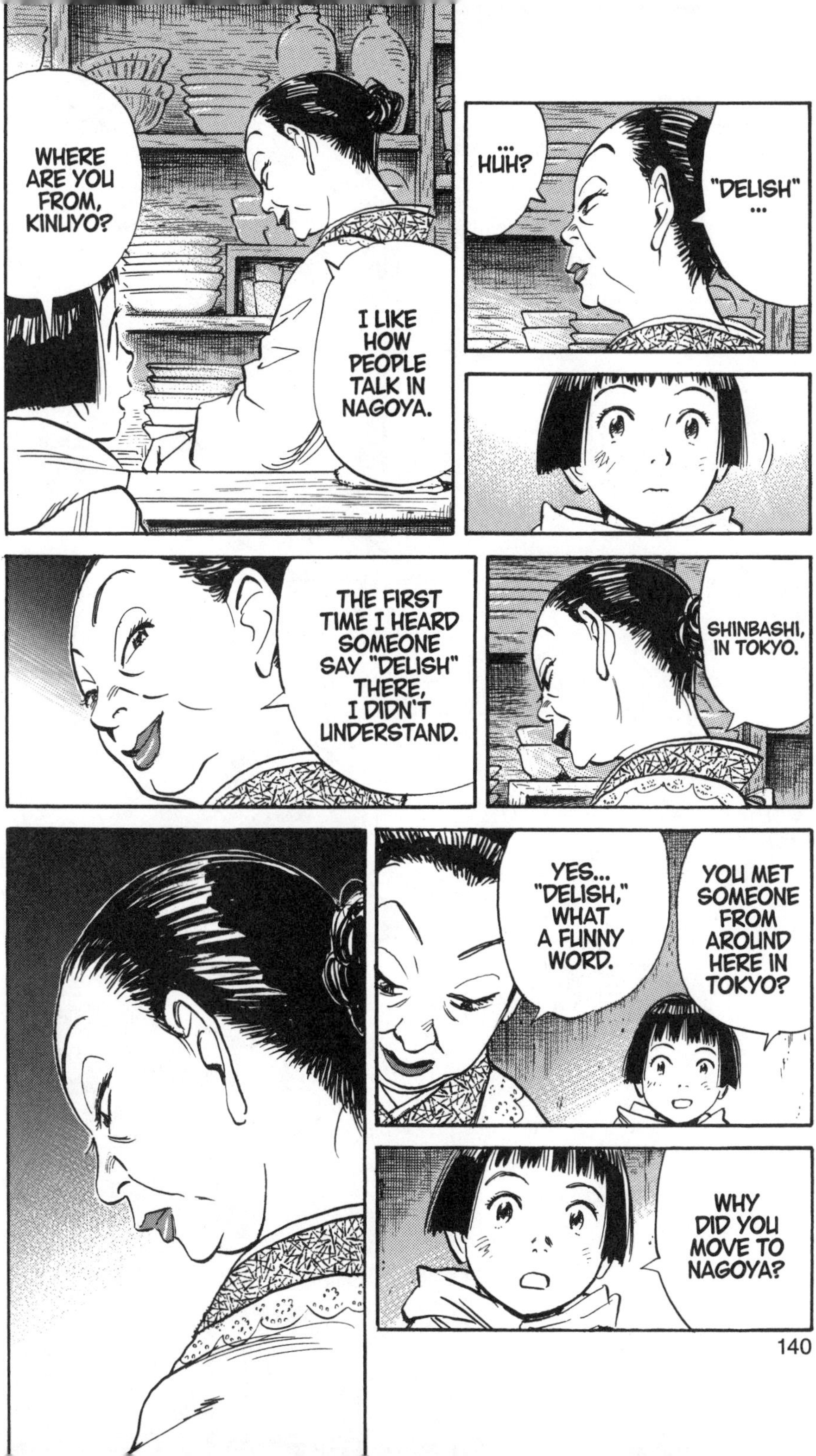
"DELISH" ...
... HUH?
I LIKE HOW PEOPLE TALK IN NAGOYA.
WHERE ARE YOU FROM, KINUYO?
SHINBASHI, IN TOKYO.
THE FIRST TIME I HEARD SOMEONE SAY "DELISH" THERE, I DIDN'T UNDERSTAND.
YOU MET SOMEONE FROM AROUND HERE IN TOKYO?
YES... "DELISH," WHAT A FUNNY WORD.
WHY DID YOU MOVE TO NAGOYA?

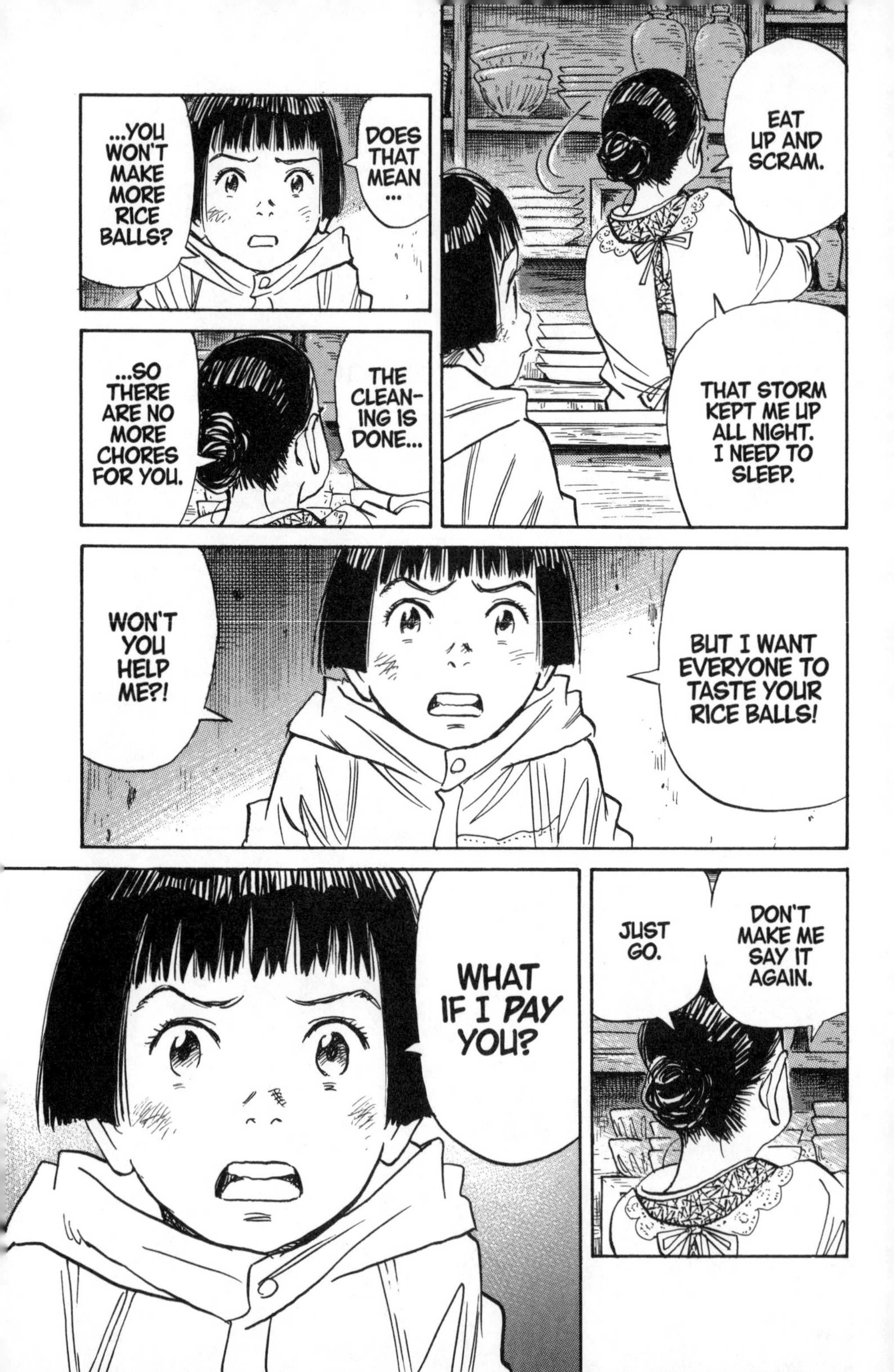
EAT UP AND SCRAM.
THAT STORM KEPT ME UP ALL NIGHT. I NEED TO SLEEP.
DOES THAT MEAN...
...YOU WON'T MAKE MORE RICE BALLS?
THE CLEAN-ING IS DONE...
...SO THERE ARE NO MORE CHORES FOR YOU.
BUT I WANT EVERYONE TO TASTE YOUR RICE BALLS!
WON'T YOU HELP ME?!
DON'T MAKE ME SAY IT AGAIN.
JUST GO.
WHAT IF I *PAY* YOU?

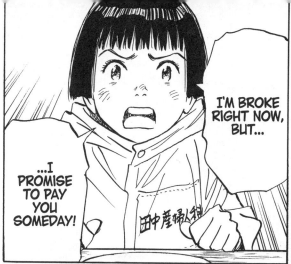

I'M BROKE RIGHT NOW, BUT...

...I PROMISE TO PAY YOU SOMEDAY!

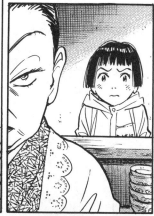

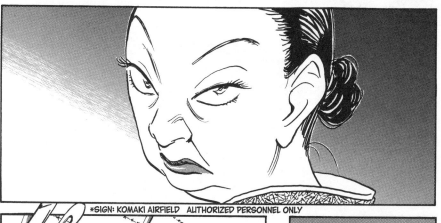

*SIGN: KOMAKI AIRFIELD   AUTHORIZED PERSONNEL ONLY

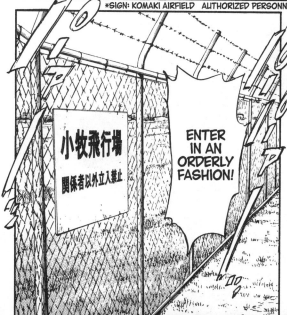

小牧飛行場
関係者以外立入禁止

ENTER IN AN ORDERLY FASHION!

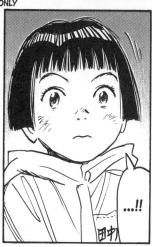

...!!

142

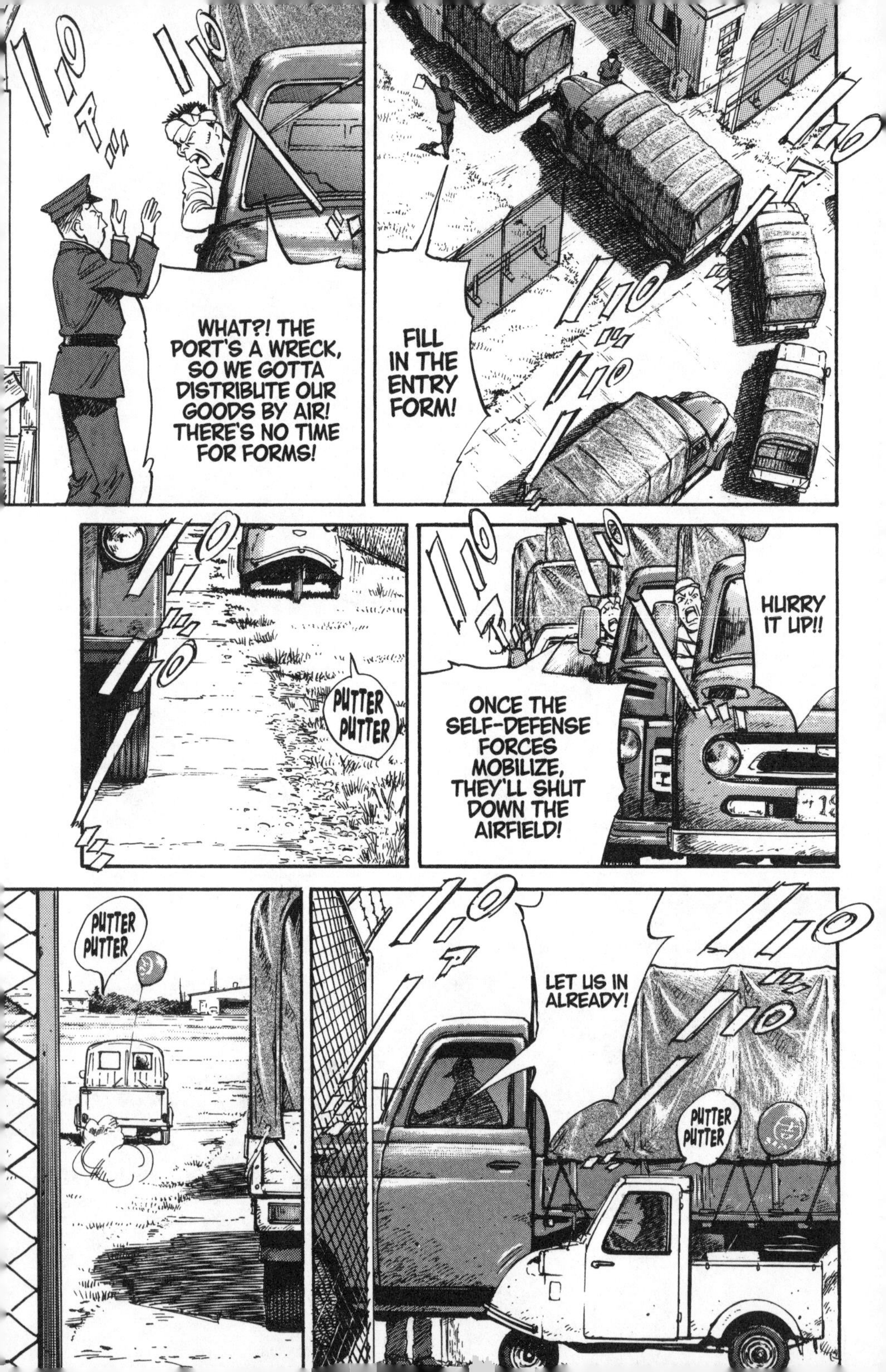
FILL IN THE ENTRY FORM!
WHAT?! THE PORT'S A WRECK, SO WE GOTTA DISTRIBUTE OUR GOODS BY AIR! THERE'S NO TIME FOR FORMS!
HURRY IT UP!!
ONCE THE SELF-DEFENSE FORCES MOBILIZE, THEY'LL SHUT DOWN THE AIRFIELD!
PUTTER PUTTER
LET US IN ALREADY!
PUTTER PUTTER
PUTTER PUTTER

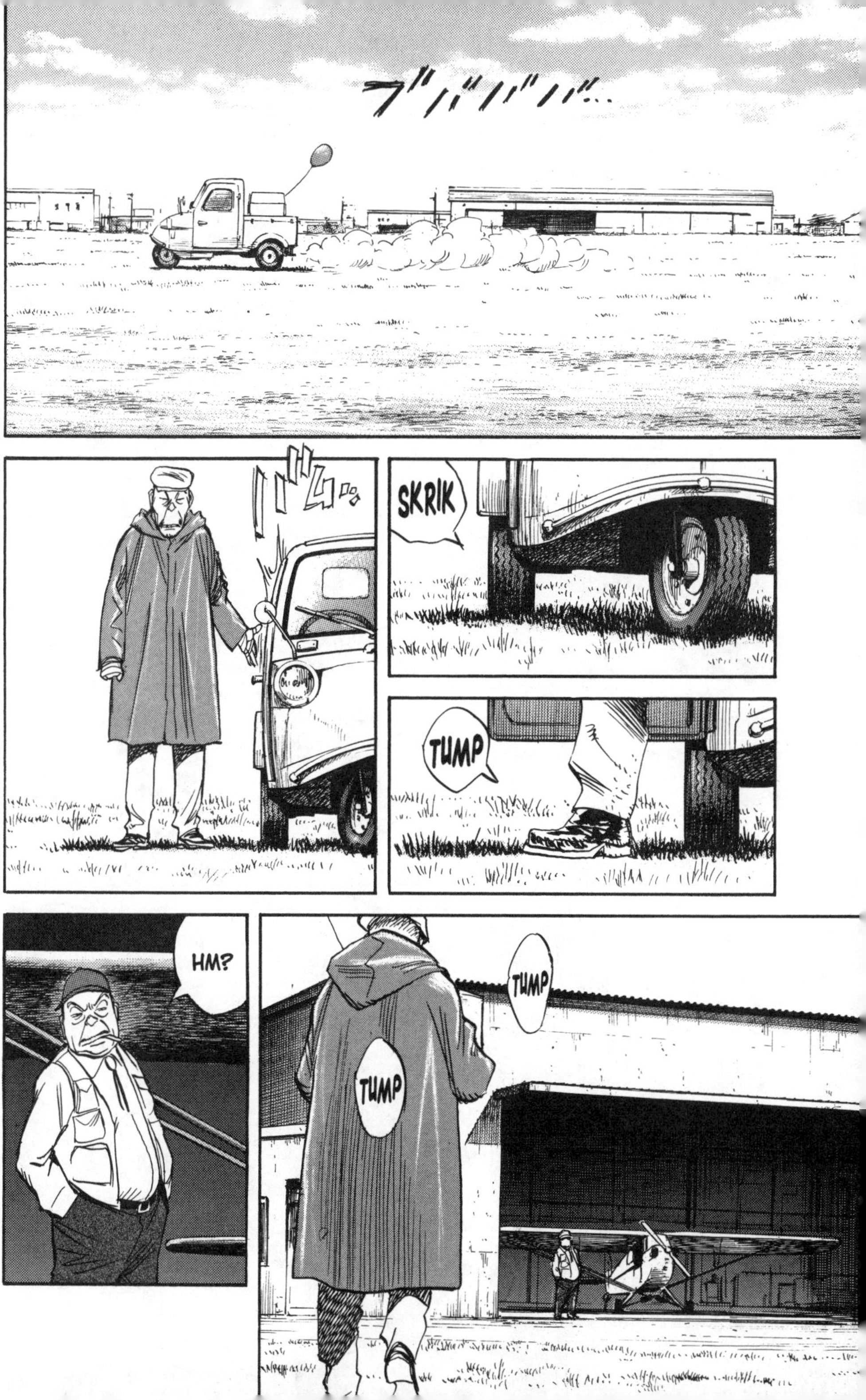
SKRIK
TUMP
TUMP
TUMP
HM?

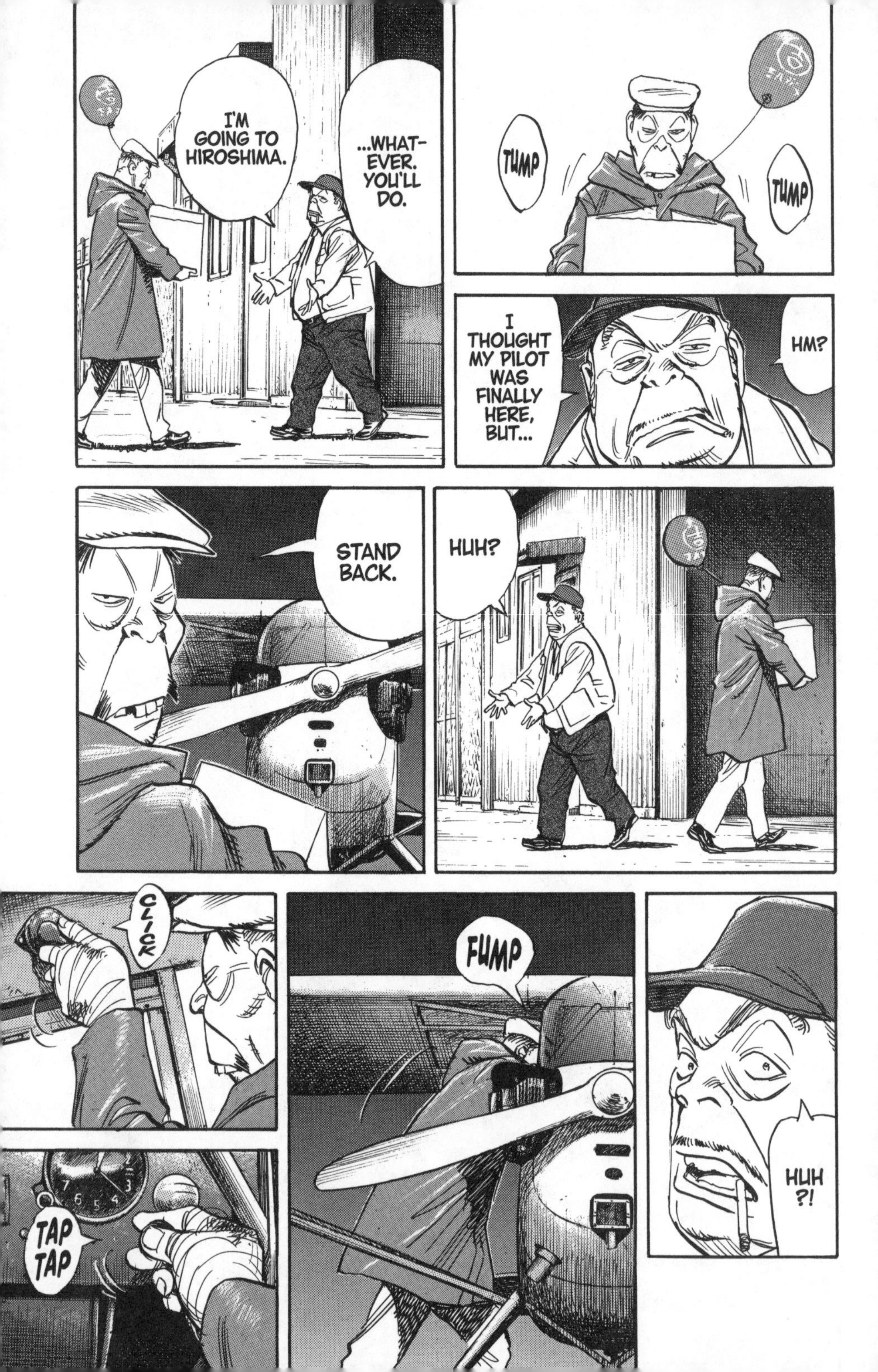
TUMP
TUMP
I THOUGHT MY PILOT WAS FINALLY HERE, BUT...
HM?
I'M GOING TO HIROSHIMA.
...WHATEVER. YOU'LL DO.
HUH?
STAND BACK.
HUH?!
FUMP
CLICK
TAP TAP

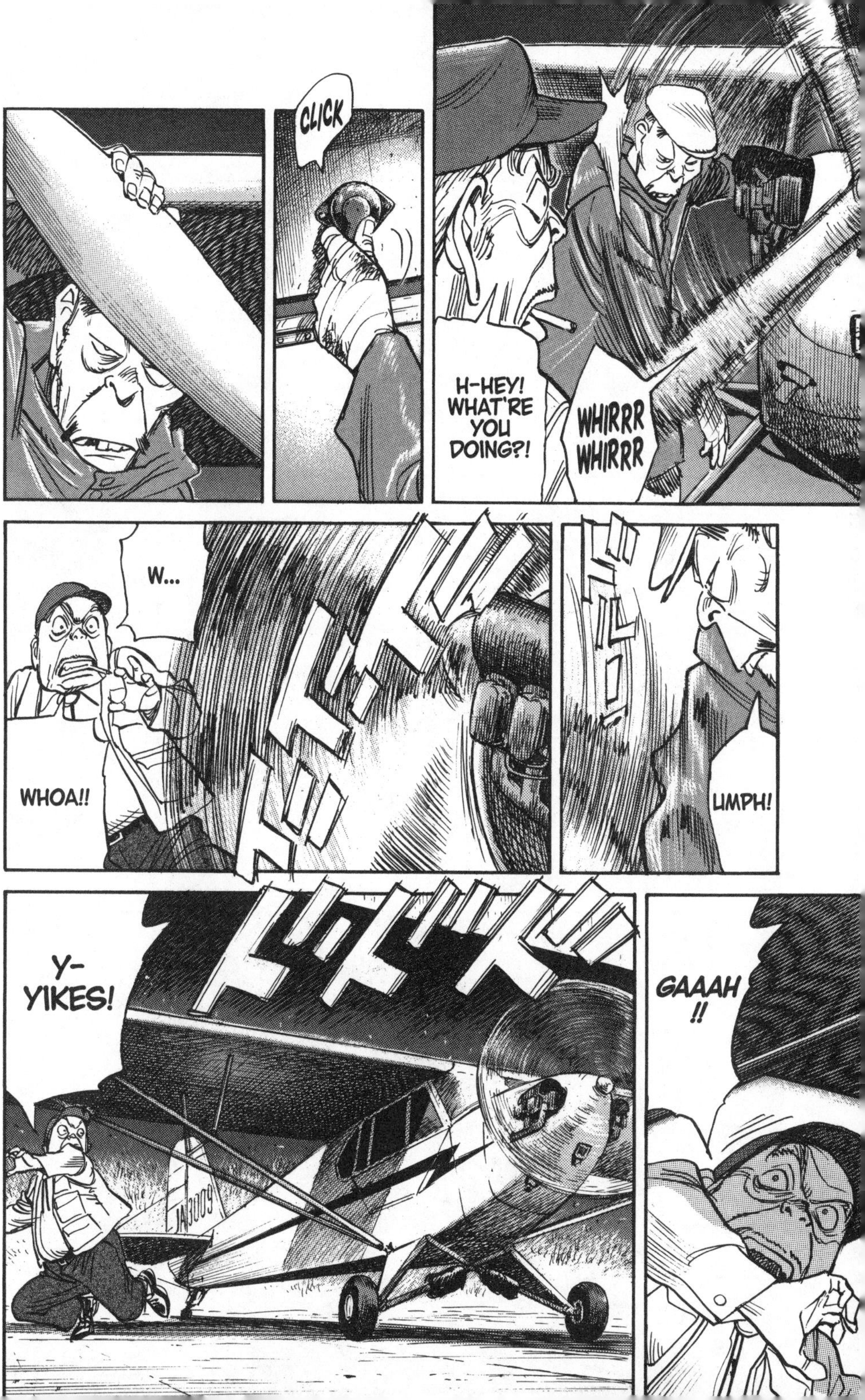
WHIRRR WHIRRR
H-HEY! WHAT'RE YOU DOING?!
CLICK
UMPH!
W...
WHOA!!
GAAAH !!
Y-YIKES!

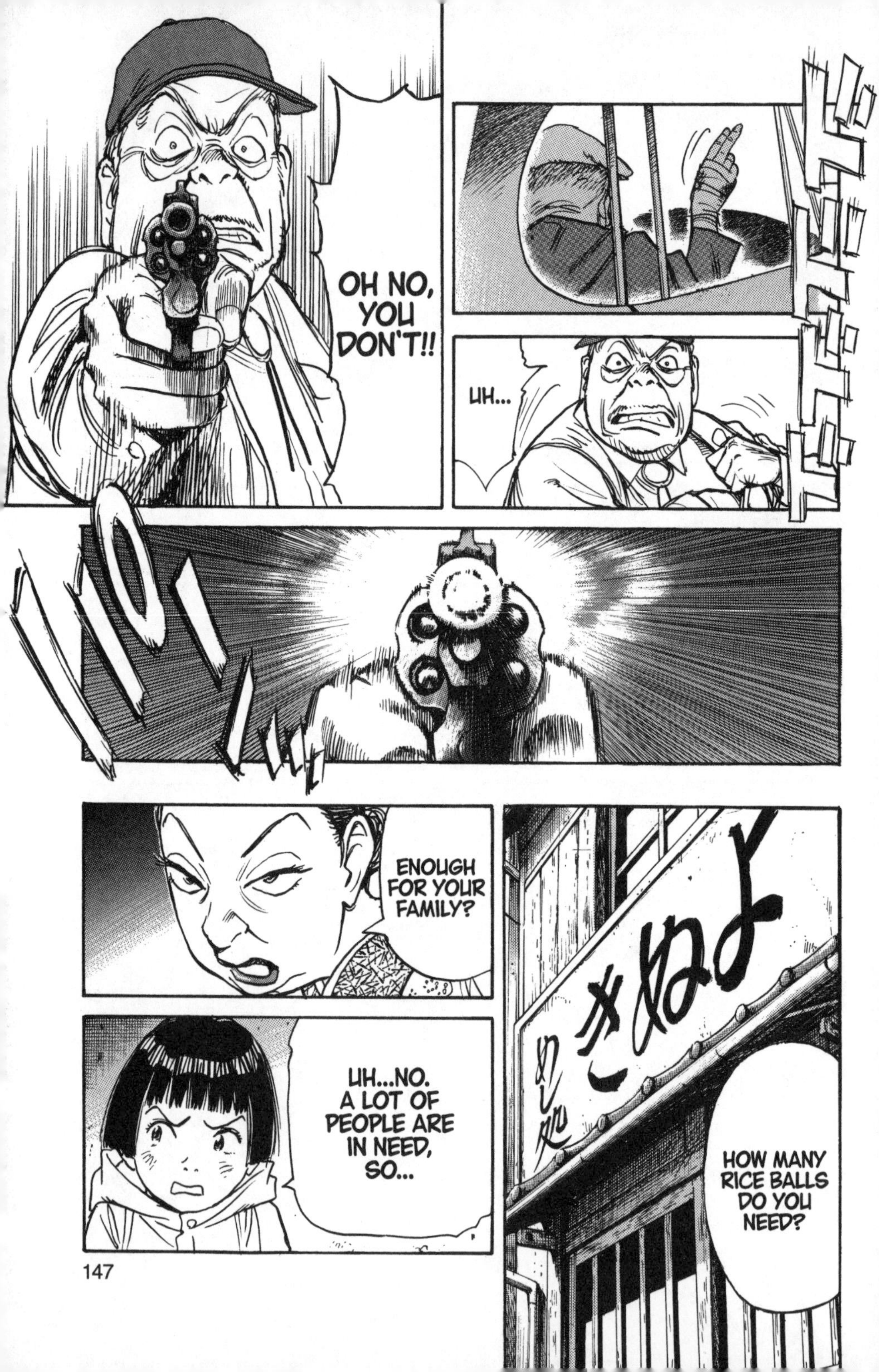
UH...
OH NO, YOU DON'T!!
きぬよ
めし処
HOW MANY RICE BALLS DO YOU NEED?
ENOUGH FOR YOUR FAMILY?
UH...NO. A LOT OF PEOPLE ARE IN NEED, SO...

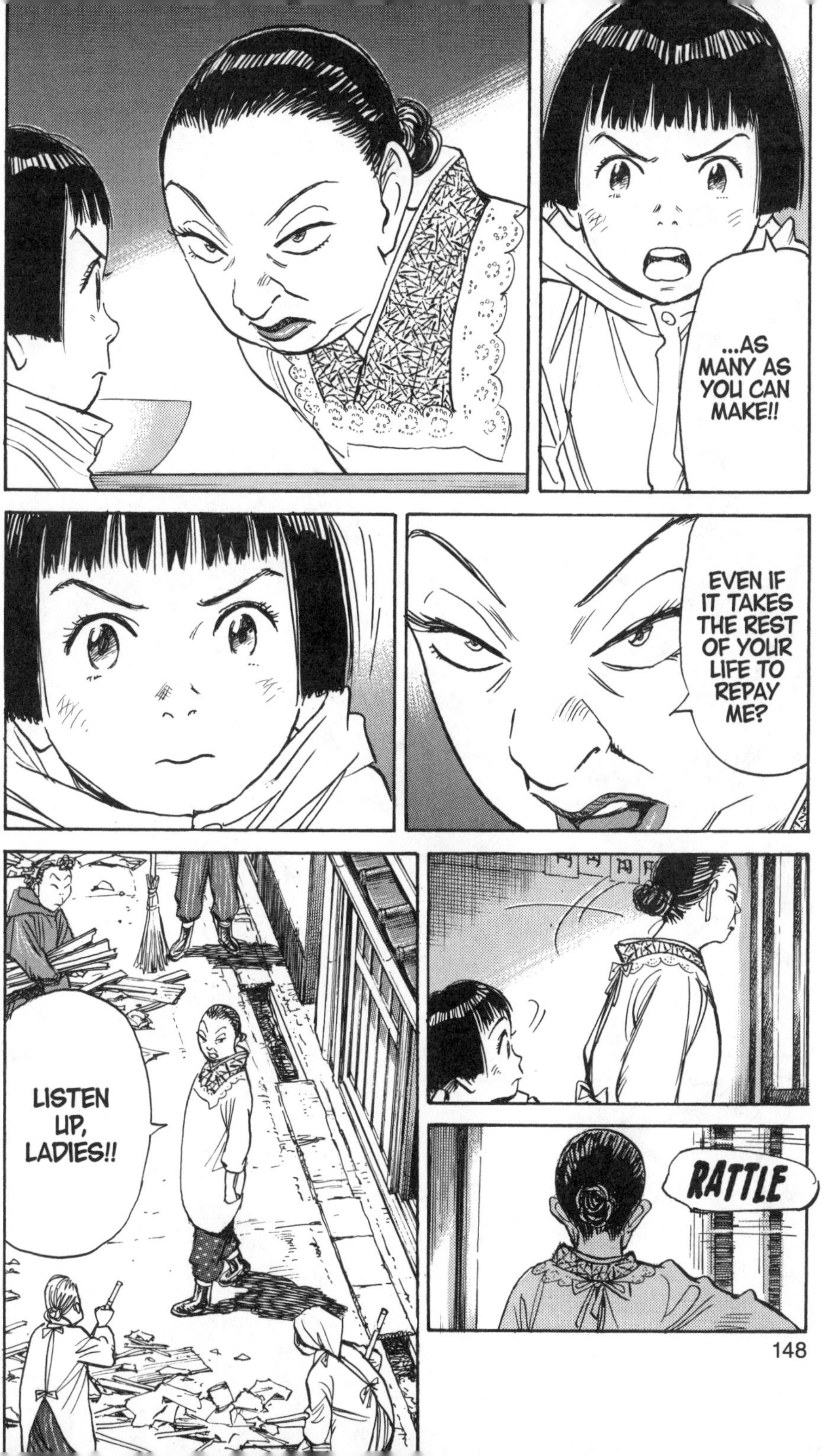
...AS MANY AS YOU CAN MAKE!!
EVEN IF IT TAKES THE REST OF YOUR LIFE TO REPAY ME?
RATTLE
LISTEN UP, LADIES!!

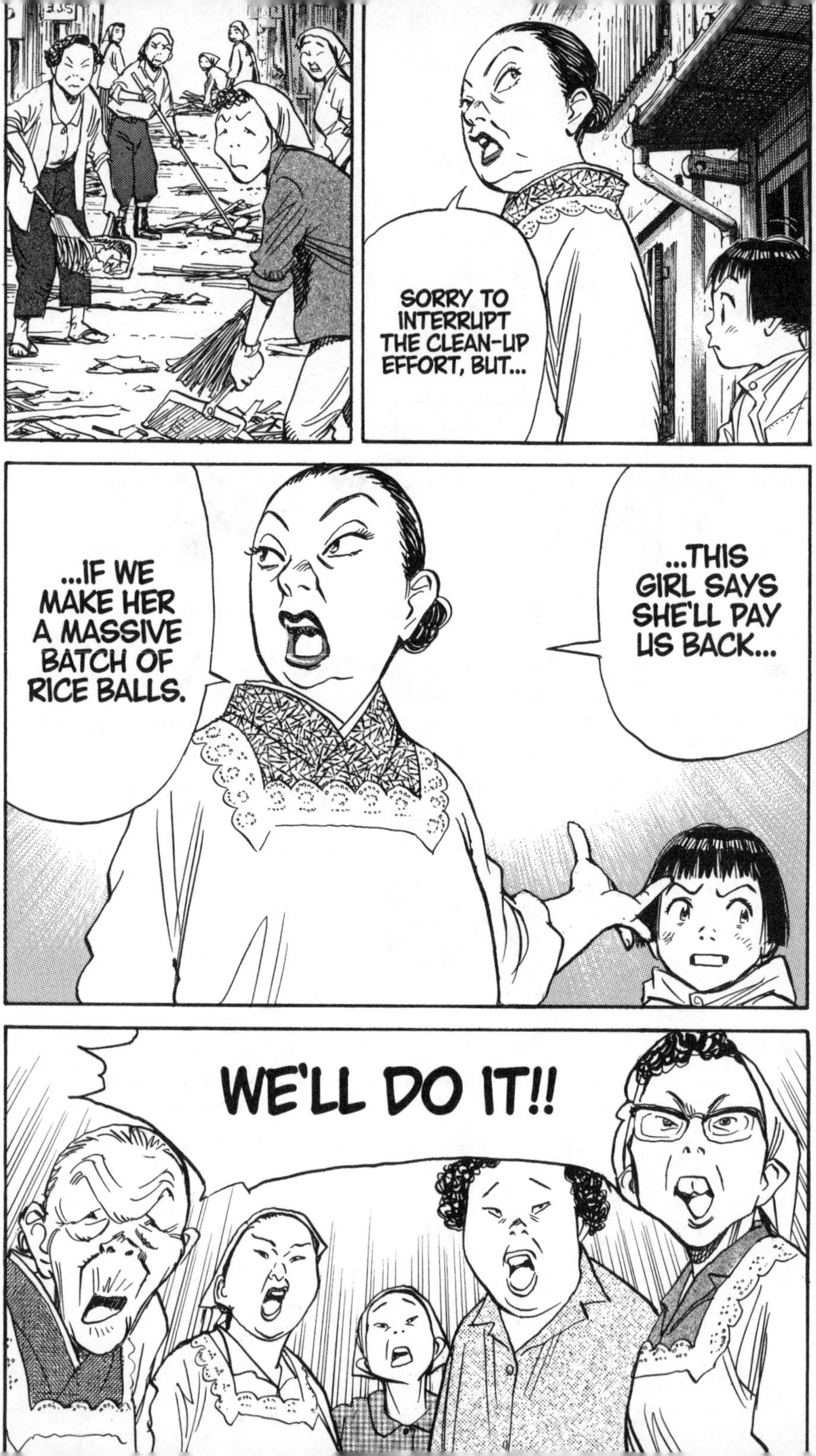
SORRY TO INTERRUPT THE CLEAN-UP EFFORT, BUT...
...THIS GIRL SAYS SHE'LL PAY US BACK...
...IF WE MAKE HER A MASSIVE BATCH OF RICE BALLS.
WE'LL DO IT!!

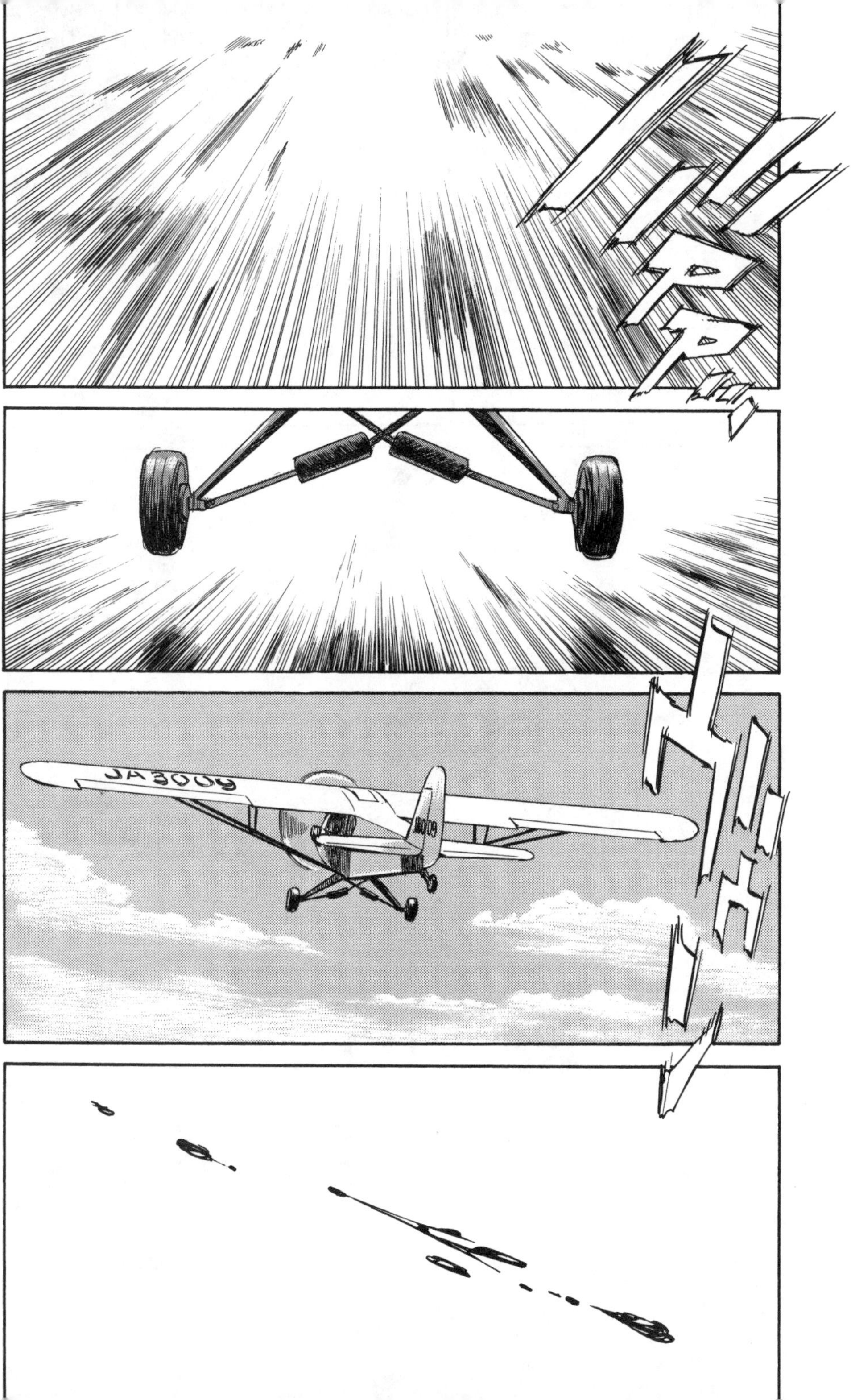
JA3009

Chapter 7 ● The Chosen One

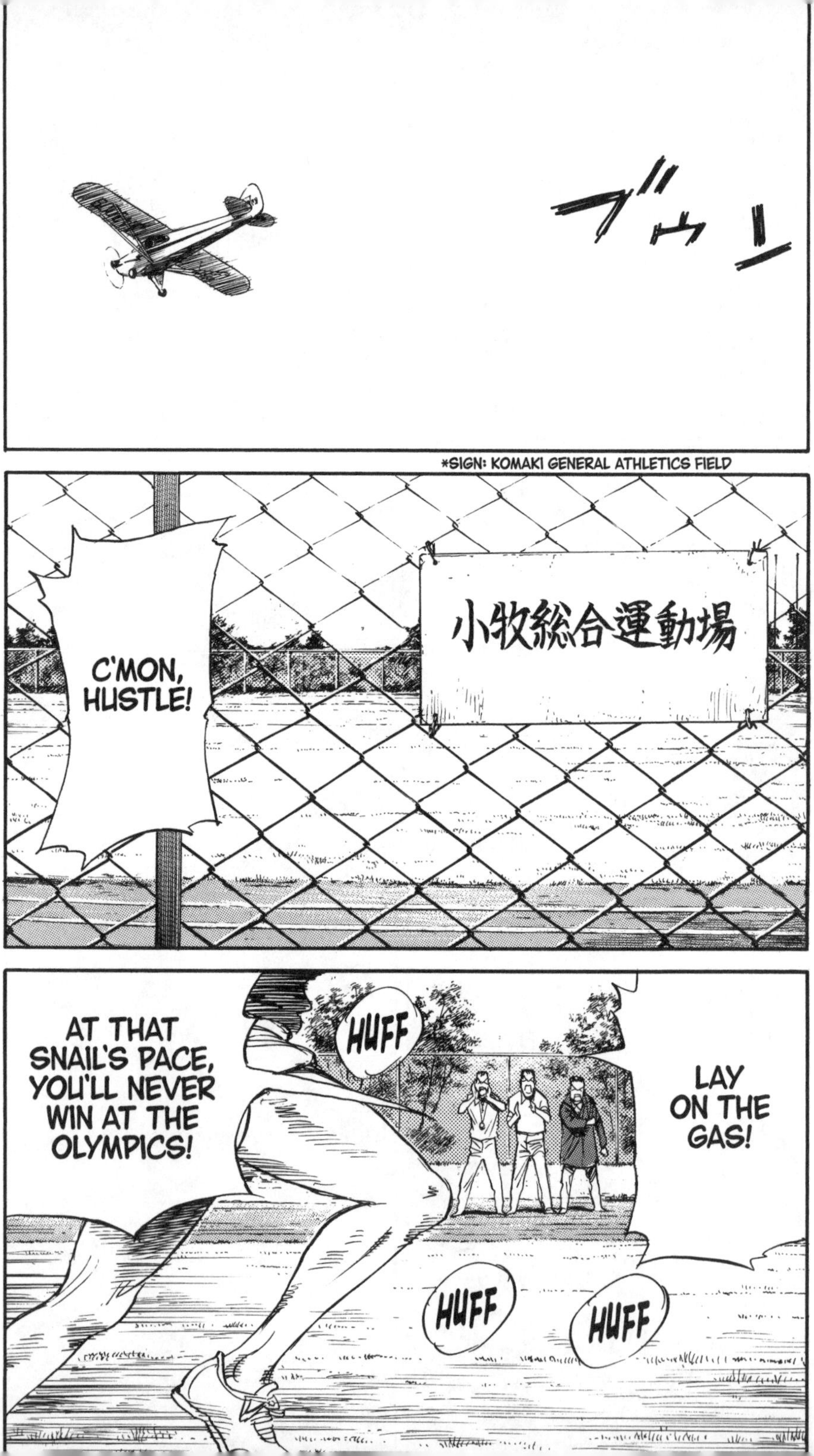
ブゥン
*SIGN: KOMAKI GENERAL ATHLETICS FIELD
小牧総合運動場
C'MON, HUSTLE!
LAY ON THE GAS!
HUFF
AT THAT SNAIL'S PACE, YOU'LL NEVER WIN AT THE OLYMPICS!
HUFF
HUFF

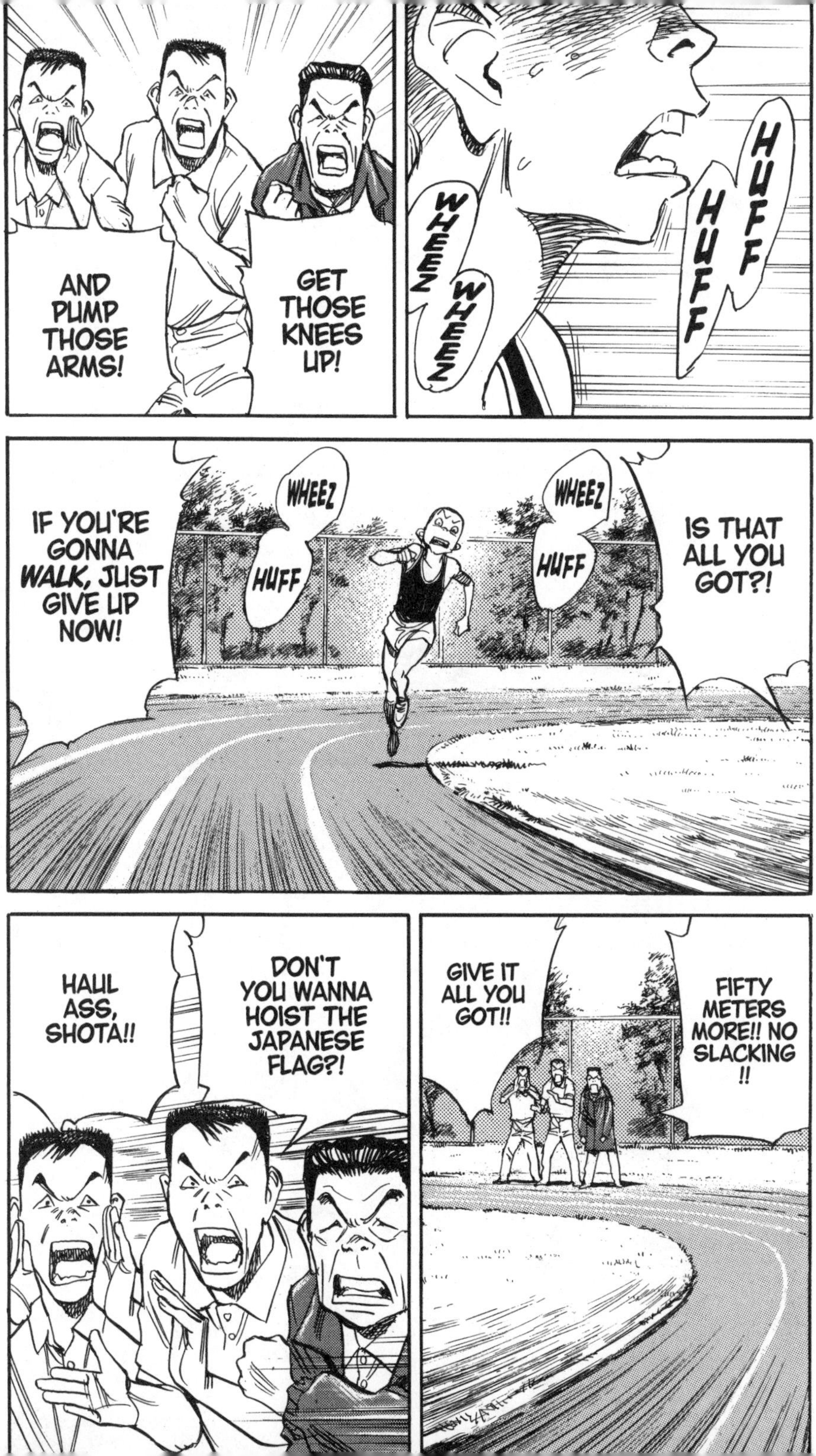
HUFF
HUFF
WHEEZ
WHEEZ
GET THOSE KNEES UP!
AND PUMP THOSE ARMS!
IS THAT ALL YOU GOT?!
WHEEZ
HUFF
WHEEZ
HUFF
IF YOU'RE GONNA *WALK*, JUST GIVE UP NOW!
FIFTY METERS MORE!! NO SLACKING !!
GIVE IT ALL YOU GOT!!
DON'T YOU WANNA HOIST THE JAPANESE FLAG?!
HAUL ASS, SHOTA!!

Chapter 7 ● The Chosen One

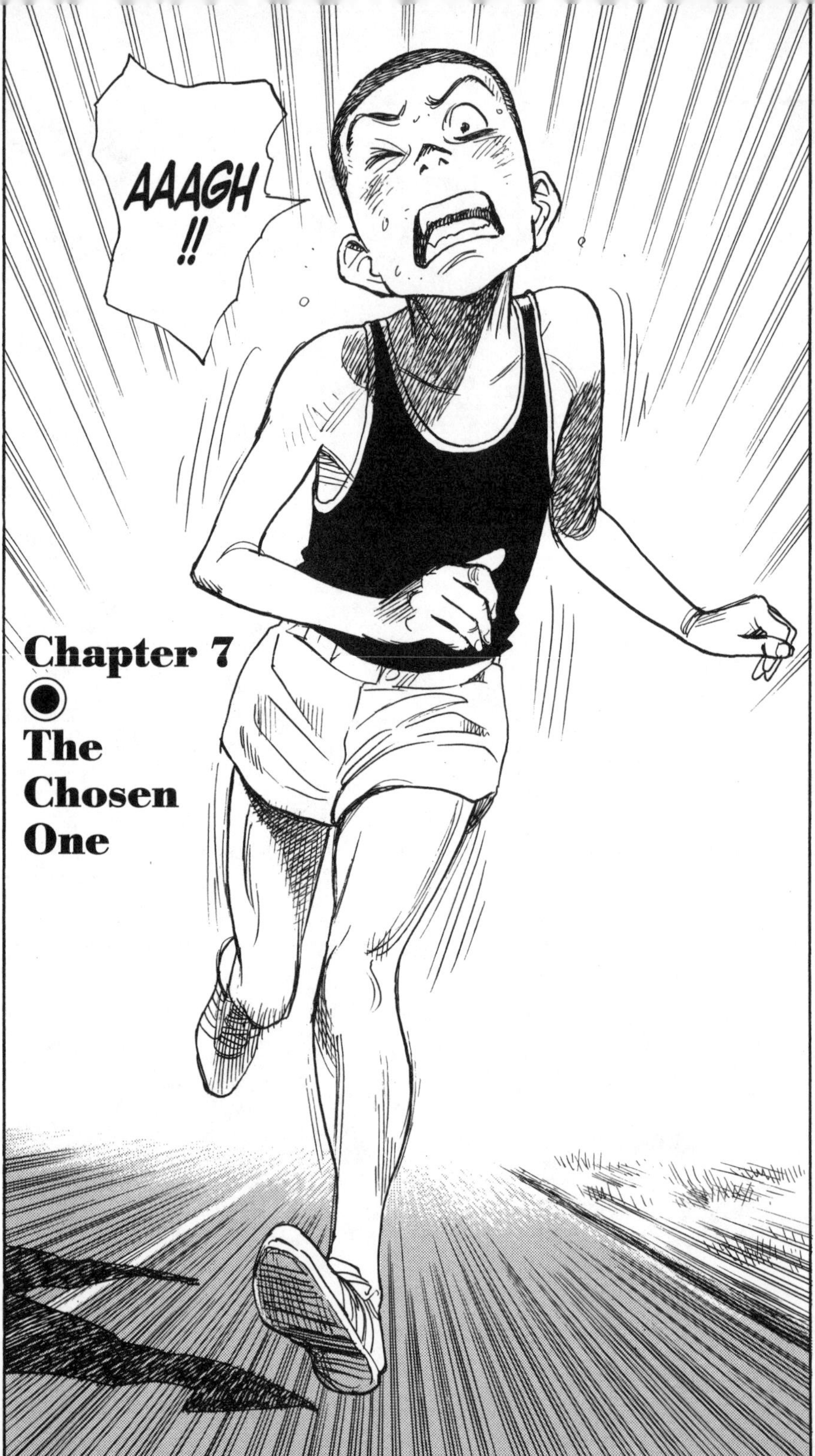
AAAGH !!

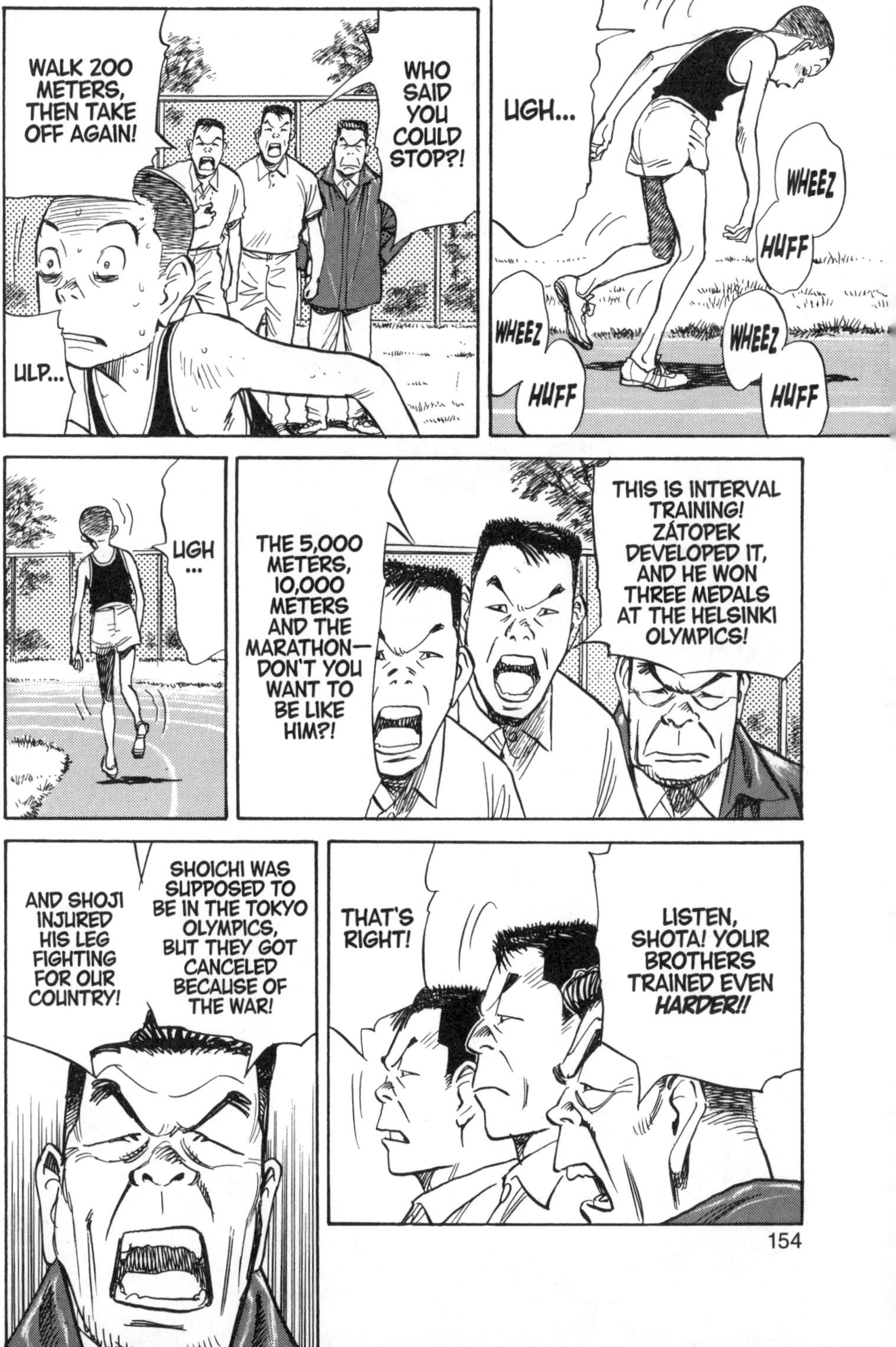
WHEEZ
HUFF
UGH...
WHEEZ
HUFF
WHEEZ
HUFF
WHO SAID YOU COULD STOP?!
WALK 200 METERS, THEN TAKE OFF AGAIN!
ULP...
THIS IS INTERVAL TRAINING! ZÁTOPEK DEVELOPED IT, AND HE WON THREE MEDALS AT THE HELSINKI OLYMPICS!
THE 5,000 METERS, 10,000 METERS AND THE MARATHON— DON'T YOU WANT TO BE LIKE HIM?!
UGH ...
LISTEN, SHOTA! YOUR BROTHERS TRAINED EVEN *HARDER!!*
THAT'S RIGHT!
SHOICHI WAS SUPPOSED TO BE IN THE TOKYO OLYMPICS, BUT THEY GOT CANCELED BECAUSE OF THE WAR!
AND SHOJI INJURED HIS LEG FIGHTING FOR OUR COUNTRY!

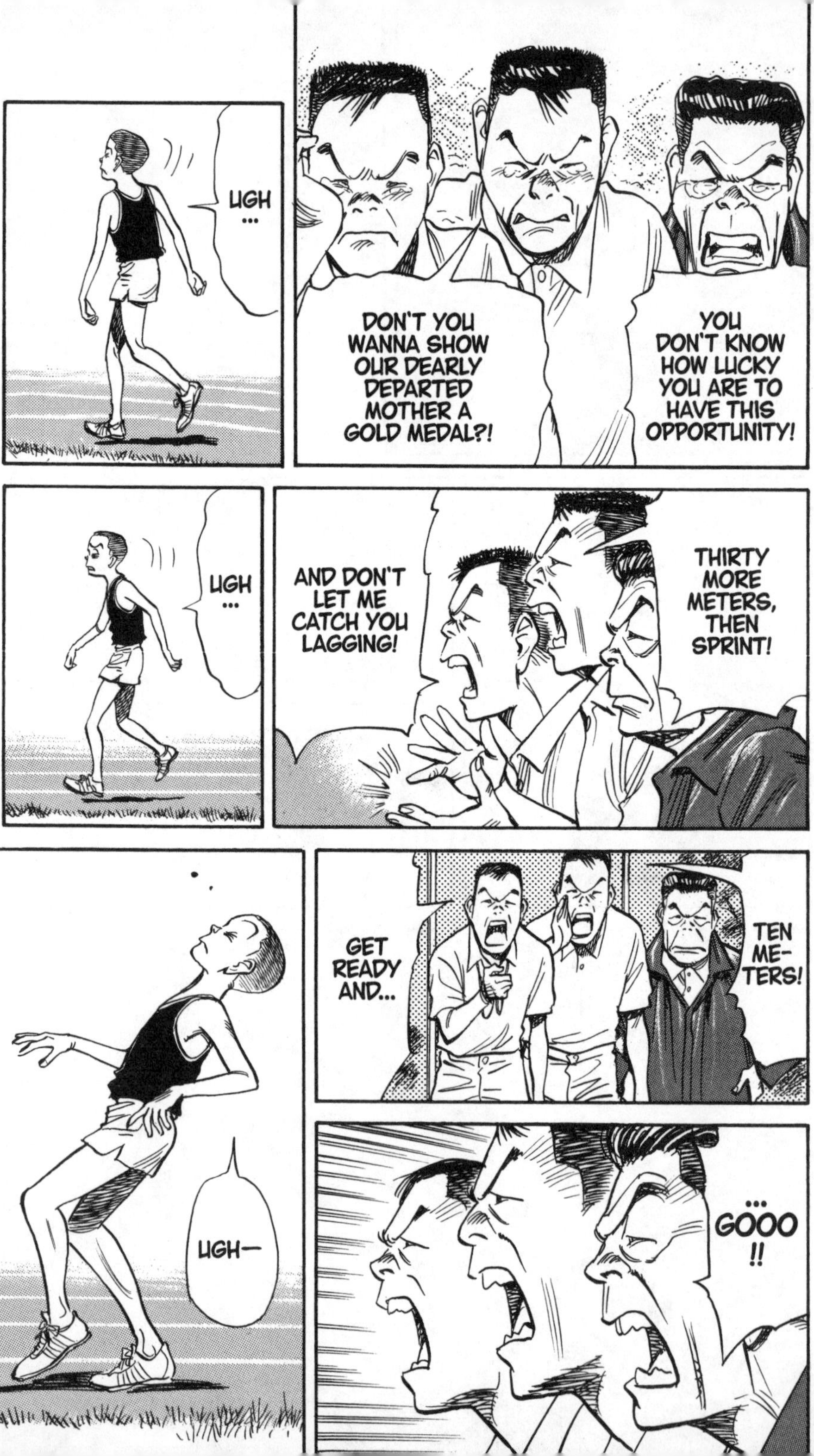
YOU DON'T KNOW HOW LUCKY YOU ARE TO HAVE THIS OPPORTUNITY!
DON'T YOU WANNA SHOW OUR DEARLY DEPARTED MOTHER A GOLD MEDAL?!
UGH ...
THIRTY MORE METERS, THEN SPRINT!
AND DON'T LET ME CATCH YOU LAGGING!
UGH ...
TEN ME-TERS!
GET READY AND...
... GÖOO !!
UGH—

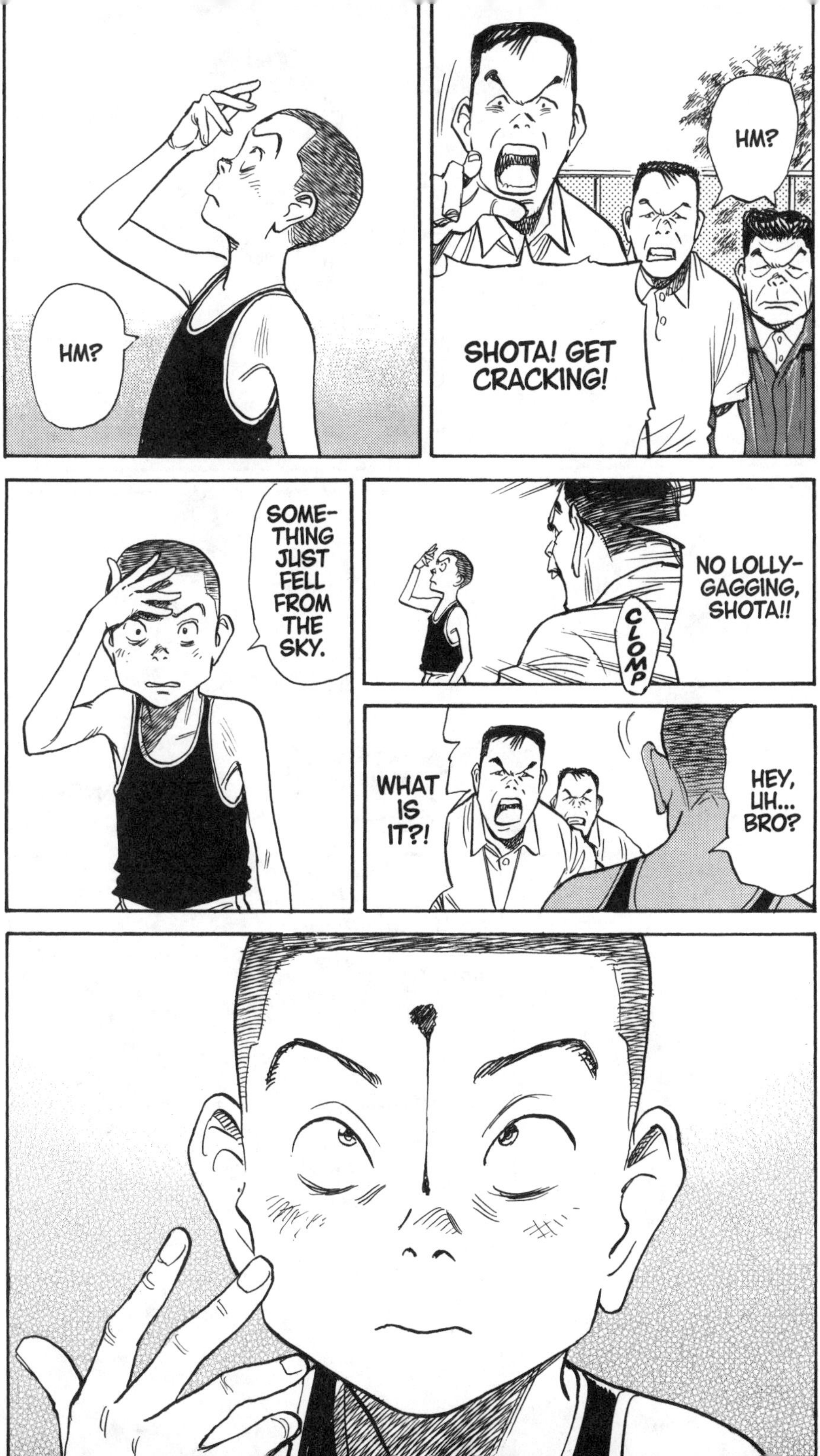
HM?
SHOTA! GET CRACKING!
HM?
NO LOLLY-GAGGING, SHOTA!!
CLOMP
HEY, UH... BRO?
WHAT IS IT?!
SOME-THING JUST FELL FROM THE SKY.

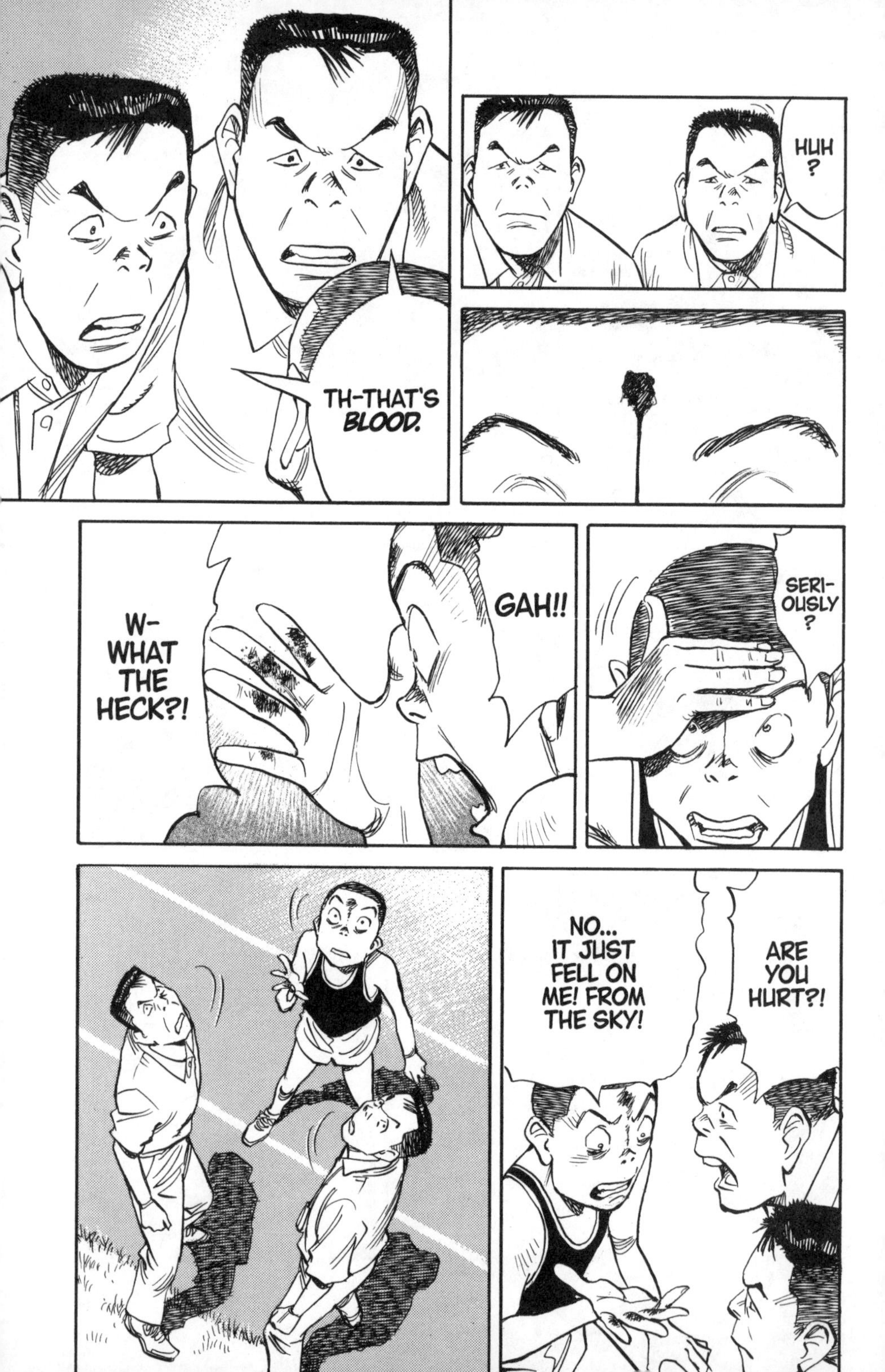
HUH ?
TH-THAT'S BLOOD.
SERI-OUSLY ?
GAH!!
W-WHAT THE HECK?!
ARE YOU HURT?!
NO... IT JUST FELL ON ME! FROM THE SKY!

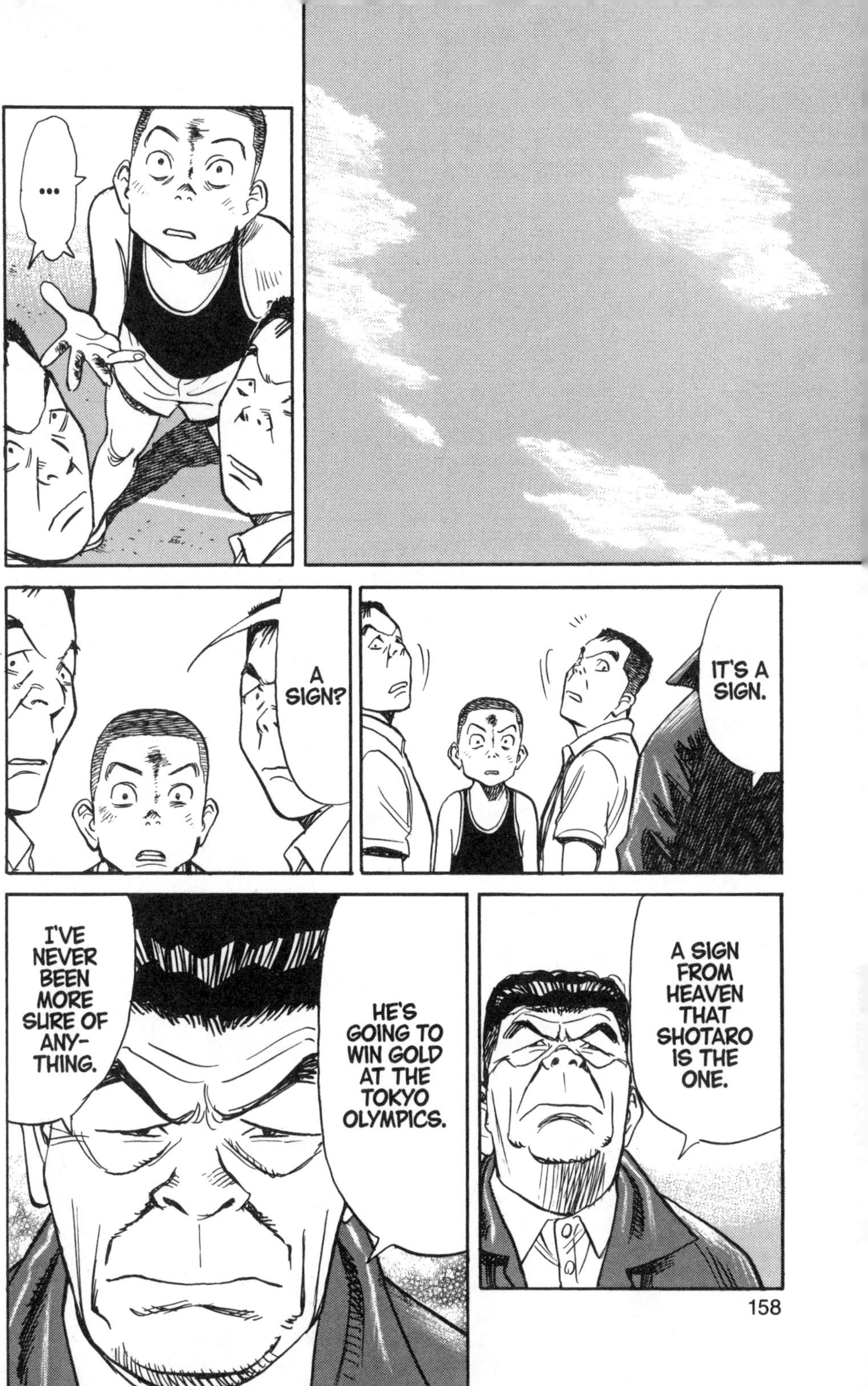
...
IT'S A SIGN.
A SIGN?
A SIGN FROM HEAVEN THAT SHOTARO IS THE ONE.
HE'S GOING TO WIN GOLD AT THE TOKYO OLYMPICS.
I'VE NEVER BEEN MORE SURE OF ANYTHING.

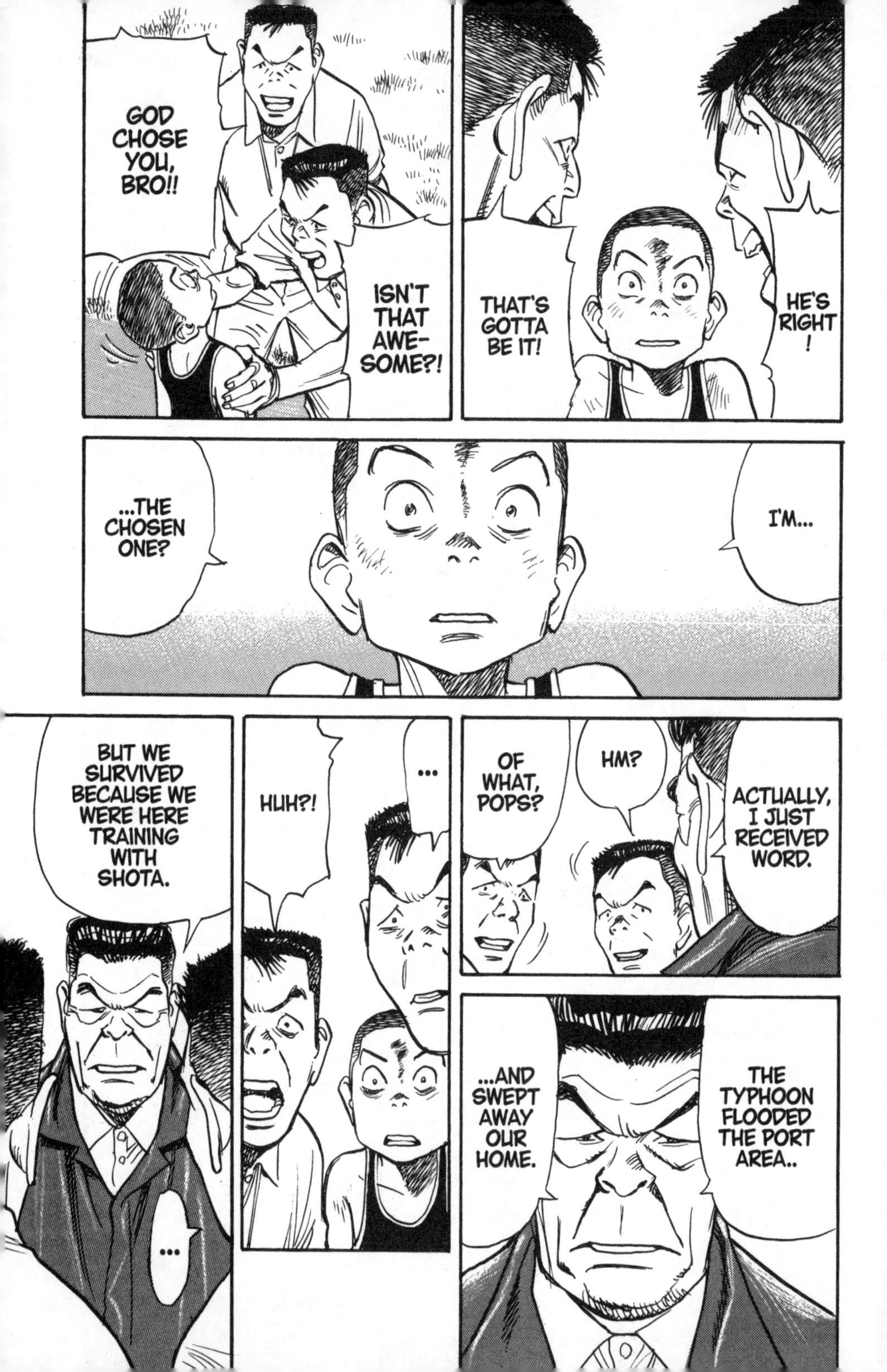
HE'S RIGHT!
THAT'S GOTTA BE IT!
GOD CHOSE YOU, BRO!!
ISN'T THAT AWE-SOME?!
I'M...
...THE CHOSEN ONE?
ACTUALLY, I JUST RECEIVED WORD.
HM?
OF WHAT, POPS?
THE TYPHOON FLOODED THE PORT AREA..
...AND SWEPT AWAY OUR HOME.
...
HUH?!
BUT WE SURVIVED BECAUSE WE WERE HERE TRAINING WITH SHOTA.
...

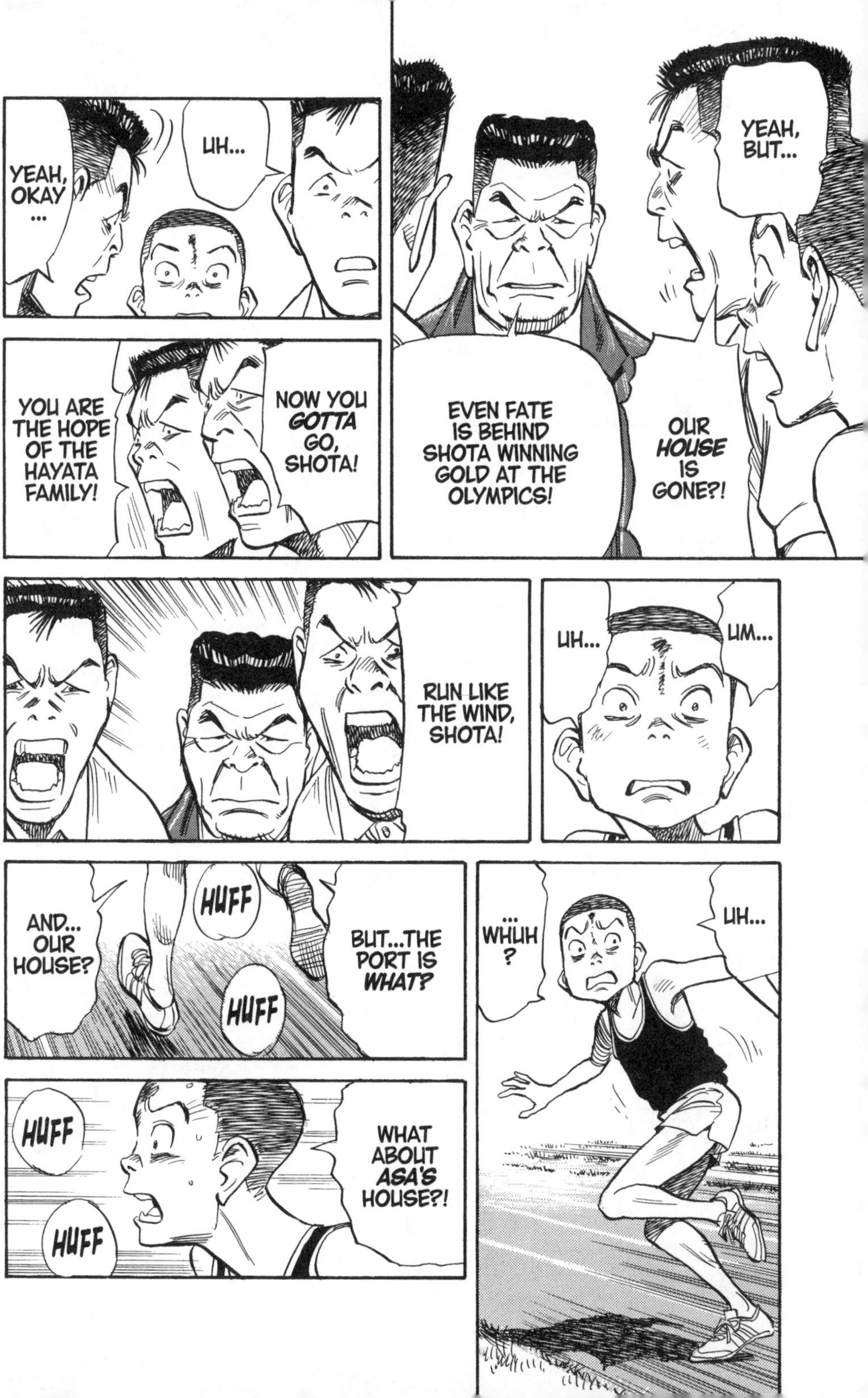
YEAH, BUT...
OUR *HOUSE* IS GONE?!
EVEN FATE IS BEHIND SHOTA WINNING GOLD AT THE OLYMPICS!
UH...
YEAH, OKAY ...
NOW YOU *GOTTA* GO, SHOTA!
YOU ARE THE HOPE OF THE HAYATA FAMILY!
UM...
UH...
RUN LIKE THE WIND, SHOTA!
UH...
... WHUH ?
BUT...THE PORT IS *WHAT?*
HUFF
HUFF
AND... OUR HOUSE?
WHAT ABOUT *ASA'S* HOUSE?!
HUFF
HUFF

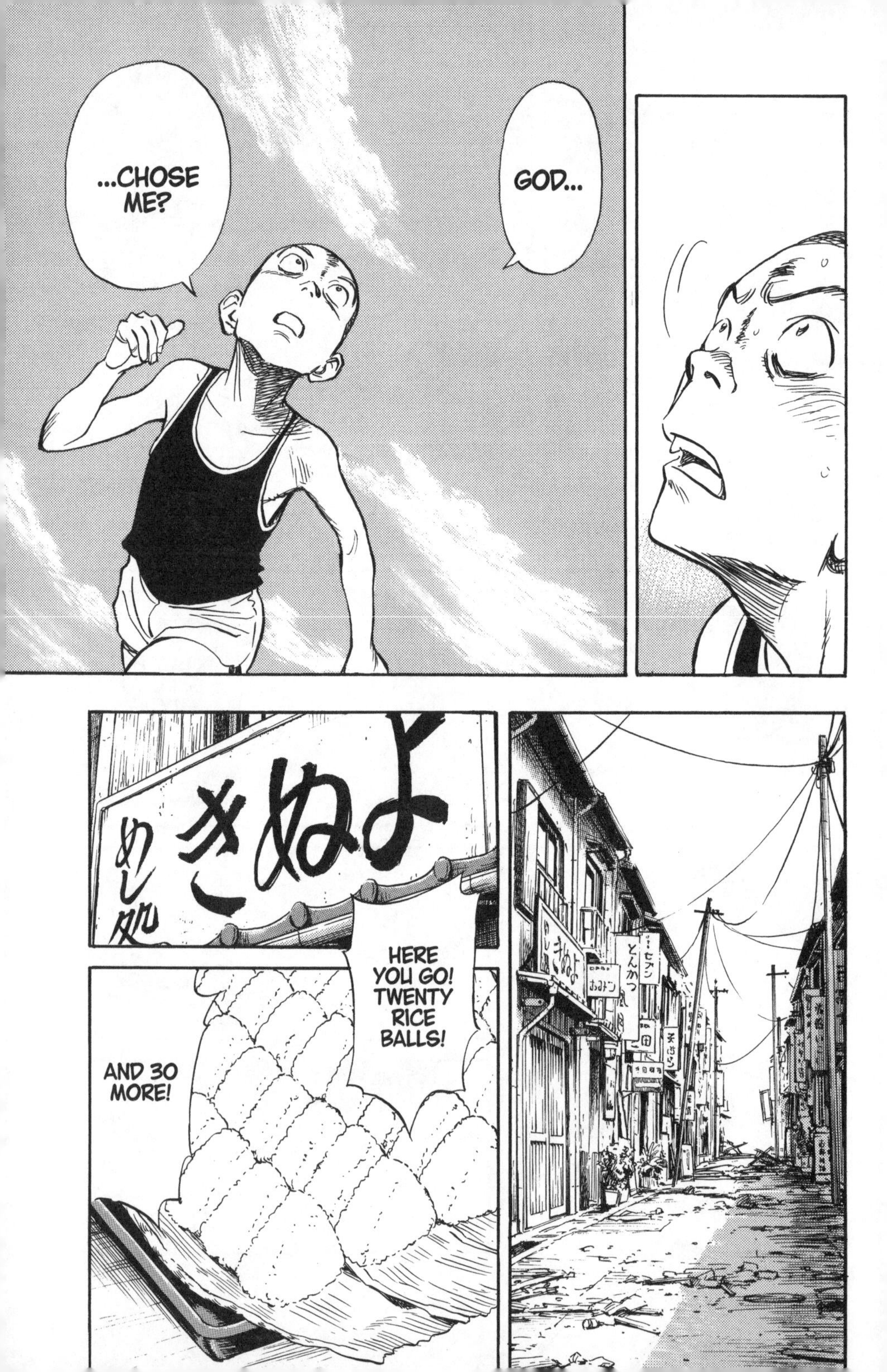
GOD...
...CHOSE ME?
めし処
きぬよ
HERE YOU GO! TWENTY RICE BALLS!
AND 30 MORE!

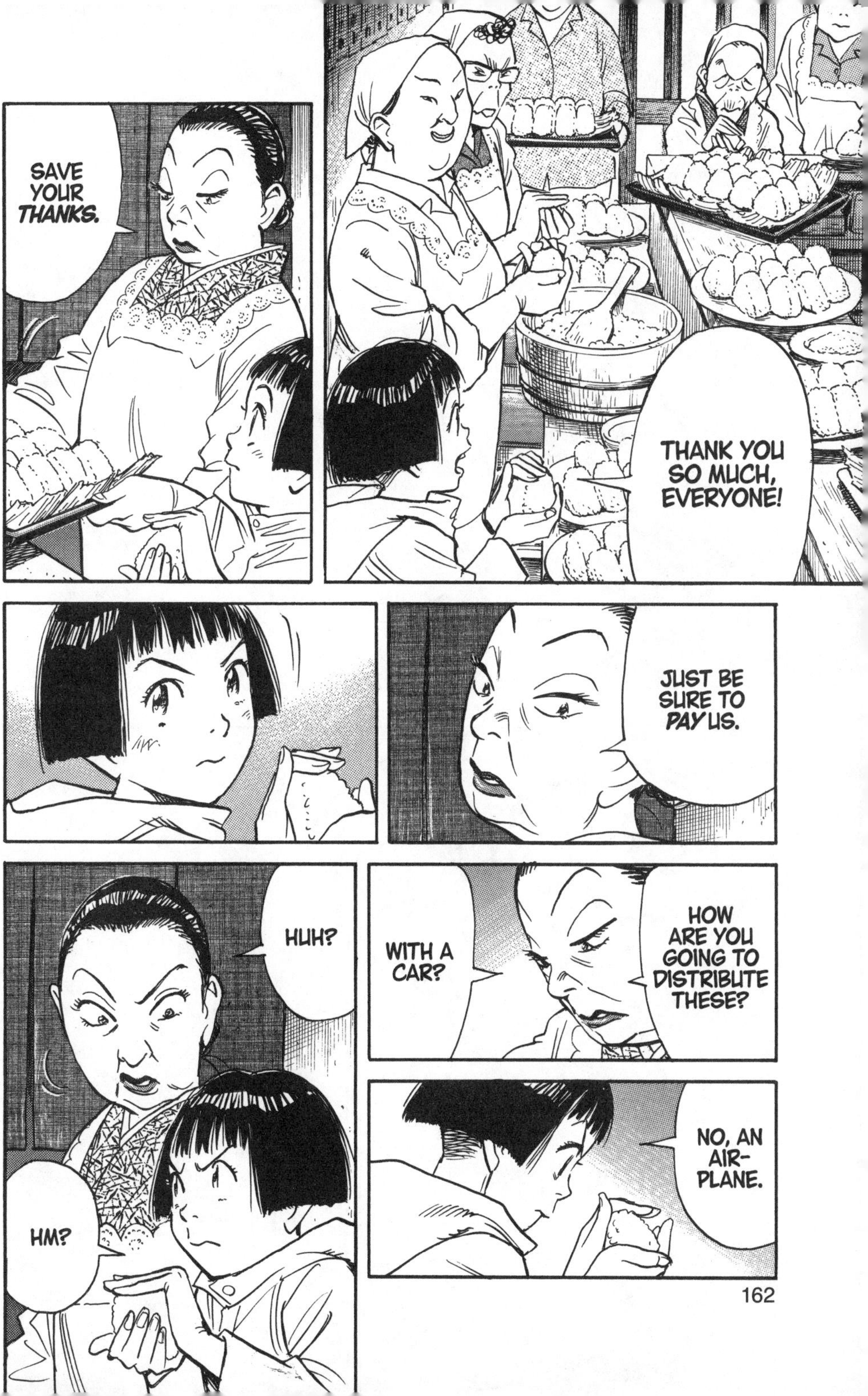
THANK YOU SO MUCH, EVERYONE!
SAVE YOUR THANKS.
JUST BE SURE TO PAY US.
HOW ARE YOU GOING TO DISTRIBUTE THESE?
WITH A CAR?
NO, AN AIR-PLANE.
HUH?
HM?

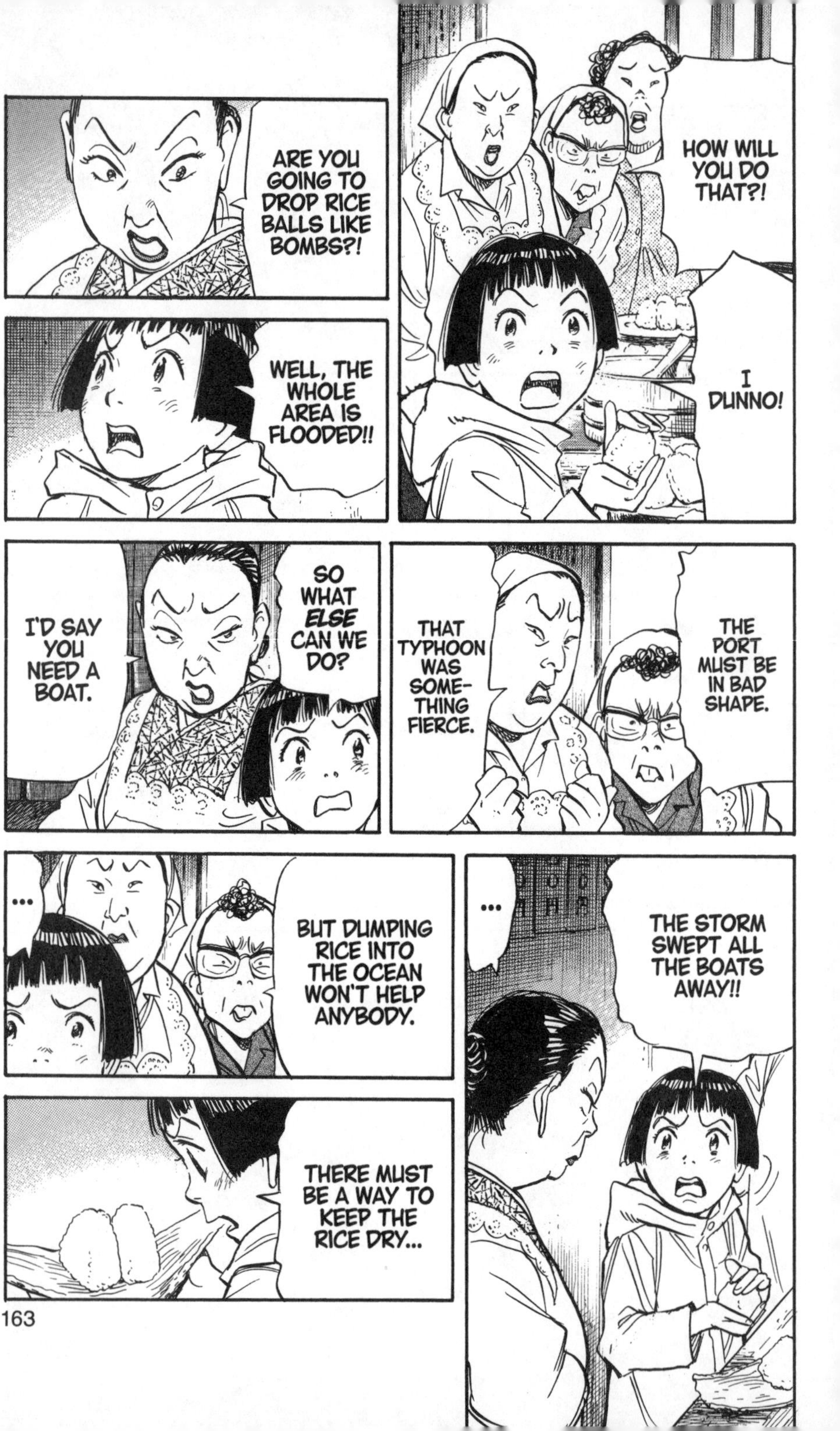
HOW WILL YOU DO THAT?!
I DUNNO!
ARE YOU GOING TO DROP RICE BALLS LIKE BOMBS?!
WELL, THE WHOLE AREA IS FLOODED!!
THE PORT MUST BE IN BAD SHAPE.
THAT TYPHOON WAS SOME-THING FIERCE.
SO WHAT ELSE CAN WE DO?
I'D SAY YOU NEED A BOAT.
THE STORM SWEPT ALL THE BOATS AWAY!!
...
BUT DUMPING RICE INTO THE OCEAN WON'T HELP ANYBODY.
...
THERE MUST BE A WAY TO KEEP THE RICE DRY...

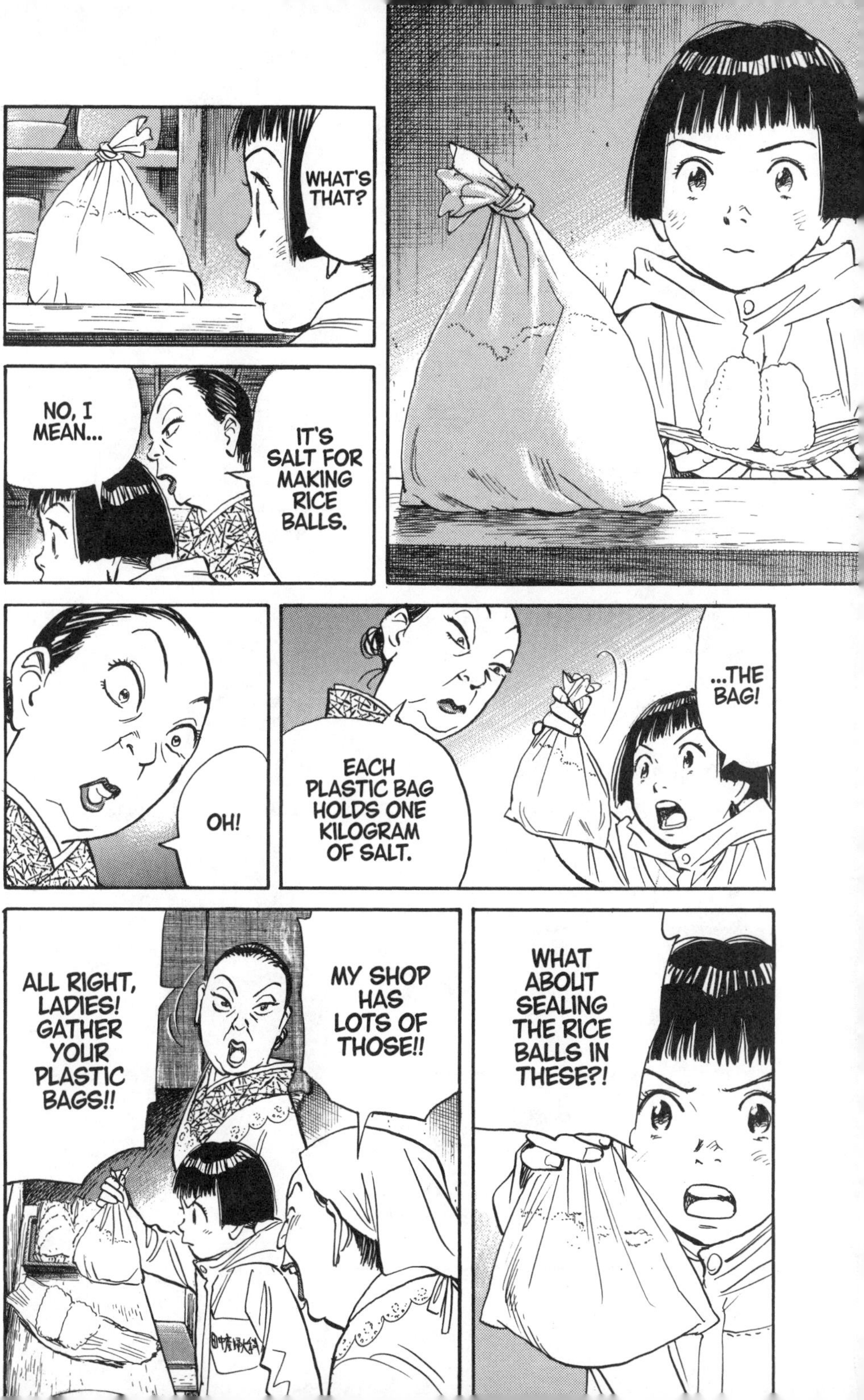
WHAT'S THAT?
IT'S SALT FOR MAKING RICE BALLS.
NO, I MEAN...
...THE BAG!
EACH PLASTIC BAG HOLDS ONE KILOGRAM OF SALT.
OH!
WHAT ABOUT SEALING THE RICE BALLS IN THESE?!
MY SHOP HAS LOTS OF THOSE!!
ALL RIGHT, LADIES! GATHER YOUR PLASTIC BAGS!!

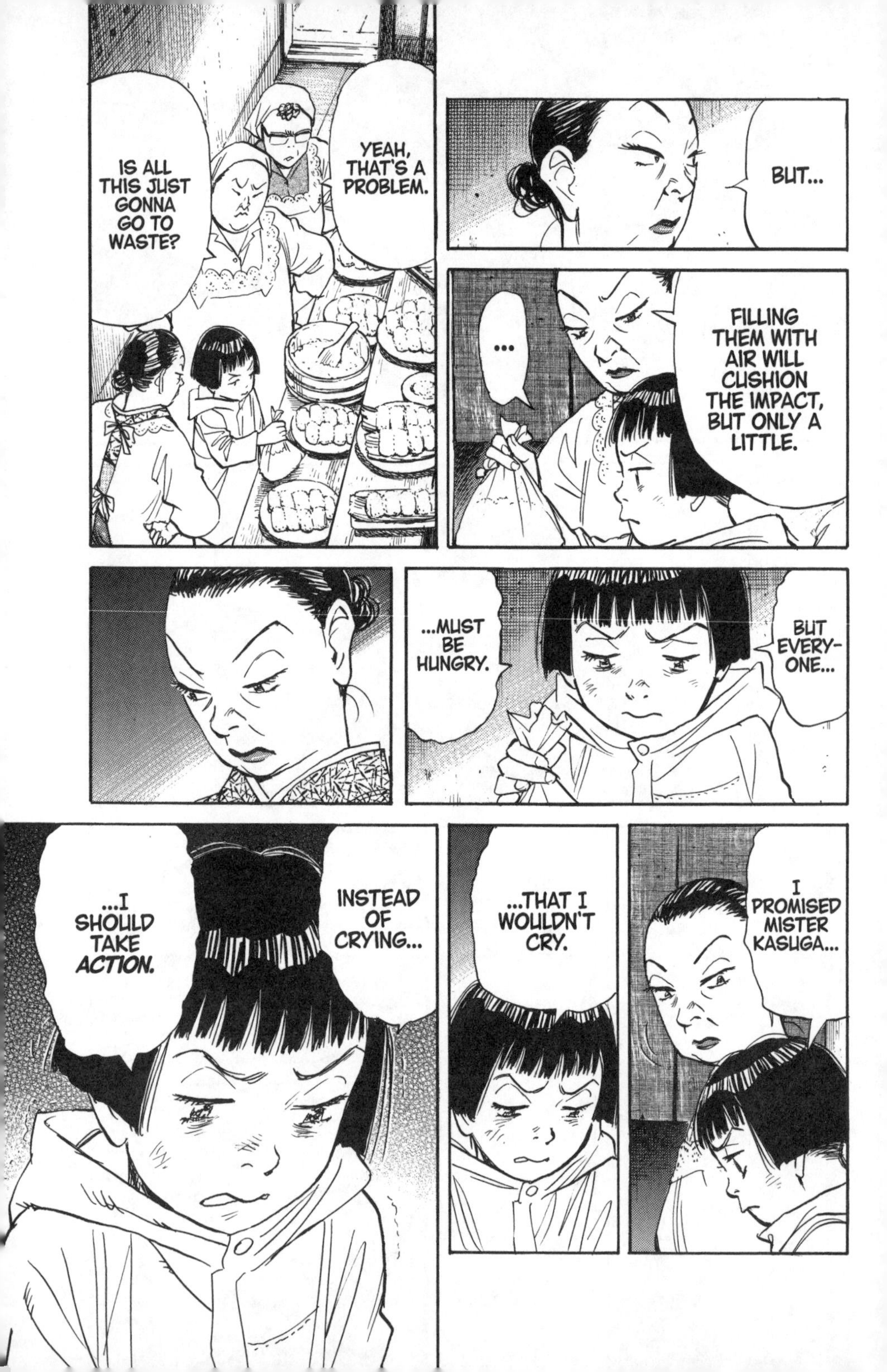
BUT...
FILLING THEM WITH AIR WILL CUSHION THE IMPACT, BUT ONLY A LITTLE.
...
YEAH, THAT'S A PROBLEM.
IS ALL THIS JUST GONNA GO TO WASTE?
BUT EVERY-ONE...
...MUST BE HUNGRY.
I PROMISED MISTER KASUGA...
...THAT I WOULDN'T CRY.
INSTEAD OF CRYING...
...I SHOULD TAKE *ACTION.*

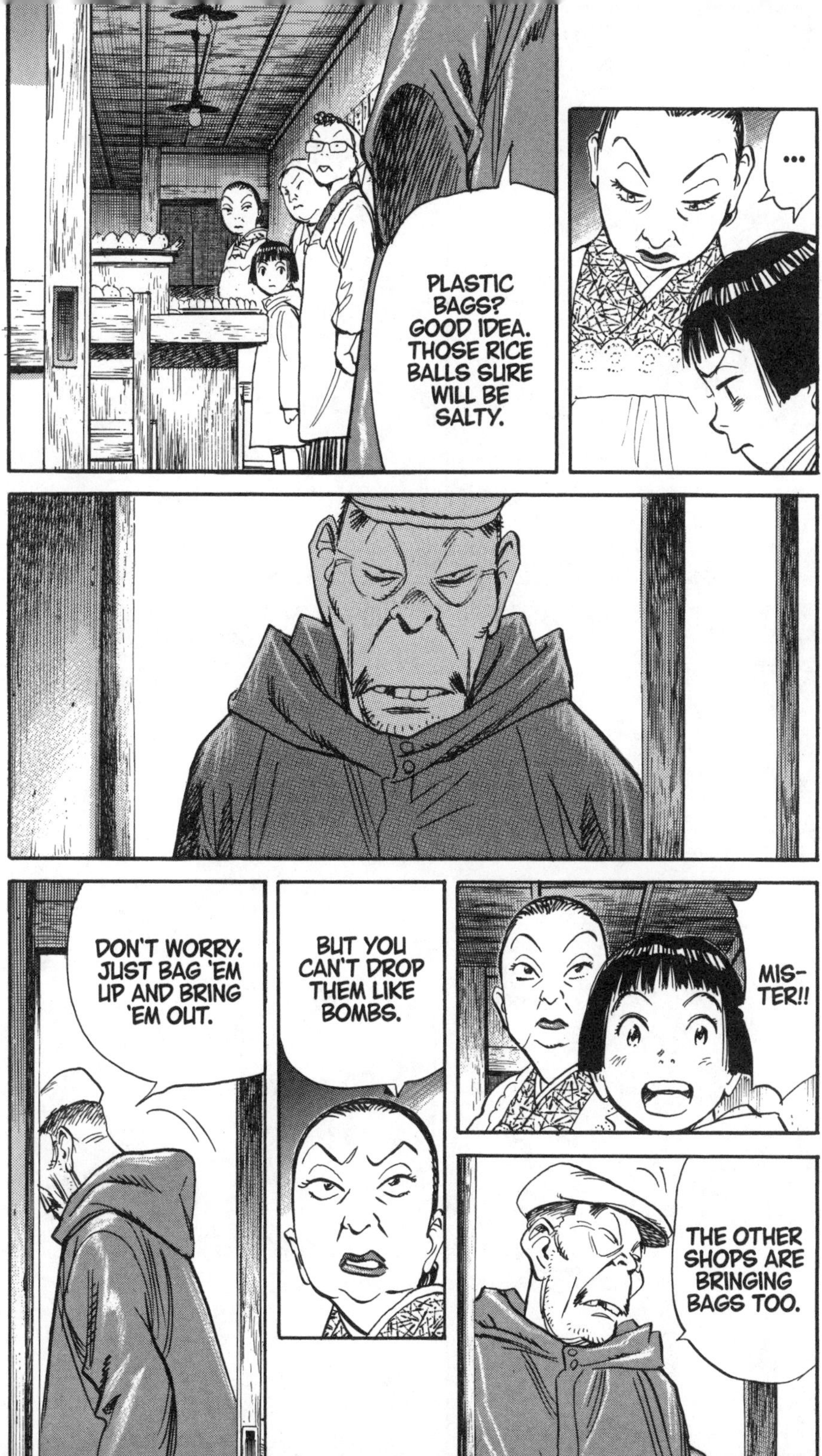
...
PLASTIC BAGS? GOOD IDEA. THOSE RICE BALLS SURE WILL BE SALTY.
MIS-TER!!
THE OTHER SHOPS ARE BRINGING BAGS TOO.
BUT YOU CAN'T DROP THEM LIKE BOMBS.
DON'T WORRY. JUST BAG 'EM UP AND BRING 'EM OUT.

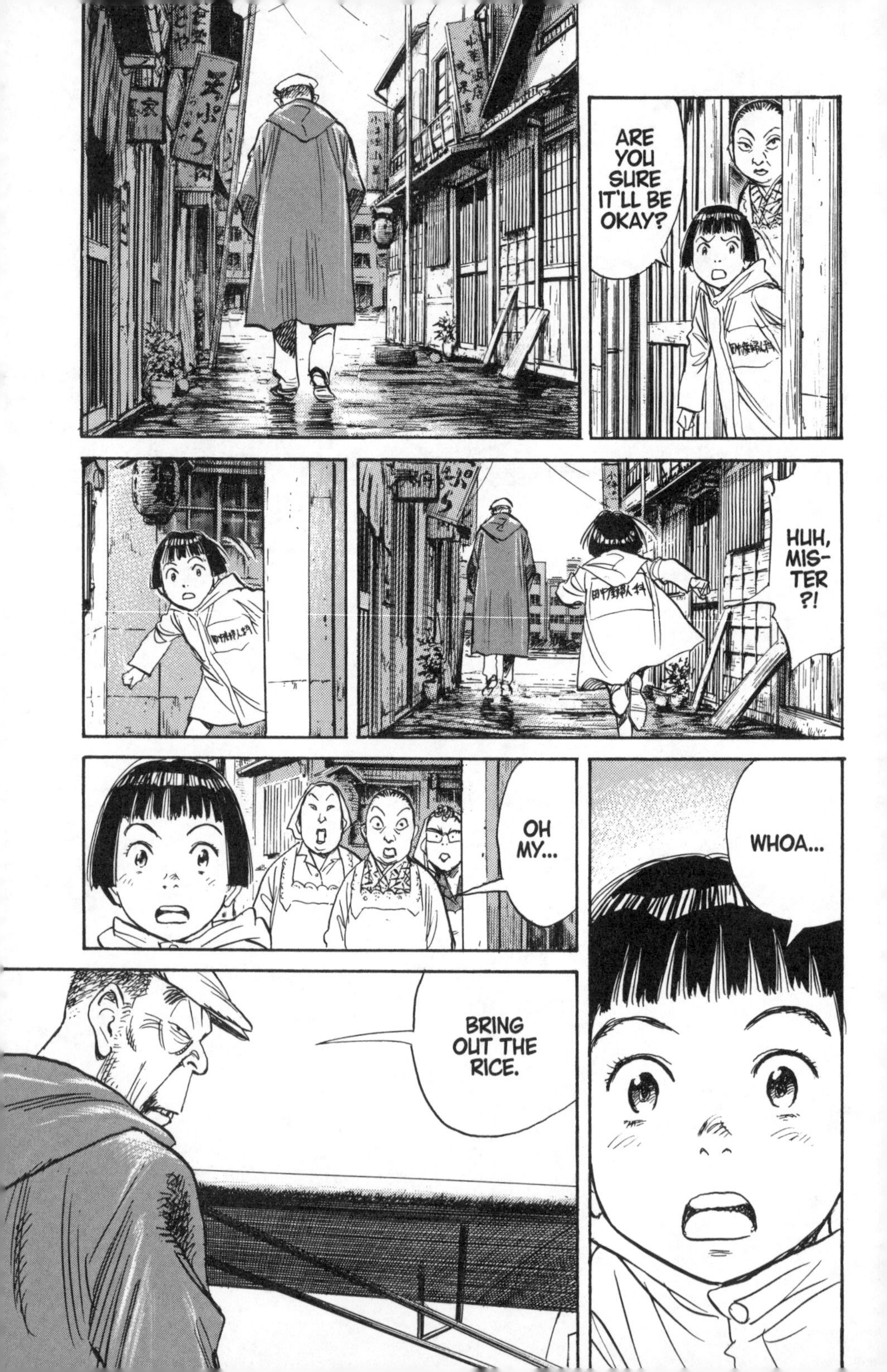
ARE YOU SURE IT'LL BE OKAY?
HUH, MISTER?!
WHOA...
OH MY...
BRING OUT THE RICE.

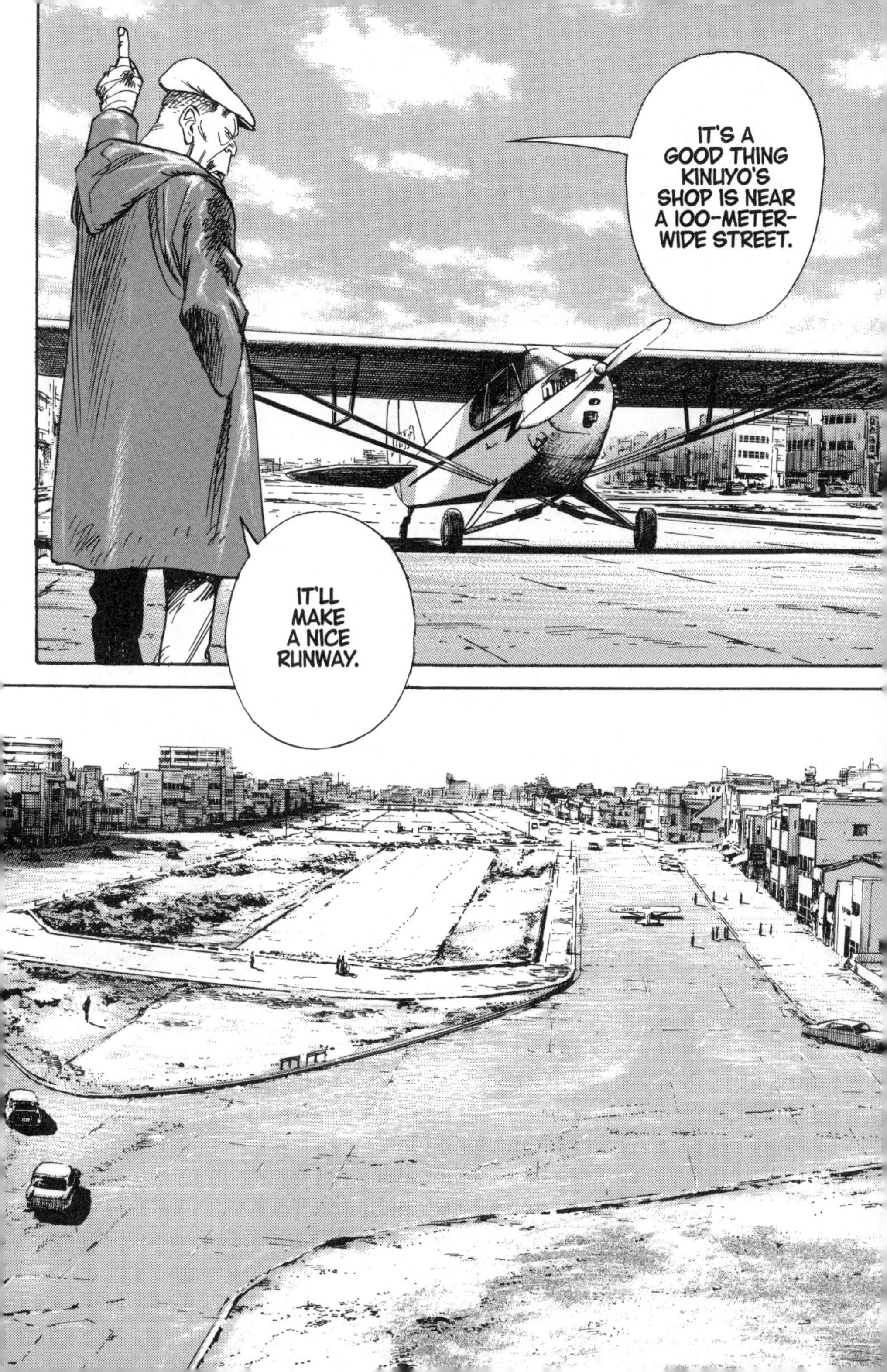
IT'S A GOOD THING KINUYO'S SHOP IS NEAR A 100-METER-WIDE STREET.
IT'LL MAKE A NICE RUNWAY.

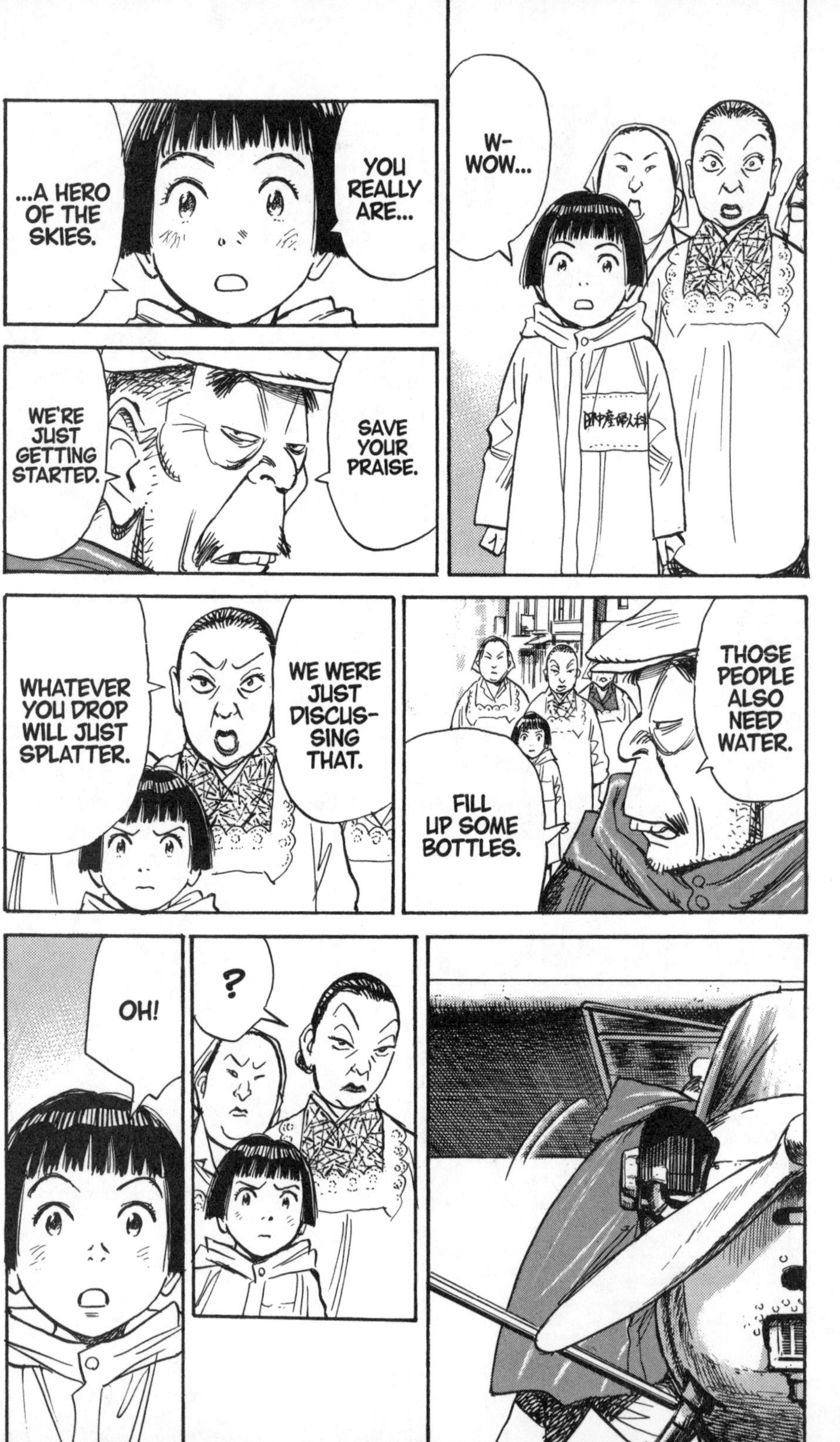
W-WOW...
YOU REALLY ARE...
...A HERO OF THE SKIES.
SAVE YOUR PRAISE.
WE'RE JUST GETTING STARTED.
THOSE PEOPLE ALSO NEED WATER.
FILL UP SOME BOTTLES.
WE WERE JUST DISCUS-SING THAT.
WHATEVER YOU DROP WILL JUST SPLATTER.
?
OH!

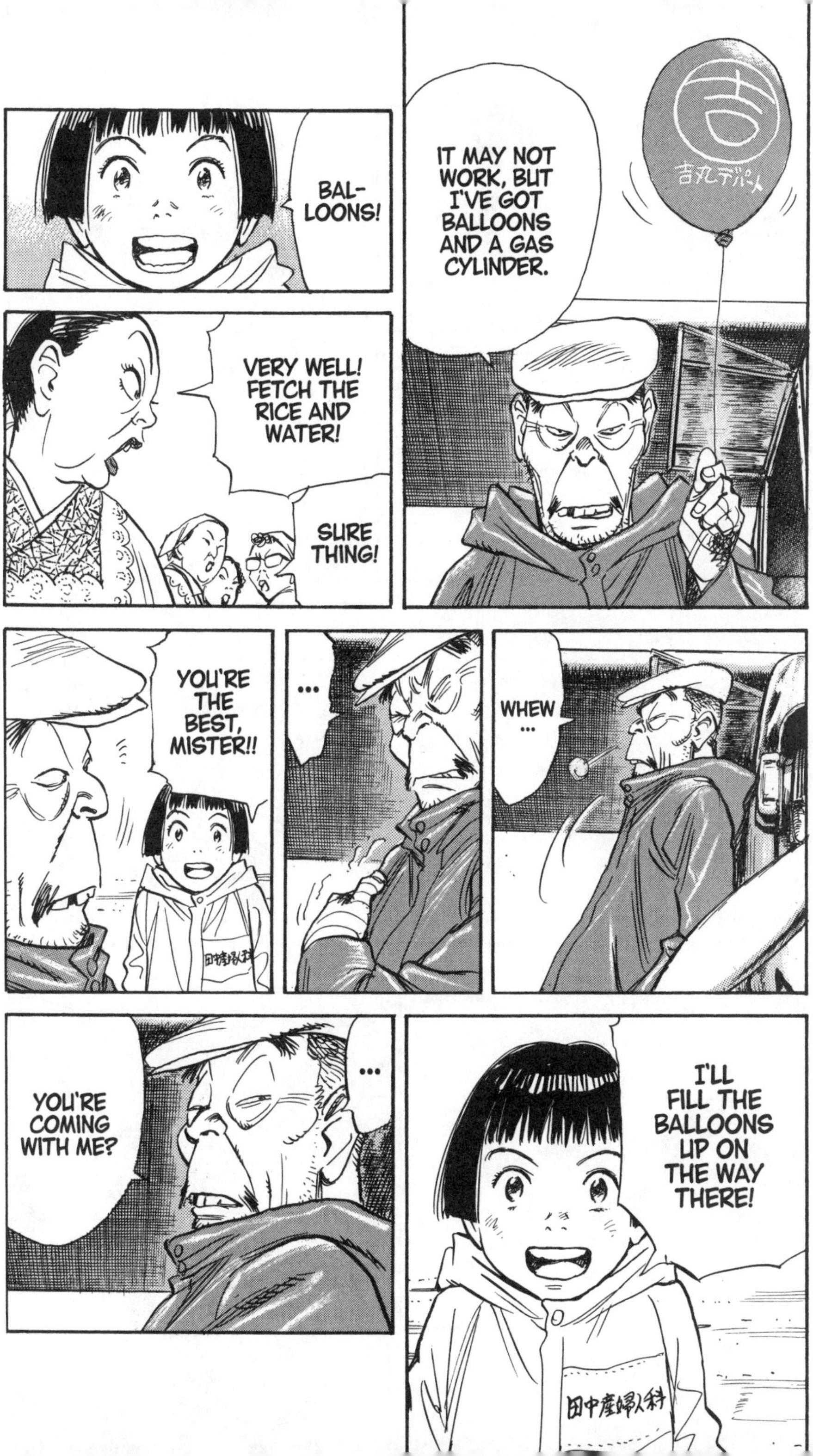
IT MAY NOT WORK, BUT I'VE GOT BALLOONS AND A GAS CYLINDER.
吉丸デパート
BAL-LOONS!
VERY WELL! FETCH THE RICE AND WATER!
SURE THING!
WHEW ...
...
YOU'RE THE BEST, MISTER!!
I'LL FILL THE BALLOONS UP ON THE WAY THERE!
田中産婦人科
...
YOU'RE COMING WITH ME?

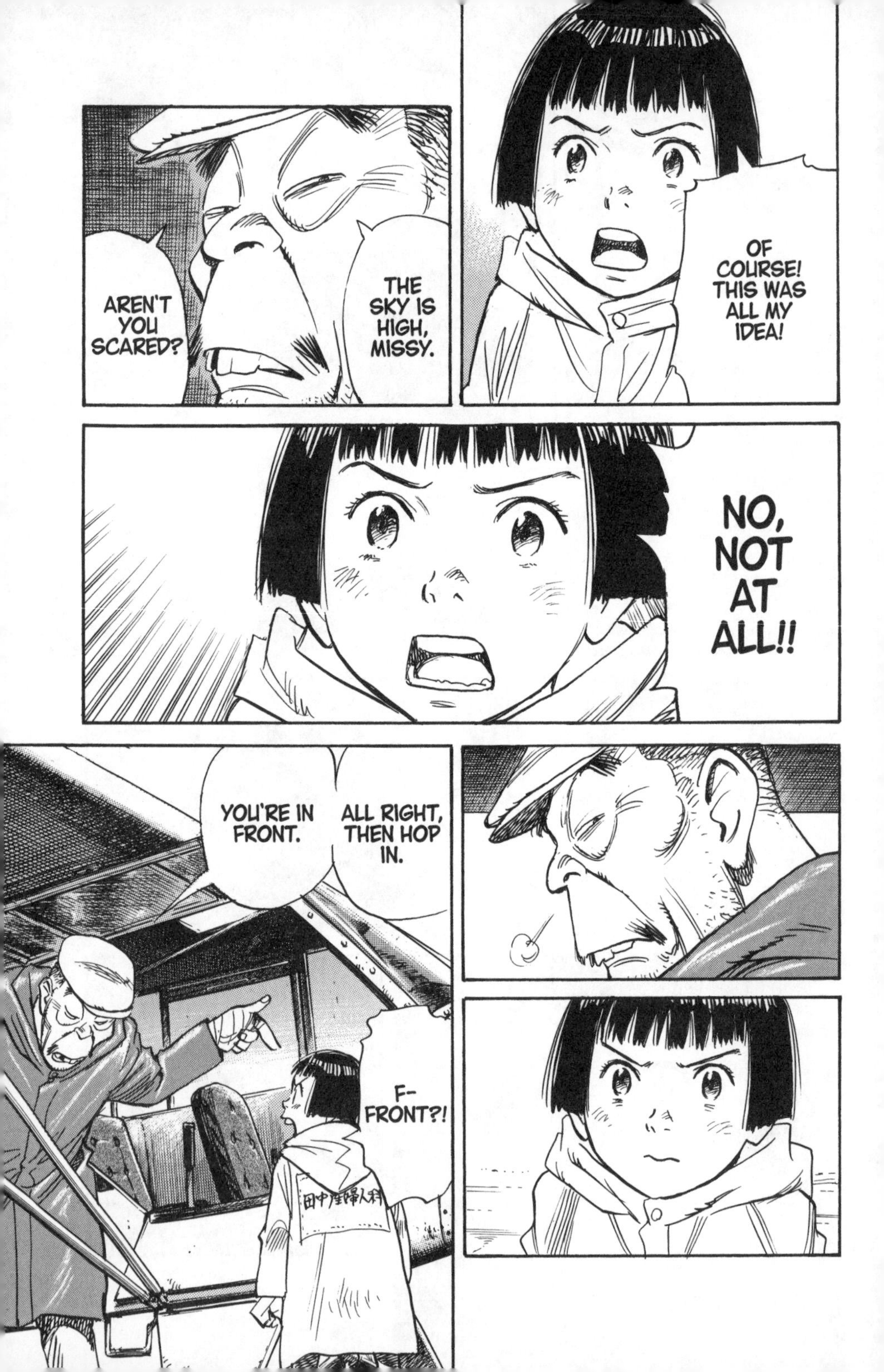
OF COURSE! THIS WAS ALL MY IDEA!
THE SKY IS HIGH, MISSY.
AREN'T YOU SCARED?
NO, NOT AT ALL!!
ALL RIGHT, THEN HOP IN.
YOU'RE IN FRONT.
F-FRONT?!
田中産婦人科

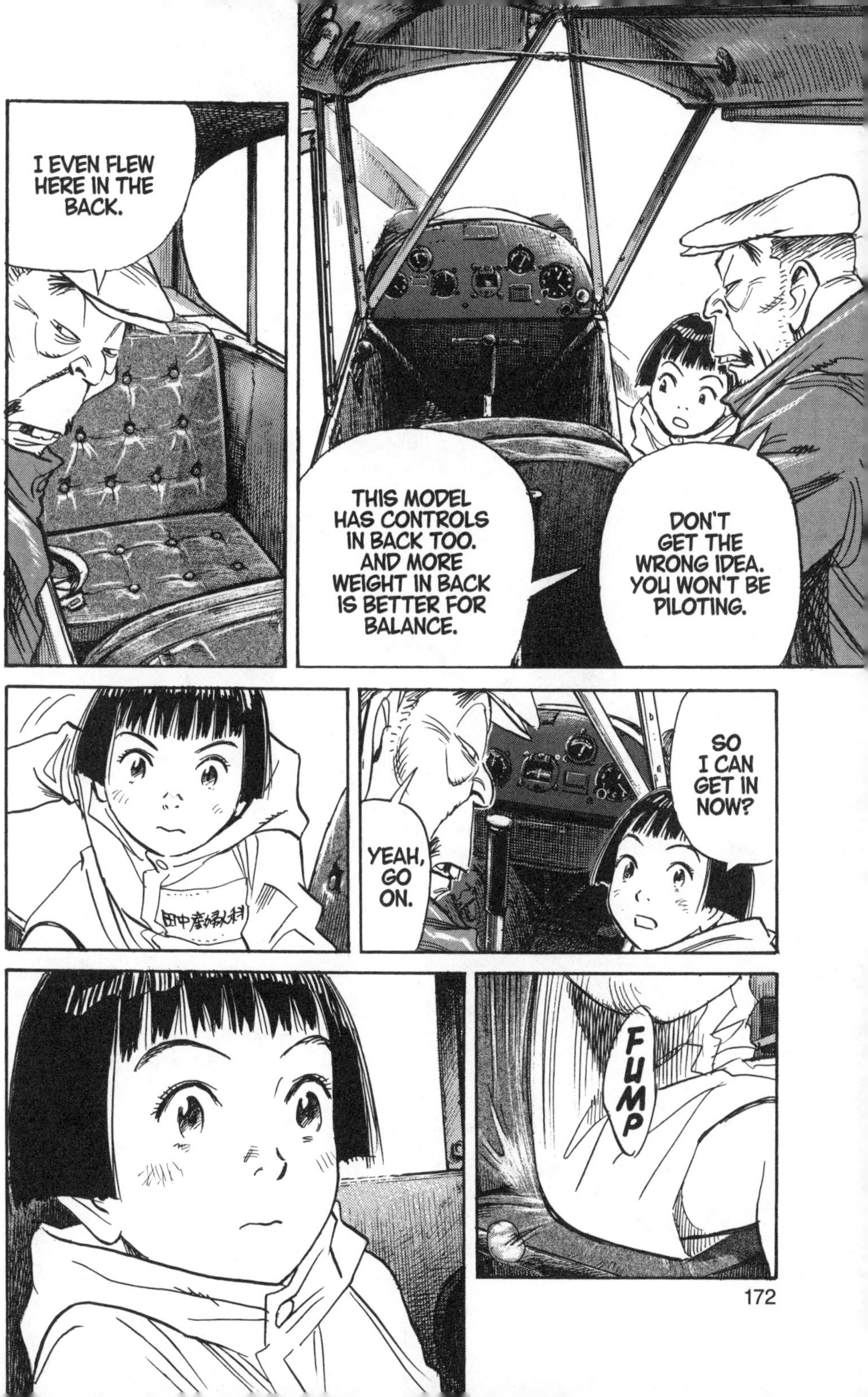
DON'T GET THE WRONG IDEA. YOU WON'T BE PILOTING.
THIS MODEL HAS CONTROLS IN BACK TOO. AND MORE WEIGHT IN BACK IS BETTER FOR BALANCE.
I EVEN FLEW HERE IN THE BACK.
SO I CAN GET IN NOW?
YEAH, GO ON.
田中産婦人科
FUMP

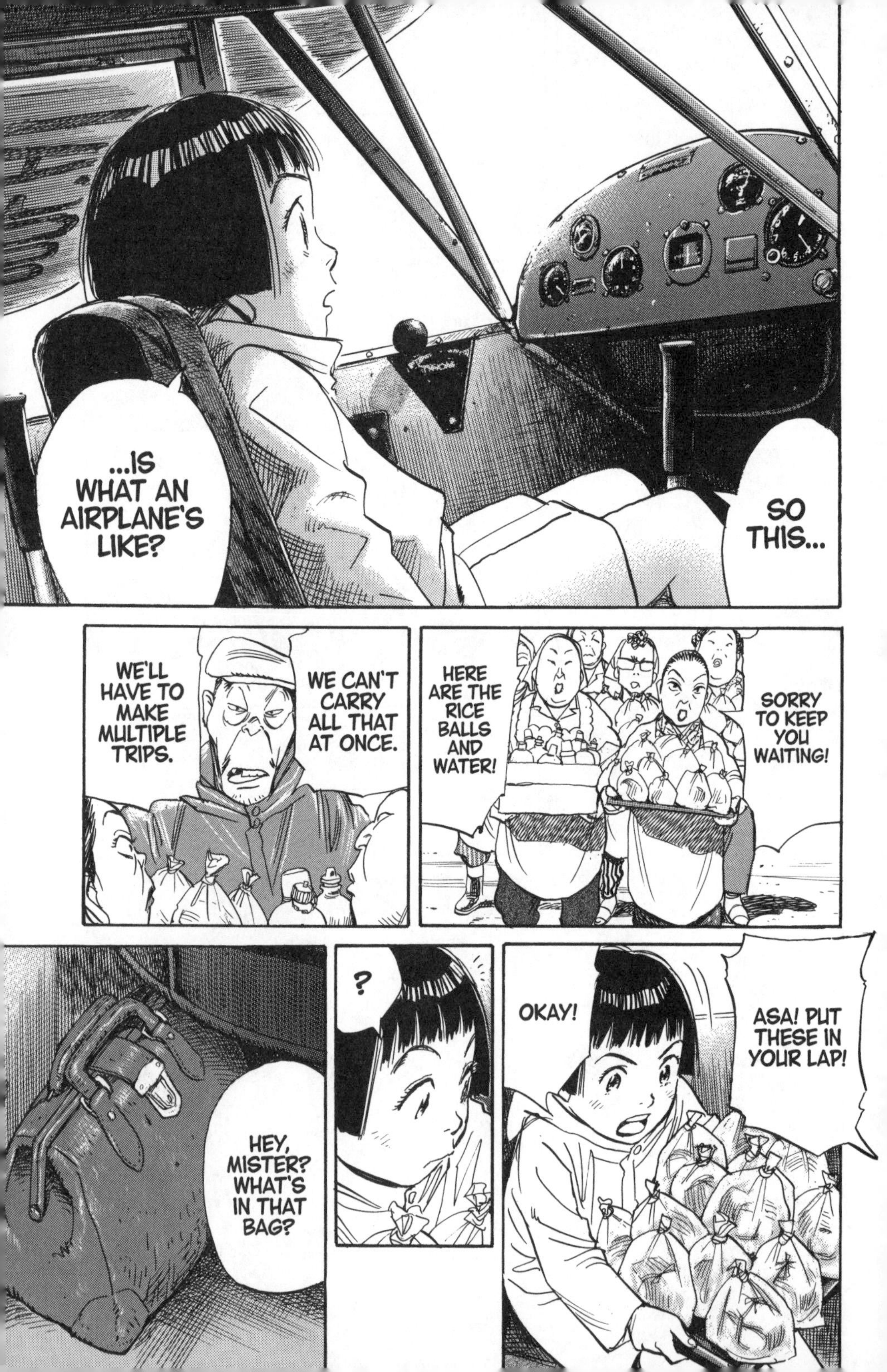
SO THIS...
...IS WHAT AN AIRPLANE'S LIKE?
SORRY TO KEEP YOU WAITING!
HERE ARE THE RICE BALLS AND WATER!
WE CAN'T CARRY ALL THAT AT ONCE.
WE'LL HAVE TO MAKE MULTIPLE TRIPS.
ASA! PUT THESE IN YOUR LAP!
OKAY!
?
HEY, MISTER? WHAT'S IN THAT BAG?

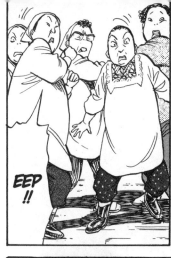

EEP
!!

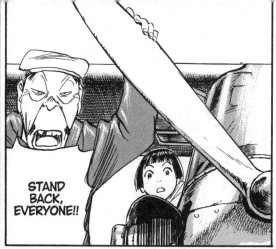

STAND
BACK,
EVERYONE!!

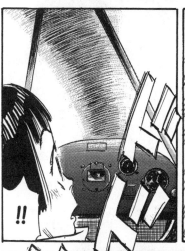

!!

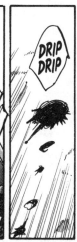

DRIP
DRIP

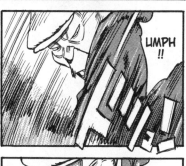

UMPH
!!

OW...

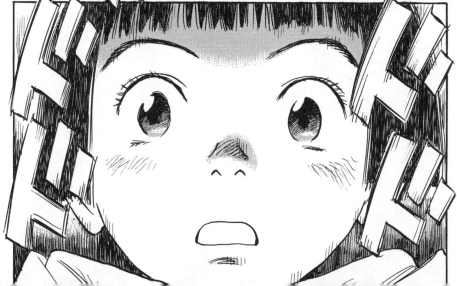

Chapter 8 ● Claw Marks

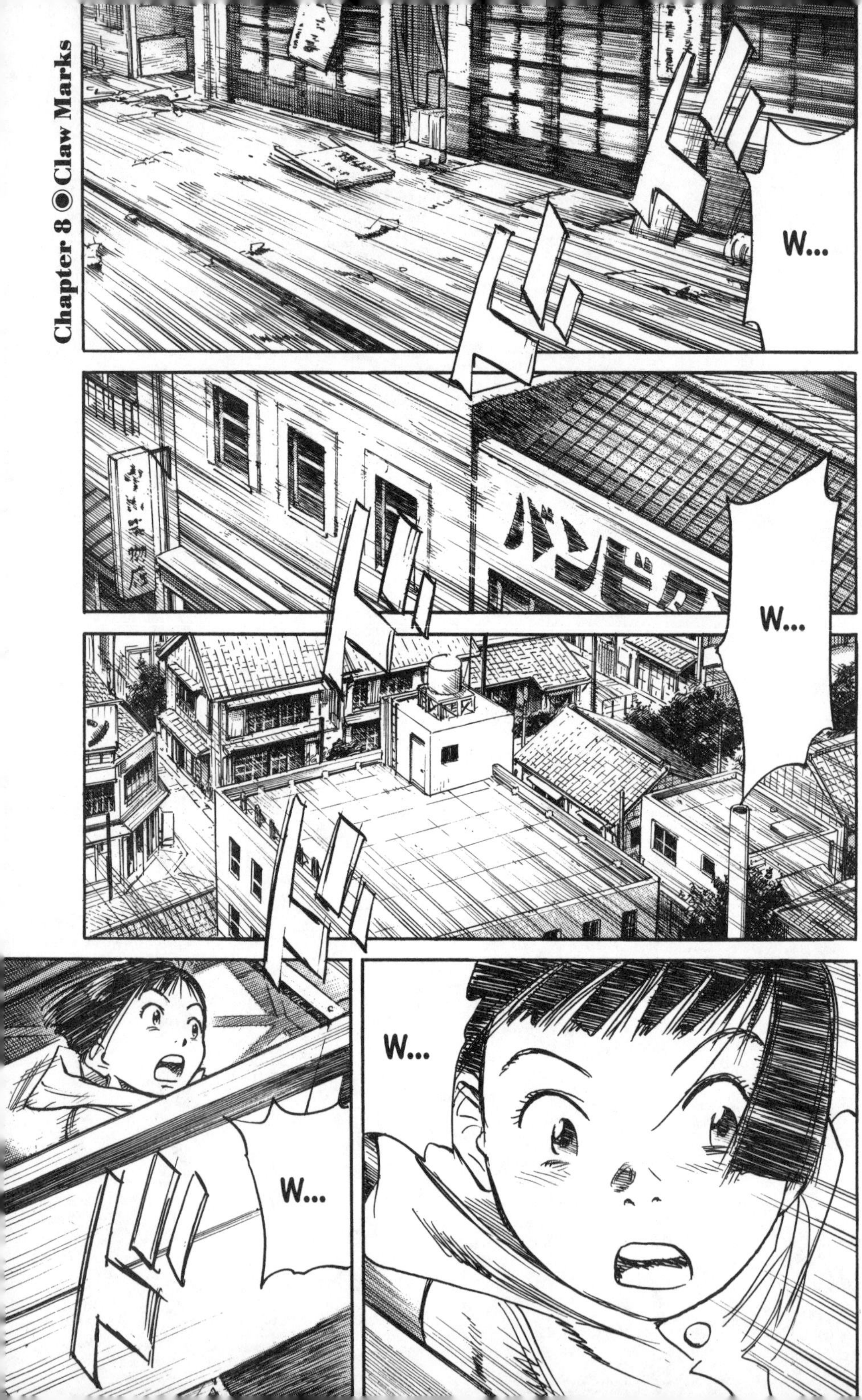
W...
W...
W...
W...
W...

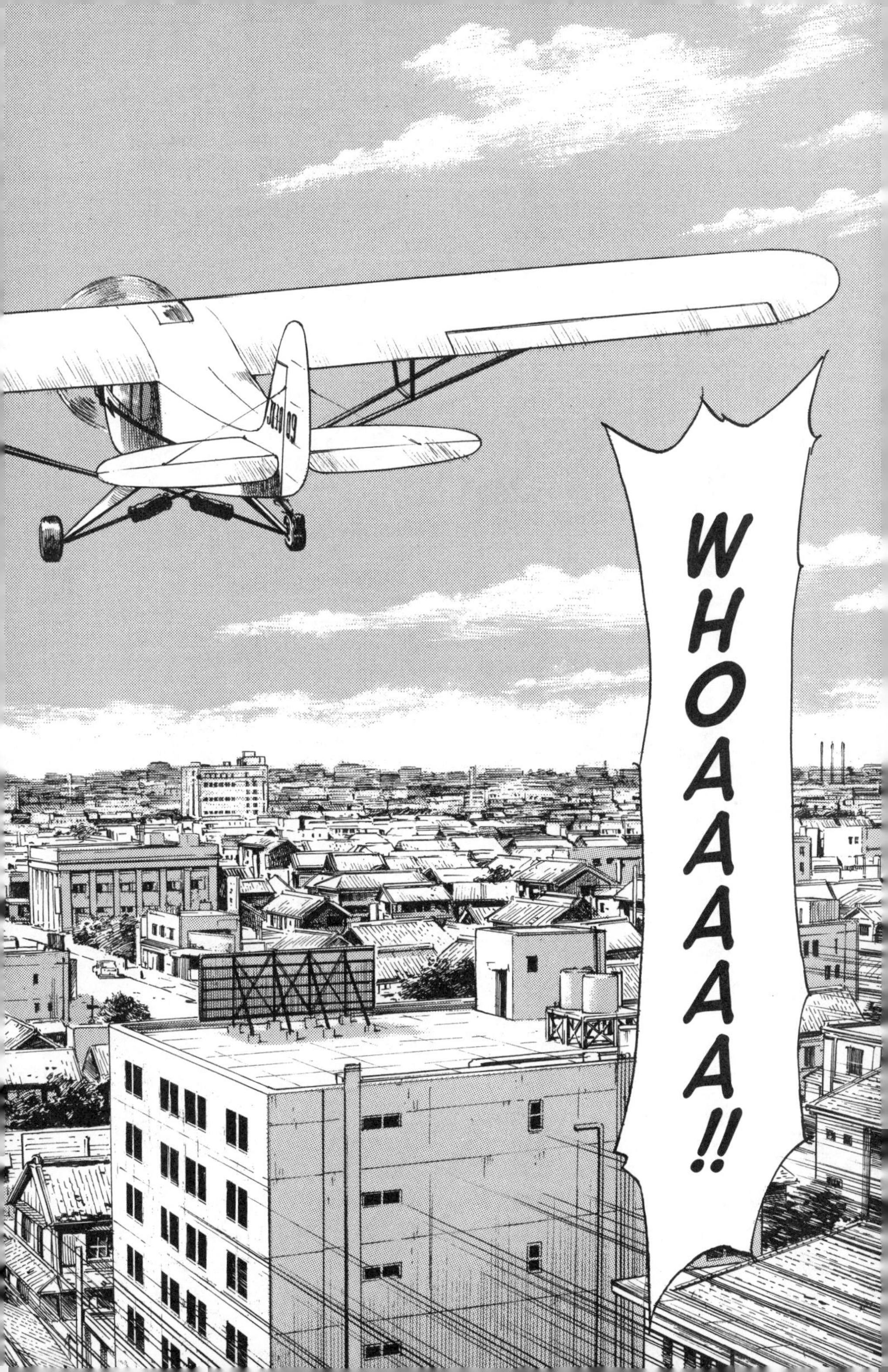
WHOAAAAA!!

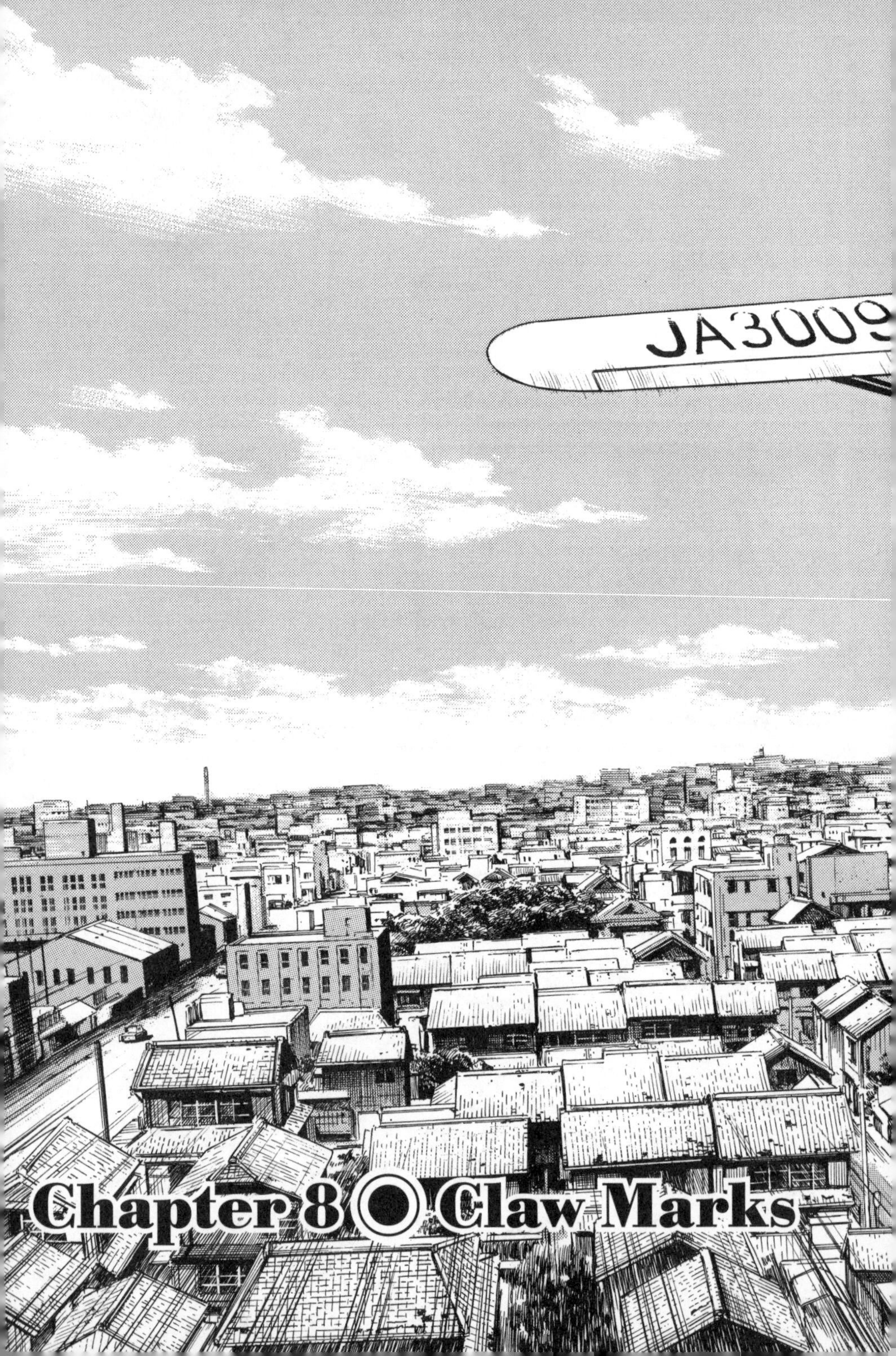
JA3009
Chapter 8 ◎ Claw Marks

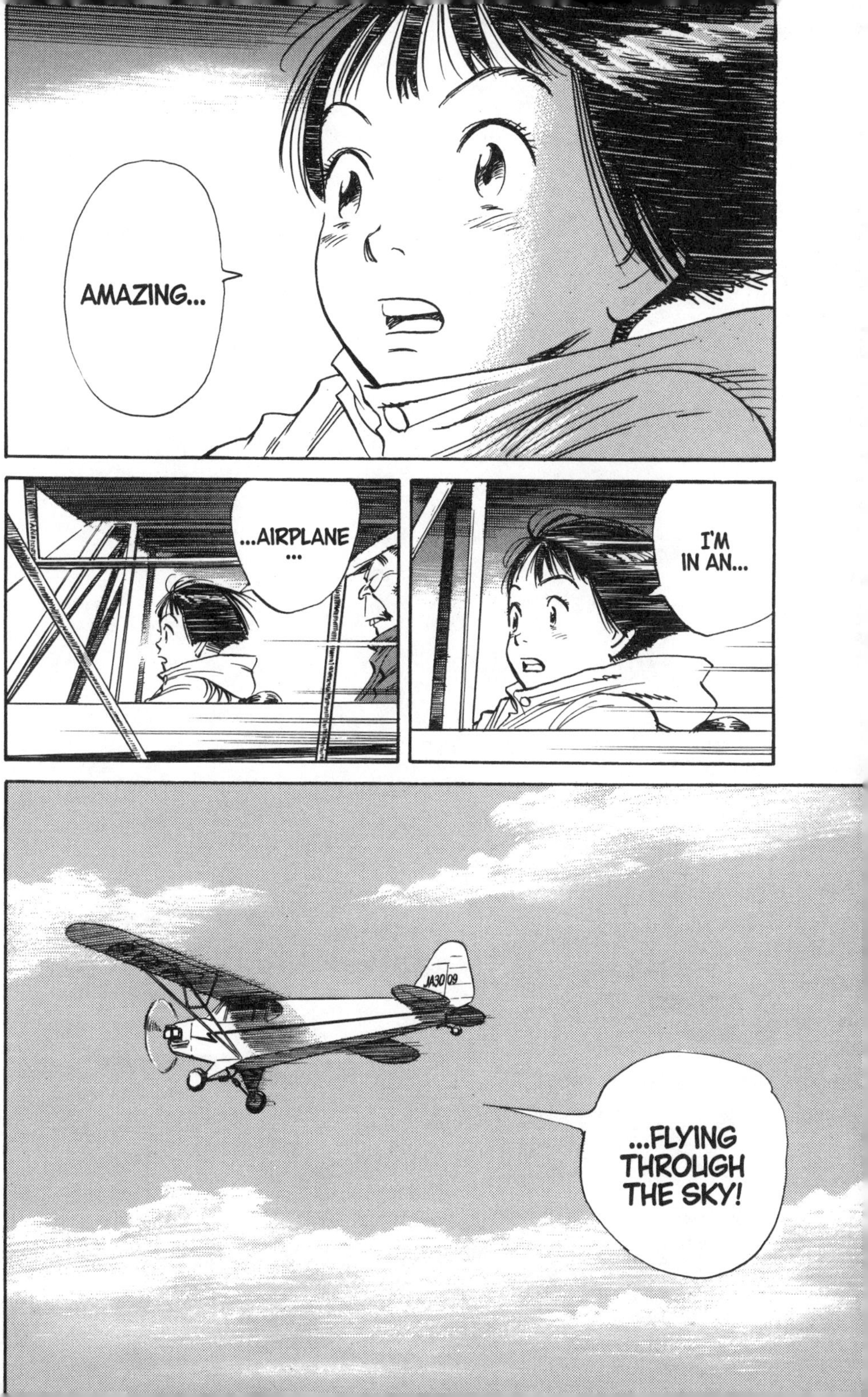
AMAZING...
I'M IN AN...
...AIRPLANE ...
JA3009
...FLYING THROUGH THE SKY!

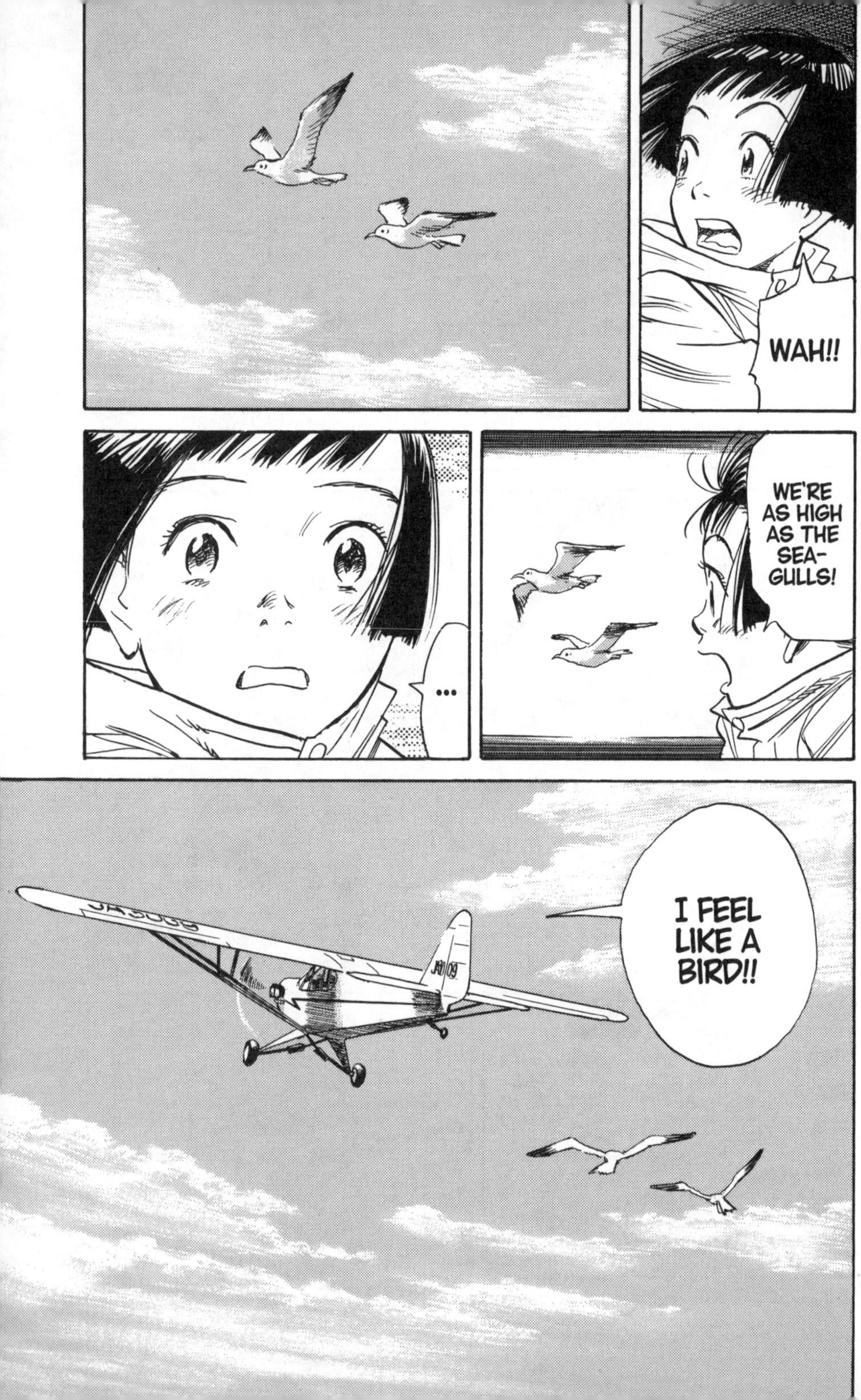
WAH!!
WE'RE AS HIGH AS THE SEA-GULLS!
...
I FEEL LIKE A BIRD!!

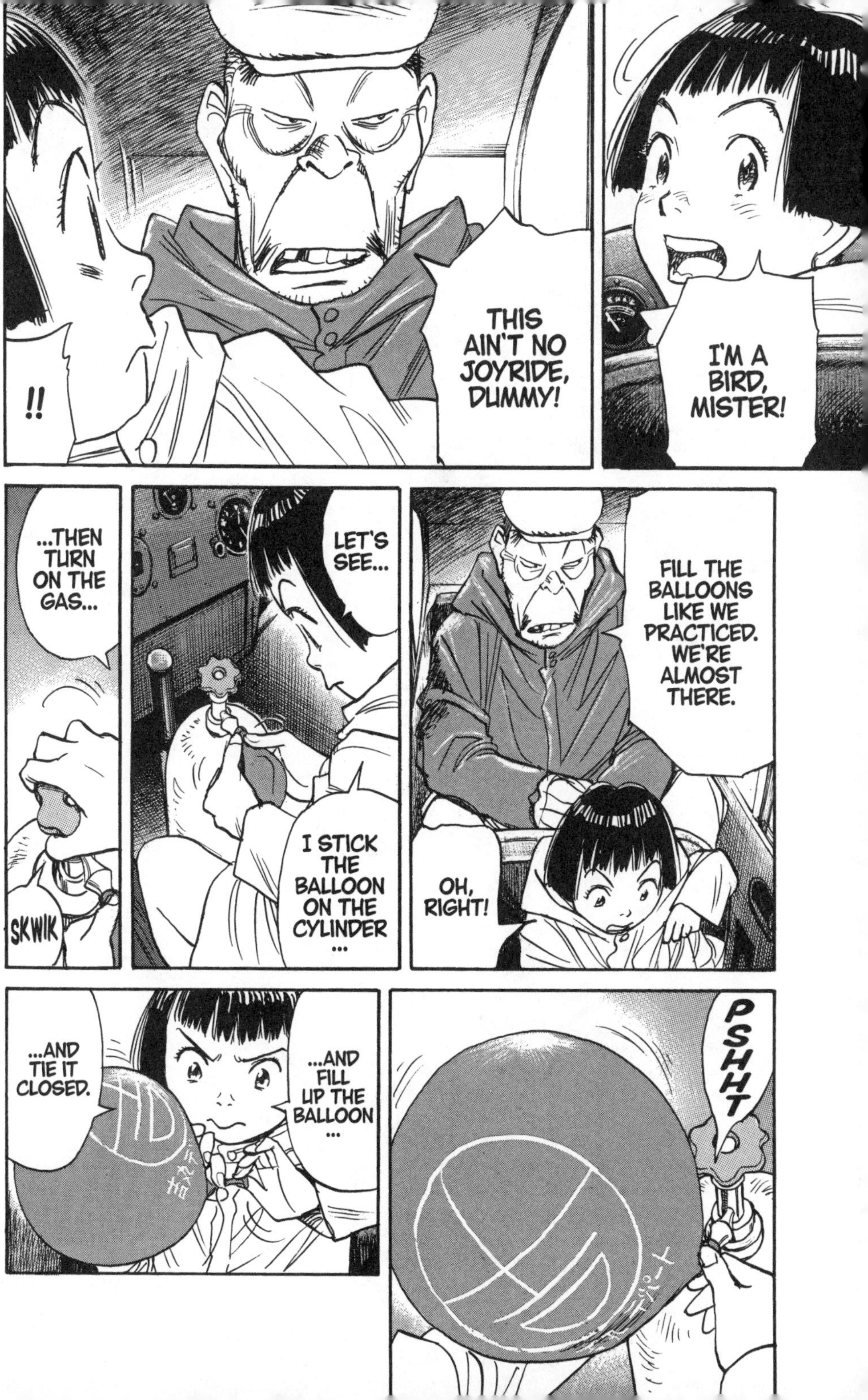

I'M A BIRD, MISTER!
THIS AIN'T NO JOYRIDE, DUMMY!
!!
FILL THE BALLOONS LIKE WE PRACTICED. WE'RE ALMOST THERE.
OH, RIGHT!
LET'S SEE...
I STICK THE BALLOON ON THE CYLINDER ...
...THEN TURN ON THE GAS...
SKWIK
PSHHT
...AND FILL UP THE BALLOON ...
...AND TIE IT CLOSED.

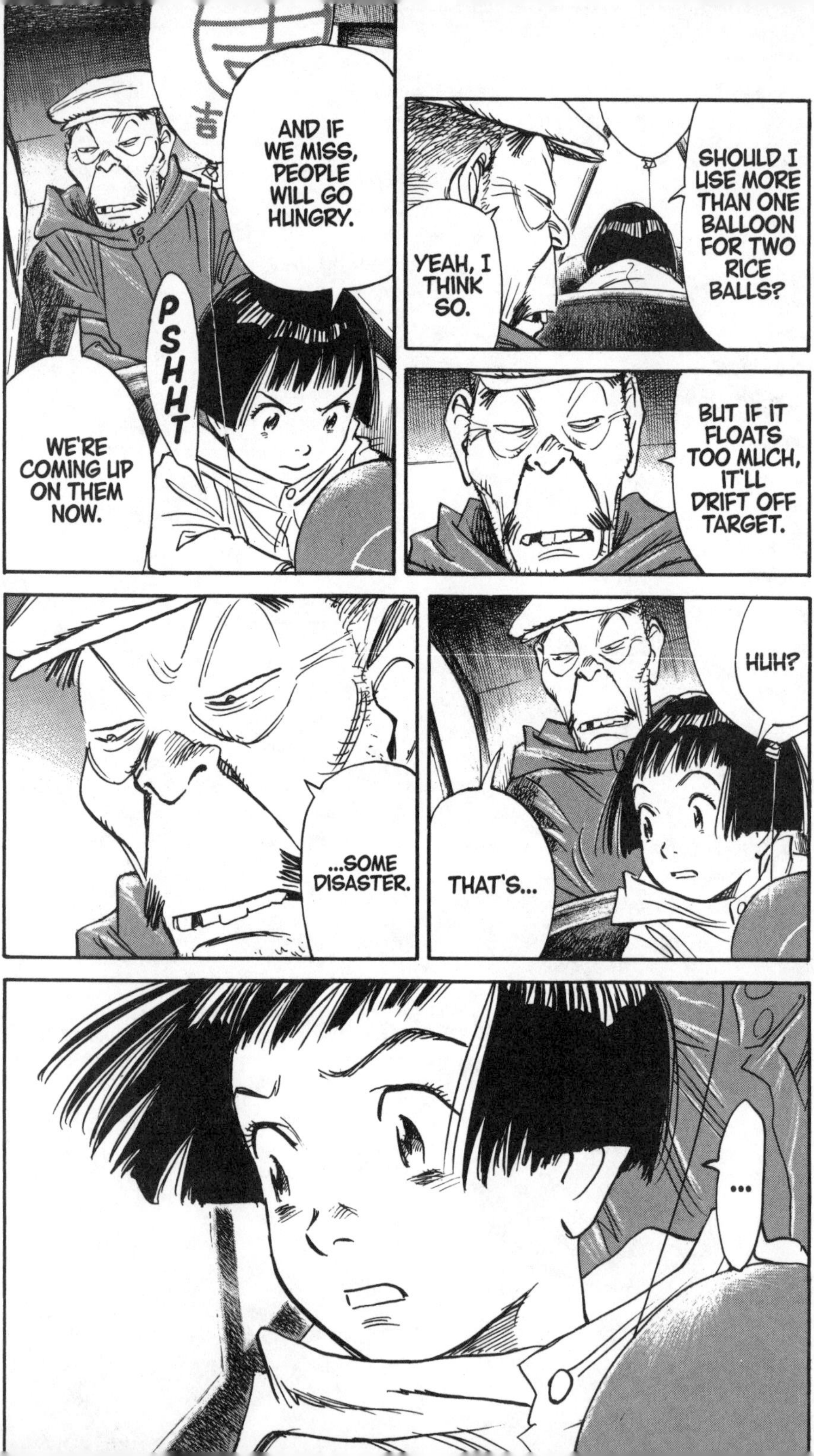
SHOULD I USE MORE THAN ONE BALLOON FOR TWO RICE BALLS?
YEAH, I THINK SO.
BUT IF IT FLOATS TOO MUCH, IT'LL DRIFT OFF TARGET.
吉
AND IF WE MISS, PEOPLE WILL GO HUNGRY.
PSHHT
WE'RE COMING UP ON THEM NOW.
HUH?
THAT'S...
...SOME DISASTER.
...

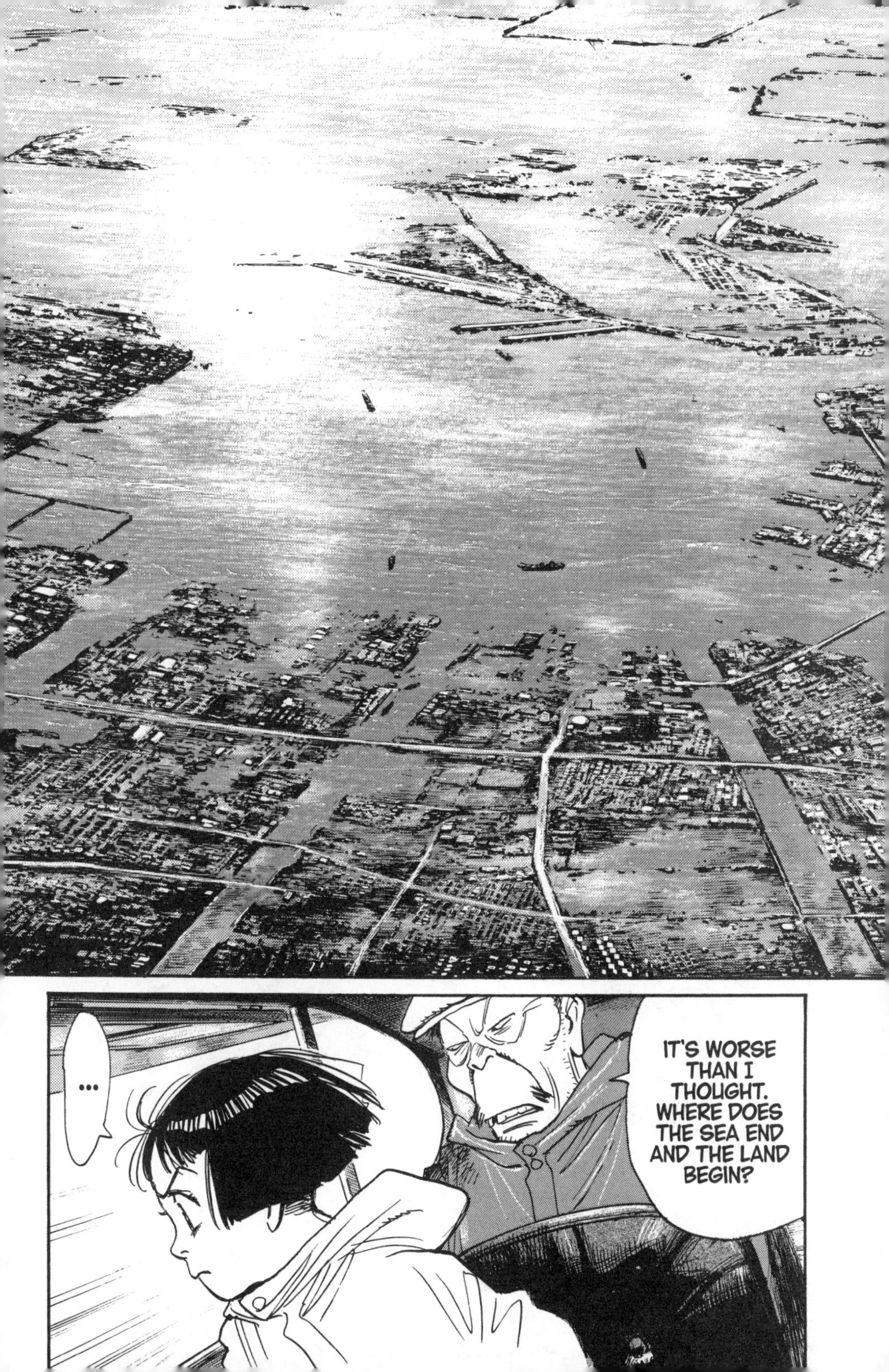
IT'S WORSE THAN I THOUGHT. WHERE DOES THE SEA END AND THE LAND BEGIN?
...

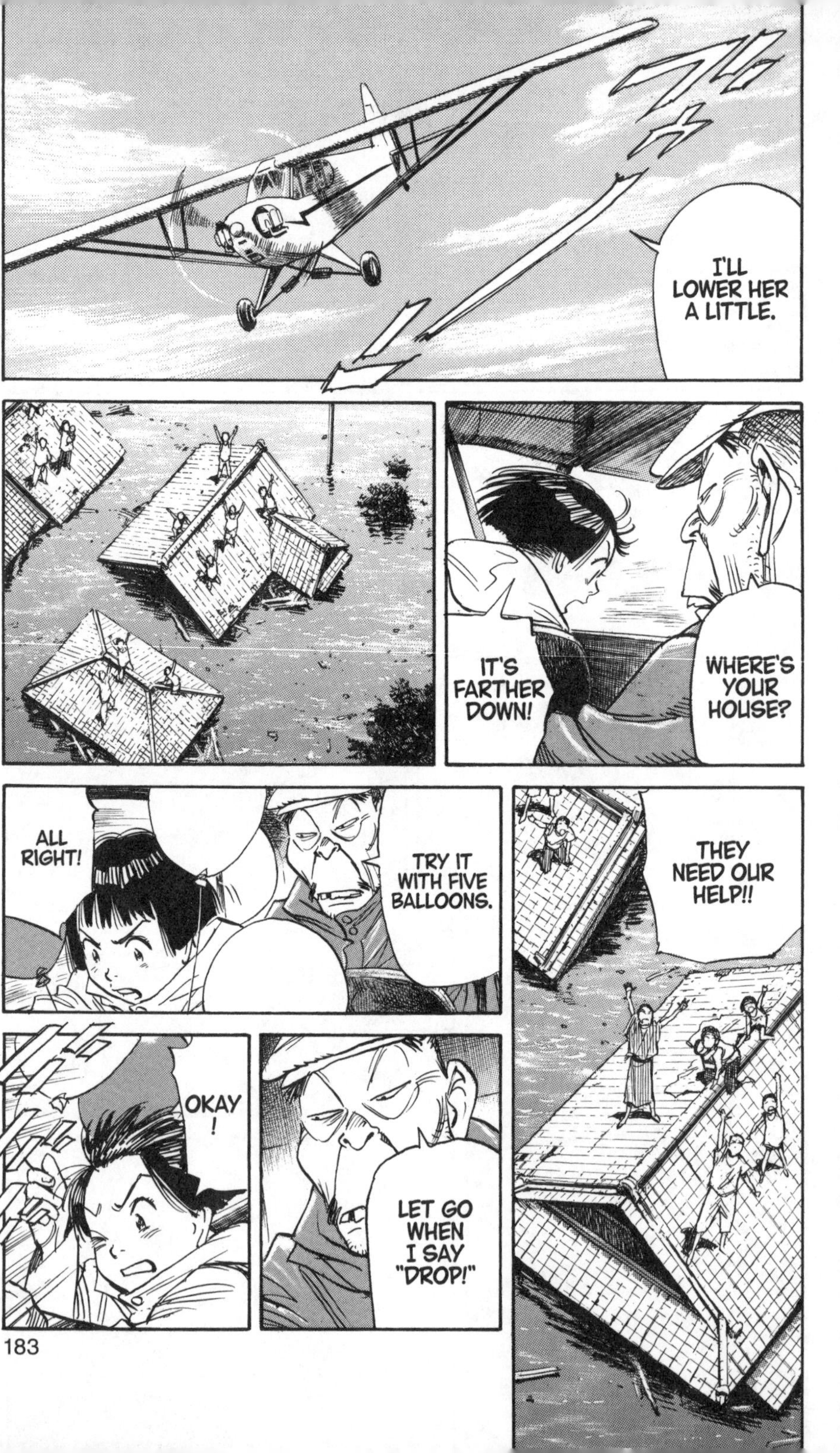
I'LL LOWER HER A LITTLE.
WHERE'S YOUR HOUSE?
IT'S FARTHER DOWN!
THEY NEED OUR HELP!!
TRY IT WITH FIVE BALLOONS.
ALL RIGHT!
LET GO WHEN I SAY "DROP!"
OKAY!

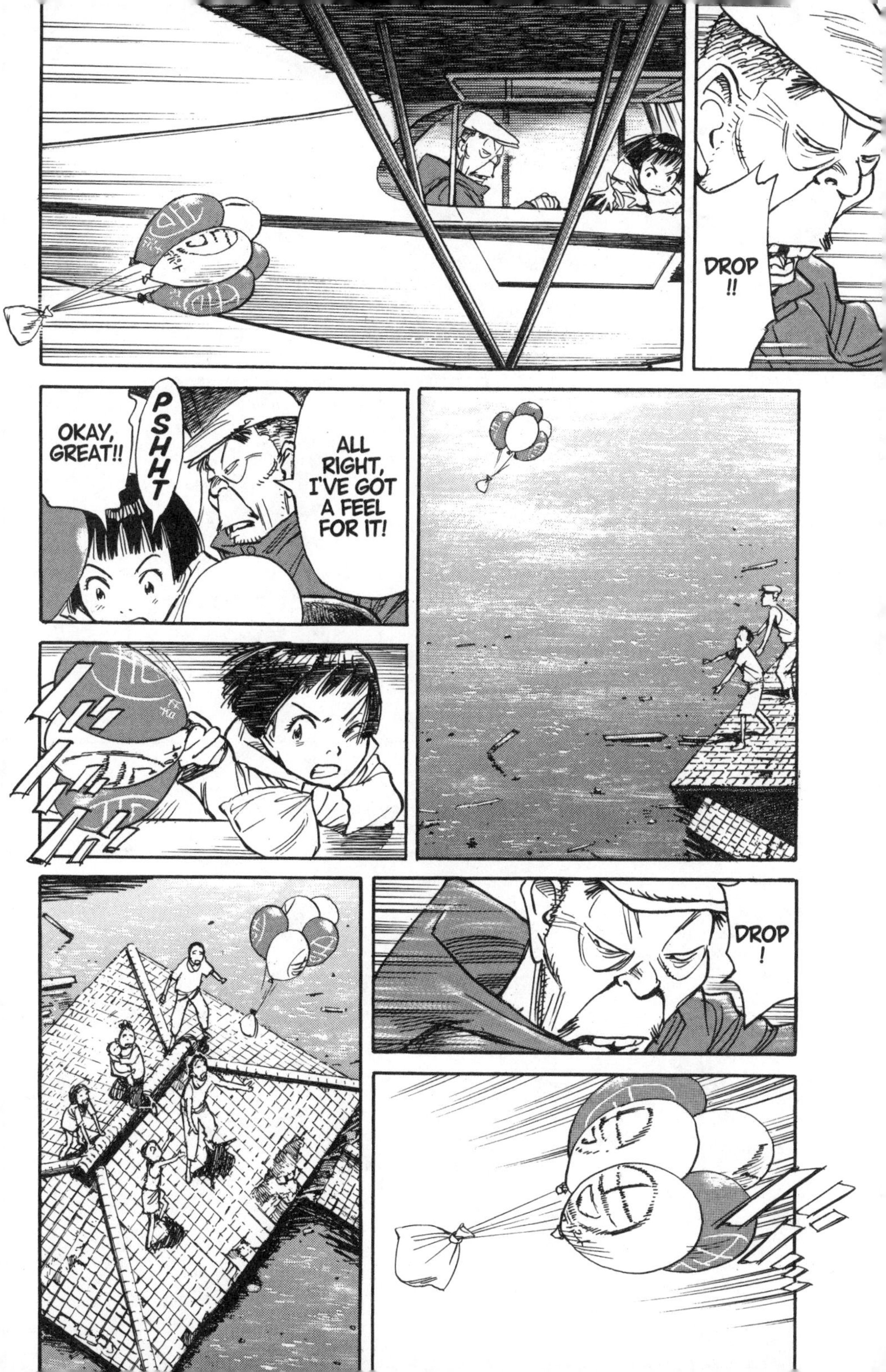
DROP !!
ALL RIGHT, I'VE GOT A FEEL FOR IT!
PSHHT
OKAY, GREAT!!
DROP !

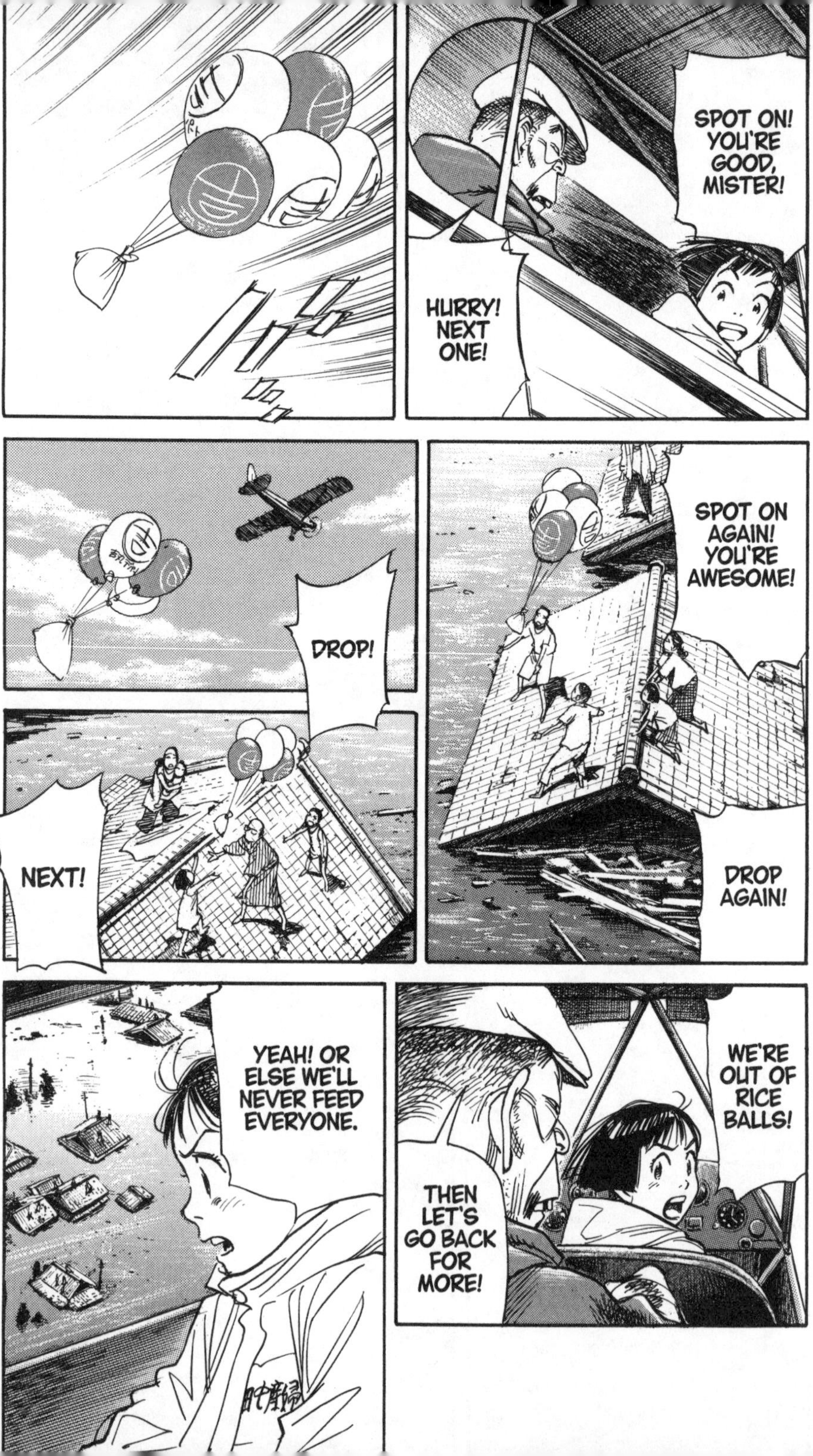
SPOT ON! YOU'RE GOOD, MISTER!
HURRY! NEXT ONE!
SPOT ON AGAIN! YOU'RE AWESOME!
DROP AGAIN!
DROP!
NEXT!
WE'RE OUT OF RICE BALLS!
THEN LET'S GO BACK FOR MORE!
YEAH! OR ELSE WE'LL NEVER FEED EVERYONE.

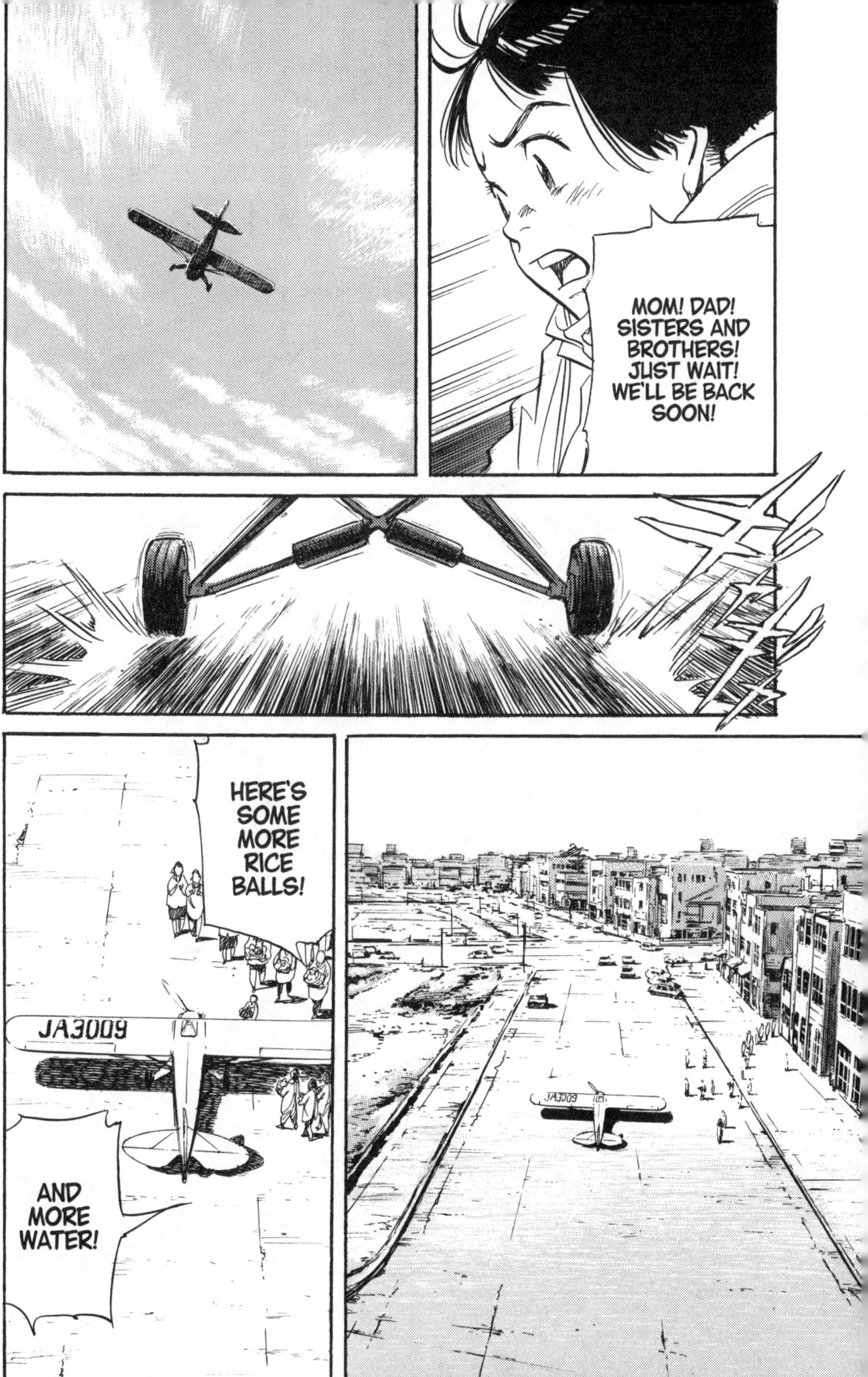
MOM! DAD! SISTERS AND BROTHERS! JUST WAIT! WE'LL BE BACK SOON!
HERE'S SOME MORE RICE BALLS!
JA3009
AND MORE WATER!

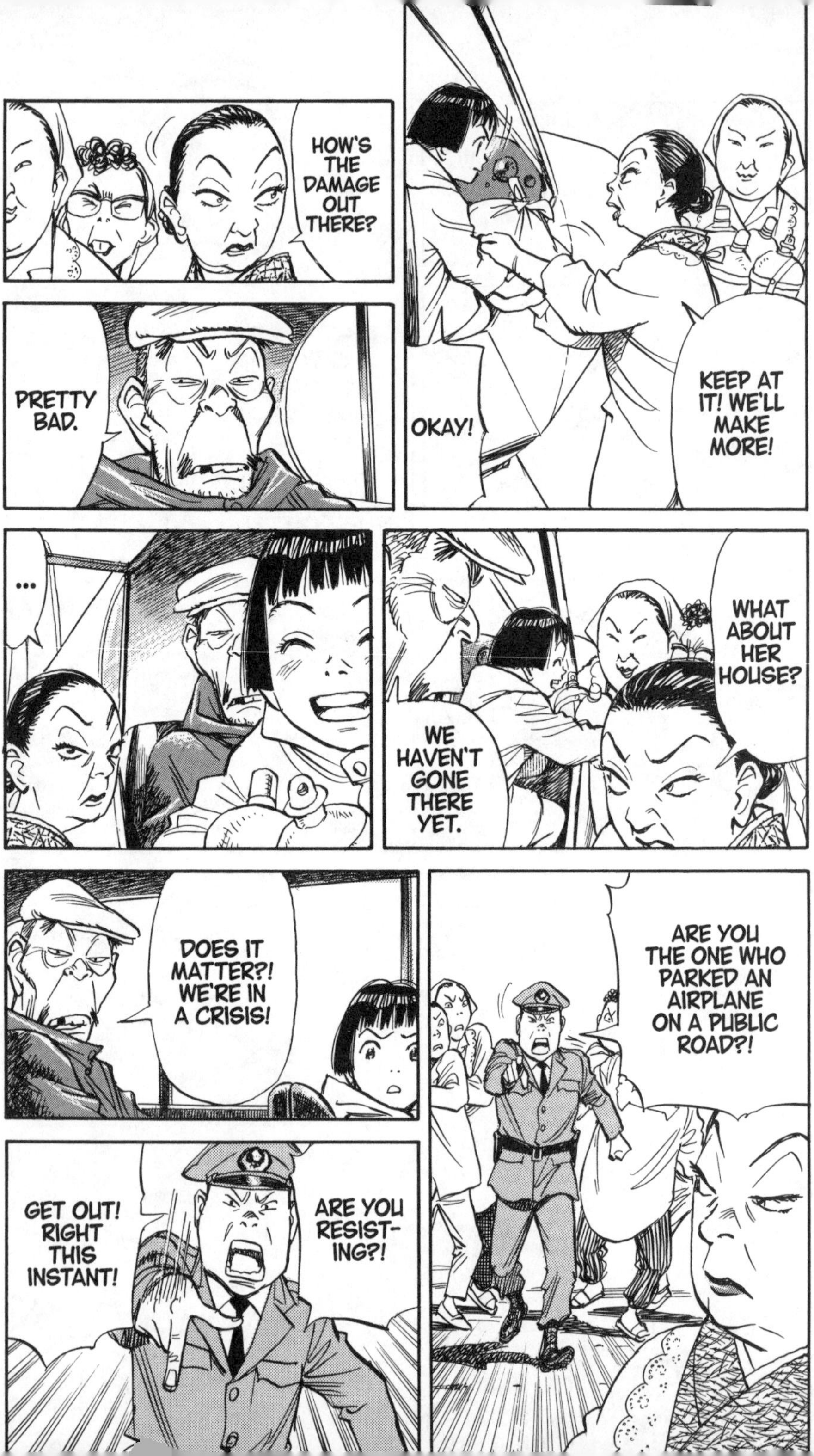
KEEP AT IT! WE'LL MAKE MORE!
OKAY!
HOW'S THE DAMAGE OUT THERE?
PRETTY BAD.
WHAT ABOUT HER HOUSE?
WE HAVEN'T GONE THERE YET.
...
ARE YOU THE ONE WHO PARKED AN AIRPLANE ON A PUBLIC ROAD?!
DOES IT MATTER?! WE'RE IN A CRISIS!
ARE YOU RESIST-ING?!
GET OUT! RIGHT THIS INSTANT!

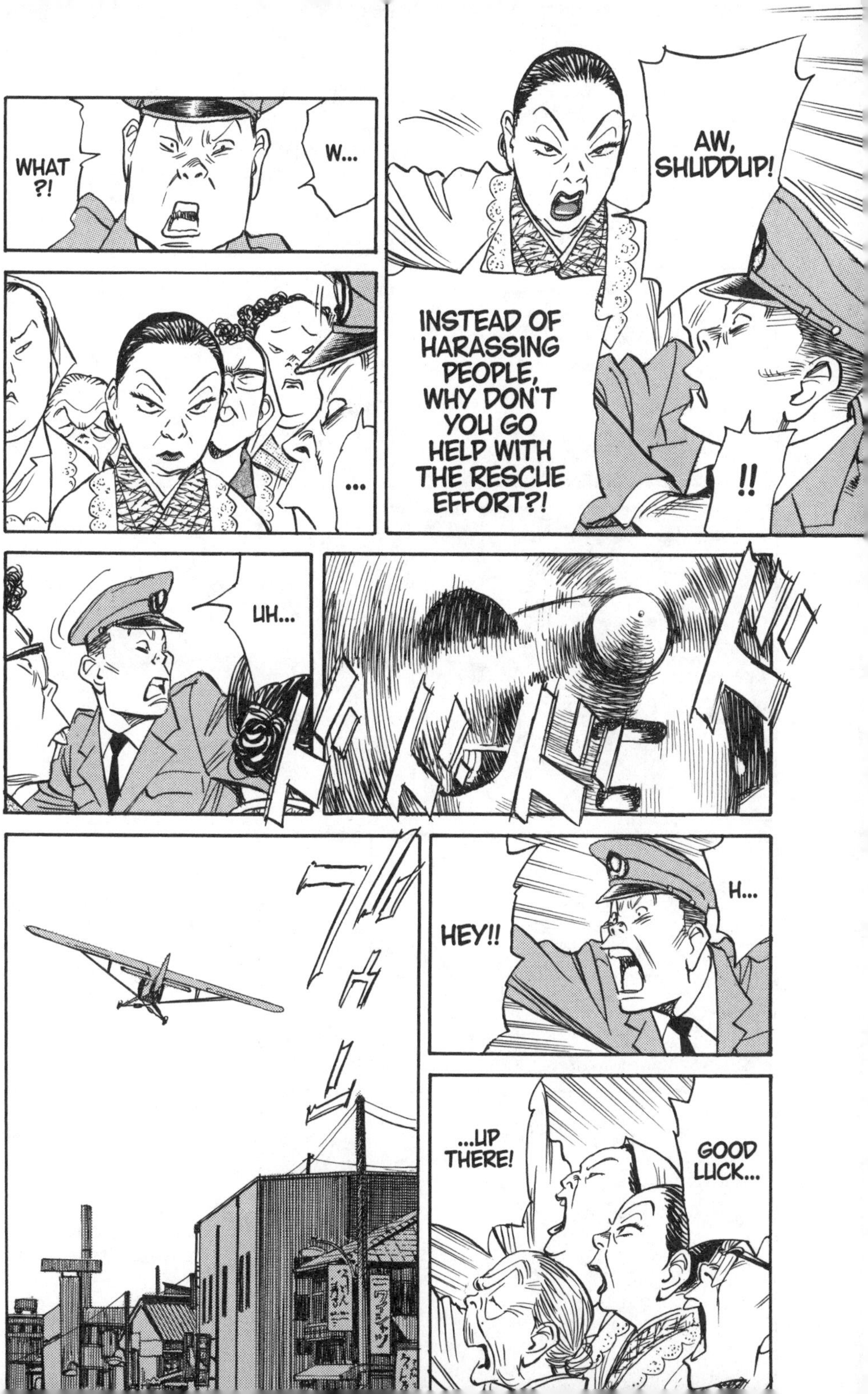
AW, SHUDDUP!
INSTEAD OF HARASSING PEOPLE, WHY DON'T YOU GO HELP WITH THE RESCUE EFFORT?!
!!
W...
WHAT ?!
...
UH...
H...
HEY!!
GOOD LUCK...
...UP THERE!

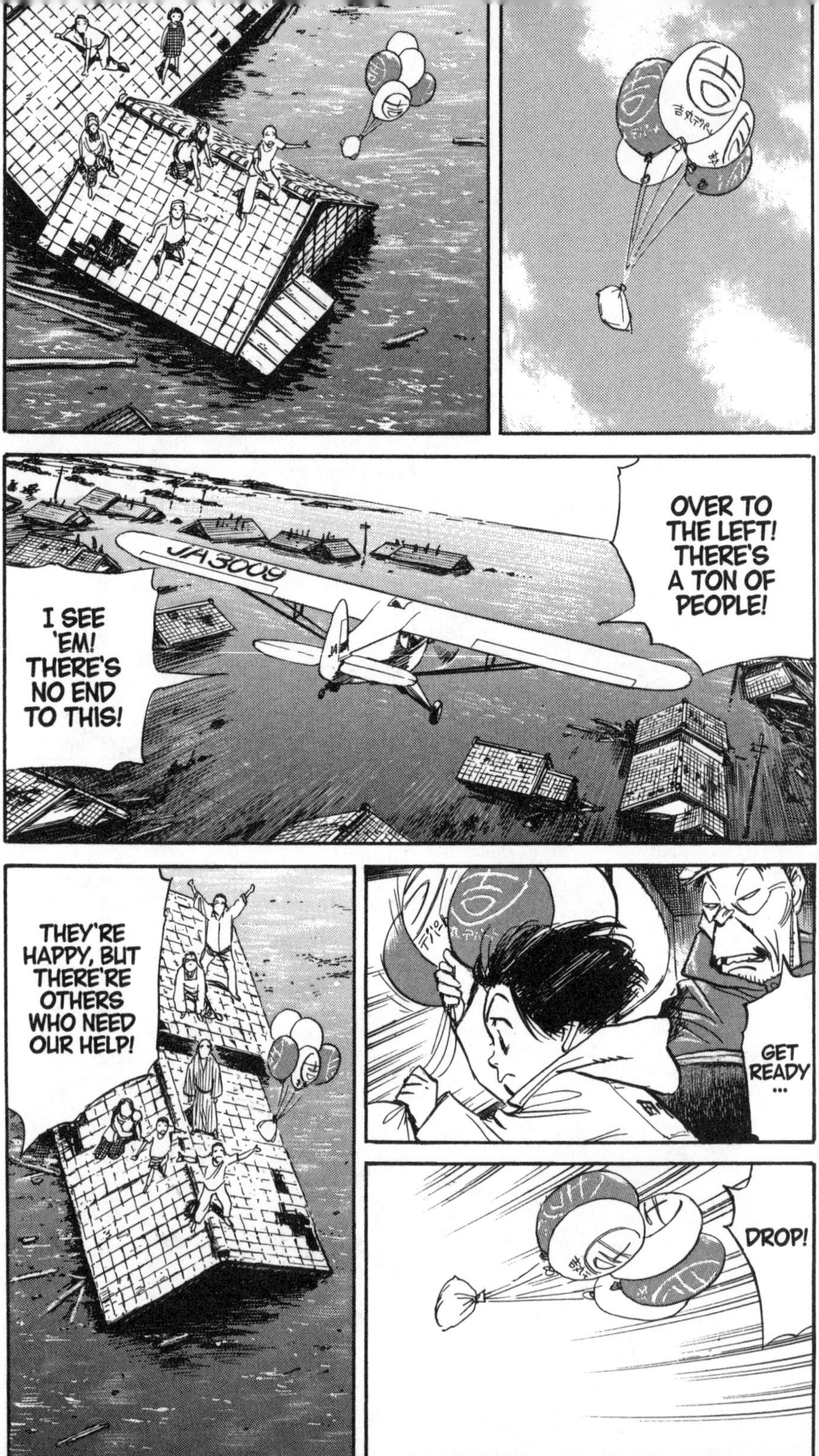
OVER TO THE LEFT! THERE'S A TON OF PEOPLE!
JA3009
I SEE 'EM! THERE'S NO END TO THIS!
GET READY...
DROP!
THEY'RE HAPPY, BUT THERE'RE OTHERS WHO NEED OUR HELP!

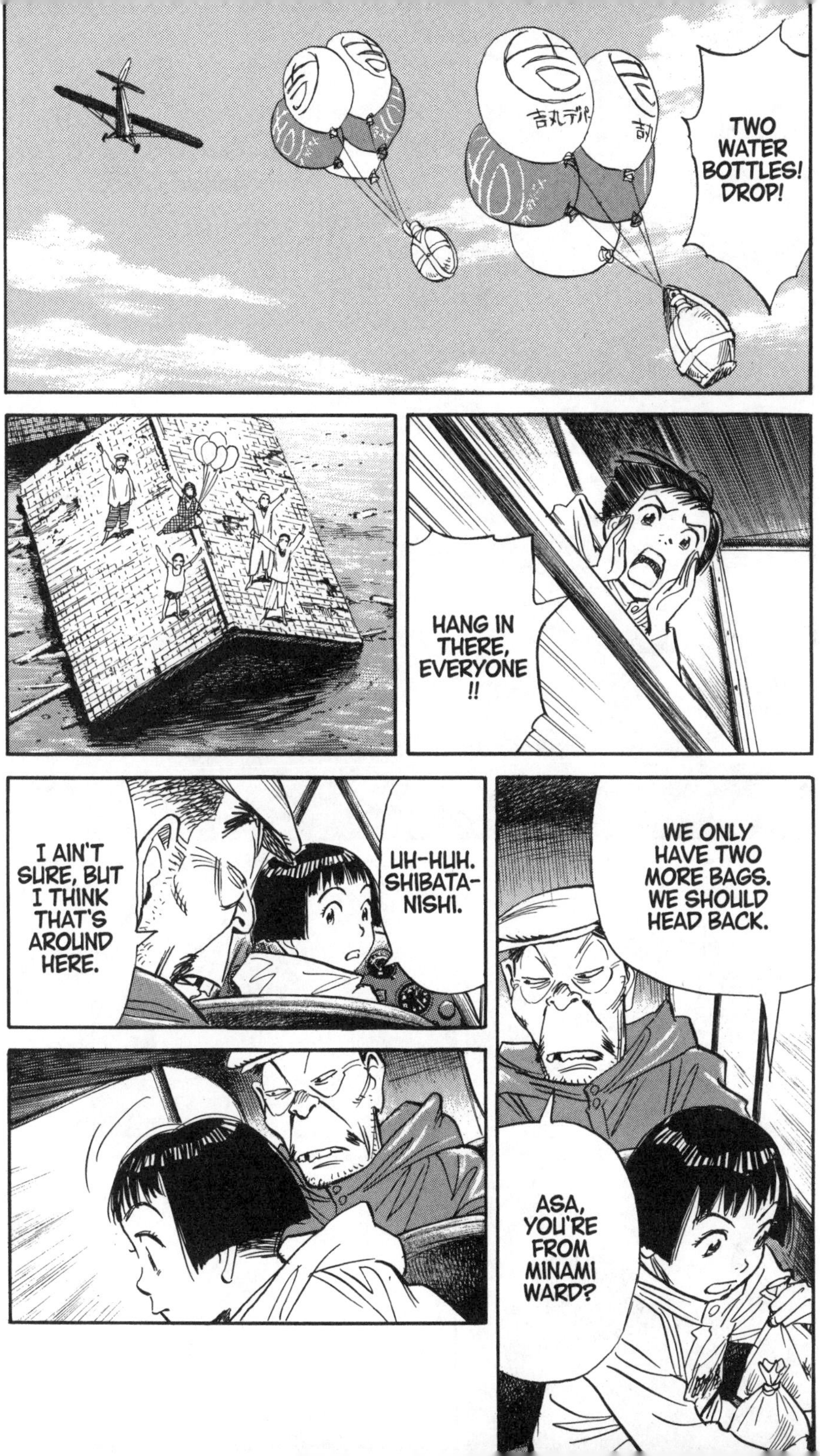

TWO WATER BOTTLES! DROP!
HANG IN THERE, EVERYONE !!
WE ONLY HAVE TWO MORE BAGS. WE SHOULD HEAD BACK.
ASA, YOU'RE FROM MINAMI WARD?
UH-HUH. SHIBATA-NISHI.
I AIN'T SURE, BUT I THINK THAT'S AROUND HERE.

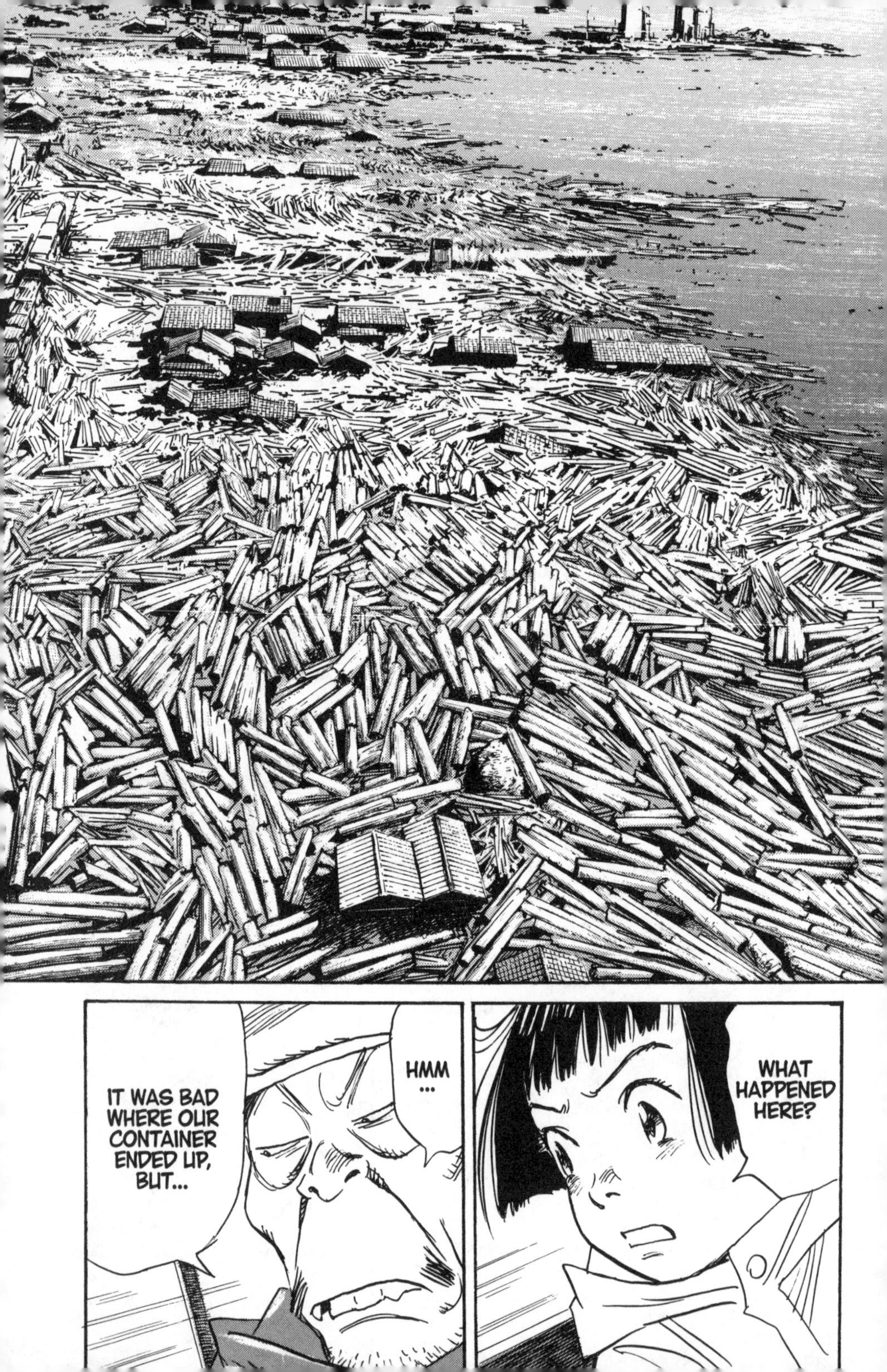
WHAT HAPPENED HERE?
HMM ...
IT WAS BAD WHERE OUR CONTAINER ENDED UP, BUT...

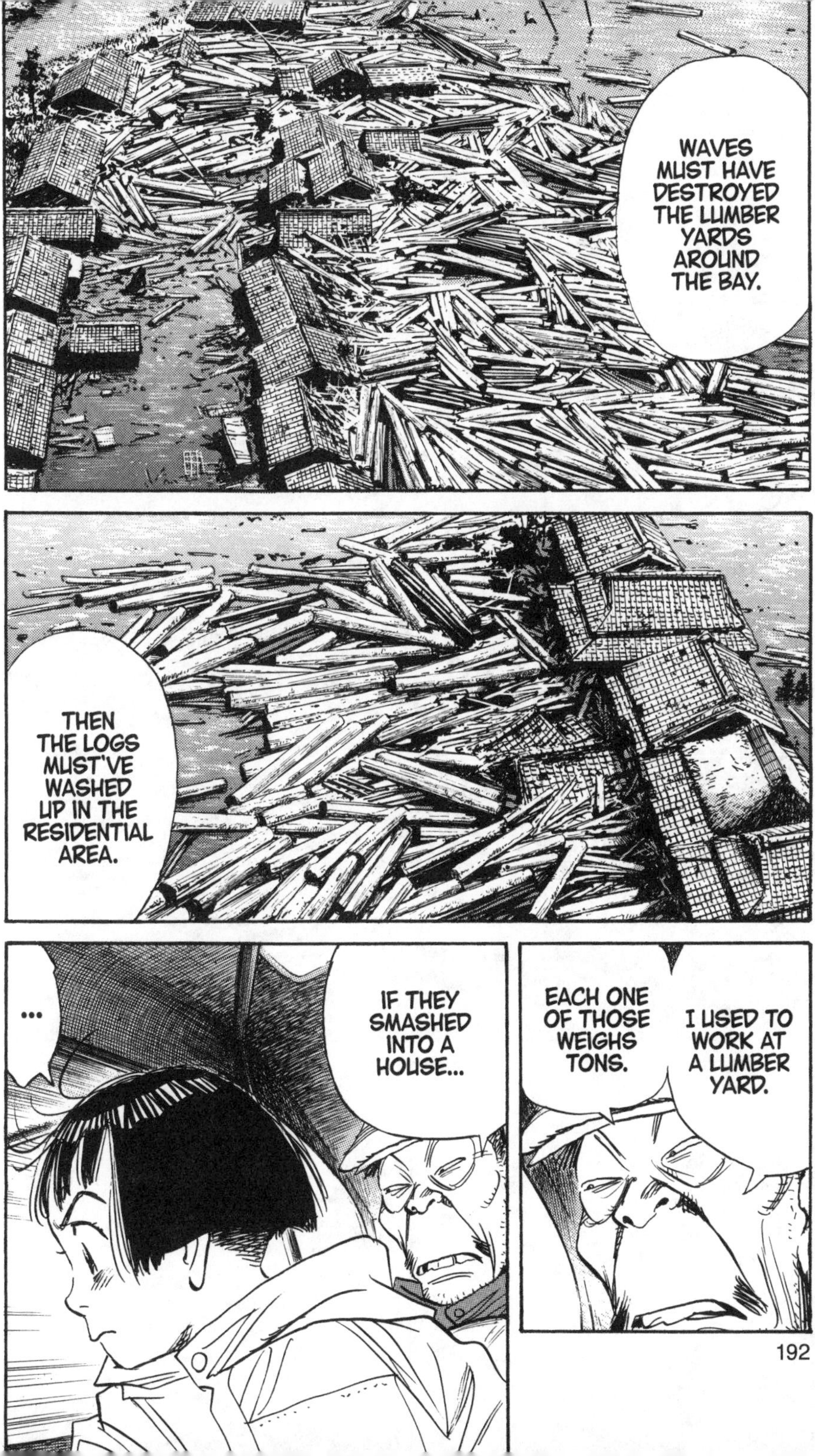
WAVES MUST HAVE DESTROYED THE LUMBER YARDS AROUND THE BAY.
THEN THE LOGS MUST'VE WASHED UP IN THE RESIDENTIAL AREA.
I USED TO WORK AT A LUMBER YARD.
EACH ONE OF THOSE WEIGHS TONS.
IF THEY SMASHED INTO A HOUSE...
...

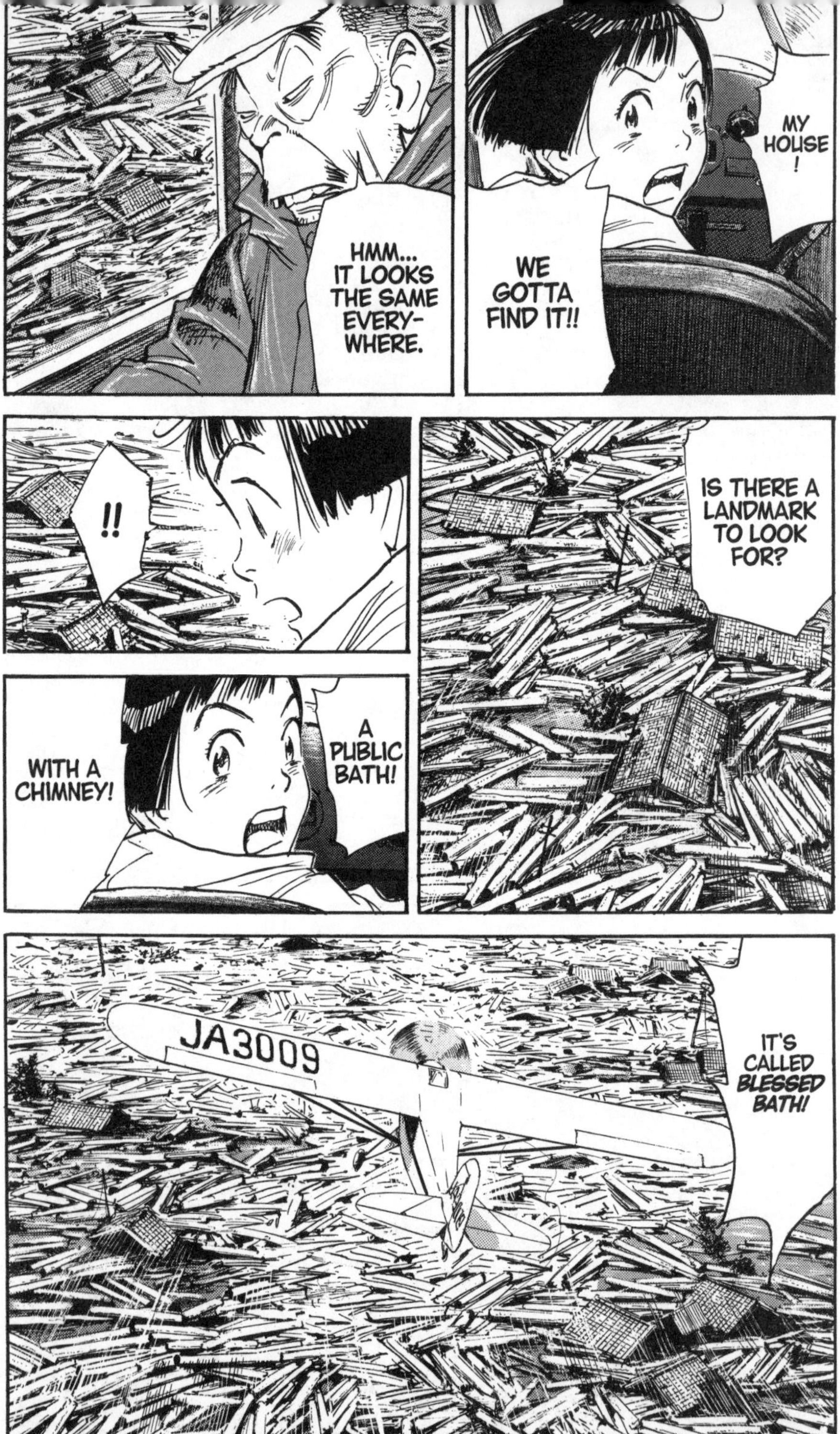
MY HOUSE !
WE GOTTA FIND IT!!
HMM... IT LOOKS THE SAME EVERY-WHERE.
IS THERE A LANDMARK TO LOOK FOR?
!!
A PUBLIC BATH!
WITH A CHIMNEY!
IT'S CALLED *BLESSED BATH!*
JA3009

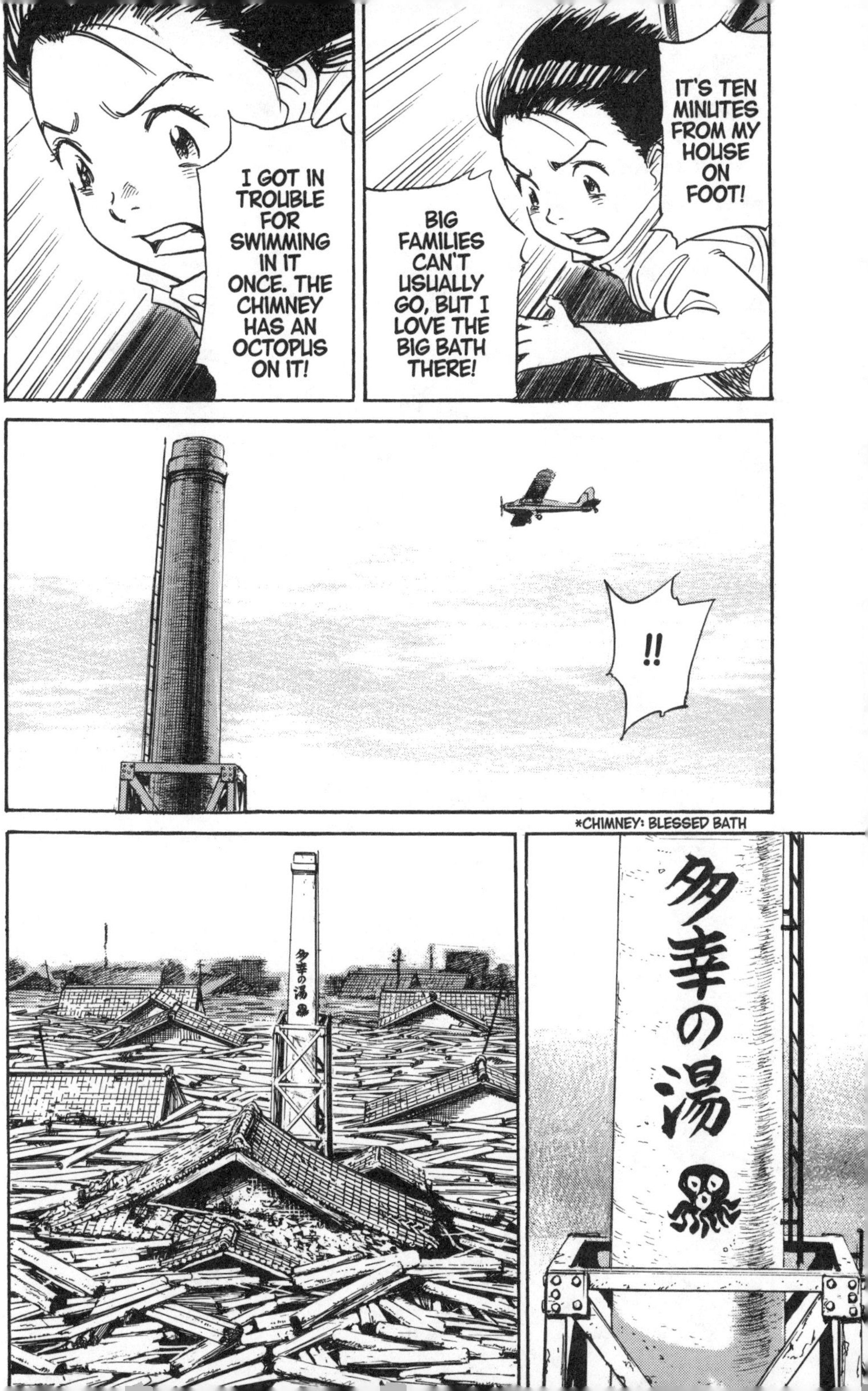
IT'S TEN MINUTES FROM MY HOUSE ON FOOT!
BIG FAMILIES CAN'T USUALLY GO, BUT I LOVE THE BIG BATH THERE!
I GOT IN TROUBLE FOR SWIMMING IN IT ONCE. THE CHIMNEY HAS AN OCTOPUS ON IT!
!!
*CHIMNEY: BLESSED BATH
多幸の湯
多幸の湯

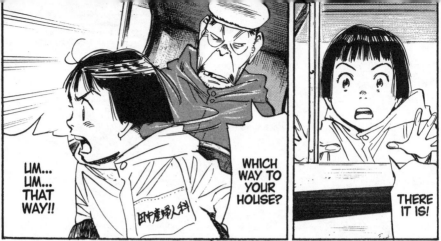

UM...
UM...
THAT
WAY!!

WHICH
WAY TO
YOUR
HOUSE?

THERE
IT IS!

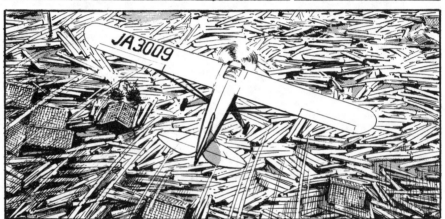

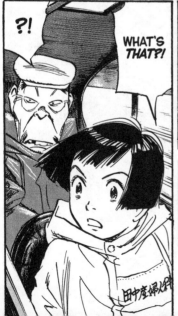

?!

WHAT'S
THAT?!

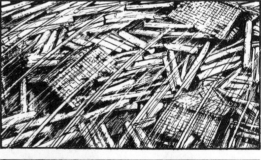

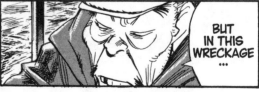

BUT
IN THIS
WRECKAGE
...

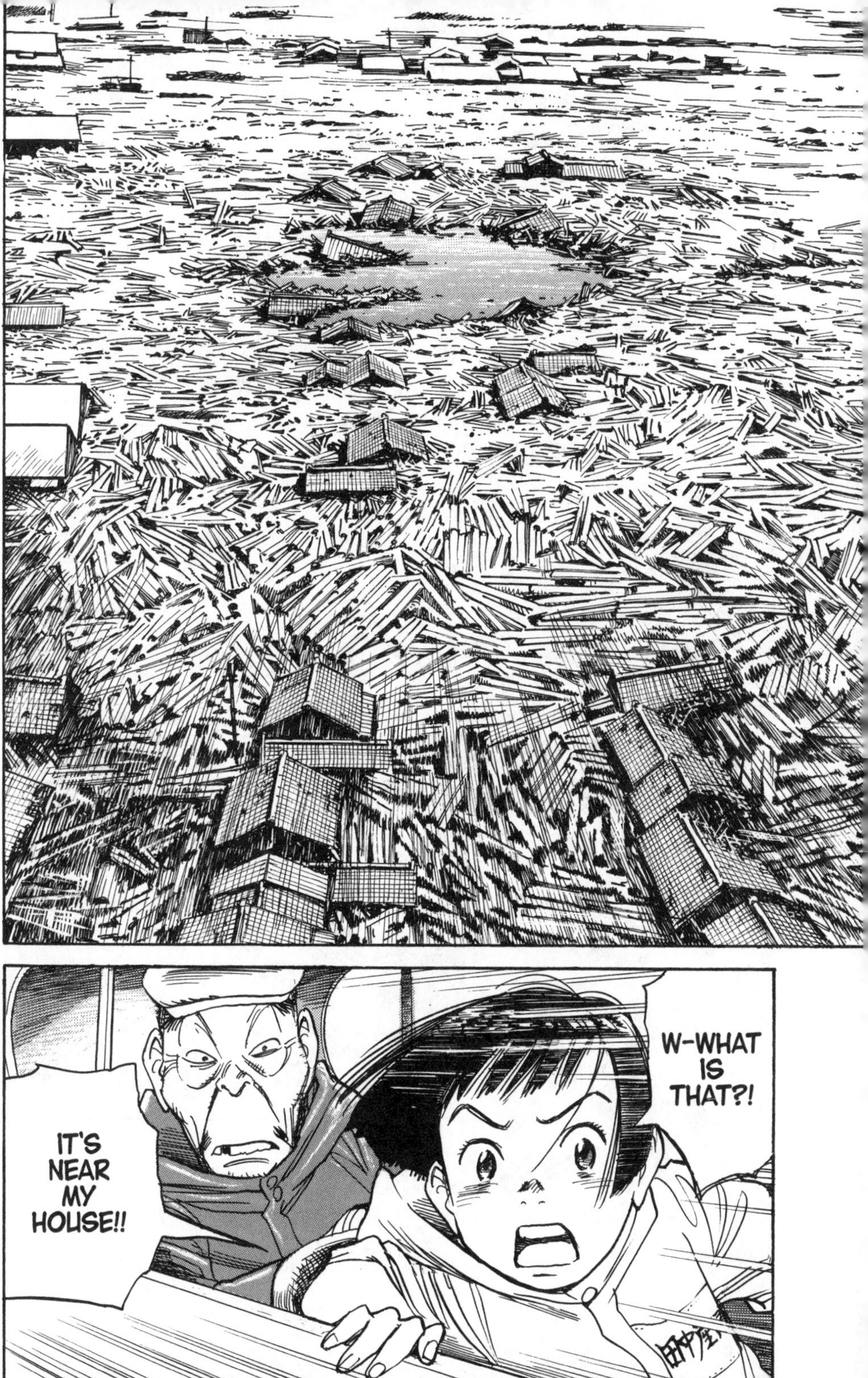
W-WHAT IS THAT?!
IT'S NEAR MY HOUSE!!

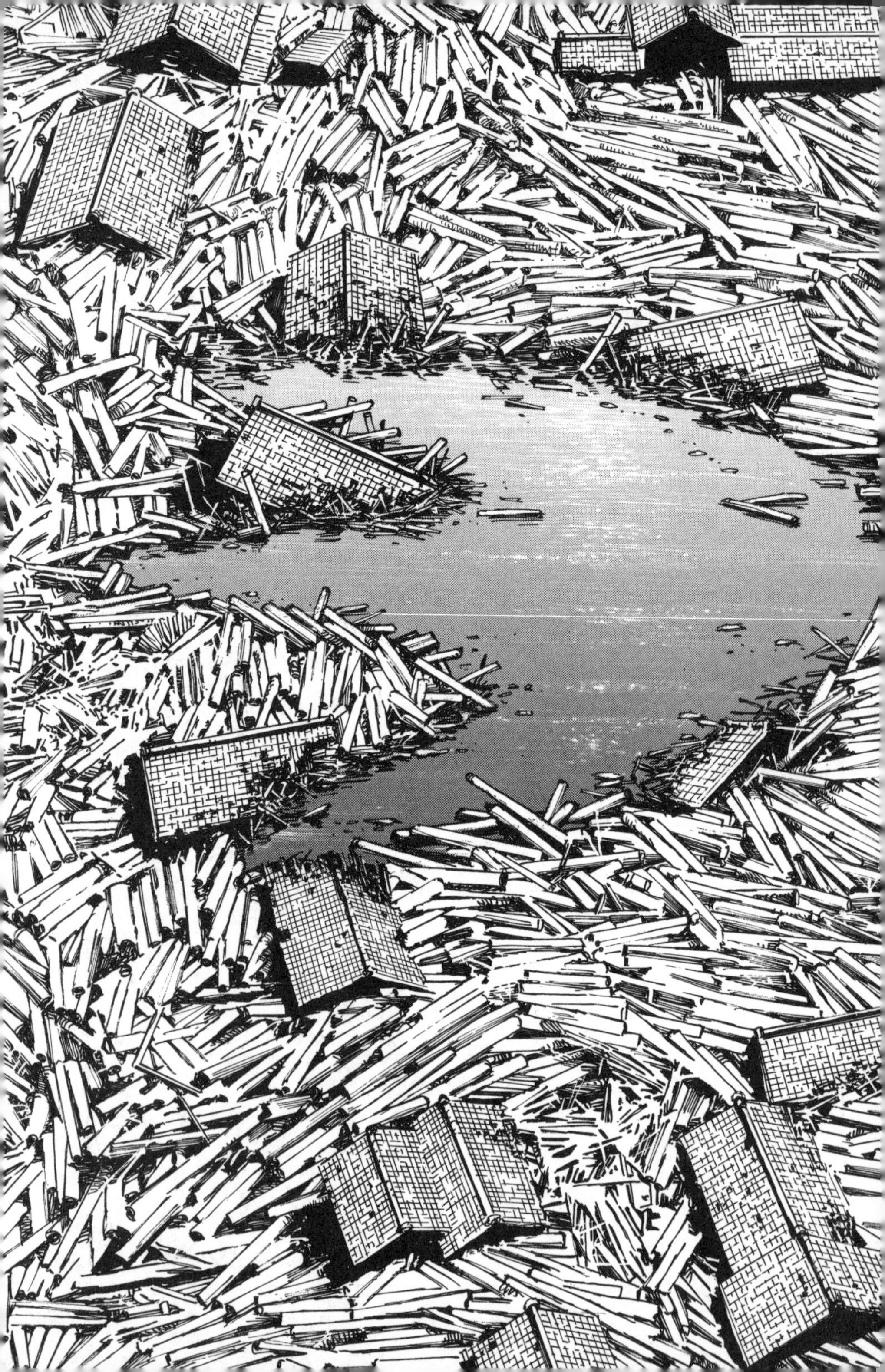

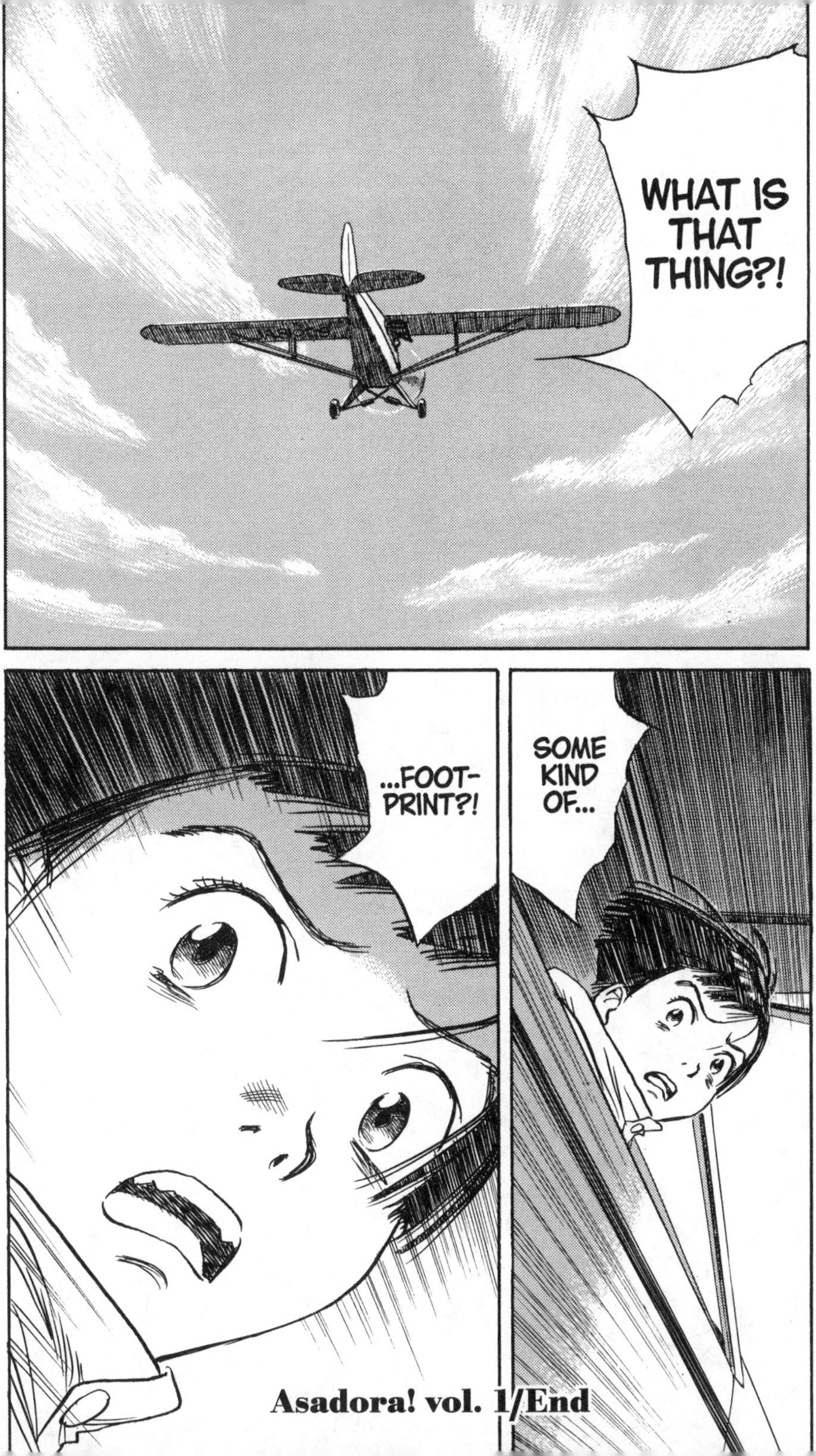
WHAT IS THAT THING?!
SOME KIND OF...
...FOOT-PRINT?!

Asadora! vol. 1/End

ASADORA!

To be continued...

Production Staff:
Hideaki Urano
Tohru Sakata

Cooperation:
Satoshi Akatsuka (TAC Photography)
Jun Takahashi
Nagoya Times, Archives Committee
Japan Aeronautic Association, Aviation Library
Takeshi Ijichi (Ikaros Publications, Ltd.)
Chihiro Katsu
Nobuyuki Kojima
Satomi Danno

Editor:
Haruka Ikegawa

References:
Takahashi, Jun. *Jun-san no Ozora Jinsei, Oreryu* (Jun's Life in the Skies, My Way).
Assisted by Masahiro Kaneda. Ikaros Publications, Ltd.

Thank you to everyone else who offered help.

PAGE 154: Emil Zátopek was a Czechoslovak runner who competed in the 1948, 1952 and 1956 Olympic Games. He is the only person to ever win the 5,000 meters, 10,000 meters and marathon at a single Olympic Games. Despite his success, many considered his running style to be inelegant. The way he panted and wheezed as he ran earned him the nickname "The Locomotive." Considered one of the greatest runners of all-time, Zátopek also served as the mastermind behind interval training (high-intensity workouts with periods of rest) and hypoventilation training (workouts utilizing reduced breathing frequency with periods of normal breathing).

PAGE 154: The 1940 Summer Olympics were originally scheduled to take place in Tokyo, making it the first non-Western city to win an Olympic bid. However, the games were moved to Helsinki amidst growing concerns over the intensity of the Second Sino-Japanese War, which started in 1937. The games were then cancelled altogether due to World War II. There wouldn't be another Olympic Games until the London Games of 1948.

Translation Notes

PAGE 15: Yujiro Ishihara, born December 28, 1934, was a Japanese actor and singer active from 1956–1982. He was a postwar icon on par with the likes of Marlon Brandon, Elvis Presley and James Dean in the US. The lyrics sung by the man in the car, "I am waiting," are from a song and movie—in which Ishihara stars—of the same name. "We're drummers! Worthless drummers!" are lyrics from the theme song for the 1957 film *Man Who Causes a Storm*, which also stars Ishihara. Tragically, Ishihara passed away from liver cancer in 1987.

PAGE 42: That "feller with the gyratin' hip" is none other than Elvis Presley, the American singer, dancer and actor affectionately referred to as "the King." Born January 8, 1935, Elvis was active from 1953 until his sudden death in 1977.

PAGE 72: The Mitsubishi Navy Type 1 attack bomber, also referred to as *Hamaki* ("leaf roll") by Japanese Naval pilots and as "Betty" by Allied Forces, was a twin-engine, land-based, medium-sized bomber used by the Japanese Imperial Navy during World War II. Despite being the most widely produced bomber used by Japan during the war, none of the 2,400 aircraft that were produced survived intact to the present day.

83.6 - wham wham wham
(gan gan gan: destruction)

83.6 - kreak kreak kreak kreak
(gishi gishi gishi gishi: creaking)

85.2 - hwam (gan: falling)

85.3 - bannng (gakon: falling)

85.4 - bwam (gon: falling)

85.5 - kreak kreak (gishii gishii: creaking)

85.6 - kreak (gishii: creaking)

85.7 - kreak (gishii: creaking)

86.3 - bwamm (gagon: falling)

87.2 - kreak (giii: creaking)

88.5 - kaslam (gagan: falling)

89.1 - kabam (gagan: destruction)

89.1 - kreaaak (kiiii: creaking)

89.2 - bang (gon: destruction)

98.3 - hwud (do: pushing)

98.4 - shuv (gi: pushing)

98.5 - fwam (don: pushing)

104.7 - slam (gachan: hanging up)

108.3-4 - hwoooo (byuoooo: wind)

110.6 - hwooo (byuuoo: wind)

121.1 - splosh (zabu: steering)

126.2 - vrum vrum (gyagyan: truck)

126.3 - vavrooosh (bobanbobobo: truck)

129.1 - vrooom (bobababa: truck)

132.4 - vroom (buon: truck)

133.2 - clatter (gatan: moving door)

133.3 - gabam (gon: falling into place)

133.4 - rattle rattle (gara gara: sliding door)

133.6 - tok tok (kan kan: hammering)

139.4 - vrooom (bobaban: truck)

142.5 - honnnk honnnk
(papaaa paaa: car horns)

143.1 - honnnk honnnk
(paaa pappaa: car horns)

143.2 - honnnk honk (paa paa: car horns)

143.3 - honnnk honk (paa paa: car horns)

143.4 - honnnk (pappaa: car horn)

143.5 - honnnk honnnk
(pappaa paaa: car horns)

144.1 - vroom (bubababa: truck)

144.4 - tunk (bamu: car door)

146.4 - vrum (dorun: starting propeller)

146.5 - vrumm (dododo: propeller)

146.7 - vrumm (dododo: engine)

147.1-2 - vrummm (dodododo: engine)

147.4 - blam (pan: shooting)

150.1 - fwoosh (baaa: lifting off)

150.3 - hwup (vuun: flying)

151.1 - vrrr (buun: airplane)

174.3 - vrum (doryun: starting propeller)

174.6 - vrumm (dodo: engine)

174.7 - vrummmm (dodododo: engine)

175.1-5 - vrummmm (dododododo: engine)

183.1 - vrooosh (buuun: flying)

183.7 - babwobble (bababa: balloons shaking)

184.5 - baflubble (bababa: balloons shaking)

184.7 - bwsh (ba: falling)

185.2 - bwsh (ba: falling)

186.3 - skrrrch (gyagya: landing)

188.4 - vrumm (dododo: propeller)

188.8 - vroosh (buun: airplane)

Sound Effects Glossary

The sound effects in this edition of *Asadora!* have been preserved in their original Japanese format. To avoid additional lettering cluttering up the panels, a list of the sound effects is provided here. Each sound effect is listed by page and panel number; for example, "6.3" would mean the effect appears in panel 3 of page 6.

3.1-3 - gwooooo (goooooo: destruction)	**52.4** - clunk clunk (gara gara: falling)
4-5.3 - angyaaaa (angyaaaa: roar)	**53.1-5** - gwooo (gooooo: wind)
6.1 - gwoom (goon: destruction)	**54.1** - gwooosh (gooooo: airplane)
6.2 - krunk krunk (gara gara: breaking)	**55.1** - vrrr (buun: airplane)
6.4 - hwomp (doon: footstep)	**56.1** - vrrr (buun: airplane)
7.1-2 - gwoooo (goooooo: destruction)	**60.2** - szzzt (jijijiji: welding)
8.1-3 - gwoooo (goooooo: wind)	**60.3** - spshhh (zaa: running water)
9.1 - whoosh (da: running)	**61.7** - thok whok wham (ga go baki: fighting)
9.6 - skid (kii: stopping)	**62.1** - vrrr (buun: airplane)
11.1 - gwooo (gooo: wind)	**62.4** - vrrr (buun: airplane)
13.4 - gwooo (gooo: wind)	**62.6** - bam bam (gan gan: hitting)
13.6 - honnnk (paaa: car horn)	**63.1** - bam bam (gan gan: hitting)
15.7 - vroom (doon: car leaving)	**63.3** - whok (ga: kicking)
16.1 - gwooo (goooo: wind)	**63.4** - whomp wham whud (go ga ga: kicking)
17.2 - gwooo (goooo: wind)	**63.5** - vrrr (buun: airplane)
17.5 - gwooo (gooo: wind)	**64.6** - vrrr (buun: airplane)
20.6 - whoosh (daa: running)	**64.8** - raaah (waaaa: cheering)
21.4-7 - gwoooooo (goooooo: wind)	**66.6-7** - vwooosh (buooooo: airplane)
22.1-2 - gwooo (gooooo: wind)	**66.6** - hwoosh (zaa: building speed)
25.1-3 - gwooo (gooooo: wind)	**70.2** - whoom (doon: wind striking)
25.4 - stomp stomp (dan dan: kicking)	**70.4** - gwooo (gooo: wind)
26.2-5 - bwoooo (byuoooo: fear)	**77.4** - gwooo (goooo: wind)
27.3 - bwooo (byuoo: spookiness)	**78.1-2** - gwoooo (goooooo: wind)
30.6 - gwooo (goooo: wind)	**78.4** - skrash (bariiin: window breaking)
30.6-8 - hwoom (doooo: wind striking)	**79.1** - skraaash (bariiin: window breaking)
32.1-3 - fwoooooo (goooooooo: wind)	**80.1** - bwooo (buoaa: wind)
34.4 - thud (dode: falling)	**80.2** - kreak (giii: creaking)
35.1 - whoosh (da: running)	**80.6-7** - rmmm (gogogogo: rumbling)
37.1 - gwooo (goooo: wind)	**81.1** - kreak (gishii: creaking)
38.1 - gwooo (goooo: wind)	**81.2** - skrunk skrunk (baki baki: breaking)
38.7 - hwap (ga: covering mouth)	**81.5** - ktoom (gogaga: breaking)
39.6 - gwooo (gooooo: wind)	**82.6** - hwooo (byuoo: wind)
40.1 - gwooo (gooooo: wind)	**82.8** - krak krak (baki baki: breaking)
40.4 - bam (gan: hitting)	**83.1-2** - rmmm (gogogo: rumbling)
44.8 - gwooo (goooo: spookiness)	**83.3** - fwud (do: falling)
50.1-2 - gwooo (goooo: wind)	**83.4** - slam (bamu: door closing)
51.1 - gwooo (gooooo: wind)	**83.5** - boom krak krak wham wham
52.2-3 - wham (gan: kicking)	(doon baki baki gan gan: destruction)
52.4 - wham (gan: kicking)	**83.6** - gwooo (gooooo: wind)

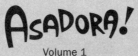

Volume 1
VIZ Signature Edition

By **Naoki URASAWA/N WOOD STUDIO**

Translation & Adaptation John Werry
Touch-up Art & Lettering Steve Dutro
Design Jimmy Presler
Editor Karla Clark

ASADORA!
by Naoki URASAWA/N WOOD STUDIO
© 2019 Naoki URASAWA/N WOOD STUDIO
All rights reserved.
Original Japanese edition published by SHOGAKUKAN.
English translation rights in the United States of America, Canada,
the United Kingdom, Ireland, Australia and New Zealand arranged with SHOGAKUKAN.

Original Cover Design: Isao YOSHIMURA + Bay Bridge Studios

The stories, characters and incidents mentioned in this publication are entirely fictional.

No portion of this book may be reproduced or transmitted in any form or by any means
without written permission from the copyright holders.

Printed in Canada

Published by VIZ Media, LLC
P.O. Box 77010
San Francisco, CA 94107

10 9 8 7 6 5 4 3 2 1
First printing, January 2021

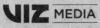

PARENTAL ADVISORY
ASADORA! is rated T+ for Older Teen and is recom-
mended for ages 16 and up. This series includes
realistic depictions of violence and disaster imagery.

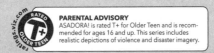

viz.com   vizsignature.com

This is the last page.

Asadora! has been printed in the original Japanese format
to preserve the orientation of the artwork.

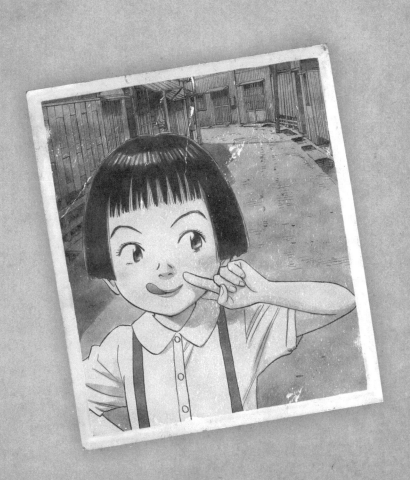